The Other Women's Movement

POLITICS AND SOCIETY IN TWENTIETH-CENTURY AMERICA

Series Editors

WILLIAM CHAFE, GARY GERSTLE, LINDA GORDON, AND JULIAN ZELIZER

A list of titles in this series appears at the back of the book.

The Other Women's Movement

WORKPLACE JUSTICE AND SOCIAL

RIGHTS IN MODERN AMERICA

DOROTHY SUE COBBLE

PRINCETON UNIVERSITY PRESS

PRINCETON AND OXFORD

Copyright © 2004 by Princeton University Press
Published by Princeton University Press, 41 William Street,
Princeton, New Jersey 08540
In the United Kingdom: Princeton University Press, 3 Market Place, Woodstock,
Oxfordshire OX20 1SY

Library of Congress Cataloging-in-Publication Data

Cobble, Dorothy Sue.
The other women's movement : workplace justice and social rights in
modern America / Dorothy Sue Cobble.
p.   cm.
Includes bibliographical references and index.
ISBN 0-691-06993-X
1. Women—Employment—United States. 2. Women's rights—United States. I. Title.
HD6095.C58 2003   331.4—dc21   2003040466

British Library Cataloging-in-Publication Data is available.

This book has been composed in Caledonia

Printed on acid-free paper. ∞

www.pupress.princeton.edu

Printed in the United States of America

1   2   3   4   5   6   7   8   9   10

FOR IRIS

CONTENTS

ILLUSTRATIONS

IN THE EARLY 1950s, my grandmother and I would ride the bus downtown for the monthly meeting of the Atlanta division of the Grand International Women's Auxiliary to the Brotherhood of Locomotive Engineers. My grandmother was in her mid-sixties (the exact year of her birth was always in dispute), and would soon resign the union office she had held since before 1930. My mother, also married to a railroad man, would step in as her replacement. Although I was only four, I was not allowed to observe the auxiliary's proceedings. Rather, month after month, I sat outside the meeting hall, next to the tightly closed door, trying in vain to make out the words being spoken. Despite my complaints, there I remained, because as my grandmother explained to me, since I had not taken the oath of loyalty to the "sisters" and to the union, I could not be trusted with the secrets of the order.

I now have the little black book in which all the secret rituals, passwords, and processional drills of the auxiliary are revealed. My mother gave it to me when she moved to a small apartment after my father's death. It's gratifying to think I have finally parted those closed doors, at least partially, and glimpsed inside. Yet the little black book of rituals did not, in the end, tell me much of what I really wanted to know about the auxiliary to which my mother and grandmother belonged. Nor did it help me in re-creating the larger world of labor politics of which they were a part. For that, I had to turn to other documents, other lives. For what mattered to me then as now was grasping what they and their union sisters believed in, what ideals inspired them, what kind of world they thought their auxiliary could help create. I wanted to understand my mother's generation of labor women, the generation who came of age in the depression, kept the factories humming during the war years, and then pioneered the now commonplace status of working wife and mother.

It's still possible I would never have undertaken this larger history had not an old friend from graduate school called and asked me for an essay on labor women for an anthology she was editing on women in postwar America. That was some ten years ago now, and I've been trying to finish the story begun in that essay ever since. Many of the ideas I tried out in that piece have weathered the archival test. Others fell by the wayside. In particular, my desires in regard to the women of my family and others like them were not to be met. Many working-class women who joined unions and labor auxiliaries—women like my mother and grandmother—are not named in the pages that follow. They did not rise to union office nor did they fashion national legislation or meet with U.S. Presidents and corporate CEOs. Yet without them, the movement that I chronicle in this book would never have happened.

My mother no longer attends auxiliary meetings. The Atlanta division of the Grand International Auxiliary disbanded on September 23, 1987. She and my grandmother were two of the four remaining members who signed the last page of the carefully kept minute book. Yet to this day, when I visit my mother, now in her nineties, she sits me down on the couch and reads me the letters from her national auxiliary officers. She is especially attentive to letters alerting her to adverse political developments in Washington affecting working people and asking her to contact her Georgia congressional representatives, a request she almost always fulfills. This book is dedicated to her and to all the women like her.

AAUW	American Association of University Women
ACWA	Amalgamated Clothing Workers of America
AFA	Association of Flight Attendants
AFL	American Federation of Labor
AFSCME	American Federation of State, County, and Municipal Employees
AFT	American Federation of Teachers
AFWAL	American Federation of Women's Auxiliaries of Labor
ALPA	Air Line Pilots Association
ALSSA	Air Line Stewards and Stewardesses Association
BSCP	Brotherhood of Sleeping Car Porters
CIO	Congress of Industrial Organization
CLUW	Coalition of Labor Union Women
COPE	Committee On Political Education
CWA	Communications Workers of America
EEOC	Equal Employment Opportunity Commission
EPA	Equal Pay Act
ERA	Equal Rights Amendment
FEPC	Fair Employment Practices Commission
FLSA	Fair Labor Standards Act
FTA	Food, Tobacco, Agricultural and Allied Workers of America
HERE	Hotel Employees and Restaurant Employees International Union
IBEW	International Brotherhood of Electrical Workers
ILGWU	International Ladies' Garment Workers' Union
ILWU	International Longshoreman and Warehouse Union
IUE	International Union of Electrical Workers
LAC	Labor Advisory Committee, U.S. Women's Bureau
NAACP	National Association for the Advancement of Colored People
NAM	National Association of Manufacturers
NCEP	National Committee for Equal Pay
NCL	National Consumers' League
NCNW	National Council of Negro Women
NCSW	National Committee on the Status of Women
NFTW	National Federation of Telephone Workers
NOW	National Organization for Women
NWP	National Woman's Party
PCSW	President's Commission on the Status of Women
SEIU	Service Employees International Union
TWU	Transport Workers Union of America
UAW	United Automobile Workers

UE	United Electrical Workers
UMW	United Mine Workers of America
UPWA	United Packinghouse Workers of America
WAGE	Women's Alliance to Gain Equality
WLB	War Labor Board
WTUL	Women's Trade Union League

The Other Women's Movement

The Missing Wave

NEAR THE END of the presidential election of 1996, political analysts discovered "Soccer Moms." It was these women, they declared, that would make or break the election. They were the undecided, the swing voters. It was their vote that Bill Clinton had to win if he were to ensure his reelection. Only much later did it become apparent that these women had been mislabeled. They were not Soccer Moms at all. Indeed, as one observer wryly noted, "Waitress Moms" might be the better catch phrase.[1] The majority of American women didn't drive new SUVs, live in the affluent outer suburbs, or spend their afternoons chauffeuring their kids around. Rather, they owned aging minivans, worked long hours for low pay, and jerry-rigged their child care through neighbors, relatives, and friends.

Once it became evident that the real swing voters were actually blue- (and pink-) collar women,[2] Clinton's advisors began to target them in their campaigns. They developed literature emphasizing Clinton's pro-abortion stand, and they touted his career mobility and employment opportunity initiatives. But as puzzled advisors admitted, they didn't seem to be hitting the right notes. It was surprising since these issues had worked in their outreach to women before. What could be going wrong? they wondered.[3]

What was wrong had to do with class. Class differences exist among women just as among men, and class has always been a salient political divide in American culture. Class distinctions did not disappear in the supposedly homogeneous, "classless" 1950s, and they persist today. Yet the prevalent cultural tendency is to operate as if class makes little or no difference. It is assumed that the experience of most women matches that of professional college-educated women. If they desire upward mobility and job opportunity over job security and guaranteed benefits, then so do all women. If reproductive freedom and breaking the glass ceiling are political priorities for professional women's organizations, then so must they be for labor women's groups. Lower-income women are no longer "absent from the agenda," as Nancy Seifer argued in 1973, but they continue to be misunderstood and misrepresented.[4] In policy and in scholarship, they remain murky and enigmatic—one-dimensional figures, depicted more by what they are not than by what they are.

The Other Women's Movement is an effort to help change that state of affairs. In writing it, I have assumed that class differences have always affected the lives of women and that their views of what reforms were desirable and possible have been shaped in a class crucible. Certainly, class is not the only difference that constructs and divides us, but as long as economic inequality flourishes and as long as our very self-definitions and moral judgments of ourselves and of each other rest on material distinctions, so class remains potent.[5]

IN SEARCH OF OUR MOTHER'S POLITICS

In 1937, 23-year-old Myra Wolfgang strode to the middle of one of Detroit's forty Woolworth's five-and-dime stores and signaled for the planned sit-down strike of salesclerks and counter waitresses to begin. The main Woolworth's store was already on strike, and the Hotel Employees and Restaurant Employees Union (HERE) was threatening to escalate the strike to all of the stores in Detroit. Wolfgang was an art school dropout from a Jewish Lithuanian immigrant family. A natural orator with a wicked wit, she had already given her share of soapbox speeches for radical causes as a teenager before settling down to union organizing in her early twenties. In the 1940s and 1950s, Wolfgang ran the union's Detroit Joint Council, which bargained contracts for a majority of the cooks, bartenders, food servers, dishwashers, and maids in Detroit's downtown hotels and restaurants. By 1952, she had become an international vice president of HERE. Nicknamed the "battling belle of Detroit" by the local media, she relished a good fight with employers, particularly over issues close to her heart. A lifelong member of the National Association for the Advancement of Colored People (NAACP), she insisted, for example, on sending out racially integrated crews from the union's hiring hall, rejecting such standard employer requests as "black waiters only, white gloves required."[6]

In the 1960s, Wolfgang, now in her fifties, led a sleep-in at the Michigan State House to persuade legislators to raise the minimum wage. She also brought Hugh Hefner to the bargaining table to talk about the working conditions of Playboy bunnies at his Detroit Club. HERE eventually signed a national contract covering all the Playboy Clubs in 1969, but Detroit was the first to go union. In these initial bargaining sessions in 1964, Wolfgang and her negotiating team debated with management over the exact length in inches of the bunny suit, that is, how much of the food server's body would be covered. They proposed creating company rules for *customers*, not just for bunnies—rules such as "look but do not touch." And they challenged the Playboy practice of firing bunnies as they aged and suffered the loss of what management called "bunny image," a somewhat nebulous concept according to the union but not in the eyes of the Playboy Club. Bunny image faded, Playboy literature warned, at the precise moment bunnies developed such employee defects as "crinkling eyelids, sagging breasts, crepey necks, and drooping derrieres."[7]

These somewhat atypical labor-management conversations came only after an extensive seven-month organizing campaign. Wolfgang launched her assault by sending her younger daughter, 17-year-old Martha, in as a union "salt." She was promptly hired, despite being underage. Martha then fed Mom a steady diet of useful information, particularly about the club's wage policies, or rather their *no wage* policies. Bunnies, it turned out, were expected to support themselves solely on customer tips. Wolfgang and her volunteers picketed the club, wearing bunny suits and carrying signs that read: "Don't be a bunny, work for money." They also secured favorable media coverage, lots of it. To the delight of scribbling reporters, Wolfgang "scoffed at the Bunny costume as 'more bare than hare' and insisted that the entire Playboy philosophy was a 'gross perpetuation of the idea that women should be obscene and not heard.' "[8]

I first stumbled across Wolfgang, or better put, she reached out and grabbed me when I came across her papers some fifteen years ago in the labor archives in Detroit. It was not just her entertaining antics that kept me awake. I was intrigued by her political philosophy, particularly her gender politics. She considered herself a feminist, and she was outspoken about her commitment to end sex discrimination. Yet at the same time, Wolfgang lobbied against the Equal Rights Amendment (ERA) until 1972, and she chaired the national committee against repeal of woman-only state labor laws. She also accused Betty Friedan and other feminists of demeaning household labor, romanticizing wage work, and caring not a whit about the needs of the majority of women. Indeed, in a 1970 Detroit debate between Wolfgang and Friedan hosted by Women's Studies at Wayne State University, things rapidly devolved into mutual name calling. Friedan called Wolfgang an "Aunt Tom" for being subservient to the "labor bosses," and Wolfgang returned the favor, calling Friedan the "Chamber of Commerce's Aunt Tom."[9]

My curiosity roused, I set out to discover more about the Myra Wolfgangs of the post-depression decades. What I have come to understand is that there were multiple and competing visions of how to achieve women's equality in the half century this book spans, and that the Wolfgangs of the world, far from being oddities, were, at times, the *dominant* wing of feminism. By the 1940s, a new generation of labor women emerged who were dedicated to making first-class economic citizenship a reality for wage-earning women. This book is a history of their reform efforts and the ideas that inspired them.

The women like Wolfgang who led this movement can best be described as "labor feminists." I consider them "feminists" because they recognized that women suffer disadvantages due to their sex and because they sought to eliminate sex-based disadvantages.[10] I call them "*labor* feminists" because they articulated a particular variant of feminism that put the needs of working-class women at its core and because they championed the labor movement as the principle vehicle through which the lives of the majority of women could be bettered.[11]

The labor feminists of the post-depression decades were the intellectual daughters and granddaughters of Progressive Era "social feminists" like Florence Kelley, Rose Schneiderman, and Jane Addams.[12] Like many of the earlier social feminists, they believed that women's disadvantages stemmed from multiple sources and that a range of social reforms was necessary to remedy women's secondary status. And they too were at odds with the individualistic "equal rights feminism" of the National Woman's Party (NWP), the prime proponent of the ERA. Yet by the postwar era, labor women had helped modernize the older "social feminism." Labor feminist goals now revolved around the achievement of what they referred to as "full industrial citizenship." That meant gaining the right to market work for all women; it also meant securing social rights, or the social supports necessary for a life apart from wage work, including the right to care for one's family.[13] They looked to the state as well as to unions to help them transform the structures and norms of wage work and curb the inequalities of a discriminatory labor market. In the pages that follow, I have tried to render visible their distinctive notions of equality and justice and to restore their political activism to its deserved place in the history of twentieth-century reform.

THE OTHER LABOR MOVEMENT

Labor women remain marginal to most narratives of political and economic reform after the 1930s. In part, this view predominates because no synthetic history of labor women's reform efforts beyond the 1930s exists. Nancy Gabin, Ruth Milkman, and Dennis Deslippe, among others, tell parts of the story I offer here in their thoughtful and compelling accounts of labor women and gender discrimination in various institutional settings, and I rely heavily on them in what follows.[14] Yet despite the growing body of case studies documenting women's activism within *individual* unions in the post-depression decades, researchers often treat each new example as *exceptional* and not part of a larger pattern of working-class women's activism.[15]

Unduly restricted definitions of what is "political" and where "politics" takes place add to the problem. Recent research on U.S. middle-class women's activism in the Progressive Era has expanded older definitions of what is political and who exerts political influence, forcing a fundamental rewriting of the political history of that period. Middle-class women may not have voted, participated in political party deliberations, or held office in the early twentieth century. But they did affect the nature of the state and the direction of public policy. Their political agenda, once viewed as "special interest" or as affecting merely the "domestic" sphere, is now recognized as having society-wide consequences, not the least being its pivotal role in shaping the emerging welfare state.[16]

Labor history of the post-depression era has yet to learn from this scholarship. It is still assumed that labor women didn't have the numbers or the positional leverage within postwar labor institutions to make much of a difference in collective bargaining or in politics, and that the concerns they did articulate would not effect widespread change in the social or economic order.[17] But these are untested assumptions this book aims to undermine.

As chapter 1 recounts, the numbers of women unionists rose after the 1930s, both in absolute and percentage terms. By the early 1950s, some three million women were union members, a far cry from the 800,000 who belonged in 1940, and the percentage of unionists who were women had doubled, reaching 18 percent. In addition, some two million women belonged to labor auxiliaries at their peak in the 1940s and early 1950s.[18] Few of these women sat at the collective bargaining table. Fewer still stood behind the podium gaveling the union convention to order. But as Karen Sacks reminds us in her study of hospital organizing in the 1950s and 1960s, the dearth of women in formal, publicly visible leadership roles should not necessarily be taken as an indication of female powerlessness or lack of influence. Sacks uncovered an informal and hidden structure of power that differed from the formal and more obvious one. In the organizing committees and unions she observed, the male union "leaders" and "spokesmen" took positions only after consulting with and gaining the approval of key women on the shop floor—women who never held formal positions of leadership but who wielded considerable influence nonetheless.[19]

Of equal significance, the 1940s witnessed the move of women into local, regional, and national leadership positions within the labor movement. Gender parity was not achieved by any stretch of the imagination, and men continued to predominate in top executive positions. But there was an increase in women's influence and the emergence in many unions of a critical mass of labor women committed to women's equality and to social justice. Myra Wolfgang was not alone. There were others: Esther Peterson, Gladys Dickason, Dorothy Lowther Robinson, and Anne Draper of the Amalgamated Clothing Workers of America (ACWA); Addie Wyatt of the United Packinghouse Workers of America (UPWA); Mary Callahan and Gloria Johnson of the International Union of Electrical Workers (IUE); Katherine Ellickson of the Research Department of the Congress of Industrial Organization (CIO); Helen Berthelot, Selina Burch, and Catherine Conroy of the Communications Workers of America (CWA); Maida Springer-Kemp and Evelyn Dubrow of the International Ladies Garment Workers Union (ILGWU); and last but not least, the group of women at the United Automobile Workers (UAW), which included Caroline Davis, Lillian Hatcher, Millie Jeffrey, Olga Madar, and Dorothy Haener. Some of the early leaders, women like Ruth Young of the United Electrical Workers Union (UE) or Elizabeth Sasuly of the Food, Tobacco, Agricultural, and Allied Workers of America (FTA), disappeared from the public stage by the early 1950s, due in large part to Cold War politics. But they were the exceptions, not the rule.

These women do not figure prominently in what are usually posited as critical turning points in postwar labor history: the 1947 Taft-Hartley Amendments to the Wagner Act, the CIO's decision in 1948 to oust the unions associated with communism, the merger of the American Federation of Labor (AFL) and the CIO in 1955, or the McClellan Committee Senate hearings on union corruption.[20] Yet the reform agenda they championed—an end to unfair sex discrimination, equal pay for comparable work, a family or living wage for women and men, the revaluing of the skills in "women's jobs," economic security and shorter hours, social supports from the state and from employers for child-bearing and child rearing—spurred a fundamental reassessment of the norms and practices governing employment that is still going on. They did not always secure the contract provisions they desired from employers, nor were they able to expand the welfare state in many of the ways they envisioned. But they were among the principal actors in the postwar struggle over the course each would take.

Indeed, a history of what labor women *thought* as well as what they *did* is crucial to understanding the course of liberalism and New Deal reform in the post-depression decades. For as chapter 2 elaborates, the majority of these women were "labor liberals" as well as "labor feminists." Not only did they embrace a political ideology distinct from the conservatism of their time, but they also promulgated a liberalism with a decidedly more egalitarian and populist bent than the version espoused by most New Deal liberals.[21]

Recent histories of the origins and nature of public welfare regimes in the United States and elsewhere reveal the myriad ways women have affected state policies. They also demonstrate how concerns over gender and race have figured as prominently in the creation of social and economic policy as has redistributive impulses and anxieties about consumer purchasing power.[22] In the United States, however, social welfare cannot be understood without analyzing the employment-based entitlements developed in the *private* sector. The United States developed a *mixed* welfare system: supplemental income, health and welfare coverage, and other benefits were as much a function of one's employment status as of one's citizenship. Labor women operated in both the public and private realms, pursuing a dual strategy of reform through legislation and collective bargaining.[23]

I contend that class differences remained salient in the new Deal and after, although in newly disguised forms, and that labor ideologies and institutions had a powerful effect on the formulation and implementation of social and employment policy. This book thus converges with the work of historians who see the labor movement as a vehicle for social reform aspirations in the post–New Deal era rather than only an engine of reaction. Increasingly historians are taking issue with a postwar narrative that assumes labor-management accord and a "tamed," conservative labor movement.[24] In *The UAW and the Heyday of American Liberalism* (1995), Kevin Boyle sees labor liberals such as UAW President Walter Reuther as continuing to "promote democratic economic planning and an expanded welfare state throughout the 1950s and 1960s." In his view, the inability to advance the left-liberal political agenda in the postwar era had more to do with the return of Republican dominance and a Democratic Party divided between southern conservatives and northern liberals than with a loss of will or vision on the part of social unionists.[25] Recent histories of steel unionism also stress the continuation of a progressive class-based politics in the labor movement after the 1930s and depict a labor movement willing to engage in considerable conflict with employers over economic and social issues. Adding his voice to this revisionist wave, Nelson Lichtenstein, in this recent survey of labor in the twentieth century, points to labor's "remarkable combative" record from the late 1940s to the early 1970s, labeling this era "the unquiet decades."[26] It was in these "unquiet decades" that labor feminism flourished, tied institutionally and intellectually to organized labor and to the battles for social justice it waged.

THE OTHER WOMEN'S MOVEMENT

The long-standing story of feminist reform as dormant in the fifty-year period following suffrage is rapidly being eclipsed. No longer is it merely the NWP valiantly carrying the banner of feminism in the supposed quiescent interlude between the 1920 triumph of the suffrage movement (the first wave) and the rebirth of the modern women's movement in the late 1960s (the second wave).[27] Rather, the activities of women in a variety of different organizations moving toward a variety of different goals become part of an expanded history of feminism.[28] The story of labor feminism that I tell here adds to these efforts to "re-wave" feminist reform.[29]

It also speaks to the need to acknowledge multiple forms of American feminism and move beyond the "equal rights teleology" that shapes the narrative of twentieth-century feminist history.[30] In this construct, labor women appear as *opponents* of feminism because they failed to pursue an *equal rights legal strategy* for advancing women's interests: that is, they opposed the ERA and advocated the retention of sex-based state labor laws. Indeed, they are often depicted as lacking a true "feminist consciousness" until the early 1970s, when at last they abandoned their support for woman-only protective laws, embraced the equal rights amendment, began a concerted push for job integration and gender-neutral treatment, and asserted an identity based more on public waged work than on household labor.[31]

In this book I try to develop a different yardstick by which to measure labor women reformers. For one, I include in the history of feminist reform those who were committed to the elimination of sex-based inequalities regardless of the *tactics* they pursued. Sex-based state laws may have frequently been used to restrict women's opportunity and income, yet it is now clear that so-called gender-neutral legislation can also be used against women.[32] The continuing inequality of women should not be laid at the doorstep of either "difference" or "equality" feminists.[33] Indeed, most labor feminists in this book never resolved the tension between equality and difference strategies, nor did they see the necessity of doing so. They wanted equality *and* special treatment, and they did not think of the two as incompatible. They argued that gender difference must be accommodated and that equality can not always be achieved through identity in treatment. Theirs was a vision of equality that claimed justice on the basis of their humanity, not on the basis of their sameness with men. Where the male standard, or what labor feminists called the "masculine pattern," didn't fit their needs, they rejected it.[34] In the 1970s, labor women adopted a more gender-blind strategy in their pursuit of equality, as did the larger women's movement. But rather than uncritically celebrate this ideological shift, I am interested in the ways in which relying on gender-neutrality and adopting the autonomous market individual as an ideal involved losses as well as gains for women.

I also include in the history of feminism those who deemed the issues of race and class to be as crucial as that of gender.[35] Feminism, in my view, need not require an unwavering single focus on gender, nor does gender-conscious reform reside only in all-female organizations. Mixed-gender institutions such as the church or the union can be sites for feminist reform. The struggle for a minimum wage, for an end to compulsory overtime, or for employment opportunities for low-income groups are examples of Denise Riley's insight that some of the most beneficial social movements for women "did not speak the name of woman."[36] For a reform agenda can be quite feminist in its conception and impact without being gender-specific. And just as a purely race-based politics may be limited as sociologist William Julius Wilson argues, so too may a purely gender-based politics, regardless of whether it speaks the language of equality or of difference.[37]

The book proceeds chronologically as well as thematically. Chapter 1 sketches the historical transformations that sparked the rise of labor feminism: the influx of women into paid work, the disrupting and reorienting experience of World War II, the new political and economic power of organized labor, and the increasing leverage of women within the labor movement. Chapter 1 also offers biographical sketches of many of the key labor feminists. Chapter 2 describes the remaking of the social feminist movement in the 1940s: the move of labor women into leadership and the emergence of a refashioned agenda for women's economic progress. During this period the labor feminist project gained some support from male allies in left unions, both communist and anticommunist, but met stiff resistance from conservative employers and politicians as well as from feminists who gathered under the banner of the ERA. Labor feminist efforts to pass new federal legislation ending "unfair sex discrimination" and setting up a president's commission on the status of women made little headway in the late 1940s.

The next three chapters (chapters 3–5) detail how labor feminists sought to transform other aspects of state policy and employer practice in the 1940s and 1950s. Chapter 3 describes the debate over women's job rights in the postwar era and the efforts of labor feminists to secure the right to employment for all women, regardless of their marital status, race, ethnicity, or age. The primary focus of this stage of the employment rights revolution was on integrating and upgrading "women's jobs" rather than moving women into "men's jobs." Wage justice emerged as a principal goal for labor feminists by the 1940s. Chapter 4 chronicles the extensive campaigns initiated by labor feminists to end what they perceived as sex discrimination in the wages paid in women's jobs. They sought federal and state "equal pay for comparable work" laws, and they pursued raising women's wages at the bargaining table. They also pushed to extend the economic benefits of the New Deal to those left out. That meant agitating for higher minimum wage ordinances and for the inclusion of all workers under federal and state labor laws. "The rate for the job" idea, a notion that was gaining ground in the larger culture, helped legitimize their case for equal pay and higher wages for women. It also collided with the older labor rationale for raising worker pay: the family or living wage.

Chapter 5 lays out the social supports for caring labor that labor feminists hoped to achieve. Although the American labor movement did not embrace family allowances, a form of social wages for caring labor instituted in many other industrialized countries, they did have a family politics. Labor feminists, with the aid of some male allies, pressed for changes in government and employee policy to accommodate childbearing and child rearing, including worktime policies that would meet the needs of caregivers as well as breadwinners. Many believed that first-class economic citizenship for women could only be won when women's unpaid labor in the home was acknowledged and valued, and when, in Nancy Fraser's phrase, policy and practice rendered "women's difference costless."[38] For this generation of labor feminists, there could be no equality without a transformation in the patterns, norms, and practices of the work world itself.

The last three chapters (chapters 6–8) trace the intellectual and organizational changes in labor feminism from the late 1950s to the present. Chapter 6 offers a rereading of the origins and impact of the dramatic federal policy breakthroughs affecting women in the 1960s. For labor feminists, the 1960s legislative initiatives to extend the New Deal and end unfair sex discrimination in employment were the culmination of a twenty-five-year reform effort. Their victories, although partial, served to open the way to the new women's movement at the end of the 1960s. Yet much of their reform agenda remained unrealized, and by the end of the 1960s the leadership of the women's movement fell to a younger generation. A new gender politics took hold in the workplace, best glimpsed in the cross-class all-female organizations formed by flight attendants and clerical workers. New issues dominated: dissolving the sexual division of labor and ending the oppressive one-way caring and sexuality expected in many female-dominated jobs. But in the late 1970s, many of the older concerns of labor feminism resurfaced. Labor women once again pursued social supports for childbearing and child rearing, and thousands joined the comparable worth movement of the 1980s, seeking to raise the pay and status of women's jobs.

The Other Women's Movement closes with some thoughts on the implications of this history for the present-day women's movement. There is, as the *Wall Street Journal* observed, a "rising chorus about the problems with modern feminism."[39] Yet all too often, the critics of feminism suffer from a kind of historical amnesia. They end up rejecting feminism per se when in fact they are simply rejecting a particular variant of feminism, one created in a different moment in history. What is needed, I think, is not a rejection of feminism, but a reconstitution of it as an intellectual tradition and as a present-day politics. If history is to help open up a way forward, it will need to encompass the multiple varieties of feminism. Twenty-first-century feminism will look in part like the feminism of the last thirty years. But if it is to succeed, it will need to build on other traditions as well. Labor feminism helped inspire the birth of a new movement in the 1960s. It can also help point the way toward the next.

CHAPTER ONE

The Other Labor Movement

A double issue is involved in the organization of women: the rights of women and the rights of labor. Both the labor movement and the "woman" movement had to wage a stubborn fight against the practice which seeks to grade human beings arbitrarily, by race and sex or class, into superiors and inferiors, and both are based on the principle of equal opportunity for all.

—*Gladys Dickason, Vice-President and Research Director, ACWA, 1947*[1]

The labor movement became the way for me to express my religious beliefs about community and collective action, about extending a helping hand, about fairness, and about giving a voice to those Eleanor Roosevelt called "the left-out people."

—*Esther Peterson, remembering her turn to the labor movement in the 1930s.*[2]

THE STORY OF union growth in the 1930s is a familiar, often-told tale. But for women, the 1940s proved just as crucial. Less than a million women belonged to trade unions at the end of the 1930s. By the early 1950s, that number jumped to three million, and another two million women had flocked into auxiliaries. A women's movement within organized labor now existed that was a force to be reckoned with. Not all wage-earning women saw themselves as feminists, nor did unionism spread to every workplace. Yet a new workplace rights consciousness and a new class militancy among wage-earning women was evident, expressed in large part through women's increasing willingness to join union institutions and to lead them.

The heightened activism among women rank-and-file helped sustain and legitimize the new gender politics being articulated by their leaders. By the end of World War II, a new generation of labor women reformers emerged. They articulated a vision of economic and gender justice that would reenergize social feminism and serve as a focal point for reform over the course of the next two decades. This chapter offers a group portrait of these women—what propelled them into gender and social justice activism and what sustained that impulse. It also locates the origins of this new feminism in the seismic shifts of the 1930s and 1940s: the movement of women into paid work, the cultural and social disjunctures of wartime, and the rise and feminization of a new labor movement.

NEW ECONOMIC REALITIES

By the end of the 1940s, many working-class women had crossed a crucial divide in their relation to paid work—a divide that would not be crossed by the majority of middle-class women until a generation later. Moreover, these economic changes were occurring without a corresponding shift toward economic equity. This yawning gap between the new realities of women's economic participation and the old ideals of second-class citizenship—what William Chafe calls "this strange paradox" of the 1940s—helped spur a new militancy among wage-earning women and made possible the rise of a labor-based feminism.[3]

For a growing number of women in the postwar decades, paid work was no longer a temporary or fleeting experience; it was an ongoing phenomenon that they combined with marriage and child rearing. In 1950, close to a third of all women were in the labor force, and the numbers were rising steadily, continuing labor force trends begun in the early twentieth century. For the first time, the typical working woman was now married, and many had children.[4]

All of these trends affected working-class women *earlier* and to a *greater degree* than they affected middle-class women: a greater proportion of working-class women worked outside the home in mid-century America, and they spent more years of their lives juggling home and work, often holding full-time rather than part-time jobs. Working-class families typically sent their daughters off to work at an early age while more elite families paid for their daughters to finish high school and even college. Upon marriage, many lower-income wives dropped out of the work force, but many others remained, often out of economic necessity. A family wage, or a single wage large enough to support all family members, was as much an aspiration as a reality for working-class families. The dual or triple earner household was not atypical. In addition, lower-income women experienced divorce, separation, and desertion more often than their middle-class counterparts. Not surprisingly, then, they sought wage work in higher numbers than other women, and they tended to be primary rather than secondary earners. Indeed, in 1940, some one-sixth supported *themselves and others*—aging parents, children, or other dependents.[5]

As more and more low-income women, married and not, saw their years in employment stretch into decades, workplace reform increasingly seemed a sound investment. And for that group of women who experienced their wage work as essential to the economic upkeep of their household, the *necessity* of changing the status quo at work was at times often painfully clear. Working-class women expressed a strong allegiance to their family roles as wives, mothers, and daughters in the post-depression decades, but their familial commitment did not preclude the development of a strong identity as a wage earner, nor did it necessarily inhibit them from engaging in workplace reform. Indeed, working-class women tended to see themselves as worker *and* mother, bread-winner *and* homemaker, and in many instances, the desire to fulfill one's family role often fueled the desire to transform one's job. Put another way, raising one's pay and increasing family income could be seen as fulfilling motherly or daughterly duties.

The difficulties that working-class women encountered on the job, height-ened by the layoffs and pay cuts in the depression years, also had a radicalizing effect on many. Once on the job, working-class women rarely derived the de-gree of satisfaction from their work that more elite women did. Professional and managerial jobs paid better, commanded higher esteem, and offered more flexibility and control than did blue- or pink-collar jobs. Further, the dual re-sponsibilities of family and market work weighed heavily on lower-income women. A high proportion of elite women who took on paid work never mar-ried, and those who did had fewer children than working-class women. The majority of professional career women also could afford to pay other women to cook, clean, and care for family members.

WARTIME DISRUPTIONS

World War II profoundly affected this generation of working-class women, heightening their expectations at work and deepening their commitment to reform. The majority of "Rosies" who entered nontraditional jobs during war-time were not middle-class housewives leaving home for a stint in the work world. Most were low-income women who were moving from waitressing, do-mestic service, or other women's jobs into higher-paying men's jobs or who were entering market work for the first time. Some had endured long stretches of unemployment. Most hoped to keep these plum jobs at the war's end. Those desires were not to be fulfilled. Yet the postwar experience for most was not a return to full-time domesticity but a return to the blue- and pink-collar ghetto of women's work.[6] The relentless expansion of the economy and the ever-in-creasing demand for female labor during and following the war heightened the contradiction between the feminine ideal and the female reality.

As working-class women moved back into "women's jobs" in the late 1940s, many brought memories of a distinctly different kind of work experience. The high wages, respect, and unionization that at times accompanied employment in war industries and in jobs vacated by men changed the consciousness of the women who held these jobs. Their ability to do a "man's job" provoked many to rethink their own capabilities. It also raised questions about the ways in which employers evaluated and compensated other jobs they had held or would hold. The majority of Rosies may have lost their place at the welder's bench at the war's end, but their sense of what was possible and what they deserved had been forever altered. Expectations had been raised that could not be buried.[7] First-time war-worker Carmen Chavez thought the women of her neighbor-

hood "changed as much as the men who went to war. We had a taste of independence we hadn't known before the war. We developed a feeling of self-confidence and a sense of worth."[8]

In the immediate aftermath of the war, women (and men) turned their attention to reconstituting family life, but societal attitudes toward female employment were changing.[9] Wage work for wives (and for mothers with older children) was gaining cultural acceptance. Even the "feminine mystique," with its
supposed celebration of women's domestic role, recognized the necessity of
and the value of wage work outside the home at various points in a woman's
life.[10] Nor were wage-earning women's morals as automatically suspect as had
been those of their wage-earning mothers a generation before.[11] The loosening
of these cultural constraints legitimized women's claims for better treatment at
work and diminished their vulnerability to charges that as wage earners or as
unionists they were transgressing gender norms and hence deserved neither
sympathy nor respect.

The disruptions of World War II and the unprecedented economic boom
that followed chipped away at racial and ethnic hierarchies as well. The labor
shortage at home opened up new jobs in industry for minorities, accelerating
the ongoing shift of blacks out of the semifeudal arrangements governing Southern agricultural and domestic labor. Factory jobs paid cash wages instead of
scrip or credit, the workday had an end, and in some workplaces, Mexicans,
African-Americans, and other new recruits sat next to white workers for the
first time. At the war's end, women of color were the first industrial workers
laid off, but many were eventually rehired, albeit into lower-paying jobs. In
1940, only 6.6 percent of black women worked on factory assembly lines; ten
years later that figure more than doubled to 14.6 percent; while the numbers
in agriculture and household work declined.[12] In contrast, a greater proportion
of white (a term that for census purposes included Mexicans in 1940 and 1950
but excluded Negroes, Indians, Japanese, Chinese, and others) women took on
office jobs over the course of the decade, while the ratio in manufacturing held
steady at one in five. In short, the occupational patterns of women changed
permanently over the course of the 1940s: large numbers of white women were
now in service, retail, and clerical jobs, and nonwhite women were a growing
proportion of the industrial workforce.[13]

Despite these occupational shifts, gender and race inequality persisted. As
the labor market absorbed thousands of new women workers over the course
of the postwar decades, both occupational segregation by sex *and* the gender
wage gap actually *worsened*. African-Americans made relatively greater economic gains in this period than did whites, but their income still averaged only
a little more than half that of whites. The majority of white-collar women's jobs
remained closed to African-American and other minority women, and, partially
as a result, a *larger* race wage gap existed among women than among men.[14]

Wartime and postwar developments emboldened African-Americans to demand change. In June 1941, President Roosevelt signed Executive Order 8802,
creating the Fair Employment Practices Committee (FEPC), and barring em-

ployment discrimination in defense industries and by government contractors. The practical effect of the executive order was limited, since it exempted most of private industry and penalties for noncompliance were minimal. Still, it was the first federal action since Reconstruction "explicitly intended" to reduce discrimination in the labor market.[15] Moreover, Roosevelt signed it in response to Brotherhood of Sleeping Car Porter (BSCP) and civil rights leader A. Philip Randolph's threat of a march of 100,000 Negroes on Washington. Randolph's new willingness to use direct action as well as the growing visibility of the NAACP reinforced the dawning societal recognition that fundamental policy changes were unavoidable. The disappointments in the war's aftermath—the loss of high-paying jobs, the shock of black veterans returning to life "within the Veil" of racial segregation—further heightened the sense of restlessness and injustice among African-Americans.[16]

THE FEMINIZATION OF UNIONS

The transformation of the labor movement in the 1930s and 1940s—its rise to power and increasing diversity in membership—laid the groundwork for a new class and gender politics among American women. Labor feminism rested on American workers' heightened sense of economic rights and their success in building permanent and influential labor institutions in the postwar era.

The American labor movement, described in 1932 by one commentator as a "collection of coffin societies" because of its losses in membership, remade itself over the course of the next decade. From a low of just under three million in 1933, labor quadrupled its membership by the end of World War II, and by 1956, some eighteen million workers were organized, a figure six times that of 1933.[17] This expansion was fueled by and in return helped fuel new demands by working people for political and economic inclusion, for an end to paternalism, and for guaranteed rights and benefits from employers and from the state. This new-found rights consciousness and sense of class power emboldened working women to make their own claims as workers and as women.

Of course, the rise of class power has never been a guarantor of the emergence of a politics sympathetic to women. Nonetheless, from the 1940s to the 1960s, a set of conditions existed that allowed for the survival and even the success of a gender politics rooted largely in the institutional soil of organized labor. Indeed, the new labor movement spurred feminism in much the same way as did the civil rights movement or the 1960s New Left organizations, albeit for a different group of women. The labor movement gave wage-earning women a new vocabulary and an ideological framework within which to justify their demands. It also frequently offered them institutional resources. And paradoxically, when labor *failed* to live up to its own rhetoric or only responded erratically, that too reinforced the escalating desires of working women.[18]

From the 1940s to the 1970s, organized labor enjoyed unprecedented political and economic power, and the prominence of labor feminists in social reform efforts in this period was tied in large part to the power and prestige of the union organizations to which many of them belonged. It also rested on the *new* power women were claiming *within* the labor movement by the 1940s.

The dramatic sit-downs and organizing drives of the labor movement in the 1930s have eclipsed the more pedestrian story of the institutionalization of labor power during World War II and its aftermath. Similarly, the growth of mass production unionism in auto, steel, and other heavy industries, with its male iconography and masculinist rhetoric, has overshadowed the equally important tale of organizing the female-dominated occupations and the increasing feminization of labor in the 1940s. The militant 1930s may have been the pivotal decade for the rise of big labor, but for working women, the seemingly less glamorous events of the 1940s loom as equally, if not more, significant.

Large numbers of women turned to the labor movement for the first time in the 1930s as CIO industrial unionism swept workers into the fold, often ignoring the old barriers of race, ethnicity, and gender. The AFL remade itself in this period as well, expanding its presence in such traditional male union strongholds as trucking and construction, while successfully organizing new sectors of the economy in which women worked such as hospitality and retail trade.[19] The number of women union members tripled in the 1930s, and by some accounts, the government guarantees of the right to organize helped "remove the stigma of 'disorderly' and 'unfeminine' conduct from the union activities of women."[20]

Yet the *proportion* of women within organized labor's ranks remained relatively unchanged in the 1930s. Women were 8 percent of union members at the end of the 1920s, and a decade later, the figure had inched up to 9 percent.[21] The story might have been different, as Dana Frank and Elizabeth Faue suggest, had organized labor adopted more community-based organizational forms and had their leadership been more attuned to the distinct needs and culture of women in the family as well as in the wage sphere. But, by and large, unions neither made special efforts to organize the jobs in which women worked nor did they adjust their ideology to embrace the differing perspective of women, a group whose lives still revolved primarily around the household and community sphere. The infusion of women into the labor movement happened as part of a general upsurge of organizing, or what Ruth Milkman terms the inclusive "logic of industrial unionism," rather than through any kind of changed gender consciousness.[22]

The 1940s, however, witnessed a more pronounced change in the relation between women and labor organizations. World War II, of course, altered the gender dynamic of unionism as women moved into positions of union leadership vacated by men and the line separating men and women's jobs shifted to accommodate the shortage of male workers. But the more profound shift in union culture and demographics was not apparent until after the war.[23]

In the immediate postwar period, the number of women in the large industrial unions plummeted, as returning veterans claimed well-paying blue-collar jobs as their own. Yet by the late 1940s, the numbers had crept back up, leaving women in a *stronger* position numerically than before the war. Some eight hundred thousand women were organized in 1940. Female membership skyrocketed to 3 million (or 22 percent of those unionized) at its wartime peak and then fell abruptly at the war's end. But the *number and proportion* of union women remained *higher* than the prewar level throughout the 1940s, and gradually exceeded the 1944 peak. By 1956, for example, three and a half million women belonged to unions, and women were now 18 percent of all union members, *doubling* their 1940 proportion of union members.[24]

The feminization of unions varied depending on industry and occupation. In manufacturing unions overall, women never recovered their wartime peak. But in many unions, they exceeded their prewar numbers, and in certain sectors of industry, they retained numerical *dominance*, due largely to the sex-segregated nature of work. Between 1946 and 1958, for example, approximately 40 percent of all UE workers were female, below their wartime peak but above their prewar level of roughly one-third.[25] In meatpacking, women had never been the majority, but between 1940 and 1950 the number of women in the industry nearly *doubled*. By the end of the 1940s, 20 percent of UPWA members were women, one-third of whom were black. And, in certain flagship meatpacking plants of Armour and Swift in Chicago and elsewhere, women were the *majority* in the workforce and in the union.[26] Even in the auto industry, where the decline of women after the war was steep, their proportion of the workforce soon stabilized at 10 percent, *higher* than before the war, with most women concentrated in auto parts production.[27]

In their traditional strongholds of apparel and food processing, women continued to dominate numerically. In 1945, women constituted 75 percent of the ILGWU and 66 percent of the ACWA.[28] These figures changed little over the course of the postwar decades.[29] Concentrated in tobacco and canning, women comprised one-half of the FTA membership in 1945, and their proportion remained the same even as overall union membership in food, tobacco, and fiber processing declined in the postwar period.[30]

The changes occurring outside the manufacturing sector were even more dramatic. As discussed earlier, many of the "Rosies" who lost their factory jobs in 1945 and 1946 returned to jobs as waitresses, telephone operators, and domestics or took on new jobs as secretaries or salesclerks. Other women joined them to swell the ranks of the burgeoning service economy. Thus, unions representing women's service jobs not only experienced a surge of membership during wartime but, in contrast to manufacturing, their female membership continued to expand after the war ended. By 1950, more than two hundred thousand female food service workers belonged to HERE, constituting 45 percent of the union's membership, almost double the prewar figure. Women also comprised 40 percent or more of the organized telephone workers, department store employees, and bakery and confectionery workers.[31]

In short, working women not only flocked to trade unions after the 1930s, but they did so in *higher* numbers than men. The labor movement continued to feminize in the 1950s and 1960s, and the numbers of women union members jumped significantly again in the 1970s.[32] The 1940s, then, in contrast to the 1930s, inaugurated the beginning of the rise of the *other* labor movement: women made substantial gains in the absolute numbers organized as well as in their share of union membership.

UNIONS AS VEHICLES FOR WORKING WOMEN'S DEMANDS

The 1940s witnessed a rise in female activism as women took to the picket lines and to shop-floor leadership. During the war and afterward, they institutional-ized the fragile new bargaining relations begun in the 1930s and built influential union organizations. Many women exercised shop-floor power as stewards and union officers for the first time during World War II. In the postwar strike wave, the largest strike wave yet seen in the United States, women further demonstrated their loyalty as union members and their willingness to take on leadership roles.

Meatpacking provides perhaps the most dramatic example of women's turn to unionism in the 1940s and their increasing leadership in the movement. During the war some twenty thousand new female employees of all races and ethnic groups passed through company gates, making women a significant con-stituency within the packinghouse workforce. Many of these women took on steward and other unpaid leadership positions within the UPWA during the wartime. Work stoppages and slowdowns were a common occurrence. The is-sues ranged from equal pay demands to how work would be organized to rest periods for women with menstrual cramps. Some stoppages were called simply to demonstrate the power of the union or to pressure undecided fellow workers into signing up. The numerous union elections held by the Packinghouse Work-ers Organizing Committee in the early 1940s could not have been won, ac-cording to Bruce Fehn, had not the women taken leadership roles in organizing and, given their numbers, voted in favor of the union.

After the war, women, along with men, participated in the acrimonious strikes that swept the industry. The 1946 strike ended in victory and the election of Ralph Helstein, a progressive closely identified with the communist faction within the union, to the presidency. The 1948 nationwide strike against the big three (Swift, Armour, Hormel) in which three strikers lost their lives proved more traumatic for the union. But in its aftermath, the UPWA rebuilt its strong shop-floor presence, paying particular attention to the inclusion of women and minorities. The UPWA set up women's leadership programs, held local and regional women's conferences, and inaugurated an aggressive antidiscrimina-tion program. These initiatives, along with the Anti-Discrimination Department set up in 1949, were crucial in facilitating the "remarkable activism" of UPWA women in the postwar period. In 1953, 200 women delegates gathered in Chi-cago for UPWA's first national conference on Women's Activities.[33] The grass-roots union activism of women in canning, tobacco, and other food-processing industries, many of which employed large numbers of African-American, Mexican, and other minority women, was also substantial.[34]

Women's activism and leadership increased in the auto and electrical industries as well. The 1930s UAW welcomed women as members and depended heavily on the energy of committed union women activists—wives and wage earners alike. Yet few women occupied paid staff positions, and the rights of married women in particular were routinely violated. But as the ranks of women ballooned to over a quarter million during the war years—the UAW tied with the UE as one of the two unions with the largest number of women members— the UAW belatedly began taking steps to better represent women. The actual practices on the shop floor, particularly in regard to pay inequalities, and women's hiring and promotional rights, would take decades to transform, but the issues had been joined. In 1944, the UAW held its first Women's Conference and established a Women's Bureau within its War Policy Division. In 1946, the UAW made the Women's Bureau a *permanent* division, putting it under the auspices of the newly created Fair Practices and Anti-Discrimination Department. By 1947, the Women's Bureau had instituted local and regional women's committees and set up a National UAW Women's Advisory Committee. These multiple bodies were dedicated spaces for women to discuss their mutual problems, devise remedies, and strategize about how to influence UAW policy and practice. The Bureau and its affiliate committees and council operated throughout the postwar decades, gaining momentum and legitimacy. In 1955, the Bureau became the UAW Women's Department, winning approval from the UAW convention to set itself up as a *separate* department within the union.[35]

In the electrical industry, women's political power within the union remained minimal in the 1930s, despite women's prominence as strike leaders and organizers. Indeed, women's issues had "no discernable place on the UE agenda" in the 1930s, according to Lisa Kannenberg. Yet over the course of the war, the influx of women into electrical jobs and into union office "dramatically altered the union's understanding of women's position and problems."[36] After the war, the overall number of women electrical workers fell somewhat, but substantial numbers of vocal women remained. In 1946 some 200,000 UE women strikers helped shut down 78 plants nationwide, responding in part to the equal pay demands UE hurled at GE and Westinghouse.[37] And, although the bitter Cold War factional battles of the late 1940s dampened gender activism in the electrical industry, by the early 1950s it was once again in full bloom. Tellingly, women's activism reemerged within the UE as well as in its new anticommunist rival, the IUE. In 1953, the UE held its *first* national women's conference in New York, attracting close to four hundred women. It continued these as annual affairs. The IUE's first national women's conference, held in 1957, also drew hundreds of enthusiastic delegates.[38]

In the expanding service-sector unions outside of manufacturing, women played an integral if not dominant part in ensuring the survival of collective bargaining and the ultimate defeat of company paternalism in the 1940s. Telephone operators had organized all-female unions in the Progressive Era and set

Fig. 1.1 Delegates to the first UAW Women's Conference, December 8–9, 1944, Detroit, Michigan. Millie Jeffrey, the first director of the UAW Women's Bureau, is seated in front, five from the left. Caroline Davis, who would become the second director in 1948, is standing in the next row, five from the right, wearing a striped dress and hat. Courtesy of: Labor News, January 1, 1945, Archives of Labor and Urban Affairs, Wayne State University.

up their own Telephone Operator Department within the International Brotherhood of Electrical Workers (IBEW), but their union had fallen on hard times
in the 1920s. Most telephone operators, like AT&T employees generally, belonged to company-led unions by the 1930s. The AT&T system—an empire
that included the Bell Operating companies and other directly owned subsidiar-
ies such as the Long Lines Division, Western Electric, and Bell Laboratories—
offered its native-born, white female workforce "genteel respectability," white-
collar status, and an elaborate benefit plan. But once the Supreme Court upheld
the Wagner Act ban on company unions in 1937, workers began shifting their
allegiance to independent unions. In 1939, many of these new independents,
along with a handful of older more company-oriented unions, created a system-
wide confederation of telephone locals, the National Federation of Telephone
Workers (NFTW). Initial membership hovered near 100,000 and included 37
percent of all Bell employees.

During the war and afterwards, women comprised over 60 percent of NFTW
members (as well as a majority of those in the telephone unions outside NFTW
ranks). Women were 72 percent of all telephone workers, concentrated in the
traffic departments, where they worked as operators (95 percent were female)
or in the clerical division.[39] They set up their own female-majority local, regional, and statewide organizations, and they negotiated and enforced their own
contracts. And because of the tendency to organize along craft as well as sex-
based lines, many of the new locals were all female. The Michigan Telephone
Traffic Union, for example, took in women operators and clerks, and by 1942
had 6,000 members statewide. Many of these new female locals were fearful of
losing local autonomy and control to a national union, even one as decentralized
as the NFTW. The Federation of Women Telephone Workers of Southern California, for example, initially affiliated its thousands of women with the NFTW
but later withdrew in 1943, ostensibly over the lack of female representation in
the national bargaining structures that were emerging.[40]

Women telephone workers and the organizations they built were the back-
bone of the 1947 nationwide telephone strike. The strike was called by
the NFTW, primarily to secure a national agreement between NFTW and
AT&T, but many of the nonaffiliated unions honored the picket lines. With
350,00 employees on strike, 230,000 of them women, the 1947 telephone strike
was the largest walkout of women in U.S. history. Carrying signs that proclaimed "The Voice with a Smile Will be Gone for Awhile," around-the-clock
pickets paraded throughout the South, the Midwest, and in rural towns across
America. In New Jersey alone, twelve thousand women operators left their
posts, defying a state law that called for jail sentences and steep fines for utility
strikers. The Washington, D.C. traffic local, emboldened by some two hundred
successful work stoppages in the previous three years having to do with such
issues as equal pay and the "usual seating, voice, and courtesy requirements,"
effectively cut off telephone access to the White House and other government
offices.[41]

The NFTW failed to win its demand for a national contract, and most of the economic issues, many of which directly affected the status and pay of operators, were settled locally. But the walkout ensured that the new system of independent collective bargaining would be retained in the industry, and that the push for a strong national union would continue. In 1948, the loosely structured NFTW reconstituted itself into a more centralized national organization, the CWA, under the leadership of former NFTW president Joe Beirne, and a year later the CWA joined the CIO.[42] A sizable number of telephone unions, including many traffic locals, remained outside the CWA, later affiliating with a rival less centralized body called the Alliance of Independent Telephone Unions. Over the course of the postwar decades, however, most independents eventually joined the CWA.[43]

The long-standing union organizations begun by women hospitality workers also expanded and stabilized in the 1930s and 1940s. In the hotel and restaurant sectors, female union activism extended back to the turn of the century, with the establishment of separate-sex HERE waitress locals in numerous cities across the country. With the advent of the New Deal, HERE moved from organizing restaurants to tackling the large hotels in urban centers, and by the end of the war initial bargaining agreements with hotel employer associations had been signed in most of the major urban areas. The majority of the newly organized hotel workers joined large industrial unions that took in everyone from bartenders and food servers to dishwashers and maids. But the older separate-sex waiter and waitress unions expanded their base in the restaurant sector, and some took in hotel employees as well. As the industry workforce feminized in the 1940s, the waitress locals moved ahead of the waiter and bartender locals in size and influence. San Francisco waitresses doubled their 1940 membership, for example, claiming more than six thousand women by the end of the 1940s; the Los Angeles membership rose from eight hundred on the eve of wartime to close to five thousand by the early 1950s.[44]

The 1940s marked the beginnings of union organization among other female-majority service and white-collar occupations. Some of these new unions, such as the ones among flight attendants, would expand over time, the flight attendant unions eventually claiming a majority of the occupation nationwide. Other unions, such as the promising but ill-starred ones among clerical workers and retail store employees, would make little headway in the 1940s and barely sustain themselves in the 1950s and 1960s, even as their potential membership base grew exponentially. Still others, such as the long-standing professional associations among teachers and nurses, retained their character as work-based collective entities in the postwar decades but did not always identify as part of a larger labor movement. The American Federation of Teachers (AFT), long affiliated with the AFL, was the notable exception, but its membership was dwarfed by the millions of teachers belonging to the National Education Association. By the 1960s and 1970s, however, the National Education Association as well as the American Nurses Association would embrace collective bargaining and turn to economic action to achieve their goals.[45]

The Invisible Soldiers

The most ignored women within the labor movement have consistently been those who joined labor auxiliaries.[46] Yet no account of women's rising numbers and influence in this period is complete without examining the auxiliaries, among the largest labor institutions built by working-class women. Indeed, at their peak, in the 1940s and 1950s, almost as many women belonged to labor *auxiliaries* as labor *unions*. Granted, these women were not counted as union members even by the international unions, central labor councils, and labor federations that issued them their official charters of affiliation. But women auxiliary members drew the movement's boundaries at a different point: they defined themselves as an integral part of the labor movement, and many saw themselves as contributing as much to the success of the movement as the men. In contrast to women labor activists outside the auxiliaries, only a few auxiliary women emerged as feminist leaders on the national level. Nevertheless, many auxiliary women supported the labor feminist agenda that was emerging, and many more provided the crucial "manpower" to preserve and extend labor's gains in the postwar decades.

Before the New Deal, large and long-standing auxiliaries existed among the female relatives of AFL railroad workers, printers, streetcar drivers, machinists, and other trades. Most of the women were wives or widows of union men, but other female relatives, including mothers, sisters, daughters, lovers, ex-wives, stepmothers, and "friends," joined. Relying on union women's "purchasing power," AFL auxiliaries ran union label campaigns, organized boycotts of non-union goods, and functioned as social, fraternal, and charitable organizations. They also mobilized during strikes and lockouts, setting up picket lines and soup kitchens.[47]

In the 1930s, auxiliary membership expanded among AFL women as unionism reemerged in a wide variety of trades and occupations. With the rise of the CIO, large and active auxiliaries also formed among women supporting the organizing campaigns among industrial workers, including auto, steel, longshore, and others.[48] And, by the early 1940s, both the CIO and the AFL auxiliaries had formed their own *national federations* to coordinate the work of the various national, regional, and local auxiliaries. The women's federations paralleled the male federations, the AFL and the CIO, in structure and governance. Yet they met separately, elected their own officers, and on many occasions formulated their own priorities.[49]

The AFL auxiliaries banded together in 1935 and formed the first national federation of auxiliaries, the American Federation of Women's Auxiliaries of Labor (AFWAL). Encouraged and financed by the Union Label and Trades Department, the new national federation hoped to affiliate the *two million* women who belonged to individual AFL auxiliaries in the 1930s and marshal their great "economic weapon" of "collective buying" in the union cause. They recognized women's "purchasing power" as an effective weapon in promoting

Fig. 1.2 The Union Label Trades Department of the AFL used this cartoon in the late 1930s to underscore the subsidiary yet vital link between the auxiliaries' work of "collective buying" and the union's job of "collective bargaining." Increasingly, many auxiliaries spoke out on issues other than those affecting "Mrs. Union Man." Credit: *American Federationist* 45 (1938), 753.

collective bargaining and helping end sweatshops, child labor, and unfair employer practices.[50]

   In the 1940s, AFWAL established a more independent relationship with the Union Label and Trades Department and took steps to move beyond its original goals. In 1942, AFWAL adopted a constitution that pledged it "to exert women's influence in the local, state, and national legislative fields." During the war, AFWAL's president, Mrs. Herman Lowe, from the National Federation of Post Office Clerks Auxiliary, spoke out against discriminatory treatment of wage-earning women, and AFWAL conventions went on record in favor of equal pay, antilynching legislation, national health insurance, and ending the poll tax. But AFWAL's more independent and activist politics of the early 1940s was not necessarily embraced by the vast majority of local AFL auxiliaries. As later chapters will detail, most AFL auxiliaries did not move far beyond their traditional focus on consumer and community service until the late 1950s.[51]

The CIO auxiliaries, however, were quick to take up gender politics as a priority, despite their origins as "support" organizations for men in the fierce economic battles to organize basic industry in the 1930s.[52] They also appeared less reticent than their AFL counterparts to challenge the priorities of the male-dominated federation to which they had linked their fate. It was the CIO auxiliaries, then, that made the greatest contribution to the rise of labor feminism.

In 1939, at a luncheon in her honor, Kathryn Lewis, the daughter of CIO and United Mine Workers of America President John L. Lewis, proposed a "permanent organization for CIO women for active participation in labor and civic affairs." And in 1941, the CIO Congress of Women's Auxiliaries, the national coordinating body for CIO auxiliaries, held its first convention in Detroit, electing as president the head of the UAW Auxiliaries, Faye Stephenson.[53] Stephenson's work experience, like that of many other auxiliary women, was not limited to the household. She had been active in the labor movement from the age of thirteen, when she left school to work in a cigar factory in 1908. In the 1930s, she lobbied for unemployment insurance and, as a forty-year-old mother of three married to an auto worker, had helped organize UAW Women's Auxiliary No. 35 during the 1936 Fisher Body strike in Cleveland.[54] Catherine Gelles, vice president of the Congress, had her first experience with the labor movement during a streetcar strike in 1919 at the age of twelve, "when she helped to stop the cars so the older girls could throw rotten eggs at scabs."[55]

The Congress, open to family members of CIO men *as well as women wage earners eligible for membership in their CIO union*, saw "legislative work in Washington" and "presenting testimony on what CIO auxiliary women think and want" as a primary purpose.[56] And in the early 1940s, they developed an ambitious legislative agenda. At its annual convention in 1944, the Congress announced its support for "free nurseries" for working mothers, "maternity leaves with re-employment guarantees," equal pay, "an end to job discrimination against Negroes," a permanent fair employment practices law, and abolition of the poll tax. Similar goals had been put forward by CIO auxiliary and union women at the local level some two years earlier. Billed as the "first trade union women in industry conference," the Los Angeles CIO Council brought together 175 delegates from auxiliaries and CIO locals in the summer of 1942. Their aspirations included equal pay for equal work, government-provided restaurant and child care facilities, free job training, no discrimination because of race, creed, or color, and wages high enough to pay for household help.[57] And as we shall see in later chapters, CIO auxiliary women joined with women active in their unions to try and make these economic rights and benefits a reality.

THE NEW WOMEN OF POWER?

To what degree did women's increase in numbers and union activism translate into greater female influence in the labor movement? The continuing dominance of men in *top* executive positions in the postwar decades should not be taken as the only or even the best indicator of female influence. To grasp the extent of female influence in the labor movement, we need to expand our definitions of leadership and power.[58]

As we have seen, male (as well as female) leaders in the postwar labor movement now had to answer to a growing and increasingly vocal new constituency of women labor activists. In addition, women moved into secondary leadership positions in the 1940s, marking yet another significant departure from the prewar labor movement. These new women union leaders held few of the *top* executive offices in national and international unions, but they occupied numerous influential positions at the national, regional, and local level. Although no systematic survey exists of the changing *percentage* of such secondary leadership positions held by women and men, the *numbers* of women labor leaders increased dramatically in the 1940s and 1950s.[59] Indeed, a critical mass was reached. Women's voices were not dominant within the labor movement by any means in the postwar decades. But given their new numbers in leadership and membership, they were able to intercede at critical moments and affect labor union policy and practice.

Who were these new women leaders? How did they differ from the generation that preceded them? What paths did they take into union leadership? And, once in leadership, how did they, like other public women of their era, reconcile the relentless demands of public leadership with their home and community responsibilities?

The 1940s witnessed the waning of one generation of women labor leaders and the emergence of another. Due to the concentration of organized women in the garment industry before the 1930s, most of the women labor leaders in the earlier era—women like Rose Schneiderman, Rose Pesotta, Dorothy Bellanca, Pauline Newman, Bessie Abramowitz Hillman, or Fannia Cohn—had institutional ties to the needle trade unions. Most were also first-generation Eastern European or Russian Jewish immigrants.[60] Well-known labor figures existed apart from the close-knit network of garment industry women—Julia O'Connor Parker of the Telephone Operators Department of the IBEW or Lillian Herstein of the Chicago Teachers' Union or Mary Anderson of the Boot and Shoe Workers Union—but their numbers were few.[61]

Born in the late nineteenth century, most reached the pinnacle of their career before the 1940s. They helped create a more inclusive "new unionism" in the decade before World War I, and they joined with National Consumers' League leader Florence Kelley and other social feminists to pass a wide array of labor standards legislation and secure the passage of women's suffrage. In the conservative 1920s, they pioneered remarkably farsighted labor education initiatives in the garment unions and at colleges like Bryn Mawr. In the thirties, they reemerged as veteran union organizers and crucial participants in the drafting of new federal laws guaranteeing labor's right to organize and extending wage and hour protection to low-wage workers, men and women.[62]

Some remained active past the 1930s, although in less prominent roles, serving as elder stateswomen to the new women leaders. Mary Anderson and Pauline Newman proved to be two of the most important. Anderson migrated to the United States in 1889 at the age of sixteen, leaving behind the declining economy of her Swedish farming village. She suffered through a succession of low-paying domestic service positions before securing steady factory work in Chicago as a shoe stitcher, a job she held for twenty-two years. She accepted the presidency of her all-female shoeworkers' local in 1900, drawn to union work in part because as Anderson recalled, the union improved conditions "for a great many people and not just for the one person who changed to a better job." Legislative work with the Chicago Federation of Labor brought her into contact with the Chicago branch of the Women's Trade Union League (WTUL), a national organization of women wage earners and wealthy "allies" dedicated to advancing the interests of working-class women. The Chicago WTUL, headquartered for a time at Hull House, included as members Hull House founder Jane Addams, crusading occupational physician Alice Hamilton, and other nationally known social welfare activists. At Hull House, Anderson discovered a women's community that sustained her throughout her life. Her closest relationships—with the exception of her sister Anna—were with other league activists, and she never strayed from the leagues' emphasis on educational and legislative work as a complement to collective bargaining. In 1911, Anderson took a full-time job as an organizer with the WTUL, and in 1917, the league recommended that the AFL name Anderson to an advisory post on women within the expanding wartime government bureaucracy. When the Women's Bureau was set up in 1920, she became its first director, serving for the next quarter century. She remained outspoken and influential into her nineties.[63]

A pre–World War I veteran of the tenement sweatshops of New York, the organizing campaigns among New York's primarily Italian and Jewish garment workers, and Socialist Party work, Lithuanian-born Pauline Newman was a frequently quoted ILGWU spokeswoman and labor feminist into the 1960s. A self-taught intellectual with an acid tongue and lingering class resentments, Newman proved to be a formidable speaker and labor newspaper columnist, particularly on issues affecting wage-earning women. In 1918, on assignment for the WTUL in Philadelphia, she met her lifelong partner, Frieda Miller, an economics professor at Bryn Mawr and a WTUL ally who would later head the Women's Bureau after Anderson retired in 1944. Both were rooming at the College Club, and when Miller fell ill during the rampaging flu epidemic, Newman nursed her back to health from near death. Except for a brief falling out in the early 1960s, she and Miller would live and work together for the next fifty years, raising a daughter together after 1923.[64]

Others of the earlier generation remained influential as well. ILGWU firebrand, suffragist, and New Deal insider Rose Schneiderman was appointed New York State's secretary of labor in 1937 and continued to speak out on such legislative matters as equal pay, government-funded child care, maternity insurance, and "a GI Bill of Rights for industrial women." An officer in the New York WTUL until it closed its doors in 1955, she also remained good friends with many WTUL women, including Newman and Miller, with whom she shared political strategy, dinners, and late-night poker games in her New York apartment.[65] Fifteen-year-old Bessie Abramowitz Hillman left her small Russian village for the United States in 1905, in part to escape the services of a marriage broker. As a button sewer in Chicago in 1910, she and several other young girls walked off their jobs at Hart, Schaffner and Marx, sparking a four-month strike of 35,000 workers in the men's garment industry. With financial and political support from the Chicago Federation of Labor, the WTUL, and Jane Addams at Hull House, the strikers leveraged a grievance and arbitration procedure that would be imitated nationwide. After the strike, Abramowitz joined the circle at Hull House, where she learned English and much of her industrial philosopohy. In 1914, Bessie Abramowitz founded ACWA, along with ACWA's first president Sidney Hillman, whom she married on May 1, 1916. Elected in 1915 as ACWA's first female executive board member, she resigned after the birth of her two daughters in 1917 and 1921. But in 1924, Hillman threw herself back into union work full-time, taking the lead in organizing campaigns and serving as the Educational Director for ACWA's Laundry Workers Joint Board in New York from 1937 to 1944. In 1946, the year her husband died, she was elected for a second time to the ACWA Executive Board, where she remained until her death in 1970. Once introduced as Mrs. Sidney Hillman, she set the record straight, remarking: "I was Bessie Abramowitz before he was Sidney Hillman."[66]

In the 1940s, a new cohort of labor women moved into leadership. Like their predecessors, the majority came from female-majority trades and occupations, where women could more easily rise to power and articulate an explicitly woman-oriented agenda. In contrast to the earlier group, however, they tended to be second-generation immigrants or from families with longer histories in the United States. They were also a more diverse group in terms of their racial and ethnic backgrounds and the industries from which they emerged. A greater proportion married and had children; in relation to the female population as a whole, however, a disproportionate number of women labor leaders of *both* generations remained childless and either never married or were divorced or widowed.[67] Of the marriages that survived, many had husbands who backed their unionism, offering verbal encouragement and taking over some of the household duties. In addition, those women with children relied heavily on other relatives or paid help in juggling their home responsibilities with the demands of public activism and employment.

Like the women leaders before them, the generation who came of age in the 1930s and 1940s held political views that put them in consistent opposition to conservative Republicans and businessmen. Some joined the Communist Party; others identified as socialists, social democrats, liberals, or were nonpartisan politically. By the early 1950s, however, the majority of labor feminists were concentrated in CIO unions that shared a left-liberal anticommunist agenda and favored close ties with the Democratic Party. These included the UAW, IUE, ACWA, and CWA. Nevertheless, strong feminist leaders continued to

Fig. 1.3 A gathering of New York Women's Trade Union League leaders at the Bryn Mawr Summer School for Women Workers, 1925. From left: Pauline Newman, Agnes Nestor, Frieda Miller, Maud Swartz, Marion Dickerman, Rose Schneiderman. Newman, Miller, and Schneiderman would be key elder stateswomen to the new group of labor feminists who emerged in the 1940s. Credit: Robert F. Wagner Labor Archives, New York University, Rose Schneiderman Photograph Collection.

operate in unions such as the UPWA and UE whose leaders sympathized with the communist left, as well as in AFL affiliates such as HERE, a union whose leaders and political allies spanned the ideological spectrum.

A few of the most promising new leaders cut short their public careers by the late 1940s: some fell victim to mounting Cold War hysteria; others simply turned their attention to less public pursuits. Ruth Young, for example, a young Jewish communist and bold advocate for gender rights in the 1930s and 1940s, joined the UE staff in 1938 and rose to become the second ranking officer in the union's huge New York and New Jersey district. By 1944, now married with a two-year-old daughter, she became the first woman executive board member. In 1950, wearied by the Cold War battles racking the union, she withdrew from union activism and settled into raising a family with her new husband, Leo Jandreau, fellow executive board member and French-Canadian Catholic leader of UE Local 301 in Schenectady. In 1954, Jandreau led the twenty thousand members of UE Local 301 into the IUE.[68] Tillie Olsen, another young 1930s radical with communist leanings, rose to leadership in the California CIO Women's Labor Auxiliary movement during World War II. She redirected her energies into her fiction writing, local community activism, and caring for her children in the war's aftermath.[69]

Fig. 1.4 Ruth Young, UE Executive Board member, speaking at a Women's Luncheon at the September 1944 UE Convention in New York. Pauline Newman is on the far left. Credit: United Electrical Workers Archives, University of Pittsburgh.

Many of the top women leaders in the Food, Tobacco, and Agricultural Workers (FTA) were lost to the labor movement by the early 1950s as well. Luisa Moreno, international vice president of the FTA from 1941 to 1947, had organized Mexican pecan shellers in Texas before her successes in unionizing the predominantly Mexican and Russian Jewish female cannery operatives in Los Angeles during World War II. She "retired to private life in 1947" and returned to her native Guatemala in 1950 under a deportation threat based on her alleged former Communist Party membership.[70] Elizabeth Sasuly, another FTA leader whose career was curtailed by the Cold War, was the daughter of Eastern European Jewish immigrants. She attended the University of Wisconsin at Madison, where she studied with labor theorists and social welfare reformers associated with John R. Commons, a leading institutional economist. Later, she enrolled in a psychology doctoral program at Columbia but was discouraged from continuing, in part because by then she was a mother. She turned to labor organizing with the ACWA and the Cannery Workers in the 1930s, and by 1940, she had risen to become FTA's legislative director in Washington.[71] Moranda Smith, FTA's first African-American regional director, died in 1950, not long after the local she had helped build into FTA's largest black-led affiliate lost the right to bargain for tobacco workers at R.J. Reynolds.[72]

Yet the *majority* of prominent women leaders who emerged by the 1940s sustained their activism over the course of the postwar decades, and some were active into the 1970s and 1980s. Mary Callahan of the UE (and later the IUE), Addie Wyatt of UPWA, and Myra Wolfgang of HERE illustrate this longevity.

Mary Callahan, third-generation immigrant of German Catholic and Protestant background, had expected to marry and spend her days raising a family, as her mother did. When her husband died in a car accident in 1934, however, leaving Mary a widow at age 19 with a two-year-old son, she became a tester in the International Resistance Company electronics plant in Philadelphia. Breaking with her early aspirations, Callahan threw herself into union and community politics and never looked back. "I became active in the union about six months after I was hired for reasons of dignity," she remembered. Soon after, she led her fellow workers out on a one-month strike for union recognition which also gained them the right to have the washrooms unlocked and a regular relief period (bathroom break). The members of newly established UE Local 105, 85 percent of whom were female, elected Callahan to union office. By 1946 she held the top position in the local, a position she retained until her retirement in 1977.

Under Callahan's leadership, Local 105 secured paid maternity leave and other benefits; it also became one of the first locals to break with the UE, voting unanimously in 1949 to join the rival IUE, where Callahan's friend and political ally, the brash young CIO "Boy Wonder" Jim Carey, served as union president. A veteran organizer at Philadelphia's Philco Corporation and elsewhere, Carey assumed the helm of the UE in 1935 at age 23. In 1938, he brought his particular brand of Catholic social theology and progressive democratic politics into the CIO as its national secretary. Defeated for the UE presidency in 1941 by a communist-led coalition, Carey continued the fight by founding the IUE.[73]

In 1959, after her election as chair of the Radio, TV & Parts Conference Board, Callahan joined the IUE Executive Board as one of two women members. She also chaired the national IUE Women's Council, and directed the political activities of Philadelphia unions in numerous local, regional, and national elections. In 1961, she accepted Kennedy's appointment to the President's Commission on the Status of Women (PCSW) and moved into national prominence as a spokeswoman on gender and employment policy. Her public life, she readily admitted, was possible because of the help she received from her mother and her second husband. Her mother lived with her for 29 years, caring for her first son, and then later her second son. Her second husband, a union activist with the Bakery and Confectionery Workers whom she met at a 1938 benefit dance for Philco strikers, was proud of her accomplishments and encouraged her union activities. He always said, "If God gave you brains, use them," she explained.[74]

Mississippi-born Addie Wyatt, like many African-American women in this period, had her first encounter with trade unionism during the war. With five younger brothers and sisters needing support at home, 17-year-old Wyatt found employment at Armour's Chicago meatpacking plant in 1941. It wasn't long before she filed her first grievance. The foreman had given her job to a newly-hired white woman and re-assigned her to a worse position on the "stew line." "I was very angry, and as I always did when there was something I didn't think was right, I spoke out." When the issue couldn't be resolved with the foreman, Wyatt and her union representative, a black woman steward, marched over to the plant superintendent's office. "What effect," Wyatt remembered thinking, could "two black women have talking to the two white, superior officers in the plant?" To her amazement, they won. Just as surprising was the union response when she got pregnant. The steward explained the union's maternity clause: Wyatt could take up to a year off and her job would be held for her. "I didn't really believe them. But I thought I'd try it, and I did get my job back." Wyatt didn't "fully understand the power and importance of the union," however, until she attended her first union meeting some years later. "That really rang a bell with me. In spite of the race problems and those situations that separated and divided us, here were workers who were learning how to band together to improve their lives. I wanted to be part of it."[75]

At age 28, Wyatt was elected vice president of her local (UPWA 437), the majority of whose members were white men. "I was scared to death. How in the world would I tell my husband and my family that now I am not only a member of this union, but I am a leader? It took me three months before I told them." Later, she took over the presidency of the local and ran successfully for the UPWA's national executive board on a platform emphasizing women's rights and the advancement of racial minorities. In 1954, she was appointed to the UPWA national staff as the first black woman national representative, a position she held for the next thirty years. Wyatt linked her union politics with the civil rights and women's movements. She acted as Martin Luther King's labor liaison in the 1950s, got deeply involved in the efforts of UPWA women to change the status of women and minorities in the workplace and the community, and helped found the National Organization for Women (NOW) in 1966 and the Coalition of Labor Union Women (CLUW) in 1974.[76]

Born Mira Komaroff in Montreal, Canada, Myra Wolfgang, as we have seen, waded into union work early on and never stepped out. She came to her union activism through radical politics, having joined the Proletarian Party, a small Marxist sect, as a teenager. Her apprenticeship in the labor movement began under the tutelage of Louis Koenig, secretary-treasurer of Detroit Waiters' Union, HERE Local 705. She chafed at being Koenig's office assistant and stretched her early assignments to include conducting strikes and sit-ins for union recognition. Marriage in 1939 and the birth of two daughters in the 1940s failed to slow Wolfgang's labor activism, in part because her husband, an attor-

Fig. 1.5 Addie Wyatt and other UPWA delegates to the 1957 NAACP convention pose with Herbert Hill, NAACP labor liaison, and Philip Weightman, AFL-CIO Representative. Weightman is second from the right; Hill stands behind him. Credit: Photograph by Edward Bailey. Courtesy of the Wisconsin Historical Society. [Whi(X3)50370]

ney, helped raise the children and encouraged Wolfgang's public life outside the home. By 1952, Wolfgang had become an international vice president of HERE and, later, with the retirement of Koenig, took over as chief executive of HERE Local 24 in Detroit, a position she maintained until her death from cancer in 1976 at the age of sixty-one.[77]

Callahan, Wyatt, and Wolfgang came from poor or working-class backgrounds, as did many labor feminists.[78] Yet the labor movement in the 1940s also attracted elite, college-educated women who tended to occupy appointed staff positions. They joined forces with the new labor feminists who were elected into leadership from off the shop floor, creating a cross-class social feminism rooted in the labor movement. Like many of their male counterparts in staff positions in the labor movement, elite women reformers of the 1930s and 1940s sought work with labor because of its progressive social program and its newfound power to influence policy. But *unlike* their male colleagues, many also ended up working for labor institutions because they faced discrimination in other sectors of the economy. Shut out of the good jobs within the university, many progressive reform-minded women with doctorates in economics and sociology turned to using their expertise in union research, education, and legislative departments. In 1953 alone, women headed some eleven union research departments, for example.[79] A generation earlier they might have been found volunteering in settlement houses or employed as social welfare professionals. The careers of Esther Peterson, Katherine Pollak Ellickson, and Gladys Dickason are typical.

Esther Eggertsen Peterson made perhaps the greatest impact of any labor feminist of her generation. The Mormon daughter of Danish immigrants in conservative Provo, Utah, where her father was the local school superintendent, she found her way to becoming the first woman lobbyist for the AFL-CIO Industrial Union Department in the 1950s and the highest ranking woman official in the Kennedy administration. Peterson claimed her "awakening" began in the early 1930s when she met her husband-to-be, Oliver Peterson, a working-class socialist and Farmer-Labor Party supporter whose heroes were Norman Thomas and Robert LaFollette. Yet Peterson was clearly ready. After receiving her B.A. from Brigham Young University in 1927, she left Utah far behind and moved to New York to attend Columbia Teachers' College. She had also decided against marrying a very different fiancé. "I can remember as a senior at Brigham Young University, having life explained to me in terms of a pocket watch, with God as the mainspring, and the man I thought I was in love with, who was doing the explaining, of course, was one of the bigger wheels, and sweet little me somewhere down in the parts you can't see, I think with the rest of the women."[80]

In New York, Oliver introduced Esther to garment union leaders Sidney Hillman and David Dubinsky, and encouraged her to teach working girls in the industrial department of the local "Y." From 1932 to 1939, Peterson spent summers as the PE and drama teacher at the Bryn Mawr Summer School— "the best education on workers' issues that I could have experienced." After a year as a paid organizer for the American Federation of Teachers, Peterson joined the staff of ACWA in 1939. At ACWA she worked first in the education department with J.B.S. Hardeman and then with Bessie Hillman during the war, organizing new shops in the South and helping "integrate the Black and White workers" on the shop floor and in the union, an assignment Peterson recalled as one of her most difficult. Finally in 1945, Peterson became ACWA's first legislative representative in Washington. Her fourth child was born in 1946.[81]

Peterson stepped down from her ACWA post in 1948 and traveled with her husband to Sweden and Belgium, where he worked as a Foreign Service officer and Peterson acted as an advisor to Swedish trade unions. In 1958, Peterson returned to full-time union work when her husband became ill—an illness brought on in part, Peterson believed, by the stresses he suffered as a result of HUAC accusations of communist activity. "He was never the same after the hearings," Peterson would often say. The ACWA leadership helped get Peterson a job on the legislative staff of the Industrial Union Department as the AFL-CIO's first woman lobbyist. From there she became head of the Women's Bureau, assistant secretary of labor in the Kennedy administration, and the

Fig. 1.6 Esther Peterson (seated on the left) with the Utah "Women's R-Day Committee."
In 1944, ACWA sent Peterson to her home state to register voters and to campaign for
Roosevelt and U.S. senator Elbert Thomas, a strong labor supporter. Credit: Esther Peterson
Collection, Schlesinger Library, Radcliffe Institute, Harvard University.

principal force behind the President's Commission on the Status of Women
and the Equal Pay Act, among other initiatives. She subsequently served as a
government official in the Johnson and Carter administrations.[82]

Jewish by birth, Katherine (Kitty) Pollak Ellickson grew up in Ethical Culture circles in Manhattan. Her father practiced law, and her mother was active
in feminist, labor, and consumer causes. Ellickson graduated from Vassar in
1926 with a degree in economics "because it was useful," and then continued
her studies in economics at Columbia. When the CIO hired her into its research department in 1942—Stanley Ruttenberg, the director, and other staffers had been drafted—Ellickson already had a decade of experience in the
labor movement as an educator at the Bryn Mawr Women's Summer School
and the Brookwood Labor College. She had also worked as a speechwriter and
assistant to Mine Worker and CIO officials and as an associate economist for
the National Labor Relations Board from 1938 to 1940. Ellickson stayed with
the CIO during the war and afterwards, due in part to a thirty-hour-week ar-
rangement that allowed her to spend time with her two young children. Later,

Fig. 1.7 Katherine Pollak [Ellickson] speaking to West Virginia mine workers in November 1931, while on staff at the Brookwood Labor School, the radical labor college started by socialist minister A.J. Muste in 1921. In 1935, Ellickson became chief assistant to John Brophy, United Mine Worker official and the first CIO director of organization. Credit: Archives of Labor and Urban Affairs, Wayne State University.

when her economist husband, John Chester Ellickson, contracted TB, Ellickson found an "English-trained Irish nurse who proved invaluable in making it possible for me to work."

In 1955 after the AFL and CIO merger, Ellickson moved onto the AFL-CIO research staff, but found it much less hospitable to women. In the AFL there was simply "not the same feeling of equal treatment for women that there was in the CIO," she recalled, especially "after my return to the CIO in the years 1942 to 1955." In the early 1960s, at the urging of her friend Esther Peterson, then assistant secretary of labor, Ellickson accepted a government job as executive secretary of the PCSW. Later, she helped set up the Equal Employment Opportunity Commission.[83]

When interviewed in 1976, Ellickson saw her "activities in the labor movement" as "unusual but not unique for a woman." She reeled off a long list of "factors" that had aided her. "I had acquired the necessary experience in the 1920s and early 1930s before I had married and before I had children. I had the option of working for the labor movement when it paid very little, [an option] somebody less fortunately placed might not have had." She continued: "I had very competent help at home—and again I could afford this. My husband did not expect me to devote myself entirely to him or to the family. My working and accomplishments may have been a threat to him but he did not protest."

Ellickson believed "the war and the drafting of men opened up opportunities which I would not have had otherwise." Finally, she saw herself as "very lucky" in working with John Brophy and, later, Stanley Ruttenberg, who felt "that women should be given opportunities and be paid the same amount as men." Their attitude was not shared, Ellickson noted, by other CIO leaders in the 1930s, including John L. Lewis.[84]

Daughter of an upwardly mobile cotton-farming family that homesteaded in Oklahoma's Indian Territory, Gladys Dickason had a conservative evangelical upbringing. She graduated from the University of Oklahoma in 1922 and then moved on to graduate work in economics and political science at Columbia and the London School of Economics before teaching at Sweet Briar College in Virginia and Hunter College in New York. She began working for ACWA as an organizer after serving on the industrial committee of the 1933 Cotton Garment Code Authority, set up under the National Recovery Act to regulate wages and prices in the cotton garment industry. In 1935, Dickason was named ACWA's research director, and later, head of ACWA's Southern department. In 1937, she launched a four-year organizing campaign against the nation's largest shirtmaker, Cluett-Peabody and Company in Troy, New York, finally securing a contract in 1941. In 1946, having established her reputation as a "tough, dedicated organizer," Dickason joined Bessie Hillman as an international vice president and the only other woman on ACWA's executive board. That same year the CIO named Dickason assistant director for the CIO Southern organizing campaign.[85]

In the late 1940s and 1950s, Dickason devoted a large share of her attention to the campaign for living wage standards in the garment industry. Surprised by her "rationality" and her "ease with figures and facts," one *Fortune Magazine* writer mused that "emotional arguments carry about as much weight with her as they would with a third grade teacher who caught Buster throwing spit balls." Dickason married Arthur Harrison, an industrial engineer, but did not have children. She retired from union work in 1963 because of ill health.[86]

Women who held influential national union office or served in high government positions were not the only women labor leaders to emerge after the 1930s, however. They were joined by a large group of women who held secondary positions of leadership. Many of these women never achieved executive board or vice presidency positions but they led union locals and district councils, served as regional representatives and business agents, and held key staff positions in research, education, and legislative departments. Many were concentrated in the large and influential industrial unions affiliated with the CIO.

In the UAW, for example, few women held *elected* leadership positions even at the local level, in part because women were such a low percentage of the workforce throughout the postwar years and in part because most locals were mixed-sex. Yet a potent group of UAW female staffers—including Millie Jeffrey, Caroline Davis, Lillian Hatcher, Olga Madar, and Dorothy Haener—created a stir felt far beyond Detroit.

Fig. 1.8 Gladys Dickason, vice president, ACWA, making a case for industry-wide bargaining in the men's clothing industry in 1953. Seated next to her is ACWA's general counsel William Isaacson. Credit: CIO News, April 6, 1953, George Meany Memorial Archives.

Mildred McWilliams Jeffrey held the leadership reins of the UAW Women's Bureau from its beginning in 1944 to 1947. After a brief leave of absence, she returned to the UAW to direct the union's public relations and community affairs divisions, working closely with the Women's Bureau and its new director, Caroline Davis, throughout the 1950s and 1960s. Born in 1911 in Alton, Iowa, Jeffery grew up in a small town where, she recalled, Irish Catholics like her family were threatened by the KKK and none held political office. From an early age, she determined to end such injustices and to use the democratic electoral process to do it. The oldest of seven children in a family supported primarily by her mother's income as a pharmacist, she earned money working at a candy bar factory and plucking chickens in order to attend the University of Minnesota in the early 1930s. There her labor politics blossomed. "I read the Webbs," Jeffrey remembered—referring to the English evolutionary (or Fabian) socialists and British Labor Party advocates Beatrice and Sidney Webb— "and the 'Y' had a profound impact on me, influencing me to be a racial liberal and a Christian socialist." At the urging of the director of the local "Y," Jeffrey applied for a fellowship to Bryn Mawr. In 1935, she received her master's degree from Bryn Mawr's Department of Social Economy and Social Research, having spent much of her time studying social problems first-hand in the poor sections of Philadelphia.[87]

After graduation, Jeffrey took a job with ACWA, organizing "baby strikes" to enforce the child labor laws in the textile industry and running educational programs for the Pennsylvania Joint Board of Shirt Makers. She also married Homer Newman Jeffrey, another labor organizer, whom she met at a rally for striking necktie workers. Their wartime work with the Labor Morale Section of the War Production Board in Washington and their political activities in the Union for a Democratic America (forerunner of the Americans for Democratic Action) introduced Millie and her husband to the Reuther brothers and other like-minded activists. They became close friends with New Deal economist and Wagner Act architect Leon Keyserling, and his wife, Mary Dublin Keyserling who later would be the head of the U.S. Women's Bureau. Their circle also included May and Walter Reuther, and electrical worker unionist Jim Carey and his wife, Margaret McCormick. "We all had young kids. We did a lot of socializing." Jeffrey's attraction to the socialist anticommunist left grew out of her "belief in the democratic process" and her embrace of what she later came to call "the middle way." She respected many of the labor activists in the Communist Party, particularly their "stance on civil rights," but "I didn't believe in their political theories—the dictatorship of the proletariat—that was a problem."[88]

Eventually, Jeffrey ended up accepting Victor Reuther's offer of a staff position as head of the UAW's Women's Bureau in 1944 despite her initial shock at discovering what Reuther meant when he promised to work out "her child care arrangements so you don't have to worry." (Reuther had contracted for foster day care for her two children, ages 6 months and two-and-a-half years, so she could travel during the week.) Jeffrey finally found an alternative child-care plan (she hired a full-time housekeeper). She stayed with the UAW for the next thirty-three years.[89]

Caroline Dawson Davis, who headed the UAW Women's Bureau from 1948 until her retirement in 1973, grew up in a poor Kentucky mining family steeped in religion and unionism. Caroline never finished high school—she left to work at a glass plant at age 15—but she was an avid reader throughout her life, ranging from Freud to political biography and history. When her family moved to Elkhart, Indiana, looking for work, she got a job in 1934 as a drill press operator in the same Excel Corporation auto parts plant that hired her father. Herschel Davis, whom she married in 1936 at the age of twenty-five, worked in the plant as well. Like her husband, Caroline Davis had a strong anti-authoritarian streak. She also had a bad habit of stepping in to stand up for anyone being mistreated. Both these traits propelled her toward union activity. "The worst thing about any job to me was authority," Davis explained matter-of-factly. "I loved people," she continued, "and I believed in people. I never saw the difference between someone who had a title and a lot of money, and Joe Doe and Jane Doe who swept floors and dug ditches. Unions give the people a voice for themselves. [They] help them make decisions—to not be robots that the boss could boss around." As she explained to *Life* magazine in 1947, in their feature story on the "strikingly attractive lady labor leader," "[if I] hadn't been a union leader, I would have been a psychiatrist." She also told *Life* that since she couldn't have children, she would "serve people."[90]

Thirty-year-old Davis helped organize her factory in 1941 and was then elected to the first negotiating committee. In 1943, she became vice-president of UAW Local 764, a 500-member local, 90 percent of whom were men. Shortly thereafter, Davis recalled, she "moved upstairs when the [union] president was drafted," becoming the first woman president of a UAW local. At the war's end, her coworkers reelected her as president. During her tenure, she negotiated four excellent contracts. Employers agreed to eliminate piecework, raise wages 80 percent above the pre-union scale, provide health and retirement benefits, and let women have more control over the timing of their pregnancy leaves. Davis also negotiated an equal pay provision in the contract that she then relied upon to win an equal pay grievance on behalf of drill press operators.

In 1946, Walter Reuther, the socialist tool and die maker who had risen to the UAW presidency after bitter fights with challengers from the right as well as from the communist faction within the union, offered Davis the directorship of the UAW Women's Department. Elected from her local as a delegate to the UAW Convention, Davis had been a solid supporter of Reuther. But Davis was reluctant to make the move. "At first I didn't think I wanted to work strictly with women. I didn't know how badly they were discriminated against because I had fought my own battles always." With the encouragement of her husband, who was now on UAW staff, she finally accepted Reuther's offer in 1948, replacing Millie Jeffrey, who took over the helm of the UAW's Community Services and Political Action Department. Davis still regretted not being able to negotiate contracts—and at one point tried to "switch jobs" despite "the resistance from some of the UAW men"—but she soon changed her mind about the extent of sex discrimination faced by women union members. As Davis remembers it, much of her new understanding came from African-American women in the union. "I was vitally interested in the problems of Negroes—as much as I was in women at that time," she recalled. "I found that Negro women said they had more problems being a woman than they had because of color. So I knew I had to concentrate more on women. . . . More and more I was seeing that the women were discriminated against. And we joined with the unfair practices department, and I worked with both women and Negroes on their problems. They were so similar."[91]

Her closest partner in this work was Lillian Hatcher. Born in Alabama in 1915, Hatcher grew up in Detroit's East Side with her widowed mother and three siblings. Hatcher graduated from high school in Detroit, and by the end of the 1930s, she was married with three children. She met her husband, one of the first black officers of a UAW local, when he was involved in a 1937 sit-down strike at Chrysler. In 1943, Hatcher was hired as one of seven black women aircraft riveters at Chrysler's Briggs-Connor Plant. A Polish chief steward helped her gain membership in the union, Local 742. In 1944, Hatcher was

Fig 1.9 One of the photos of Caroline Davis from *Life* magazine, June
30, 1947. The caption read: "After a hard day the lady president of
Local 764 relaxes at home with the union newspaper and a book by
Freud." Her choice was Freud's *A General Introduction to Psycho-
analysis*. Credit: Gordon Coster/Timepix.

elected to the local's executive board and then appointed by the International
as the first black woman staff representative, working in tandem with the UAW's
Women's Bureau and its Fair Practice and Anti-Discrimination Department,
established in March 1946, until her retirement in 1980. Hatcher and Davis
went everywhere together, responding to complaints of discrimination from
women and minorities across the country and speaking to local after local about
race and gender equity.[92]

Jeffrey, Davis, and Hatcher shared leadership with Olga Madar, the second-
generation Czech shop-floor leader at Ford's Willow Run plant who took charge
of the UAW's Recreation Department in 1947, becoming, as one newspaper
explained, "the girl sports director of the he-man UAW." "An inveterate sandlot

Fig. 1.10 (page 56). Caroline Davis (far left), Lillian Hatcher (standing), and William Oliver of the UAW Fair Practices and Anti-Discrimination Department welcome Dorothy Height of the National Council of Negro Women to the 1955 UAW convention. Credit: Archives of Labor and Urban Affairs, Wayne State University.

softball player," Madar was voted one of Detroit's top ten women athletes before coming to the UAW. She had also finished Michigan Normal College and tried her hand at teaching before returning to factory work during the war. As one of her first assignments, she took on the integration of the American Bowling Congress and the Women's International Bowling Congress, both of which barred Asian-Americans as well as African-Americans. By 1952, both associations had dropped the "all-white" clauses from their constitutions.[93]

In the 1950s and 1960s, Dorothy Haener joined the group, becoming more prominent in gender politics nationally after 1960 when she moved from the UAW's Office and Technical Division to the Women's Department. Raised a strict Catholic on "a hardscrabble Michigan farm run by a single mother," Haener recalled her wartime experiences as formative. Fired in 1939 for union organizing in her auto plant, Haener managed to secure a coveted position in 1941 as a B-24 small-parts inspector at the Ford Willow Run Bomber Plant. It was then that she began to reevaluate her life. Before, "I had always expected to get married and raise a family." She never did, in part because, as she explained, "by the time the war ended, I was too independent to get married." When she lost her job in the summer of 1944 to a new male hire with less seniority, she ended up at a toy factory assembling plastic toy guns for much lower pay. She fought to gain her old job and salary back but lost, finally accepting a clerical position in the same auto plant in 1946. Yet she never really gave up: much of her postwar career with the UAW she spent pushing for the promotional rights of her fellow female factory workers, first as a local officer and then in 1952 as an international representative.[94]

All five UAW women, like the majority of labor feminists, combined their union work with other organizational commitments. All were staunch supporters of the Democratic Party and active in the civil rights movement early on. Jeffrey joined the NAACP in the 1940s, as did Lillian Hatcher, who also belonged to the National Council of Negro Women (NCNW). Davis was elected as NOW's first secretary-treasurer in 1966; Hatcher and Haener were among NOW's founding members.[95]

Few unions could match the UAW in terms of the number of women on its *national* staff, but almost all the progressive industrial unions had women in key positions as local and regional union officers as well as on national staff. And, in many of these unions, African-American women stepped forward to take leading roles as activists and leaders—sometimes in numbers greater than their percentage of the workforce would warrant.[96] In the UPWA, Addie Wyatt was joined by numerous other African-American women leaders in Chicago and elsewhere. In the IUE, Gloria Tapscott Johnson, an African-American with B.A. and M.A. degrees from Howard University in economics and statistics, was the principal national staffer in charge of women's activities from 1954 until her retirement in the 1990s.[97] And, as Susan Hartmann has detailed, she was not the lone African-American feminist within the IUE by any means.[98]

As the number of black women in apparel increased fourfold over the course of the 1940s, black women emerged as leaders in the garment unions as well— although Jewish and Italian men retained the top executive positions (nationally and locally) even as the membership shifted to black, Asian, and Spanish-speaking immigrants.[99] Panamanian-born Maida (Stewart) Springer-Kemp, for example, became one of the first black ILGWU union officials in the early 1940s. Springer-Kemp's politics were shaped by her mother's affinity for Marcus Garvey, the Black Nationalist leader, and later her close friendship with BSCP leader and socialist A. Philip Randolph. Much of her loyalty to the labor movement, however, derived from first-hand experience. With her husband out of work in 1932, Springer-Kemp found a job first as a hand sewer and then as a pinking-machine operator. Encouraged by her union president, Charles Zimmerman, she rose quickly in Local 22, an offshoot of the famous Dress and Waistmaker's Local 25 that had earlier nourished Fannia Cohn and Rose Pesotta. She joined the executive board of the union in 1938, and in 1943 Zimmerman appointed her to a full-time staff position as an education director. In 1948, she became the first African-American woman to be an ILGWU district business agent, servicing some sixty shops. When the manufacturers' association protested, saying their officers would not be seen with her, Springer-Kemp recalled Zimmerman's defense of her. "My own union leader, Zimmerman, said, 'All right, nobody will function. You don't want her—you won't see her—you won't see any of us. She's an officer of our union.' " They relented, and only later did Springer-Kemp find out what had happened. Springer-Kemp's long career in international affairs had begun two years earlier with her 1945 appointment by the AFL as one of its two representatives to England as part of an Office of War Information Exchange—the first African-American so honored. In Europe, Springer-Kemp met a group of young African trade unionists and became intensely interested in Pan-Africanism and the role of trade unions in the struggle against colonialism. In 1960, she joined the AFL-CIO's Department of International Affairs full-time.[100]

Other black feminists spent valuable years in the ACWA. Laundry workers remained virtually unorganized until 1937, when a wave of strikes brought thirty thousand New York City laundry workers under contract for the first time. Dorothy (Dollie) Lowther Robinson led the 1937 strike at Colonial Laundry, where she and some 300 other women sweated 72 hours a week for six dollars. She went on to become the education director of the majority-black Laundry Worker Division within the ACWA, encouraged by Bessie Hillman. She and Springer-Kemp became close friends and collaborators in this period as well, drawn together through their activities in the New York WTUL and their involvement in labor education programs at the WTUL-supported Hudson Shore Labor School. They served together on the New York State Minimum Wage Board during the war, along with Pauline Newman, and they worked together on labor and civil rights issues with A. Philip Randolph, the NAACP, and the NCNW. Later, Robinson served as an official in the New York State Labor Department and graduated from law school. In 1961, Robinson accepted Esther Peterson's invitation to join her at the Women's Bureau.[101]

White women held the positions of greater authority in the garment unions, however. Gladys Dickason and Bessie Hillman's connections with the ACWA (both sat on the ACWA Executive Board after 1946) have already been noted. Of ACWA's regional directors, Anne Draper, the Union Label Director for the western states, had perhaps the most influence. Born Pauline Kracik to Polish-Ukrainian immigrants of Roman Catholic faith, Draper grew up poor in Manhattan's Lower East Side. As a teenager she joined the Young Socialists (YPSL) after reading the works of Trotsky. She continued her involvement in radical movements at Hunter College, where she also studied math and economics, supported by the earnings of her older siblings and her own work as a store clerk. After a brief interlude with the Steel Workers Organizing Committee in

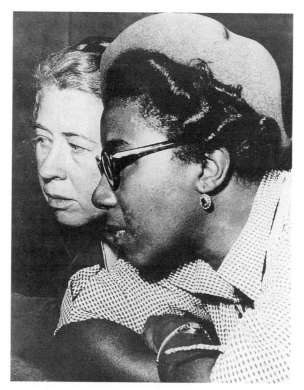

Fig. 1.11 Esther Peterson and Maida Springer-Kemp
listening to an equal pay debate at an International Labor
Organization meeting in Sweden in 1951. Springer-Kemp
toured Sweden under the auspices of the American-Scandi-
navian Foundation before studying at Oxford University's
Ruskin Labor College. While in Sweden, she stayed with
Peterson, a friend since their garment union organizing days
of the late 1930s. Peterson lived in Sweden from 1948 to
1952 during her husband's tenure as labor attache. Courtesy
of Murry Weisz and the George Meany Memorial Archives.

the late 1930s and a job as a unionized welder during World War II, Draper
settled into a position as a business representative for the United Hatters Union
in New York that lasted for over a decade. In 1958, Draper moved to California,
where she took a job with ACWA and quickly became a prominent spokeswoman on behalf of California's large agricultural workforce. She organized
labor and community support for the United Farm Workers and represented
ACWA in lobbying for farmworker coverage under California's minimum wage
laws. In 1971, along with other labor women, she founded Union WAGE (Wom-
en's Alliance to Gain Equality), an inter-union organization of labor women
dedicated to solving the problems of low-wage women.[102]

In the ILGWU, Jennie Matyas and Angela Bambace occupied executive board seats throughout most of the postwar era. They replaced Rose Pesotta, the first woman on the ILGWU Executive Board, who resigned her vice presidency in 1944 after serving three terms, and returned to the dress shop and membership in Waistmakers' Local 25 in New York.[103] None took as prominent a role in the women's movement, however, as did Evelyn Kahan Dubrow, the ILGWU's first female legislative representative. Raised in a socialist working-class family in New Jersey, Dubrow managed to graduate from New York University with a degree in journalism in the middle of the depression before turning to labor work as education director for the New Jersey Textile Workers Union. During the war, Dubrow worked with the New Jersey Industrial Union Council, where she chaired women's political activities in the 1944 election. After "a bad experience with a very brief marriage" and nearly a decade as the director of organization for the Americans for Democratic Action, Dubrow took a job as executive secretary of the ILGWU's political department in 1956, eventually becoming their legislative representative in 1961 and an international vice president in 1977.[104]

Outside of manufacturing, in unions such as CWA and HERE, almost all the women leaders were white, in part because few minority women worked in the jobs these unions represented. The phone companies, for example, did not hire black women until the 1960s. And, although black and Spanish-speaking women worked as maids, cooks, and other "back-of-the-house" positions, the leadership of HERE in the postwar period was drawn almost wholly from the "front-of-the-house" crafts such as bartending and food service.[105]

Despite the large numbers of women members in HERE and CWA, fewer women held positions of national or regional leadership in these unions than in the large CIO manufacturing unions. Indeed, over the course of the postwar era the number of prominent women labor leaders in both the telephone and the hospitality industry *declined* somewhat as the numbers of separate-sex and female-majority locals dwindled. In HERE, sex separatism lasted in some cities into the 1970s, providing women with a base of support and ensuring women at least some representation in national and regional bodies. Exceptional leaders like Myra Wolfgang managed to win elections in mixed locals, but overall the number of women leaders in HERE fell after 1950 as women had to compete more directly with men for the few leadership slots.[106]

The situation in the telephone industry was worse. Women found it hard to get elected to office as industrial-style mixed locals replaced the old separate-sex locals and the numbers of women telephone operators dropped with the introduction of direct dialing.[107] In addition, women with long and distinguished records of local activism found it difficult if not impossible to get appointed by the national CWA as regional or district staff representatives.[108]

Nevertheless, exceptional women did move into leadership positions—women like Catherine Conroy of Wisconsin, Selina Burch of Alabama, and Helen Berthelot of Michigan. These women, like most CWA women leaders, were white; they also tended to be from rural and lower-middle-class, old immi-

Fig. 1.12 Anne Draper (far left) marching with the grape strikers in the United Farm Worker-organized caravan to the California State Capitol on Easter Sunday, April 10, 1966. She is joined by Clara Cotruvo, ILGWU; Tina Wall, Office and Professional Employees; and Myrtle Banks, ILGWU. Courtesy of the Labor Archives and Research Center, San Francisco State University.

grant backgrounds—all characteristics typical of the women Bell hired before World War II.

Adopted daughter of a down-on-his-luck art dealer, Catherine Conroy managed to finish high school before settling into a secure job as a phone operator with the Wisconsin Phone Company in 1942. In 1947, with the national telephone strike in full swing, Conroy was 28 and her life was, in her words, "at a turning point." Her mother wanted her to marry and have a family, but Conroy "wasn't eager to marry just to marry, and I hadn't met anyone that I could see myself tied down to and spending a lifetime with." Instead, she ended up serving as a picket line captain during the strike, and later became a steward and local officer in her NFTW telephone operators' local. "It was such an exciting time . . . building the union, writing a constitution, long debates. . . . At five in the morning we were still arguing should it be this way or [that]. I wouldn't have missed it for anything." In 1951, when her local affiliated with CWA, Conroy was elected president. In 1960 she became one of the few women on CWA staff. By the end of the 1960s, Conroy had served on the Wisconsin Governor's Commission on the Status of Women and as the Chicago NOW chapter's first president.[109]

Selina Burch's life and union career paralleled that of Conroy. A high school graduate and farmer's daughter, Burch started working in the Dublin, Georgia, Southern Bell office in 1945. She was active in the 1947 strike. Later, union work became an alternative to a marriage gone bad. By 1952, Burch was divorced, childless, and giving all her time to the union as the local's secretary-treasurer. "I guess the rebel in me really began to come out somewhere between 1952 and 1954 when I saw that I was doing all the work and a male was getting all the credit. In 1954, I decided I would run for local president." With more women in the local than men, Burch won. The violent nine-state, nine-week walkout in 1955 affecting some 50,000 Southern Bell employees catapulted Burch into district leadership. Three years later, she moved on to CWA southern regional staff, a position she held into the 1970s.[110]

Berthelot, also from a rural background, became an operator for Michigan Bell in 1923. She returned to working for Bell in the 1930s when her husband died, leaving her with two children to support. Berthelot used her earlier experience as an employee representative in the company union to help organize an independent union in the late 1930s, and by 1942 was secretary of a 6,000-member statewide operators (traffic) union. She and Fran Smith led the operators out in 1946 and again in 1947. "It was a great shock to the Telephone Co. in Michigan." Nothing like this had ever happened before, Berthelot explained, especially in the rural areas. Later, she became vice president of the Michigan Division of the NFTW and then, in 1953, with her kids grown, moved to Washington to become CWA's first female legislative representative. "It was rough. I will never forget the looks on the men's faces—this is when . . . all the legislative people were men. I was the first gal that came in and they looked at me as if I had crawled out from under a stone, even our own fellas didn't want to be associated with me too much, being a gal . . . the two men from the UAW were the ones who adopted me." She persevered for the next sixteen years, retiring in 1969.[111]

The labor women who have been introduced here led the other women's movement in the postwar period. Their power rested in part on women's growing numbers in the labor movement—both as activists and as leaders—as well as on women's rising expectations about what they deserved at work. Yet their influence would have been minimal had they worked in isolation or had they stayed within the institutional confines of trade unionism. As the next chapter will show, what enabled them to have a national impact on the social policy of their era was their ability to forge organizational links to each other and to female allies outside the labor movement. It is to the social feminist alliances they created in the 1940s and 1950s that we now turn.

CHAPTER TWO

Social Feminism Remade

> The woman problem in industry is equally a labor problem. Equal rights and
> equal opportunities for women workers can not be separated from the
> question of industrial justice for all workers.
>
> —*Mary Anderson, in* Good Housekeeping, 1925.[1]

THE STORY OF social feminism often trails off in the 1940s as national figures
such as Secretary of Labor Frances Perkins or WTUL leader and Roosevelt
White House advisor Rose Schneiderman recede from public view. Yet the social feminist movement after the 1930s included new women's organizations like
the National Council for Negro Women (NCNW), founded in 1935 by Mary
McLeod Bethune, as well as older yet still vital groups like the American Association of University Women (AAUW) and the YWCA. These groups, joined
loosely into what Cynthia Harrison has called the "Women's Bureau network,"
represented a large segment of all women organized into all-female associations.[2]

The social feminist wing of the women's movement in this era also included
the labor women reformers described in chapter 1. It is these women who
moved into leadership positions in the movement in the 1940s and reenergized
it. They brought their ties to the economic and political resources of organized
labor, the largest social movement of the day, and they brought their own ideas
of how to advance the status of women. The labor women who led the social
feminist movement in the postwar era were not devoid of reform ideas, nor
were they animated solely by a negative politics of opposition to the equal
rights feminists who supported the ERA. Indeed, by the early 1940s, they had
articulated a concrete and broad reform agenda around which they and their
allies in the broader social feminism movement would organize for the next
quarter century.

THE LABOR WOMEN'S SEAT IN GOVERNMENT

The Women's Bureau and its labor-oriented directors played a crucial role in
instigating and sustaining the national alliance that emerged among labor
feminists by the 1940s.[3] From its onset, the Women's Bureau had close ties to
labor women and the broader social feminist community. As the Chicago
WTUL leader and shoe worker Mary Anderson remembered it, Jane Addams,

WTUL President Margaret Dreier Robins, and other women associated with the WTUL in the Progressive Era had long been interested in "having some division of the federal government look after the interests of women in industry." The forerunner of the Bureau, the Women in Industry Service, with Mary Van Kleeck of the Russell Sage Foundation in charge and Anderson as her assistant, was inaugurated during World War I. In 1920, pressure from the National WTUL and other groups secured an act of Congress setting up a permanent federal bureau within the U.S. Department of Labor. Its mandate was to "promote the welfare of wage-earning women, improve their working conditions, and advance their opportunities for profitable employment." Mary Anderson, as we have seen, took the reins in 1920 and held them for the next twenty-five years.

Under her leadership, the Women's Bureau adhered to its initial charge as interpreted by Anderson and the group of social feminists with whom she worked, including her close associates at the WTUL, the National Consumers' League (NCL), and other women's organizations. The Women's Bureau led the campaign to derail the ERA beginning in 1923, and its research proved instrumental in the passage and continuation of labor standards legislation for women. Such legislation included statutes mandating minimum wages, rest and lunch breaks, maternity provisions, proper safety devices, and restricting daily and weekly work hours, night work, and industrial homework. Anderson felt a special passion for raising the wages of low-income women and countering the myth of women as secondary earners, in part because she was the primary breadwinner for herself (a single woman), and later her widowed sister and her sister's daughter. Infuriated by the "pin money" notion that women got jobs to buy frivolous extras, Anderson commissioned numerous studies showing that most women took jobs out of economic necessity. Anderson also pressed for adequate female representation on governmental and labor bodies and for policies that addressed the special needs of women, noting more than once that when officials "spoke of 'the people,' they meant the men."[4]

The Women's Bureau network still included many women's organizations among its supporters after the 1930s, but labor women and the institutions they represented became the *dominant* constituency. Older women's organizations like the NCL were in decline, their membership dwindling and their bank accounts barely in the black. In contrast, labor women represented organizations with millions of members, ample treasuries, and an impressive degree of political and economic clout; they also simply outnumbered the other groups. The vitality of social feminism after the 1930s, then, no longer rested on the persistence of the older Progressive Era women's groups. The political weight had shifted. Labor and working-class women had a greater voice in the social feminist movement than ever before, and the network gathered around the Women's Bureau drew its power from its connections to labor institutions as much as to women's organizations.

In 1945, for example, when the Equal Pay Bill was introduced in Congress for the first time, Women's Bureau director Mary Anderson appeared to testify before the Senate committee representing a coalition of some 42 organizations. Unions constituted the *majority* of the organizational members, including the many new CIO unions with large and vocal female memberships—auto, electrical, garment, communication, and other unions—as well as a number of labor women's auxiliary groups.[5] The constellation of this new social feminist ad hoc coalition, as well as other similar groups formed in the 1940s, would change little over the course of the next two decades.

After Anderson stepped down in 1944, labor women and their organizations continued to hold special cachet at the Women's Bureau. With the exception of Republican-appointee Alice Leopold's tenure, which lasted from 1953 to 1961, all the Women's Bureau directors before the 1970s took great care to involve union women in every aspect of their work. Women's Bureau directors asked union women to keynote at Women's Bureau conferences, even those involving a cross-section of women from government, business, and the community, and union women's advice was sought in determining Bureau priorities. Most tellingly, in 1945 and 1946 the Women's Bureau held two special national conferences for union women, out of which emerged a concrete and comprehensive agenda for raising women's economic status and an institutional mechanism for helping realize such an agenda. In 1945, following the first national conference for "women labor leaders from unions having large numbers of women members," the Women's Bureau set up a "Labor Advisory Committee" (LAC), which served as a policy think tank for top women in the labor movement.[6] It met frequently between 1945 to 1953 under Frieda Miller's directorship, more sporadically between 1953 and 1961, and then was reconstituted in 1961 when Esther Peterson took over.

LAC consisted of a shifting group of some fifteen top women labor leaders from both the AFL and the CIO. It included, among others, Esther Peterson, Gladys Dickason, and Dollie Lowther Robinson from ACWA; Lillian Hatcher and Caroline Davis from the UAW; Katherine Ellickson (CIO Research Department); Myra Wolfgang (HERE), Pauline Newman (ILGWU), and Helen Berthelot (CWA). In LAC's first few years, the UE's Ruth Young and the FTA's Washington legislative representative Elizabeth Sasuly, both of whom worked for unions closely associated with the Communist left, were also on the committee, and among its most vocal and far-thinking participants. But within a few years both Young and Sasuly were gone, casualties of the cold war split in the labor movement. The women remaining, unified in part by their affinity with the left-liberal wing of the Democratic Party, led the social feminist movement until the late 1960s. They shaped the policy direction of the Bureau in the postwar era, and they provided the political muscle needed to help realize that policy in legislative enactment and employer practice.[7]

The movement might not have coalesced nationally without the initiative and persistence of the labor-oriented women who headed the Women's Bureau. Such an institutional home facilitated a national conversation among labor women; without it they might have remained isolated and their energies dissipated. Mary Anderson sought out and encouraged labor women's leadership

Fig 2.1 A meeting of the Women's Bureau Labor Advisory Committee, June 4, 1946. Women's Bureau chief Frieda Miller is seated in the center. To her left is: Lillian Hatcher, UAW; Helen Blanchard, ACWA; Pauline Newman, ILGWU; Elisabeth Christman, National WTUL; and Dollie Lowther Robinson, Laundry Workers Joint Board, ACWA. Gladys Dickason, ACWA; Katherine Ellickson, CIO; and others are not shown. Credit: Frieda Miller Collection, Scheslinger Library, Radcliffe Institute, Harvard University.

largely because of her own sympathies with the political program of the labor movement and her belief in its viability as a mechanism for improving the lives of wage-earning women. Anderson could be critical of male union leaders and their policies toward women, yet she never stopped believing in the necessity for *collective* representation in the workplace. The labor movement, she even once suggested, offered an alternative to marriage for working-class women. At least that's how it felt in her life. "I thought as a young girl that I would get married too, but somewhere I lost myself in my work and never felt that marriage would give me the security I wanted. I thought that through the trade union movement we working women could get better conditions and security of mind."[8]

Frieda Miller, director from 1944 to 1953, continued these traditions. Although from quite a different class background than Anderson—Miller's father was a lawyer, and she had a college degree plus years of doctoral work in law and economics at the University of Chicago—Miller's basic assumptions about unions and the problems of working women overlapped considerably with those of Anderson. Before becoming New York State's industrial commissioner in 1938, a position she would hold until 1943, Miller had worked for the Philadelphia branch of the WTUL, taught at the Bryn Mawr Summer School, and been instrumental in the passage of New York's 1933 minimum wage law for women and minors. Miller was a close friend of Roosevelt's secretary of labor Frances Perkins, and part of the tight circle of WTUL activists based in New York, including Rose Schneiderman and Pauline Newman. In 1918, as discussed in chapter 1, she had met and developed a lifelong relationship with ILGWU organizer Newman. While on a trip to Vienna in 1923 for the Third International Congress of Working Women with Newman, Miller gave birth to a daughter, Elisabeth. She and Newman raised Elisabeth in their Greenwich Village apartment and later in their Connecticut home, with Newman increasingly holding down the domestic front while Miller traveled throughout the United States and abroad in her capacity as a government official.[9]

Of the women who succeeded Miller in the 1950s and 1960s, only Alice Leopold, appointed director by President Eisenhower in 1953, failed to fit the labor mold. A Goucher College 1927 graduate, Leopold pursued a business career in retail, first as a personnel director for B. Altman & Company and then as a designer and manufacturing of children's toys, before she entered Connecticut politics as a Republican legislator in 1949.[10] Esther Peterson (director from 1961 to 1964), as we have seen, had strong labor sympathies, as did Mary Dublin Keyserling, who took over in 1964.

Keyserling grew up in a prosperous New York City household, the daughter of Eastern European Jewish immigrants. Her mother, a social worker, had served as head of a settlement house in Philadelphia and her father, a statistician and vice president of the Metropolitan Life Insurance Company, was a prominent public health expert. Following in her mother's footsteps, Keyserling attended Barnard College, graduating in 1930. She then pursued graduate studies in economics at the London School of Economics and, like a number of other prominent labor women reformers of this era, passed her qualifying exams in economics at Columbia University before dropping out to put her theories into practice through labor reform work and teaching. By 1938, at the age of twenty-eight, Keyserling became executive director of the New York branch of the NCL. She later worked with Eleanor Roosevelt in the Office of Civilian Defense during the war, as an economic analyst in the Department of Commerce in the late 1940s and early 1950s, and then, with her husband, Leon Keyserling, as a consultant on labor and social welfare issues. She established her labor sympathies and social reform agenda early, and never strayed far.[11]

Without the Women's Bureau, the emerging generation of women labor leaders might have remained isolated and even unknown to one another, their time and imagination absorbed by the problems of their individual unions. After all, no national organization of labor women existed in this period. Although it did not formally disband until 1950, the national WTUL, the cross-class organization that provided a home for an earlier labor feminism, had died a quiet death in the late 1930s for all practical purposes. The committees and conferences sponsored by the Bureau helped fill the vacuum. The labor women who led the postwar social feminist movement met each other at the behest of the Women's Bureau, and it was the Women's Bureau directors who urged them to devise a new policy agenda and then to organize for its achievement. And, although the Bureau itself lost resources and independence after 1947, "its network proved hardier than the agency itself."[12]

Yet labor feminism in this period extended *beyond* the confines of the Women's Bureau network. Labor women leaders in Washington, especially the full-time staffers working in national union legislative and research departments, formed their own ad hoc groups, which pursued policies independently from the Women's Bureau network. Particularly in the 1950s, with Alice Leopold in office, few if any of the political groups formed by labor women found a home at the Bureau. The National Committee for Equal Pay (NCEP), for example, the principal group coordinating the state and federal equal pay campaigns from 1953 to 1963, operated out of the IUE headquarters and kept its distance from the Women's Bureau until 1961 when Esther Peterson came in as director.

But even more importantly, labor feminists sought to realize their social reform agenda in league with the mixed-sex labor, civil rights, and political organizations to which they belonged—organizations whose reach extended into workplaces and communities across the country. As we have seen, labor feminists were active in the NAACP, the NCNW, and other civil rights coalitions as well as the full range of Democratic Party politics. Their greatest political resource, however, was their access to their own union organizations. Unions knew how to mobilize their members as well as their "auxiliaries" for large-scale political and economic action. They were effective lobbyists at the state and local as well as the federal level. Further, collective bargaining procedures allowed for a wide range of issues to be raised and negotiated *directly* with corporate policy-makers. Indeed, labor feminists spent as much time transforming employer policies through economic pressure as they did lobbying for new government rules and regulations. Thus, to characterize the postwar women's movement as a small, beleaguered, Washington-based lobbying network lacking a grassroots constituency or a national presence misses the extensive campaigns labor feminists conducted *outside* of Washington. It ignores the leadership of women in labor's postwar efforts to extend economic citizenship to new groups of workers through *state*-mandated rights and benefits and through union contracts in numerous local settings.

After the 1930s, labor women breathed new life into the social feminist movement by connecting it to the energy and power of organized labor. They also helped refashion the social feminist agenda, recasting received tenets from an earlier era and pushing for the needs and perspectives of labor and working-class women to be given greater credence. An earlier generation of labor women leaders, grouped principally in the WTUL, had often articulated their own labor variant of social feminism, what Annelise Orleck calls "industrial feminism," and it could differ quite sharply from the "maternalist" feminism more typical of middle-class women active in social reform. Class tensions were palpable in the early WTUL, with labor women often favoring policies that encouraged worker organization and self-determination and objecting to those that smacked of charity or that set up middle-class notions of femininity as the assumed ideal.[13] By the 1930s, the influence of labor women reformers was gaining ground, particularly in the formulation of labor and social policy in the Roosevelt White House.

The labor women of the post-depression decades extended these working-class traditions into the postwar era, creating a gender politics that reflected the historically specific realities of their generation. During the war, a consensus crystallized among labor feminists that the next step in the march toward gender equality was the achievement of first-class economic citizenship, or what Mary Anderson called "full industrial citizenship."[14] The struggle for the vote, once won, "only inaugurated a more important campaign," a UAW leaflet proclaimed, "one that is still being waged, the fight for economic equality."[15] In 1943, the Women's Advisory Committee of the War Manpower Commission proclaimed its opposition "to discrimination in employment on the basis of sex in time of peace or war" and its plan to protect "the rights of women" at war's end. During the war, the committee pointed out, women "adjusted their family life and found a new, often hard won economic status which they do not wish to lose."[16] Yet lose it they did. And it was the wartime *taste* of economic advance in conjunction with the *loss* of these gains at the war's end that intensified women's desire for full economic citizenship.

Economic rights and equality, then, were at the heart of the social feminist movement by the 1940s and would remain so until the rise of a new generation of feminists in the 1960s and 1970s. Yet labor feminists conceived of economic rights and equality *broadly*. Achieving first-class economic citizenship meant transforming women's market work; it also meant paying attention to women's household labor. Labor feminists cared about raising women's status in employment, particularly in what Frieda Miller referred to as the "traditionally feminine occupations" where women were "grossly underpaid."[17] Yet that goal could never be achieved without securing recognition and compensation for women's domestic labor in the home. As Esther Peterson succinctly put it: "Women's jobs are traditionally low paying because we've never put value on work that's done in the home."[18]

Labor feminists also accepted the permanence of women's wage labor, and they claimed a right to wage work equal to that of men (as will be more fully detailed in chapter 3). Yet many labor feminists also argued that women's claim to full economic citizenship required "special" accommodations for women's maternal responsibilities, what they later called "social rights." As Gladys Dickason summarized in 1947: "Special measures of protection and adjustment" such as "maternity leave without loss of seniority" are "essential for the health of mother and child and to insure that women are *not penalized for motherhood*."[19]

First-class economic citizenship for women translated into a number of specific goals. Whether articulated by women on the Communist left like Ruth Young or government bureaucrats like Mary Anderson and Frieda Miller, whether from national union leaders or from the shop floor, the sentiments were remarkably similar. In a 1942 article in the *American Federationist*, Mary Anderson labeled "sex discrimination undemocratic and unbusinesslike" and the "double wage standard pernicious." She demanded the elimination of both.[20] Ruth Young extended Anderson's analysis in the *CIO News* in 1944, calling for "the right of all women to work," "equal pay and the opportunity to advance," and "government responsibility for accommodating maternity and child rearing."[21] The diverse group of AFL and CIO women who formulated the postwar goals of the women's movement in the Women's Bureau conferences held in April 1945 and October 1946 reached the same conclusions. The reports, model contracts, and summary statements flowing from these meetings self-consciously set forth a new "positive program of action for elimination of discriminations" faced by women. Their program included ending discrimination due to sex, color, national origin, age, or marital status; "abolishing wage differentials based on sex rather than job content"; creating a "wider appreciation" for "woman-employing" occupations and industries; raising labor standards; "equal opportunity for promotion"; and supports for women during pregnancy and child rearing.[22]

Rank-and-file women working within their unions echoed the ideas being voiced by their national representatives. ACWA women, for example, in their 1948 "Resolution of Women's Rights," passed by the union convention, judged women to be "widely discriminated against" and decried efforts "to undermine the status women had achieved in the war effort." Others agreed, laying out a concrete program to turn the situation around. At their 1947 convention, UPWA women condemned "employer attempts to dislodge and downgrade women from the positions they held in wartime." They resolved to "fight to ensure equal rights for women on and off the job, equal pay, equal opportunities for promotion and advancement, adequate maternity leave, and protections against discrimination in hiring and firing."[23]

As labor feminists came to the helm of the social feminist movement, the balance among social feminist concerns began to shift. The rhetoric of "rights" increasingly competed with the rhetoric of "protection," and the post-1930s social feminism movement pointed to women's position as citizens and workers as frequently as it noted women's status as wives and mothers.[24] Of course, social feminism had never been merely a maternalist movement concerned solely with enabling women to fulfill their responsibilities as mothers, wives, and daughters. Nor did all Progressive Era social feminists valorize motherhood to the exclusion of other social roles. There had always been a competing discourse of workplace justice and the right of women to wage earning.[25] It was this strand of feminism that now came to the fore. Attention to the needs of mothers *continued*, but the goal was how to *balance* wage-earning and household responsibilities and how to enable women to function in multiple roles.

As we will see later, in the aftermath of World War II, labor women and their allies in the broader social feminist movement debated and reconceived the meanings of "discrimination," "equal pay," and "family wage." Notions of how to achieve their goals evolved as well. Debates over the proper place of sex-based state laws intensified, as did arguments over the advisability of a "family wage," even one expanded to include female heads-of-household. Disagreements erupted over how much emphasis to give a government-centered strategy, particularly in regard to income supports for women's caring labor. Should maternity benefits, for example, "be bargained or costs spread over the whole society through some form of social insurance?"[26] How should the economic and emotional needs of dependents be met? Should labor women push for state income subsidies like the family allowances that existed in Canada and Western Europe? Would emphasizing state-centered approaches and social wages undermine labor's traditional strategy of obtaining a higher market wage—which for many still meant a wage sufficient to pay for household labor and dependent care? How could a right *not* to work be secured in tandem with the right *to* work? What were the best mechanisms for limiting work time so that family and community life could be sustained? These were among the many questions tackled by the postwar labor feminists and their social feminist allies.

A SHARED FRAMEWORK

Much of this debate took place within a shared ideological framework. Like many unionists and left-liberals in the postwar era, labor feminists believed the government should take action to rectify economic injustices. And, although views could diverge sharply over how much government intervention was necessary and the proper relationship between corporations and the state, left-liberals differed from conservative Republicans and businessmen in their willingness to use the state to ameliorate the inadequacies of an unregulated market. By the late 1940s, many left-liberals were pursuing a strategy of social provision that can best be described as *mixed*: it combined public social insurance with private nongovernmental entities such as union-negotiated health and welfare funds.[27]

Unlike some New Deal liberals, however, labor women believed that a more "moral capitalism" needed greater economic democracy and control from below. Increasing state regulation of capital was not enough.[28] Labor feminists believed in the importance of labor institutions both as vehicles for democracy in the workplace and as mechanisms of economic redistribution. Moreover, for a mixed system of provision to work optimally, union institutions were essential. Union political power ensured that government would do its job and curb the abuses of the market; union economic power helped establish fairer and more democratically determined policies in the *private* sector. Without unions, the expansion of New Deal entitlements in the private sector was simply a continuation of paternalistic welfare capitalism. Private provisions should be *negotiated* with workers and their representatives, and they needed to be *guaranteed* through a union contract. Further, labor feminists deemed worker organizations valuable because they *enforced* the rights that government granted. Rights could be inscribed in statute, but worker organizations were necessary for those laws to be more than formal abstract rights. Relying exclusively on government could be dangerous for working people, as AFL leader Samuel Gompers had proclaimed years earlier. What government gave, government could take away.

Labor feminists tried to formulate policies that responded to the particular needs of working-class women because they saw them as the majority of women and because they assessed their problems as more pressing than those of elite women. Economic security loomed large among the concerns of working-class women who came of age in the 1930s; hence, labor feminists took economic security seriously and saw it as one of their top priorities. Moreover, although policies that focused on moving individual women into higher-paying jobs were not discouraged, their limits were recognized. Labor women sought more solidaristic approaches to low pay and economic injustice, such as living wage statutes and paid maternity benefits. They saw these as efforts to change the larger system in ways that offered advancement in income and status to the majority, not just the few.

Post-1930s labor women, both leaders and rank-and-file, felt they deserved higher pay and greater recognition for their labor at home and at work, but they did not necessarily embrace policies of equal treatment or workplace sexual integration. Rather, they believed that differential treatment did not always disadvantage women, and that sometimes the best approach to gender equality was revaluing women's sphere rather than dissolving it. Why valorize men by using them as the standard to which women should aspire? The work world had been constructed with the needs of men, their bodies, and their social roles in mind. Women should not have to become *like men* in order to deserve first-class citizenship. The goal, Frieda Miller offered, is to "achieve an equality which takes account of the differences between men and women." Any other approach risks imposing "identity under a masculine pattern." The world of work should change in response to the women who were now its citizens. That meant raising the pay and status of the "traditional female occupations"; it also meant rethinking work norms and structures.[29] In short, first-class economic citizenship for women would entail the extension of economic rights and benefits to women; it would also require a redefinition of citizenship.[30]

Labor feminism, as an American ideology, existed within the bounds of American political discourse at mid-century. Yet it pushed against these cultural bounds even as it embraced them. Labor women held notions of the market, of the legitimate power unions should have, and of the extent to which working people deserved rights and benefits which were at odds with the dominant political and economic philosophies of their time. And, as we shall see in their debates with equal rights feminists over the ERA, they, like the "equal righters" with whom they disagreed, also held ideas of women's rights that were subversive of the established gender order.

THE CONTINUING BATTLES OVER THE ERA

Ever since the word "feminism" came into common usage in the United States in the early twentieth century, there have been debates over who was and wasn't a feminist and what the appropriate ends and means for a movement on behalf of women should be.[31] That debate intensified after the passage of suffrage in 1920 when two groups of women reformers faced off against each other over how best to advance women's equality. One group, the equal rights feminists, led by NWP head Alice Paul, focused single-mindedly on the passage of a constitutional amendment, the ERA. When introduced into Congress in 1923, the ERA declared that "men and women shall have equal rights throughout the United States and in every place subject to its jurisdiction." NWP leaders had earlier debated and rejected the addition of a clause exempting woman-only labor laws and other kinds of "special legislation," the position advocated by NCL secretary Florence Kelley and other social feminists. After 1923, social feminists formed a "counter-lobby" to the ERA, which included such women's organizations as the WTUL, the League of Women Voters, the General Federation of Women's Clubs, the YWCA, and others.[32] Labor women were particularly bitter in their opposition. As Pauline Newman declared at a trade union woman's conference in 1922:

> We know what equality is and what it is not. Experience has taught us that. There are so-called equal rights which furnish thrills for the few, but have no regard for the lives of the many. We want to remove discriminations, but a blanket law that threatens to take away rights already won we will fight, and fight to the finish.[33]

The battle continued full-blown into the World War II years and beyond.[34] The ERA's perceived threat to the numerous sex-based state laws that regulated women's wages, hours, and working conditions was certainly a major reason for the unrelenting condemnation of social feminists. In the heartfelt words of one labor union activist in 1946, echoing Newman's words from the 1920s: "Frankly, I feel that the protection of the gains that we have made is extremely important and I for one don't ever want to support a bill or bills that will jeopardize those gains. The fight has been too severe and the victory too sweet."[35] Harvard professor and long-time WTUL member Alice Hamilton pondered in the *Ladies Home Journal* in 1945: "Why should we who call ourselves feminists oppose such a measure?" Her answer: "It is in connection with labor legislation that my opposition is strongest. Women will lose more than they will gain."[36]

But the intensity of the battle over the ERA can not be understood without putting it in the larger context of clashing class interests, fundamentally opposing philosophies of economic and political reform, and deeply held but divergent views on gender and women. As historian Carl Brauer observed, from the 1920s to the 1960s "the debate over the ERA had distinctly class, interest group and ideological overtones, pitting affluent, business-oriented, and politically conservative women against poor, union-oriented and politically liberal women."[37] Amy Butler's recent study of the clashes over the ERA in the 1920s makes a similar point. Both sides wanted "full citizenship for women," she concludes, but each had "competing political philosophies and class allegiances that prevented them from finding common ground."[38]

Class resentments and divergent political philosophies surely fueled the enmities between labor union women and ERA advocates in the 1940s and 1950s. As the ILGWU's legislative representative Evelyn Dubrow summarized, women in the labor movement opposed the ERA not because we "didn't believe in equality" but because we "thought it was a class piece of legislation."[39] Unionists saw the ERA as an attack on workers by the elite class, and many within the small and in-grown NWP fit that description.[40] The left-led FTA condemned the ERA in 1946 as a "fake" reform "touted by leisure-class women and employer interests."[41] Frieda Miller relied on the same rhetoric, describing the NWP as "a small but militant group of leisure class women" who were out of touch with "women of the laboring people."[42]

Moreover, many felt a deep disaffection with the "conservative economic ideas" of the so-called "women of property" who supported the ERA.[43] NWP members, for example, rarely favored legislative measures designed to enhance labor standards or worker rights to collective representation. Women, like men, they insisted, should be allowed to traverse the market without hindrances or protections. Theirs was a free-market rhetoric, touting "liberty of contract" and a mythic kind of "individualism." One NWP pamphlet argued that unions supported labor standards for women not to help women but to protect men from the competition of women. Without such laws, women would be free "to contract on the same terms as men"—an approach they favored.[44]

Many of the NWP's congressional allies held similar views, as did prominent backers of the ERA such as the Chamber of Commerce and the National Association of Manufacturers (NAM). Indeed, these business groups were among the most strident in their resistance to government-established labor standards and their advocacy of an anti-union, "pure competition model" of the market.[45] To the ERA opponents, a legal equality that brought with it the conservative doctrine of "liberty of contract," meaning employer freedom from government and union regulation, would be at odds with achieving women's industrial equality.[46]

Alice Paul, the founder and charismatic leader of the NWP, epitomized the fervent individualism and single-issue focus of the NWP. Paul grew up in a strict Hicksite or "inner light" Quaker family in New Jersey where her father worked as president of the Burlington County Trust Company and owned several successful businesses. According to one biographer, her approach to equality for women rested on a strong early belief that "each individual had the capacity to achieve his or her goals" without interference or restraint. Her political philosophy solidified in England, where she abandoned her early interest in social work and turned with an unremitting intensity to the issue of suffrage, enduring force-feedings and other torments when jailed for picketing and civil disobedience on behalf of the cause. With suffrage secured in 1920, she fixed her sight on yet another constitutional amendment. Like many of the women grouped around her, she firmly believed that women should enjoy the same freedoms as men, including "freedom of contract."[47]

Labor feminists objected to the narrowness of the NWP's *political* program, seeing its relentless focus on ending all sex discriminations in the law as regrettable. Mary Anderson, for example, saw the ERA as a bill that promised "doctrinaire equality" without any "social justice." In her view, the "woman question" was interrelated with "other great social questions," and to insist only upon women's legal rights no matter what happened to other rights could result in *greater* inequality.[48] In 1944, she expressed her relief that the women reformers with whom she was now working did not take such a "narrow feminist view," one she associated with the NWP feminists. Rather, they realized that women's problems stemmed from a number of sources and should be considered "on a broad humanitarian basis." She was heartened that the new generation of social feminists neither "overlooked" nor "minimized the vital and traditional role of women in the home and the valuable services they have to render in the community."[49] Union leaders such as UE's Ruth Young and FTA's Elizabeth Sasuly echoed her criticisms of the ERA a few years later. Young found the ERA a "nebulous abstraction" that did not address "pressing human problems"; Sasuly characterized it as "an empty concept of equality" that would only offer women "the right to be exploited."[50]

Labor feminists also lit into the NWP's political program for its wrongheaded notions of how the laws affecting women's status could best be transformed. They disagreed vehemently with the NWP about the *definition* of sex discrimination and the *appropriate legislative remedies* for ending such discrimination. These disagreements were particularly evident in the Women's Status Bill, the

63

federal legislation proposed by labor feminists in 1947 "to eliminate unfair discrimination based on sex."[51] The Women's Status Bill did not get far, but the content of the bill itself and the debates over it help clarify the competing visions of gender reform that animated each side, and show why it was so difficult for them to find a middle ground.

The Women's Status Bill was introduced into both houses for the first time on February 17, 1947, sponsored by social feminist allies Democratic congresswomen Mary Norton and Helen Gahagan Douglas, among others. A New Jersey congresswoman first elected in 1925, Norton had grown up in a working-class Irish Catholic household and worked as a governess before marrying a successful businessman. As a congresswoman, she supported labor standards legislation, government funding for child care, and other social feminist programs.[52] Douglas, another New Jersey daughter, starred in Broadway plays in the 1920s before she met and married Melvyn Douglas in 1931. She then moved to Hollywood, where she raised two children, continued an acting and operatic career, and involved herself in raising money for California's migrant workers. In 1937, after a singing tour of Europe, she joined the Anti-Nazi League and the Women's Division of the Democratic Party, becoming vice chair of the California State Committee. She won election to the House in 1944 and again in 1946 and 1948, representing a primarily blue-collar and mixed-ethnic Los Angeles district. In 1950, she ran for U.S. Senate against Richard M. Nixon, who won the election largely by slinging red-baiting insults at Douglas, accusing her of being "soft on communism."[53]

With the support of Douglas in the 1940s and then later in the 1950s under the sponsorship of Brooklyn congressman Emmanuel Celler, the Women's Status Bill was reintroduced each year until 1954.[54] Mary Anderson, now retired as director of the Women's Bureau, chaired the National Committee on the Status of Women (NCSW), the group that lobbied for the bill. Organizations who joined included both garment unions, the auto, electrical, and packinghouse unions, the telephone and teachers unions, four national labor auxiliaries, the National Council of Negro Women, the YWCA, and others. Of the thirty-four organizations that signed on as sponsors of the Women's Status Bill in 1948, twenty-one were labor groups.[55]

The Women's Status Bill was in large measure "a way to meet the threat of the ERA," as Cynthia Harrison points out.[56] In 1944 Mary Anderson had set up the National Committee to Defeat the UnEqual Rights Amendment, the forerunner of the NCSW, to deal with what she perceived as a political crisis. The Republicans had already endorsed the ERA in their platform in 1940, and in 1944, the Democrats joined them. In 1945, the Senate held hearings on the ERA in which Maida Springer-Kemp, Frieda Miller, and Mary Anderson, among others, vied for the support of those in the crowded gathering against the pointed and patriotic speeches of women from the NWP, business and professional associations, and numerous college sororities.[57] By 1946, the ERA was ready for a vote in both houses, having been favorably reported out of committee for the first time since its introduction in the early 1920s.

But the women who belonged to the NCSW had more on their minds than simply stopping the ERA. These same women were pursuing a comprehensive and ambitious reform agenda on multiple fronts, sponsoring new policies in their unions and lobbying for a range of legislative initiatives affecting women's economic status. They viewed the Status Bill as a part of this larger reform effort and as a vehicle for expressing their very real desire to end discrimination against women.[58]

The Women's Bureau Labor Advisory Committee (LAC), one of the incubators from which the bill sprang, described it at their January 1947 meeting as "a positive policy to get the wheels moving for elimination of discriminations." The "heart" of the bill, Frieda Miller claimed, was a recommendation for a presidential commission on the status of women. The commission would study "not just the legal status but the general status" of women and would propose policies "to eliminate unfair discrimination based on sex." Esther Peterson and Kitty Ellickson were particularly strong advocates for such a commission when it was discussed in LAC meetings in early 1947. Their model, the President's Commission on Civil Rights, established by Truman's executive order in December 1946, had issued a report, "To Secure These Rights," with a host of policy recommendations. Many of the recommendations were not enacted until the 1960s, but the report was an important national acknowledgment of the race problem and of the need for government intervention to help solve it. The labor feminists behind the Women's Status Bill hoped for a similar report that would stir the nation and inaugurate a national debate over "the political, civic, economic, and social status of women."[59]

Like their equal rights opponents, labor feminists indicted American society in the postwar years for its discriminatory treatment of women, and they called for an end to such policies. But they differed from equal rights feminists over how to define discrimination and how to overturn statutes deemed discriminatory. First of all, unlike the NWP feminists, labor feminists and their allies did not think that *all* differential treatment based on gender was unfair or discriminatory. *Some* sex-based policies benefited women and should be retained. Sex-based labor laws were a case in point, but there were others as well, such as custody laws and criminal statutes related to underage marriage and sexual intercourse. By the 1940s, labor feminists had reached the conclusion that many of the sex-based labor laws did indeed discriminate against women. There was general unanimity, for example, that laws which prohibited the employment of women in certain jobs constituted sex discrimination, and a growing minority concluded the same about night laws and other laws restricting work time for women.[60] These needed to be either amended or taken off the books. Nonetheless, *other* sex-based statutes did *not* "unfairly disadvantage" women. Because they believed sex differences—anatomical and social—*did exist*, policies that explicitly addressed the results of these differences were necessary to achieve equality.

Second, because some sex-based laws were thought to benefit women, an amendment that threatened to remove *all* such legislation without any guarantee of comparable replacement protections risked harming women and, in their minds, doing so unnecessarily. There were *other* ways of removing the offending laws. They recommended, for example, a review of the legislation on a case-by-case basis—an approach that came to be referred to as "specific bills for specific ills." Those laws deemed harmful to women would be removed, and those deemed beneficial would be retained or amended to cover men. Esther Peterson proposed in 1947, for example, that the President's Commission she and others had inserted in the Women's Status Bill could list the "distinctions that should be kept, those that should not, and those in the middle ground."[61] In this sense, then, the Women's Status Bill embodied a contingent approach to equality. Difference was never automatically understood as discriminatory: each case had to be judged in its context and in its particular effect.

The two sides squared off most dramatically in 1948 before the House Judiciary Committee in hearings called to consider the relative merits of the ERA and the Women's Status Bill.[62] As Helen Gahagan Douglas saw it: "we agree on the need to get rid of discriminatory laws"; the problem, however, was that the ERA *might* end *all* protective laws, and the two sides clearly disagreed over whether that outcome would be a net gain or loss for women.[63] Each side evaluated the situation from a particular class vantage point. The ERA supporters, primarily business and professional women competing directly with men, assessed the bulk of the laws as "outmoded and discriminatory." As women with substantial training and education, the lawyers, business executives, and others who led the ERA drive didn't particularly need labor standards legislation to ensure their own satisfactory working conditions. Moreover, as women competing against men in largely male-dominated arenas, sex-based protections put them at a disadvantage. On the other hand, the working-class women, for whom labor feminists spoke, had fewer individual "skills" that would enable them as individuals to negotiate an acceptable status in the market, and only a minority belonged to unions. Further, in contrast to many of the professional women, the majority toiled in "female-majority occupations," did *not* compete directly with men, and thought there was little possibility they ever would. Thus, many concluded that the advantages of the laws outweighed the disadvantages.

Nor was there agreement on how best to address women's disadvantages in the market or even *what* those disadvantages were. Educated in Europe and "presented at the Kaiser's Court" before her stint as executive vice president and treasurer of her husband's coal brokerage company, New York Republican congresswoman and ERA supporter Katharine St. George saw few obstacles facing women except discriminatory laws. Women didn't need help at work, she insisted. They simply "want to be free to work as equals asking for no special privileges."[64] NWP's Nina Horton Avery agreed: "All adults should be treated alike."[65] Frieda Miller countered this line of argument, pointing out that "identity of treatment" is not the same as equality, and that the ERA's blanket approach to ending discrimination was ill conceived. She preferred the Status Bill: it "declares a general policy of equality" but "takes account of the differences between men and women" and "offers a specific, fact-by-fact approach" to determining "which changes would actually achieve equality."[66]

Selma Borchardt, representing the AFL, joined Miller in arguing that the ERA was the wrong *tactic* to use in addressing women's disadvantages. Borchardt, who by 1948 had a law degree and had served twenty years as the Teachers' Union representative to the Women's Joint Congressional Committee, favored "giving rights to women" through "specific legislation" rather than the "broadly framed panacea" of the ERA. Such an approach was "more effective" and would not "endanger the benefits we now enjoy."[67]

On the other hand, the two sides *agreed* that sex discrimination existed, that it should be ended, and that the ultimate goal was equality between the sexes. At times it even appeared that there was considerable sentiment on both sides for extending protective laws to men and keeping maternity benefits as a special case that "in no way conflicts with the idea of equality."[68] As Frieda Miller said, echoing Helen Gahagan Douglas, "everyone is for equality for women"; what was not clear was "what in fact would provide equality for the great majority of women."[69]

Yet the bitter disagreements over how to get to these shared goals, combined with a deep distrust of each other's motivations, made it impossible for a compromise position to even begin to emerge. The hearings degenerated frequently into name-calling and insults, with each side delivering ripostes with equal gusto. NWP members attacked male labor leaders mercilessly and called the labor women who worked with unions "lackeys," denying these women any independence of mind or action. They red-baited union representatives as well, pointing out that the ERA was "vital to the American way of life" and that many of the unions opposed to it were "communist." They dismissed the middle-class supporters of the Women's Status Bill as "do-gooders" and "lady bountiful" sentimentalists.[70]

Labor feminists and their allies dished it back. Pauline Newman had been perfecting her attack since at least the 1920s. Decades later, she was still in the ring. She charged the proponents of "this so-called ERA" with being "selfish careerists" who were "numerically insignificant, industrially inexperienced, economically unsound, and intellectually confused."[71] By the end of the hearings, the personal insults had taken their toll. As one ERA opponent sadly observed, "We need a real discussion of the issues." But the movement remained divided into "hostile camps," stuck in what William Chafe has called "a politics of mutual recrimination."[72]

On Hold

Neither the Women's Status Bill nor the ERA made much progress after 1948. The Women's Status Bill was quietly dropped after 1954. The ERA fared only marginally better. In 1956, when the Senate held hearings once again on the ERA, it appeared less likely to pass than ever. Only a small group came to testify, mostly the usual suspects. Congresswoman Katherine St. George, the chief sponsor of the ERA in the House since 1948, Emma Guffey Miller, chair of the NWP, and Michigan congresswoman Martha Griffiths led the delegation of proponents. Their thrusts were parried and returned by AFL-CIO Legislative Department Director Andrew Biemiller, representatives from the NCL, and NCNW, and Mary Anderson, now in her eighties. Many of the labor opponents simply sent letters.[73] The next serious consideration of the ERA would not occur until 1971.[74]

In part, the attempts of feminists to end sex discrimination in the 1940s were wrecked on the shoals of "difference," class and gender. Neither side knew how to cross the class divide separating them. Neither side knew how to find a middle ground between those who believed gender differences could not be denied and those who believed that the denial of "difference" was exactly what *was* needed. In part, the problem then was what it still is today. Attempts to legislate gender equality can become a vehicle to re-inscribe inequality. Until the power balance between the sexes is transformed socially, economically, and politically, statutes premised on equal treatment as well as those allowing gender differentiation can be used against women. And for postwar feminist reformers, as for those in the present, the question is what to do in the meantime.

The labor feminists, for their part, believed that gender difference needed to be acknowledged in policy and its acceptable uses specified. The problem, as Gladys Dickason formulated it in 1947, was to distinguish "false discriminations between men and women workers" from "genuine differences—physical, social, and psychological—which create special problems for women workers" and need to be remedied.[75] Yet what constituted "genuine gender differences" or what were "valid and invalid distinctions," to use Frieda Miller's phrase, was not always easy to decipher.[76] The NCSW, the Mary Anderson-led group pushing the Status Bill, reached a measure of agreement on these matters, but even in the short period in which they pursued the bill, their notions of legitimate reasons for discriminating between men and women changed.

In the first version of the bill, introduced in 1947, for example, they proposed that "no distinctions on the basis of sex" were acceptable except "such as are reasonably justified by differences in physical structure, biological or social function."[77] Later, however, they revised this language, reflecting a new consensus. No longer would "biological functions" automatically be seen as a legitimate rationale for making distinctions between the sexes. Rather, in 1949, they agreed that the phrase "maternal function" would be substituted for the phrase "biological function."[78] "Gender differences" were still "real" and could not be ignored in policy, but they were now increasingly social and hence carried less of a sense of immutability or "naturalness."

Ideas of what constituted sex discrimination or what were "unwarranted gender distinctions" would further evolve, as later chapters will convey.[79] But by the early 1950s, the push for a Women's Status Bill ground to a halt, stymied in part by the lackluster consensus on "difference," but also in reaction to the growing number of conservatives in office. Olya Margolin of the National Council of Jewish Women wrote Kitty Ellickson in 1954 that the likelihood of the bill's passage was "not too great" and that many on the committee now felt that it "might be easier to secure a Presidentially-appointed Commission on the Status of Women."[80] Labor feminists and their allies continued to oppose the ERA, but by the 1950s their principal approach was no longer the Women's Status Bill. Instead, they relied on the Hayden amendment to the ERA, a proviso that the ERA "shall not impair any rights, benefits, or exemptions now or hereafter conferred by law" on women.[81] The Hayden amendment, they thought, would preserve beneficial sex-based laws while allowing those that harmed women to be overturned. Supporting the Hayden amendment also meant they could put aside the vexing issue of finding a definition of "reasonable differences" that could be agreed upon and written into law. Yet the language of the Hayden amendment appears more to confirm the status quo than to engage the issue of how to evaluate and amend the labor laws in line with women's changing sense of their needs and capabilities.

The NWP for its part "solved" the problem of gender difference by avoiding it. Its approach was to claim equality on the basis of sameness or identity. The NWP refused to support an ERA with the Hayden amendment, although such a bill passed the Senate in 1950 and again in 1953; they held firm to their position that allowing sex-based differences in treatment was untenable and would open the door to discrimination against women.[82] And there the conversation was stuck until the 1960s.

CHAPTER THREE

Women's Job Rights

The old fear sits again in the hearts of women. back . . . back to women's place in woman's industries. will it have to begin all over again? the right of a woman to any job she can do, the right of a woman to advancement.

—Tillie Olsen, novelist and president, California State CIO Women's Auxiliary[1]

There are people who say a woman's place is in the home. No one can say where anyone's place is. I say a woman's place is everywhere. No longer is she content to be told she is a second class citizen.

—Caroline Davis, Director, UAW Women's Department, c. 1955[2]

THE ANSWER TO the perennial question "Should women work outside the home?" has changed dramatically over time. The early nineteenth-century mill owners had to convince a skeptical public that wage-earning for young, single, white women would neither endanger the moral codes of acceptable womanhood nor undermine the stability of the patriarchal family.[3] A century later, the terms of the debate had shifted. The question was no longer whether women could engage in paid employment but *which* women, in *which* occupations, and with *what* rights. The debate was never fully resolved in the sense that, even today, in the minds of some, women's claim to wage work is secondary to that of men's. Nevertheless, in the mid-twentieth century as in the mid-nineteenth, significant transformations occurred in the cultural norms and social policies affecting women's job rights.

Labor women were at the center of the debate over women's job rights in the 1940s and 1950s. And the positions they advocated were not always ones that corresponded to those offered by their union brothers or by their employers. Many claimed the right to employment for all women. That meant opening jobs to married women, older women, pregnant women, and mothers as well as challenging discrimination on the basis of race, religion, and ethnicity. Ensuring women's job rights also meant ending what was often referred to as "unfair sex discrimination." Here a distinction was made between those sex-based practices and policies that harmed women (and hence were discriminatory) and those that did not. At times the route to equality was through differential treatment; at other times the path lay through rejecting such practices.

Some labor women believed, as Tillie Olsen did, that women's job rights entailed "the right of a woman to any job she can do," but that demand did not emerge as the dominant rallying cry.[4] Rather, the primary (although not exclusive) approach to women's job rights was to focus on upgrading the status of "women's jobs," or what Frieda Miller called the "woman-employing fields."[5] At times, that meant redefining certain "men's jobs" as female or shifting the boundaries between men's and women's work to expand the female sphere, but only rarely did it mean challenging the sexual division of labor per se. Later, in the 1960s, union women would file some of the first grievances and lawsuits under Title VII of the Civil Rights Act, claiming the right to move into so-called men's jobs. But in this period, most labor women believed that dividing work into men's jobs and women's jobs did not *necessarily* condemn women to a secondary status. What mattered was how the separate spheres were valued, who defined the boundaries between them, and who decided when sex-based or differential treatment was appropriate.

RUMBLINGS FROM BELOW

The campaign for women's job rights began on the factory floor, among blue-collar women, and then filtered up to women in white- and pink-collar jobs. Blue-collar factory women were the first to challenge restrictions on women's rights and the first to experience some success. The effort to transform women's secondary status outside of manufacturing came later and was a much harder fought battle.

This trickling up of gender activism should not be surprising. Many factory women had little choice but to seek the expansion and protection of their opportunities for wage work. Their income often was essential even in a multi-income family economy, and many were the *sole* support of themselves and their dependents.

Moreover, blue-collar manufacturing women had powerful and progressive institutional vehicles through which to express their concerns: the large industrial unions that were firmly established by the 1940s. They had a mechanism through which individual and collective grievances could be advanced. Despite the paternalistic and hostile attitudes sometimes directed toward blue-collar women by their male coworkers and fellow unionists, the reigning ideology of industrial unionism was one that emphasized fairness through securing policies that treated all workers alike. The inexorable logic of bureaucratic, industrial-style unionism pushed for an end to differential treatment based on gender, race, and other personal or sociological characteristics. Unions sought to replace managerial prerogative and favoritism with impersonal, jointly established rules—the legitimacy of which depended on allowing few exceptions and insisting on the interchangeability of *all* workers.[6]

Whether or not employers shifted their actual practices, however, had as much to do with the nature of the industry and the inclinations of particular employers as with the protests of women and their unions. Employer resistance to ending marital, age, and race bars was strongest outside of manufacturing—in the pink-collar service sectors where employers depended upon and favored the labor of young, single, attractive, white women. For these employers, profit depended on the low wages paid to young single women as well as the earnings they could extract from the "femininity" and sexuality of their female workers. Individual foremen in an auto plant may have desired youth and beauty in female employees, but the exigencies of manufacturing productivity pushed toward hiring those women who were backbreaking workers, regardless of their physical attractiveness.

Ironically, in some instances, prejudices based on class, race, and ethnicity undercut gender stereotypes and helped open up low-level blue-collar occupations to excluded groups of women. Some employers were more amenable to hiring non-whites into dangerous, difficult, and unhealthy jobs or ones that required long hours away from home and community—all jobs frequently seen as unfit for white women. They also worried less over preserving the reproductive functions and household responsibilities of immigrant working-class women than of the more elite native-born women who filled the ranks of pink- and white-collar jobs.[7]

Married Women's Job Rights

Before World War II, the right of married women to wage work was tenuous at best. Married women, it was feared, could not successfully combine the responsibilities of employment and domesticity. Public skepticism about the advisability of married women working outside the home turned to hostility during the economic crisis of the 1930s. Despite the high numbers of wives in the labor force, many leaders in business, government, and labor proposed solving the problem of unemployment by restricting the job rights of married women.[8]

Working-class opinion divided on the question, with large numbers of working-class women as well as men supporting employment policies that gave lesser jobs rights to married women than to other workers. Some reasoned that in times of unemployment, the need to distribute the remaining work (and income) among as many households as possible took precedence over guaranteeing the rights of individuals. Married women, it was assumed, were part of a household economy that included a second wage earner, and households with two earners could better afford to lose a job than could households depending on only one. And married women should be laid off before married men, the thinking went, because they were better suited for household labor.

Others disagreed. ACWA rejected a proposal at its 1936 convention that married women be laid off before "heads of families and men and women who are self-supporting." Labor women also defended the equal right of married women to employment in the pages of the *American Federationist*, pointing out that "married women worked out of economic necessity," and that "whether or not a married woman should work is an individual personal problem. Suitable employment for women, as for a man [*sic*], means the right to utilize their abilities in the occupations of their choice, whether it is homemaking or an outside occupation."[9]

In the 1940s, as the wartime shortage of labor and the ensuing postwar prosperity created a demand for married female labor, hostility toward wage-earning wives and mothers lessened. Nevertheless, women's *equal right to wage work* was not yet established. Women were judged as *secondary* workers entitled to *secondary rights*. In response, a growing number of labor women turned to their unions to defend and expand the job rights of women, seeking equal rights regardless of sex or marital status.

Our picture of the relationship between labor unions and women in the decades following World War II is still shaped largely by the influential accounts of the reconversion period immediately after the war and the ways in which unions failed to protect women's job claims at the war's end. And indeed, in many instances, seniority provisions protecting women were not enforced, and some contracts explicitly discriminated against women by "providing that women shall be laid off first."[10]

Yet the reconversion period is a poor guide to the willingness and ability of labor to defend women's job rights in the postwar era.[11] Indeed, if one looks at the overall record of unions in the 1940s and 1950s, it appears that women's claim to equal job rights, including the claims of married women, achieved a new legitimacy within organized labor circles in the postwar decades. In part, labor unions were responding to women's own changing sense of their rights and needs; in part they were compelled by the logic of industrial unionism with its stress on seniority, equity of treatment, and the interchangeability of workers.

The large industrial unions had embraced seniority as a basis for layoff decisions in the 1930s. It was accepted as an equitable and rule-based alternative to arbitrary management power and as a way of protecting older workers. And, although seniority was not enacted in order to foster individualism and gender rights, it did just that. The union principle of equitable treatment of individual workers helped erode older notions of employment rights based on family status. Defending the seniority principle from management attack, for example, often meant arguing that married women be treated just like any other worker, male or female.

The shift in policy and practice within the UAW is a case in point. In the 1930s few locals defended the rights of married women workers in the UAW, and even when they did, they had little power to change employer practice. By the war's end, however, the situation was different. The first UAW women's conference in 1944 pointed to the importance of protecting all women's rights to wage work in the postwar years, including the rights of married women. Millie Jeffrey, then head of the UAW Women's Bureau, told her union sisters at the 1945 gathering in Washington that "we are emphasizing at this point no discrimination on the basis of marital status." The efforts of the UAW Women's

Bureau brought protests from single women as well as from men. "In one Michigan local," Jeffrey told those assembled, "where the contract provided that married women would be laid off first, this became a very hot issue. You had a division among the women themselves, you had the single women lined up against the married women. It came out well, but by a very close vote . . . the local union voted to eliminate this clause."[12]

The 1946 UAW convention resolution to end discrimination based on marital status was neither fully enforced by the international nor honored by all locals during the re-conversion period. Nonetheless, under pressure from the now-permanent UAW Women's Bureau, located within the Fair Practices and Anti-Discrimination Department, wayward locals began to fall into line. The international stepped up its rhetoric as well, with national leaders like Emil Mazey proclaiming that "a married woman is an economic citizen in her own right."[13] Locals changed their contract language to end differential treatment on the basis of family status, and they filed grievances on behalf of married women's job rights. Lillian Hatcher kept a running list of the growing number of locals that changed their bylaws to conform to the international's nondiscrimination policy, and by the 1950s discriminatory contract language against married women had been virtually eliminated in UAW agreements.[14] Other CIO unions took up married women's job rights aggressively in this period as well. In 1951, for example, the IUE threatened to strike GE until certain concessions were secured, one of which was the addition of "no discrimination because of marital status" to the union contract. Two years later they threatened strike action over what they perceived as the unfair discharge of married women.[15]

Yet prejudice against married women continued, especially during recessions. In response, the UAW tried to change opinions as well as policies: Lillian Hatcher, for example, spent a lot of her time in the late 1940s holding educational programs with locals concerning enforcement of married women's job rights. Still, with the industry in a slump in the early 1950s, women on the UAW Women's Advisory Board complained bitterly about the resurgence of hostility against married women from single women as well as from men. The Buffalo local, one advisory board representative worried, almost put through a motion to lay off married women—"we had a weak president, new man . . . and the number of single women against married women working is surprising. In a good many places, you were threatened if you took the wrong stand on married women working." The board also expressed dismay that employers still resisted hiring women, especially married women, into any new jobs that were high paying.[16]

At the 1955 UAW convention, women proposed the reaffirmation of the "democratic principle that all members shall be guaranteed full protection without discrimination based on sex or marital status." In what one paper headlined as the "Battle of the Sexes," delegates confronted each other in a spirited two-hour floor debate revolving around married women's job rights. After a number of male delegates offered various objections to married women in the factories, Mildred Szur of Detroit's Local 17 reminded the delegates of women's basic civil rights: "Where is our democracy in this country if a woman cannot be a free individual and make up her own mind? I think that when you start telling women you can or cannot work, you are infringing upon their civil rights which I, as a woman, resent." In the end the resolution passed unanimously.[17]

In the late 1950s, unions continued to improve their policies toward married women, spurred by the logic of their own ideology and the increasing numbers of married women in their ranks. Employers initiated changes as well. The range of acceptable jobs was limited of course, especially for middle-class women. But part-time office work emerged as one good choice for married women, and, according to economist Claudia Goldin, the "marriage bar, which at its height affected about 50 percent of all office workers, was virtually abandoned in the 1950s."[18]

Nevertheless, bars to the employment of married women and mothers persisted, particularly in "white-collar" occupations that historically had been preserved for young, white, single women. In part because women preferred these more "respectable" jobs, employers could be more choosy in whom they hired. Blue-collar and manufacturing employers opened the door to a wider range of women earlier because they faced a more restricted supply of applicants. But employers of white native-born women also continued to express concern over the ability of their female employees to fulfill the duties of marriage and motherhood. Many school districts, for example, persisted in firing married women once they got pregnant. As classroom teacher lore put it, the correct response to the personnel office inquiry as to how long you intended to teach was "from here to maternity." In defending their policies, school districts explained that visibly pregnant teachers might harm their young pupils by raising questions about sexuality, and that women with young children should be at home.[19]

The airline industry provides an even more revealing contrast to the progress blue-collar women made in establishing married women's job rights. The airlines resisted hiring married women longer than any other major industry. Despite the declining number of young single white women available for hostess positions in the 1950s, most major airline companies insisted upon their need to restrict hiring to that group. Airlines expressed concern that stewardesses simply couldn't combine marriage and airline travel because of the long absences from home. But just as important was the market advantage they felt they gained by hiring "young, attractive, and unencumbered" attendants. Indeed, as air travel expanded in the postwar era, the airlines built an industry in which profit margins rested heavily on the sexual allure of unmarried hostesses for the male business traveler.[20]

Ironically, the advantages of hiring young single women as hostesses had not been immediately apparent to the airlines. When air transport companies first began offering commercial flight services, Eastern and Pan American followed the traditions of the railroad and steamship companies and hired male stewards or pursers to attend to passengers. But after United offered Ellen Church, a nurse and aspiring pilot, a job as a passenger assistant in 1930, other airlines began to see the several advantages of hiring young single women as stewards, and they followed United's lead. Young women stewards, it was thought, particularly those with some nursing background, would reassure a public who might fear for their safety: if young women could fly, then how could any adult man admit to trepidation? Moreover, the companies soon realized that they could compete for market share based on the attractiveness of their hostesses. By the end of World War II, the airlines quietly dropped their nursing requirement, but the single-only rule stuck.[21]

Many flight attendants married despite the single-only rule, and simply kept their marriages secret.[22] And married or not, flight attendants had to remain childless. Children were not as easily hidden as marriages, and airlines refused to hire mothers, claiming that pregnancy inhibited the performance of flight attendant duties and that child rearing was incompatible with the travel schedules of stewardesses. When the airlines discovered married and/or pregnant flight attendants, they generally fired them, regardless of job performance. One transgressing employee had kept her infant secret for three years. Upon discovery, the airline insisted that she either resign (in which case she could keep her child) or put her child in an orphanage. Another airline offered the following "grisly maternity leave" in the early 1960s: if the pregnant flight attendant had a miscarriage or the baby died within a year, she could return to work with no loss of seniority.[23] Faced with company policies such as these, flight attendants delayed marriage and children and considered abortions or adoption—all to keep their jobs.

Before the 1960s, protest against these policies was minimal and generally ineffective, despite the high rate of unionization among attendants (all the major carriers, with the exception of Delta, were unionized). In part, the lack of an effective challenge to the airline policies had to do with the nature of the male-dominated unions representing flight attendants. The first flight attendants had organized independently from their male coworkers: United Airline attendants organized their own union in 1944 and bargained a first contract in 1946. But this small independent organization was no match for the large corporation against which it was pitted. In 1949, it merged with the Air Line Stewardesses and Stewards Association (ALSSA), a division for flight attendants set up within the Air Line Pilots Association (ALPA) in 1946. Other transportation unions organized flight attendants as well in the 1940s and 1950s, but in fewer numbers: the Transport Workers Union or TWU (primarily inter-city bus drivers and subway workers) and the International Brotherhood of Teamsters (local and long-distance truck drivers). Like ALPA, both unions were male-dominated and uninterested in (or at best unfamiliar with) the particular kinds of discrimination experienced by airline hostesses.[24]

In 1951, ALSSA held its first convention and elected its first set of officers. The existence of a separate section for stewardesses and stewards within the Pilots union was an official recognition of the separate and distinct issues of attendants; unfortunately, the attendants also held a separate *and* unequal status within the organization. (Throughout the 1940s and 1950s, the ALPA Constitution expressly forbade anyone but a pilot from heading the union. Pilots, the captains on the plane, were also to be captains in the union.) Mary Alice Koos served as the first president of ALSSA, but perhaps to fight fire with fire, as flight attendant historian Georgia Nielsen observes, ALSSA members chose one of their few male members, Rowland Quinn, as their president in 1953. Quinn, a University of Michigan graduate with a degree in industrial management, led ALSSA until 1963. The high turnover rate of female attendants, averaging 18 months in the 1950s, and the no-marriage rule also meant that stable female leadership was almost impossible to achieve.[25]

When the companies began firing married stewardesses in large numbers in the postwar era, the unions representing flight attendants largely acquiesced. Between 1945 and 1967, for example, over eight thousand attendants left United because they married. United refused to retain any married attendant. Yet the company's actions met little resistance from the union representing attendants, in this case ALSSA. Unions did file grievances in protest, but with little effect. Arbitrators denied TWU's grievance against Pan Am's marriage bar in 1948; ALSSA grievances against TWA and Eastern over their firing of married attendants also met defeat.[26] Arbitrators rarely ruled in favor of an aggrieved party unless the contract language had been violated, and airlines obstinately refused to include no-discrimination provisions in their union agreements, leaving the unions little ground upon which to mount a successful arbitration case. The primary weapon left to the unions was organized economic action. This alternative was never pursued before the 1960s, in part because of the reluctance of the leadership, but also because the flight attendants themselves were ambivalent about the airlines' restrictive hiring policies.

When flight attendants were hired, many signed explicit contracts with the airlines promising to "voluntarily resign" upon marriage. In the minds of some, these no-marriage contract terms could not be abrogated or altered. Many attendants also preferred marriage to long-term wage work and entered the occupation with the hope that indeed they could "retire" into marriage.[27] Others may have supported the rule because they saw it as adding to the glamour and status of their occupation. Their occupation was exclusive and reserved for only the select few; they were set apart from other women based on their desirability and attractiveness.

Nevertheless, a growing number of flight attendants begin to chafe at these restrictions over the course of the postwar era. Many flight attendants left the industry to marry but later realized that they did not want to remain full-time housewives. Like many other women, they sought to follow the path blazed by blue-collar women who combined marriage and work. In addition, as the working conditions in their occupation began to decline in the 1950s, flight attendants responded by becoming more involved in their unions.[28] To their surprise, they found that they now commanded more power in their unions because their numbers were growing relative to the pilots: the shift toward wide-body jets meant more attendants and fewer pilots. With the passage of the Landrum-Griffin Act in 1959 requiring unions to comply with more majoritarian principles of governance, the flight attendants within ALPA also had a legal basis upon which to question the union rules limiting office holding and voting to pilots. By the end of the 1950s, flight attendants had won concessions from their unions and achieved greater autonomy and power.[29] Although the airlines continued their firm resistance to changing their hiring practices, the stage was now set for flight attendants to join other unionized women in the employment rights battles that were to emerge in the 1960s.

THE OLDER WOMAN WORKER

Age discrimination began to recede in the postwar era as cultural norms shifted in regard to married women, older married women sought employment once their children left for school or work, and the pressures of a tight labor market eased employer restrictions.[30] Resistance to hiring and retaining older women declined first among large industrial employers, where the racial, ethnic, and class makeup of the labor force lessened employer concern for preserving women's family functions, and where unions made an issue of age discrimination. By the 1950s, fewer barriers blocked access to jobs for older women in manufacturing, although prejudice still remained, and, reversing historic patterns, seniority provisions provided older women employees with *more* job rights than younger women.

Progress was slower outside of manufacturing, particularly in occupations in which appearance played a large part in the labor and customer exchange. Not surprisingly, the airline companies resisted hiring older women just as tenaciously as they had resisted hiring married women. Alarmed over their aging stewardess workforce, almost all the major airlines instituted formal policies in the early 1950s requiring stewardesses to "retire" once they reached their thirties. Some airlines routinely fired any flight attendant over 32; others waited until the hostesses reached the ripe old age of 35. One company official explained why, pointing out that "the average woman's appearance has markedly deteriorated at this age."[31] "It's the sex thing, pure and simple," another executive said. "Put a dog on a plane and 20 businessmen are sore for a month."[32]

The male-dominated unions representing flight attendants took the issue of age discrimination more seriously than they had marital discrimination. Age discrimination, after all, happens to men as well as women, while marital discrimination is more peculiarly a female problem—since employers tend to favor married men over single. Ending discrimination against older women also did not threaten the male head-of-family notion (with its attendant expectation of a higher wage and of employment priority) in the same explicit way as the issue of ending marital discrimination.

ALSSA's first president, Mary Alice Koos, who served from 1951 to 1953, refused to agree to a mandatory retirement age for stewardesses. When American Airlines became the first airline to institute age ceilings for attendants, requiring "retirement" at age 32, the TWU protested as well. The only concession they wrested from American, however, was a "grandmother clause" exempting those hired before November 1, 1953 from the policy.[33] After the defeat at American, unions made little headway, since most carriers simply introduced the policies unilaterally and refused to bargain over the decision.[34] As with discrimination against married women and mothers, real progress against age barriers for attendants would not be made until the 1960s.

OPENING BLUE-COLLAR "WOMEN'S JOBS" TO MINORITY WOMEN

Women of color, whether young or old, married or single, were already engaged in wage work in large numbers before World War II, and indeed, in many cases, wage labor had for them been as much coerced as prohibited. Thus, their issue was not claiming the right to wage work per se. Rather, it was *which* jobs could they claim, and with what rights. The legitimacy of job segregation by race and ethnicity and the practice of restricting women of color to certain jobs came under intense scrutiny in the postwar era.[35] Yet the postwar campaigns to end race discrimination differed from the later antidiscrimination efforts of the 1960s and 1970s in a fundamental way: the racial-ethnic division of labor was much more frequently challenged than the sexual. As Karen Anderson notes, black women's employment gains "occurred almost entirely through the integration of job categories historically assigned to women."[36]

Labor women's reform goals, especially concerning gender segregation in employment, appear limited from the perspective of the present day. Yet historic shifts were occurring in attitude and practice. Minority and white women workers had rarely if ever worked in the same occupations, and when they did, as in nursing and teaching, they were highly segregated.[37] From the days of slavery to the present, people of color in the United States, particularly African-Americans, had been restricted not only to the lowest-paying, most arduous work, but also to those sectors of the labor force lacking full "free labor" status. Agricultural work, domestic service, and other jobs disproportionately held by minorities after the Civil War never enjoyed a fully waged, at-will status.[38] Rather, in their restrictions on labor mobility, in the lack of wage guarantees, in their reliance on tip rather than wage income, and in the heightened expectations of loyalty and personal service, their jobs retained more of the character of bound labor than did the jobs of whites.[39] The postwar campaigns to gain *industrial* job rights for minority workers was, in this sense, a continuation of the long struggle to claim a free labor status. They were about breaking down entrenched patterns of racially segregated labor among women as well.

Labor women and their unions played a significant role in these postwar campaigns, a role often underestimated.[40] Indeed, a focus on the reform efforts of labor women in the postwar decades reveals the continuation of a substantial and at times effective civil rights movement within a range of unions. And, of crucial importance, this movement was not limited to the advancement of minority men; expanding job opportunities for minority women was central to it. Race reform was a *woman's issue* in the postwar era, and labor women, minority as well as non-minority, were key actors in the movement. Despite the lack of consensus among white women about integrating women's jobs,[41] many jobs held by white women, especially in manufacturing, opened up to women of color in the 1940s and 1950s. White women had to adjust and they did.

The history of the UPWA provides one of the richest illustrations of the dynamics and impact of the movement to expand job rights for minority women. The UPWA's commitment to civil rights rested on a peculiarly auspicious set of institutional circumstances: the UPWA leadership give racial justice a high priority and the union had a critical mass of African-American workers within its ranks. With 30 percent of its membership black, the UPWA had one of the largest group of organized African-American workers outside of the Sleeping Car Porters.[42] Many of these workers held union leadership positions. And, unlike the situation in most other industries, African-American men occupied a strategic position of power within the production process. The first step in the meat-processing line was killing the animal, a job done almost exclusively by African-American men. They had the power to shut down the entire production process, and they used it.[43]

A decade before the upsurge of the civil rights movement in the mid-1950s, black women launched a full-scale assault on the race discrimination suffered by women within the Packinghouse Workers. They formed coalitions with black men, and with other sympathetic workers, white and Hispanic (a small number of Hispanics had gained jobs in meatpacking by the 1940s).[44] Chicago Armour activist Addie Wyatt became a mainstay in this struggle, as did Jarutha Cole-man, Elizabeth Mayo, and others in the Chicago Swift plant. African-American women outside Chicago in Kansas City (Kansas), Waterloo (Iowa), and else-where also took part. For Wyatt, as for many other black women, the union was a site where the racial/ethnic as well as the gender status quo was disturbed. When Wyatt attended her first local union meeting, she was stunned. "I saw a picture I have never been able to forget. It was a room full of blacks, white workers, Hispanic workers, young and old, middle-aged workers, male and fe-male. And they were talking about problems of decent wages and working con-ditions. But in addition they were talking about the struggle of black people and women."[45]

Ending racial discrimination in female hiring was one of the first priorities. During the 1930s and World War II, a sizable number of African-American women were hired into meatpacking jobs, but they were consistently assigned to the dirtiest, least desirable positions. White women trimmed the meat or weighed, sliced, packed, and wrapped it after the animal had been killed, cut into sections, and cleaned. Black women could be found in the offal depart-ment, flushing worms and feces from the intestines of the animals.[46] As one white UPWA activist explained to an interviewer in 1939: "I'm in Sliced Bacon. That's supposed to be the lightest, cleanest place to work. They wouldn't take on a Negro girl if she was a college graduate. There's plenty of them doing all kinds of dirty jobs in the yards, but Sliced Bacon, oh, that's too good to give a colored girl."[47]

The rigid pattern of racial job segregation among women altered somewhat during the war, but employers attempted to reconstitute it at the war's end. The UPWA Women's Committee, an interracial group, protested employers' attempt "to dislodge and downgrade women from the positions they held in wartime" in the immediate postwar years, and they extracted numerous promises from the union to take action against racial discrimination, but little changed.[48]

As the numbers of women in the industry approached 20 percent in the late 1940s, pressure for change mounted.[49] Women in Chicago's black-led Local 28 worked together to set up a separate women's committee where women could talk about their grievances. Separate meetings were necessary, the organizers lamented, because "women are still afraid to speak in mixed groups and men don't take their problems seriously."[50] In 1950, the women's committee began documenting the discriminatory hiring practices of Swift and Company by sending black women to apply for jobs in the all-white pork trim unit and systematically recording the number turned down for employment. The newly established UPWA Anti-Discrimination Department joined in the effort by sending out white women applicants, who were subsequently hired for the same jobs. In protest, the local filed a grievance alleging violation of the union's nondiscrimination clause, and union activists engaged in work stoppages and slowdowns. Finally, in 1951, a government arbitrator ruled in favor of the union grievance, requiring Swift to hire thirteen black women job applicants and give them back pay to the date they had first applied.[51]

Other locals now stepped up their antidiscrimination efforts, emboldened by the success of the Swift local, whose story received widespread publicity in the union pamphlet "Action Against Jim Crow." Local 28's Coleman told the 1952 UPWA Convention, "We want action. We don't want just words." And she got it. New contract provisions prohibiting racial separation inside plants, national union conferences on antidiscrimination and on women's activities in 1953, and the consistent backing of the Anti-Discrimination Department and the international, all boosted local efforts.[52]

Breakthroughs occurred at a number of plants. In Waterloo, Iowa, when Rath Company hired black women in the sliced bacon department for the first time, white women threatened a walkout. Only when black men in the hog kill department countered by refusing to work did the company decide to retain its new hires. The company offered white women the choice of working in the integrated department or not working at all. At the Cudahy plant in Kansas City, black and white women (mainly Croation) worked in the same room but at different tables: the blacks worked on hog casings and the whites on sheep casings (lighter work). When Marian Simmons, a black woman, was elected steward for the entire casings department, she helped change the situation so that seniority applied *across* tables. Thus, "all women were given the privilege, regardless of color," of working on sheep casings.[53]

At the Armour plant in Chicago, the employer made the mistake of attacking the union's overall control over job transfer as well as refusing to honor UPWA's no-discrimination policy, thus uniting members in support of the local's position on both issues. The union leadership at Armour had encouraged black women to use the transfer provision of the contract to move into previously all-white women's departments such as sliced bacon, and when the employer refused, they had filed grievances. The employer might have prevailed. But when the company instituted "aptitude tests" for all new hires in sliced bacon, bypassing the transfer clause, a spontaneous walkout of some three to four thousand workers ensued. The walkout resulted in the end of "aptitude tests" as well as the hiring of black women into sliced bacon for the first time.[54]

The UPWA Women's Activities Committee, along with the Anti-Discrimination Department, continued its efforts to "secure full integration of non-white women in plants where they are employed, and the hiring of such women in plants where they are not presently employed" throughout the 1950s.[55] As Elizabeth Mayo of Local 28 told convention delegates in 1954: "Too long have the women been pushed aside. I ask other women not to be quiet. Get up and speak your minds, because the men [still] feel that now is not the time for you. Who is going to tell us when it is time for us?"[56] And, in many plants, the time did come. White and black women now worked together in the same departments, used the same rest rooms and locker rooms, ate in the same cafeteria, and were entitled to the same union rights and benefits.

The UPWA campaign to end employment discrimination against African-American women in the postwar period, although unusual in its sweep and intensity, was not an isolated case.[57] The UE, the UAW, the ACWA, and other unions shared the progressive racial politics of the UPWA. Scholars disagree sharply on how to assess the overall record of these unions on civil rights; but by the end of the 1950s many of these unions had helped secure job rights for women of color in areas historically reserved for white women.[58]

To supplement their efforts at the firm level, CIO unions pursued legislative changes as well. The creation of a permanent Fair Employment Practices Commission, similar to the lapsed wartime agency that had enforced Executive Order 8802 prohibiting discrimination in defense industries and government, was a major plank in the national CIO's legislation program against race discrimination. Indeed, labor's continuing support for a federal agency to oversee racial discrimination issues would prove crucial in the final shape and ultimate passage of the Civil Rights Act. The CIO also supported state-level FEP laws, banning racial discrimination in the armed forces, the passage of an anti-lynch law, and ending the poll tax. The UAW, IUE, UPWA, ACWA, UE, and other unions actively supported this agenda, and later when the two federations merged in 1955, these unions helped push the AFL toward a more progressive racial stance.[59]

Finally, unions forged coalitions with community-based groups to address race discrimination in the community as well as in the plant. UPWA women called on the NAACP to help them boycott local retail establishments, particu-

larly those near UPWA plants that refused service to minorities.[60] Unions such
as the BSCP, the UAW, District 65, and the ILGWU actively assisted the Montgomery Improvement Association (MIA) campaigns in the South to end segregated practices such as those requiring blacks to give up their seats to whites
on public buses.[61] Indeed, one of Addie Wyatt's first assignments when she
joined the International UPWA staff in 1954 was raising money for the MIA
bus boycotts among predominantly white male union members in Wisconsin,
Illinois, Michigan, Ohio, and Kentucky. Later, she served as one of Martin
Luther King's labor advisors.[62] With the encouragement of the ILGWU, Maida
Springer-Kemp coordinated a successful Madison Square Garden rally in 1956
to raise money for the MIA boycotts as well. Earlier, in 1946, the ILGWU
had released Springer-Kemp to organize a Madison Square Garden rally
on behalf of establishing a permanent FEPC. The event drew over seventeen
thousand people.[63]

INTEGRATING WHITE WOMEN'S SERVICE JOBS

Discrimination on the basis of race and ethnicity eroded more slowly in wom-
en's service and semiprofessional jobs than it did in blue-collar and manufacturing jobs.[64] Many pink- and white-collar occupations did not open up to minority
women until the 1950s and 1960s, and then only marginally. Employer resistance to the integration of minority women into "interactive service jobs" was
particularly strong.

Women of color predominated in many low-paying service jobs, but outside
the South they rarely held ones that were "visible" or involved sustained personal interaction with white customers. In the hospitality industry, for example,
white women worked in "front of the house" jobs such as hostess or waitress or
front desk attendant; women of color worked in "back of the house" positions
in housekeeping or in the kitchen. Even as wait work expanded in the postwar
period, almost doubling between 1940 and 1960, employers refused to hire
nonwhite women in "front of the house" positions. After returning to its prewar
numbers in 1950, the percentage of waitresses who were African-American, for
example, actually declined, reaching a low of five percent in 1970. Some employers argued that customers preferred white women because only white
women could achieve the desired standards of femininity, beauty, and "professionalism." Others, primarily outside the South, believed that the (white) public
wanted waitresses like their mothers, wives, or daughters and would reject an
intimate service encounter with a nonwhite server.[65]

Cultural and racial prejudice shaped the hiring practices of employers even
in jobs in which interpersonal contact was just voice-to-voice. During the war, a
sprinkling of African-American women, some graduates of leading universities,
gained entry into telephone operator jobs after black activists associated with
A. Philip Randolph's March on Washington movement and others filed suits

with the wartime FEPC and picketed in St. Louis, Baltimore, and elsewhere. But by 1960 less than three percent of the female telephone workforce was black, almost all concentrated in large northern cities.[66] Telephone executives, like employers in many other industries, claimed that (white) employee morale would be lowered if white women worked side by side with nonwhite. As one interviewer told a teenage Maida Springer-Kemp when she applied for an operator position, "What white mother do you think would want you to sit beside her daughter?" In addition, telephone representatives detailed a host of "social skills" needed in a telephone operator that, they insisted, nonwhite women lacked. African-American, Hispanic, and other minorities couldn't speak with the precision or the correct accent that was required. Nor could they inspire confidence enough to comfort and calm those calling in emergencies.[67]

Like other service sector employers, the airline companies pinned their discriminatory practices on the needs and desires of the customers they served. Their standards of beauty were European: women of color were ipso facto defined as "unattractive." In defending their all-white hiring policy in 1956, one airline explained that they "hesitated" to employ blacks because of "possible unfavorable reactions from passengers from the South and from other employees." Another worried that "the ranks of white stewardesses would dwindle fast if the glamour of the job were down-graded by employment of Negro girls."[68]

A few airlines hired black attendants in the late 1950s, after much public pressure, but the larger pattern of egregious discrimination would not change until the passage of the Civil Rights Act in 1964. In 1957, Mohawk Airlines, a New York State carrier serving mainly northeast routes, hired the nation's *first* black flight attendant, a 25-year-old nursing school graduate. In May 1958, TWA became the second airline to break the racial bar by also hiring *one* black attendant. These limited concessions came after African-American women sought and received the help of the New York State Commission Against Discrimination. The Commission, established in 1945, received sixteen formal complaints of race discrimination from black women denied flight attendant positions before they initiated "a broad inquiry into the hiring policies and practices" of the airlines. They ruled in favor of the plaintiffs, and after five months of negotiations with the airlines, gained a pledge in 1956 from eighteen carriers (all of whom flew out of New York) not to "practice racial discrimination."[69] The Michigan Fair Employment Practices Commission pursued a similar course after receiving complaints of racial discrimination in airline hiring. Yet in 1962, after three years of "persuasion and negotiation," they still had not convinced Northwest Airlines to integrate its hostess ranks.[70]

The unions representing service workers did not pursue racial justice in the 1940s and 1950s with the same determination as the unions representing factory workers. There were fewer minority members within these organizations to raise the issue. In addition, these unions were less influenced by the racial progressivism of the left, especially that of the Communist Party. Because many service unions were organized along occupational lines, their membership reflected the racial and ethnic composition of the occupations they represented: all white. White women in "pink-collar" jobs had more to lose in the way of "status," since these jobs were constructed in part as "respectable" jobs for "white ladies."[71]

Unions representing white service workers largely acceded to the prevailing racial norms. The all-white flight attendant unions, for example, raised few objections to the racial hiring bars of the airlines. Indeed, the African-American job applicants who sued in 1955 charging race discrimination did so with the support of the National Urban League's Committee on Discrimination in Airline Flight Employment and other community-based black organizations, not the all-white unions.[72]

The CWA's record of organizational effort on behalf of racial justice in the postwar decades is similarly tepid. Race was a highly volatile political subject within the union. The CWA had few nonwhite members; it also had an unusually large proportion of Southern workers, many of whom felt strongly about defending racial segregation and white supremacy in the postwar period. Racial justice issues rarely surfaced at the national union level, and when they did, the outcome was not always positive. At the 1953 CWA convention, for example, a proposal for the creation of a Fair Practices and Anti-Discrimination Department "to work for the elimination of discrimination based on sex, race, color, creed" was soundly defeated.[73]

Although the national union did little, certain individual CWA officers, especially in the South, took great personal and political risks to advance the rights of minorities. By the late 1950s, Selina Burch was working as the CWA regional representative in Atlanta, making herself unpopular by advocating an end to the segregated practices at the Southern Bell companies. Later, in the 1960s, when as a result of the 1964 Civil Rights Act, the telephone companies finally began hiring African-Americans in the South for the *first* time, the white fury directed her way reached a fever pitch. "When Southern Bell started hiring blacks as switchboard operators, the phone in the CWA office was ringing off the wall. Members of the union were demanding that we stop it, hollering that if niggers came to work, they were going to walk off their jobs. My answer was always the same: you have the right to walk off your job, but the union will not protect you if you do. Then, when blacks began to show up at union meetings and voting in elections, my home phone began ringing all night, members calling to shout 'nigger lover' into the phone and hang up. It got to where the first thing I would look for when I came home in the evening would be two double martinis." Burch's emotional and physical health deteriorated, and she eventually ended up in the hospital for a month. When she came out, she redoubled her long-standing efforts outside the union to change the racial status quo: she volunteered for Andrew Young's congressional campaign and Maynard Jackson's mayoral bid in Atlanta. Jackson became Atlanta's first African-American mayor in 1973.[74]

PRESERVING WOMEN'S FAIR SHARE OF JOBS

As was clear in the immediate postwar years and again in the recessions of the 1950s, women's equal right to wage work was meaningless without strategies of job *retention* as well as *access*. The logic governing employer decisions about layoffs and rehiring was as crucial to women as how employers decided whom to hire in the first place. At times, wage-earning women disagreed among themselves, as well as with their brother unionists, over the principles that should determine who would be employed and who unemployed. Yet they shared with wage-earning men an allegiance to certain values and strategies not fully embraced by the culture at large. Many believed that economic security took precedence over economic opportunity; that bureaucratic rules were preferable to supervisor discretion; and that seniority and work sharing were fairer distributors of jobs than earlier systems based on "merit," productivity, family status, or personality. Also, although they debated where the lines separating men's jobs and women's jobs should be drawn and whether certain sex-based policies were desirable, few women, if any, objected to the notion that in some circumstances men and women should do different jobs.

By the postwar era the belief that layoffs and rehiring should be governed by the seniority principle had taken deep root in many blue-collar union cultures.[75] Working-class women embraced the seniority principle in the 1930s, just as did men, and they defended it from attack or modification throughout the postwar period. Workers favored seniority because it offered a predictable, impersonal, and clear-cut system by which layoffs and rehiring would occur. A strong seniority clause lowered anxiety about how economic downturns would affect individual workers; it also improved the daily experience of blue-collar work by undercutting the ability of foremen to exercise their power in a wanton and abusive way. With seniority systems in place foremen lost much of their control over the distribution of work.

Yet seniority could also be cruel in its blindness to the needs and talents of individual workers, and although nominally a race- and gender-blind policy, it could have a negative effect on minority and women workers. For one, since longevity of employment was the sole characteristic being rewarded, those hired last—often women and minorities—had the least protection. In addition, many seniority systems operated on a departmental rather than a plant-wide basis, meaning that the job claims of workers based on their tenure extended only to the jobs in their department. Since many departments tended to be segregated by race and sex, departmental seniority could be (and was) used to preserve the jobs of white men. Employers simply laid off whole departments of women and minorities and kept open departments in which white men predominated. Departmental seniority also reinforced occupational segregation by race and sex, since few workers wanted to lose their seniority rights by transferring to a new department.

Nonetheless, particularly in the 1930s and 1940s, working-class women often preferred *departmental* seniority to *plant-wide* seniority. In an era when women's departments appeared to be *more* resistant to economic downturns than did men's, many women thought that departmental seniority would help *alleviate* the inherent inequalities in a plant-wide system that favored those workers hired first. At least theoretically, with departmental seniority, newly hired women and minorities could *retain* their jobs as more senior white men *lost* theirs. Moreover, the advantages departmental seniority offered in obtaining employment security outweighed its disadvantages in promotion and job transfer. For many working-class women, job security trumped job opportunity.

By the 1950s, however, the issue became more contested, with some women pushing hard for plant-wide seniority and others holding fiercely to departmental. For some, the rejection of departmental seniority was a rejection of a sex-based system that upheld a particular sexual division of labor they saw as outmoded and/or characterized by limited promotional opportunities. But most abandoned departmental seniority because it no longer offered the best route to economic security. By the 1950s many women had accumulated at least a decade or more of service; hence, plant-wide seniority gave them more protection than it had in the 1940s. Of equal importance, in many industries, women's departments now were more subject to layoff than men's.

At least in some manufacturing sectors, as jobs unionized and women's wages moved up relative to men's, employers reacted by laying off women. Especially in blue-collar jobs that were not strongly sex-linked—that is, they required neither women's supposedly special physical talents (women were thought to excel at jobs requiring detail or tedious, repetitive motions) nor their vaunted emotional and nurturing capacities—employers began shutting down women's departments and firing women. The problem was especially acute for African-American women. Their status in high-wage full-time jobs was precarious. Indeed, black women often were able to break into jobs that historically had been reserved for white women because these jobs were becoming less desirable. This was the case in telecommunications, for instance. African-American women moved into telephone operator jobs as the shift from manual to direct dialing (first for local calls and then for long distance) reduced the skill, prestige, and job security of operators. Among telephone operators, it was a revolving door in which black women entered as white women were leaving.[76]

A similar trend appeared in meatpacking, where African-American women gained access to jobs that, by the mid-1950s, were being eliminated. Employers automated many "women's jobs," closed down women's departments, combined men's and women's jobs, hiring men for the new combined jobs, and made it perfectly clear that if pushed to improve women's wages and working conditions, they preferred to hire men. Some of the hardest hit areas were the ones with the largest concentrations of black workers.[77]

In response, many women, particularly women of color, abandoned their allegiance to departmental seniority and began a decade-long search for alternative job security measures. Some women argued for shifting to plant-wide seniority and "combining male and female seniority."[78] Others searched for a third way, one that expanded women's job rights but continued to specify at least *some* jobs as either male or female. Marian Simmons, a respected African-American activist who became the first woman UPWA district director in 1955, proposed "triple seniority" because "certain jobs women can't do and certain jobs men can't do." Triple seniority would preserve these jobs as either male or female, while creating a third category of jobs open to men or women.[79] She saw her proposal as a way to "straighten out this seniority thing." She wrapped up her appeal to UPWA convention delegates by linking sex discrimination to race. It's not fair that women are jobless and "walking the street," she argued, "just because they happen to be women, something they have no control over any more than we have on the color of our skins."[80]

In 1958 and 1960, the UPWA convention continued the search for an effective response to women's job losses. They agreed at one point to combine male and female seniority "provided that women will not suffer more job losses as a result of such combination."[81] Later, the convention adopted the Women's Committee's recommendation that "the union make a survey as to what jobs now being handled by men can be handled by women . . . and that women be sent to apply."[82] Finally, in desperation, the Women's Committee demanded in 1962 that "all elements and segments of female jobs be *frozen as female*" (italics added) and that employment opportunities be increased "for women on jobs they are capable of performing." Addie Wyatt called on men to be fair and "refuse to accept a woman's job."[83] Unfortunately, none of these proposals turned the situation around. Employers continued to lay off women.

The job protection measures that women devised in other unionized sectors of the economy were more effective, in large part because employers were not as resistant to female employment as in meatpacking. These proposals, like many suggested by UPWA women, attempted to enhance women's economic security while simultaneously respecting the sexual divide.[84] The primary job security strategy relied upon by unionized waitresses, for example, was to redraw the boundaries between "men's" and "women's" jobs so that a greater proportion of work fell within the female domain. Waitresses historically had respected men's claim to certain strata of food service jobs—those involving liquor service or formal dinner service, for example—but increasingly they insisted that some of these men's jobs properly belonged to women. These jobs would remain sex-typed but would be relabeled as female.[85]

Many labor women in the postwar decades tried to save jobs for women in these ways, but few were ready to embrace gender-blind job assignments or unimpeded competition between men and women. In part, their support of job segregation by sex reflected deeply held, almost unconscious beliefs. Yet women's advocacy of sex-based practices as well as their support for more gender-neutral treatment must be understood as arising as much from *pragmatic* considerations as from *ideological*. Their views on departmental seniority, for example, could shift depending on the industry and the perceived impact of the policy. Would it provide women with the economic security they needed?

Would it help them claim the jobs they preferred? At times, men's jobs were desirable, and women claimed them. Other times, men's jobs were heavier, dirtier, and less attractive; men could keep them.[86]

Mary Callahan captured this mix of motivations among working-class women when she looked back on the postwar decades in a 1976 interview. On the one hand, she explained, everyone, including herself, took job segregation in the 1940s and 1950s as a "way of life." Yet part of the reason the system went unquestioned was that it was not felt to be objectionable; neither was it judged unfair or "discriminatory." "We never questioned it when they posted female and male jobs . . . we didn't realize it was discrimination. I never thought of it. I figured who the heck wants a job over there; it's a male job, you know."[87]

ENDING UNFAIR SEX DISCRIMINATION

Although most working-class women did not experience the sexual division of labor per se as objectionable in the postwar period, many identified "discrimination based on sex" as a problem. It is important to stress that what labor women meant by "discrimination" in this period often differed from what it would come to mean by the 1960s and 1970s. As Mary Callahan's comment suggests, many sex-based practices were simply not seen as discriminatory. Nonetheless, labor women recognized that discrimination against women because of their sex existed, that it needed to end, and that governmental and union action might be required. After consulting with a group of women labor leaders, the Women's Bureau issued a pamphlet in 1945 asking unions to reject "discrimination based on sex, color, creed, and national origin in all matters pertaining to hiring, upgrading, lay-off, wages, and seniority." In subsequent conferences, union women reiterated their commitment to this goal. Despite, in the words of Ruth Young, it "being damn hard to sell this [no discrimination on the basis of sex] to a lot of the workers, including some of the leaders of the union," labor feminists forged ahead.[88]

CIO wartime publications committed the organization to "the eradication of discrimination against women workers," and it reiterated its position in the years following. In 1951, the CIO passed a resolution on women workers declaring that "women must be accepted as full union members, entitled to all rights. We must," the resolution continued, "eliminate discriminations based on outworn tradition rather than current ideals and needs." For these reasons, "we continue our support for the Women's Status Bill, and urge our affiliates to support actively protection of women's rights through clauses in union contracts against discrimination in pay, hiring, up-grading, and layoff."[89]

Clauses prohibiting discrimination on the basis of sex were already common in the UE by the 1940s, and they became more widespread, both within the UE and in other unions, over the course of the postwar period.[90] By the mid-1950s, a number of unions reported considerable progress in carrying out this mandate. The IUE, for example, by 1956, had gained provisions prohibiting sex discrimination in hiring, layoffs, promotions, and transfers in a number of its local contracts, although GE and other corporations resisted nondiscrimination clauses in national bargaining.[91]

Labor women sought government as well as union help with ending sex discrimination. But no one really knew what kind of government policy would be feasible or effective. The Women's Status Bill garnered the most support among union women in the late 1940s and early 1950s. There was also support for adding "sex" to the FEP statutes that many CIO unions were pursuing.[92] The IUE, for example, passed convention resolutions urging the inclusion of sex with race in all laws banning job bias beginning in 1950.[93]

Yet all these approaches had problems. Neither the Women's Status Bill nor the fair employment legislation made much headway in Congress against what A. Philip Randolph called the "unholy alliance" of Republicans and Southern Democrats. The 1950 Fair Employment Practices Bill, which included a ban on sex discrimination, met defeat despite Randolph's threat of a "silent, non-violent march on Washington of Negroes, Japanese-Americans, Mexicans, Protestants, Catholics and Jews, trade unionists, AF of L and CIO, men, women and children."[94] The political support needed to pass FEP statutes was shaky, particularly if they included a sex amendment. The New York State FEP law, passed in 1945, prohibited discrimination on the basis of race, religion, and national origin but did not include a clause forbidding sex discrimination. Of the other FEP laws to pass before 1964, only two departed from the New York model and included provisions against sex discrimination, despite much testimony about the pervasiveness of the problem by labor women.[95] Millie Jeffrey remembered ruefully that we "couldn't get to first base" when it came to including sex in the FEP laws. "The whole tenor of that period was that you could not put sex into FEPC because that would lose the support of the Catholic Church and others. If you had [to make] a commitment, the dominant problem was race."[96]

When the UPWA women attempted to mount a civil rights campaign that linked race and sex, their first hurdle was getting people to even think of women as a minority group. When a resolution came before the UPWA convention in 1947, for example, calling upon Congress "to enact a civil rights law that will protect the right of every person regardless of race, creed, color, nationality, or religion," a female delegate rose to amend the proposal and include the word "sex." "I feel that in speaking of discrimination against minority groups we sometimes forget that women are also considered a minority group. The employer, when he uses the method of divide and conquer he uses black against white, Jew against Gentile, and he also uses men against women." Those submitting the resolution apologized for "not having it in there," and after the applause died down, the resolution passed overwhelmingly.[97] Although later UPWA antidiscrimination proposals also "forgot women"—Addie Wyatt had to add "sex" from the convention floor in 1964 in a replay of 1947—the UPWA's political action platform of 1956 did not. It proposed the passage of FEP legislation to "insure equal job rights of women workers" and called for adding sex to the 1941 executive order forbidding discrimination in defense and government employment.[98] The UAW also sought to have sex included in presidential executive orders and committees, beginning with the FDR's 1941 proclamation. They urged Truman's Committee on Government Contract Compliance to consider forbidding discrimination on the basis of sex, a forerunner of their later efforts in the 1960s to get sex included in Kennedy's 1961 Executive Order 10925.[99]

Efforts to link sex and race discrimination faced other problems. "Sex discrimination" was not yet recognized as a problem by many male union leaders, and certainly not one as pressing as race. Women unionists had their reservations too. Some feared that a focus on sex discrimination would undermine the struggle against race. Others were uncomfortable with the equation of race and sex discrimination in public policy: the two were different in origin and intensity, it was thought, and required different kinds of interventions. Putting them side by side in public statutes would confuse the issue rather than clarify it.

But others thought the two should be linked. For one, the indignities of women of color stemmed from sex discrimination as well as race. In addition, for many white women, there was a logical as well as emotional connection between the problems they experienced and what they observed being done to minorities. The UAW's Caroline Davis, for example, always began her speeches explaining that women too were a minority and that they, like Negroes, experienced discrimination. In part she drew on this analogy because of its inherent logic and because she knew her audience would be receptive. It also felt right to her because of her own emotional investment in ending racial discrimination, a commitment that had deepened over the years as she encountered racism close up in her travels with Lillian Hatcher. When asked in 1973 about what had kept her going, Davis wrote back a letter filled with anecdotes about the harshness and illogic of racial prejudice in the postwar era. "What can I tell you," she began, "of the time Lillian and I were in Georgia and no cab would stop for us?"

> They were all marked "Colored" or "White". The drivers would take a look at us and pass us by because none of them knew where we fitted—we laughed. Or—of the time in 1954 when Lillian and I brought suit against a Drive-In in Royal Oak, Michigan, because we were served cold, fat slabs of pork for a pork barbecue and drinks in paper cups instead of the china cups others were using. When I complained and refused to pay and demanded to see the manager, I was told to go to the back door. We did, and got into an argument. He finally was disturbed enough to call the Royal Oak police and said, "We got two colored women here who refuse to pay their bill." We all went to the police station and started the same proceedings there until we got a court date set. We were assigned to an old blind judge who when questioning me, asked if I were white. I guess up until that point, everyone was trying to make up their minds because in those days, it was inconceivable that a black and white were friends. Well, we lost the case.[100]

A COMPETING STRATEGY

Although still faint in the 1940s and 1950s, another discourse could be heard among labor women that emphasized sex-blind treatment and the integration of women into men's jobs. Women who held jobs in male-dominated sectors and who were in more direct competition with men were often among the first to see persistent disadvantages in differential treatment and the rigid division of jobs by sex.[101] Some UAW women, as Nancy Gabin observes, began to favor equal rather than differential treatment as an appropriate strategy in the 1940s and 1950s and consistently objected to a wide variety of sex-based employment practices, including the exclusion of women from so-called men's jobs.[102]

Still, even among UAW women, the realization that policies based on "gender difference can limit women's opportunities" sat alongside a continuing belief in sex differences and the viability of differential treatment as a means to improve women's situation. In 1963, the UAW Women's Department issued a widely distributed pamphlet entitled *How to Be Equal Though Different: Working Women Today*.[103]

African-American women also tended to be more skeptical of sex-based differential treatment and a rigid sexual division of labor than did other women. The different reactions of black and white waitresses to the sexual division of labor among hotel and restaurant workers are telling. Black waitresses, for example, asserted their right to serve liquor (a job traditionally handled by male waiters only) more quickly than did other waitresses. They also parted ways with white waitresses in the postwar debate over whether bartending should remain a male preserve. In 1951, three hundred barmaids belonging to the all-black Waitresses', Bartenders', and Cooks' Local 444 in Chicago successfully resisted the adoption of a Chicago City Council ordinance prohibiting women from dispensing alcoholic beverages. That same local had raised the only objections in 1948 when the international launched its national crusade to pass new state laws restricting bartending to men.[104] In other industries such as meat-packing and electrical, it was also often black women who first raised the possibility of abandoning the separate spheres framework in the search for job security and advancement.[105]

Black women had both material and ideological incentives for questioning the sex typing of jobs. Because of the racial discrimination against black women as well as black men, the economic alternatives for black women were more limited than those for white women while the economic pressures for them to contribute to family support were greater. Fewer jobs were open to black women than to white, and fewer black men received a breadwinner wage. Moreover, historically, black male and female workers were less differentiated by sex than white. Black women as well as men, for example, performed physically demanding agricultural labor as well as other low-paying, heavy jobs in the industrial and service sectors. In part because the daily experience of black women largely conflicted with the reigning ideology of "separate spheres," black women developed, in Linda Gordon's words, "an autonomous gender system, one distinct from white mainstream norms but also from those of white feminists. The normative femininity they created was never as subordinate or as confined to the domestic as was the white."[106] Neither did black female identity depend as much on performing sex-typed work tasks. Finally, the system of racial segregation itself, with all its attendant indignities, made black women deeply skeptical of a separate-but-equal doctrine—whether based on race or on sex.

CONCLUSION

Accounts of the postwar decades that see little change in women's work lives because gender segregation and the gender wage gap remained firmly entrenched are missing much of the drama of the era. Indeed, if those were the only indicators of change, one would have to conclude that not much had happened in the nature of women's wage work for hundreds of years. Yet much did change for working women in the 1940s and 1950s. Bars to the employment of women based on marital status lowered. Combining marriage and wage earning for women became the norm, and minority and older women moved into a range of jobs that heretofore had been the preserve of younger, single, white women. Problems remained. Although women of color moved into factory work, the opening of white women's jobs to all women was just beginning. Discrimination against mothers and pregnant women was rife too, even in so-called "women's jobs." But the transformations of the postwar decades, albeit incremental, set the stage for the next wave of reform in the 1960s and 1970s.[107]

In particular, labor women's persistent challenge to unfair sex discrimination in employer policies and their demands for a *right to jobs for all women* helped spur the employment rights revolution of the 1960s and 1970s. By arguing for women's equal job rights, they expanded notions of industrial citizenship and labor rights. By raising the question of which sex-based differences were "discriminatory" and which were not, they expanded the meaning of discrimination and narrowed the range of acceptable differential treatment. Moreover, their efforts to establish sex discrimination as a social problem that required union and even state intervention helped legitimize federal government intervention and oversight of employer decisions affecting hiring, layoffs, promotions, and other conditions of employment.

Of course there were tensions over how to define women's job rights and how to create a movement that addressed the needs of all women. Yet despite potential fissures along the lines of industry and occupation, of race, of family status and other differences, the political consensus and coalition that labor feminists had forged by the end of the war remained intact. And, as the next two chapters will detail, that consensus rested on a shared understanding that the campaign for women's job rights and for access to wage work was always intertwined with other concerns. Along with equal job rights, postwar labor feminists sought to transform the pay and working conditions of the jobs held by women, ensure the market did not reward only the strong and the unencumbered, and gain the right to leisure and to a life apart from wage-earning.

Wage Justice

> Doesn't it come to this question: "Are wages paid as compensation for work or are they paid as a social obligation?"
>
> —*Senator Tunnell, 1945 Senate hearings on the Equal Pay Bill.*[1]

> This business of thinking of a job as something that can be defined separate from the person who is doing it is a very new idea."
>
> —*Frieda Miller, Director, Women's Bureau, October 1946*[2]

IN DECEMBER 1944, Frieda Miller, newly appointed director of the U.S. Women's Bureau, offered her thoughts to the hundred and fifty UAW women who had come to Detroit as delegates to the first National Women's Conference of the UAW. Introduced as a long-time advocate of equal pay for equal work, Miller returned to that theme more than once in her talk, always eliciting the enthusiastic response of the crowd. Yet Miller reminded her audience that the campaign for wage justice was not limited to equal pay, nor would women's problems be resolved only through collective bargaining. She called on the UAW women, often considered the elite of working-class women because of their high-wage unionized jobs in a male-dominated industry, to help out their lower-paid unorganized sisters. Use your influence on state legislators, she urged, to improve the working standards in the "traditionally feminine occupations, such as beauty parlor operators, sales clerks, and domestic workers," where women are "grossly underpaid."[3]

Her call did not go unheeded. In the 1940s, wage justice for women emerged as a principal goal of the social feminist wing of the women's movement.[4] In the decades following World War II, labor women and their allies initiated widespread campaigns to raise women's wages through collective bargaining and through the passage of improved minimum wage statutes and equal pay protections. These campaigns were a major component of efforts to extend the benefits of the New Deal to those left out. Indeed, the nature of the employment system that would emerge, as well as the economic well being of wage-earning women for years to come, rested in part on the success or failure of labor feminists to secure wage justice for women.

From Protectionism to Wage Justice

In the nineteenth century, demands for local, state, and federal legislation regulating wages and hours arose chiefly from the labor movement, and the proposed protections were often class-based, covering both male and female wage workers. But by the turn of the century, AFL President Samuel Gompers and many of the other top AFL leaders favored *voluntary* rather than *state-centered* solutions, at least for men. That is, they preferred that wages, hours, and working conditions be determined through the voluntary give and take of collective bargaining rather than by state fiat. There were exceptions, such as the AFL support for laws regulating workplace health and safety, but by and large the labor movement approved of protective legislation for women and minors only. As was also true of the courts, the AFL judged minimum wage coverage as less legitimate than other protective laws, such as those that set maximum hours, required lunch breaks, rest periods, seats, and other amenities, or prohibited night work and employment in hazardous industries.[5]

By the early twentieth century, women social reformers, most prominently among them Florence Kelley of the NCL, had become the principal advocates of state intervention on behalf of workers. They met resistance from the labor and business community as well as from the courts. In 1905, decrying labor standards regulating adult men as an unconstitutional interference with "liberty of contract," the Supreme Court, in *Lochner v. New York*, overturned the New York state law that limited the hours adult *male* bakers could work. The ruling dashed the hopes of reformers for state protective laws covering men and women. Yet three years later, the Supreme Court affirmed the constitutionality of maximum hour legislation for *women* in *Muller v. Oregon*, allowing that women's "power of contract" could be restricted because of public interest in protecting their health and "maternal functions." *Muller v. Oregon* reenergized the movement for protective legislative, at least in regard to women and children. A flurry of state laws followed. By the early 1920s, all but four states had enacted maximum hour laws for women, and almost every state had laws guarding women's health and specifying when and where they could work.[6]

Far fewer states had minimum wage laws. Such laws, some feared, might raise women's wages and prompt them to choose employment over household duties. In contrast, statutes limiting hours and safeguarding women's health appeared to encourage women's responsibilities in the home by limiting their access to higher-paying jobs and protecting their maternal functions. Nonetheless, Massachusetts passed the first minimum wage law for women in 1912. Fourteen other states, the District of Columbia, and Puerto Rico followed suit over the next decade. The movement stalled in 1923, however, hamstrung by the Supreme Court decision in *Adkins v. Children's Hospital*, which struck down the District of Columbia minimum wage law, holding that "even women's need for protection was not adequate justification for state intervention."[7]

The dramatic economic and political disruptions of the 1930s reopened the door to federal regulation of working conditions. Reformers now argued that federal intervention was justified on behalf of *both* male and female workers, relying upon the commerce clause in the Constitution that allowed for federal regulation of interstate commerce in order to maintain fair competition and a healthy economy. In 1937, the Supreme Court upheld the Wagner Act and, in *West Coast Hotel Co. v. Parrish*, it overturned *Adkins*, clearing the way for a new class-based regulatory regime covering wages, hours, and working conditions for men and women. The Fair Labor Standards Act (FLSA) followed in 1938 and was upheld by the Supreme Court in 1941.[8]

The FLSA established the same minimums across region and industry, unlike the earlier National Recovery Act (NRA) wage codes. It also had broad coverage in one sense: men were included for the first time.[9] Yet when the dust of debate cleared, Congress had set depressingly low minimums—twenty-five cents an hour, which would rise to forty cents by 1945—and the statute covered only about a third of the workforce.[10] Despite its reliance on the seemingly neutral category of "worker," the lowest paid workers, the group who stood to benefit the most, were disproportionately excluded. Southern conservatives specifically targeted agricultural and domestic labor, the two leading occupations for minorities and a mainstay of the Southern economy, for exclusion. In addition, most retail and service occupations fell outside the law. ACWA's Sidney Hillman had insisted on coverage for the textile and garment trades, but the service and retail trades were largely unorganized and lacked political clout. Their inclusion also raised "constitutionality issues," since it was unclear whether hotels, restaurants, and other such industries were engaged in interstate commerce and hence subject to federal regulation.[11]

In short, the passage of the FLSA left labor feminists with much of their agenda still unrealized. As a result, raising wage minimums and broadening statutory coverage to the vast number of men and women still without protection would remain an integral aspect of women's efforts to achieve wage justice after the 1930s. Other strategies would be pursued as well. Indeed, by the 1940s, equal pay was no longer a slogan advanced chiefly by men; it was one of the core demands of the women's movement.

EQUAL PAY BECOMES A WOMEN'S DEMAND

The emergence of equal pay as an issue pushed primarily by women was a significant departure from the past. Before World War II, women divided sharply on the issue, and equal pay demands were as likely to be advanced by men as by women.[12] Most employers preferred to hire men for high-wage jobs. Thus, if employers were forced to pay a woman a "man's wage," many would either not hire her at all or employ her temporarily until a man could be found. The demand for equal pay, then, was often proposed by men as a strategy to protect their jobs and wage levels.[13]

Yet by the mid-1940s, many of the friends as well as the enemies of equal pay had rethought their positions. Equal pay was no longer a policy pushed largely by men with the primary goal of preserving male privilege.[14] It became a rallying cry of those seeking economic justice and higher wages for women. Women dominated the leadership of the national coalitions devoted to equal pay in the 1940s and 1950s. In particular, labor women from unions with large female memberships—ACWA, UE, IUE, and CWA—provided the political muscle behind equal pay efforts at both the federal and state level. Some male-dominated unions continued to support equal pay as a job preservation strategy for men. But others, such as the UAW, adopted their favorable stance toward equal pay in part because of consistent pressure from strong feminists inside the organization.

Why did equal pay emerge as a significant female demand in the 1940s? Some women, of course, supported it because they believed it would preserve the earning power of men and stabilize traditional gender roles. But there is little evidence to suggest that the prime motivation on the part of most women was to protect men's jobs and wages. Rather, the explanations given by women themselves, both public and private, suggest that the crucial issues for them were those of fairness, of improving women's economic standing, and of ensuring women's ability to support themselves and their dependents.[15] These ideas gained increasing salience as working-class wives entered the labor force, joining the growing numbers of female heads of household and self-supporting single women. One of the oldest divides over equal pay—married women against single—was dissolving.

World War II also changed the minds of many women about their own capacities and about what constituted wage justice. Many never forgot the experience of doing exactly what a man had been doing the day before and receiving half his wages. For others, doing a man's job demystified the work of men and prompted a new assessment of the worth (and hence wages) of men's jobs in comparison to women's jobs. The 1942 War Labor Board's General Order 16, which allowed union claims for wage increases on the basis of equal pay for equal work, and the board's subsequent rulings favoring the equal pay principle, also helped legitimize the idea of pay equality between men and women.[16] By the end of the war, a growing number of women believed they deserved equal pay. They embraced equal pay as an important statement of women's inherent equality with men, and they supported it regardless of its economic consequences.

The long-term shift toward a service economy and the corresponding rise in the demand for female labor also spurred a reassessment of the economic impact of equal pay. By the 1940s many women began to think differently about how equal pay statutes would affect employer behavior and their own job opportunities and income. Increasingly, they saw equal pay as a strategy that would benefit rather than penalize them economically.[17] Where employers continued to prefer men and hired women only when they could pay them less or when no

men were available—often the case in the automobile and other male-dominated heavy manufacturing industries and occupations—equal pay demands
frequently did cost women jobs. But in other sectors of the postwar economy,
particularly those in which large numbers of women already worked, employers
were willing to hire women and/or retain them even if they had to pay them
the same as men.

REDEFINING EQUAL PAY

The typical equal pay demand before World War II merely required that when
women took on "men's jobs" they would be paid the same as men. In a world
in which few women held "men's jobs," the potential for raising women's pay
through equal pay demands defined on these narrow grounds was minimal.

This dilemma is precisely why labor feminists took care to define equal pay
broadly. "Equal pay for equal work is a catchy slogan," Mary Anderson judged
in 1944, but its effect is limited to situations where women "take the place of
men in the same work that men have been doing." For Anderson and others,
this situation was unacceptable. Equal pay needed to be applied to a much
larger group of women: those doing *comparable* work as well as those doing the
same. To reflect this more encompassing definition of equal pay, labor feminists
used the slogan "equal pay for *comparable* work" instead of "equal pay for *equal*
work." The older notion of equal pay, as UPWA leader Addie Wyatt later told
an interviewer, "did not solve the problem of low pay for women's jobs." These
jobs, she continued, sometimes had "greater skill and training requirements"
than men's jobs but "had long since been categorized as female jobs and [paid]
a female rate. We talked about comparing the jobs."[18]

Labor feminists combined this notion of comparing dissimilar jobs with a
related idea, what was called "the rate for the job." The idea of a "rate for the
job" in management circles simply referred to the setting of a wage rate by
experts who evaluated job duties and set a scientific and supposedly fair rate.[19]
In the hands of labor feminists, however, it was often used as a way of supporting the equalizing of wages between women and men—or ending what Mary
Anderson called "the double wage standard."[20] Mary Van Kleeck, director of
the Women-in-Industry Service (the forerunner to the Women's Bureau), and
her assistant Mary Anderson used the phrase "rate for the job" in their World
War I era efforts to raise wages for female employment, as did British feminists
Eleanor Rathbone and Beatrice Webb.[21] In 1944, the International Labor Organization (ILO), relying upon "rate for the job" language supplied by the U.S.
Women's Bureau, resolved that "steps should be taken to encourage the establishment of wage rates on the basis of job content, without regard to sex."[22] And,
soon after, the April 1945 Women's Bureau conference for women labor leaders,
dominated by younger activists like Kitty Ellickson, Ruth Young, Maida
Springer-Kemp, Millie Jeffrey, and Dollie Lowther, reached a consensus on a

new meaning for equal pay that incorporated the "rate for the job idea." "The old method or approach, that is, equal pay or the same pay for women if they do the same work as men, was much too limiting. The rate for the job was the proper approach . . . that is, no discrimination in the rate of pay because of sex."[23] For the first time, enthused Frieda Miller, "we were thinking about a job apart from the person doing it."[24]

These definitional changes had enormous implications practically and theoretically. Equal pay could now mean abolishing "dual wage structures," or situations in which men and women in *comparable* job classifications were paid unequally. In its most sweeping application, it questioned the very basis by which the "so-called traditional women's occupations" were evaluated and assigned pay grades. Ridding these jobs of gender bias or establishing a fair "rate for the job" could mean raising women's pay whether or not comparable male jobs existed. The potential for lifting the wages of the "women-employing occupations" was thus vastly improved.[25]

Elaborating upon the implications of this new definition of equal pay, labor women even questioned the gender bias of the job evaluation or wage-setting process itself. At the April 1945 Women's Bureau Conference for Trade Union Women, Cornelia Anderson of the FTA commented on the concept "from the point of view of industries like canneries and tobacco plants, which are largely women employing." In these industries, "you can very beautifully establish the principle of equal pay for equal work and yet have large numbers of women making less than the men, simply because of women working in . . . entire jobs and categories that are always women-employing. When you talk about rate for the jobs . . . there is a possibility of re-studying and reevaluating jobs throughout the plant [and of asking] why should a woman who sits and packs be paid 20 to 25 cents less than a man who sweeps the floor?"[26] Other delegates echoed these sentiments, pointing to the importance of reevaluating the skills of traditional women's jobs and adjusting the "wage rates" assigned women's jobs. One delegate suggested a study analyzing what each job "means and what it takes in skill and experience." "Women's skills have been under-estimated," Frieda Miller stated in support of the idea. Such an evaluation "would give us some basis for upping many of the types of occupations that women have had in the past."[27]

This more expanded definition of equal pay is evident in the language of the state and federal equal pay laws proposed by labor feminists as well as in the contract language they hoped to insert in collective bargaining agreements. Equal pay contract provisions and legislative statutes should, they declared, "cover situations where women replace men, where men and women are employed on comparable jobs, and employment of women in so-called women's jobs or women's departments." The federal Equal Pay Bill submitted for the first time in 1945 prohibited wage differentials for "work of a comparable character" or work requiring "comparable skills"; it also proposed industry committees that would analyze the current job classification and wage-setting systems for gender bias.[28]

Pursuing Wage Justice at the Bargaining Table

After 1940, the real wages of American workers grew steadily for the next three decades.[29] The rise was due to a number of factors: the insulation of the U.S. economy from global competition, the income and tax policies of New Dealers, and the productivity advances in basic industry. But the expansion of unions and the enhanced ability of workers to exert economic and political pressure in support of wage demands also contributed to the high wage economy of the postwar years.

Women workers shared in these economic advances, particularly unionized women. Economistic studies calculating the economic impact of unionization routinely find that the income of organized workers exceeds that of unorganized, even within industries and occupations. Moreover, the "union wage effect," or the amount unionization raises wages, is greater for women than for men because women as individuals have less bargaining power in the labor market than do men.[30] Unionized women in the postwar era also benefited from the industrial union principle of wage solidarity. Wage solidarity often meant equalizing wages across regions, employers, and different categories of workers. In "pattern bargaining," an approach to negotiations that became almost a "party line" for industrial unions in the postwar era, unions would target a high-wage employer in the industry, settle with that employer first, and then use that settlement to raise standards in the rest of the industry. These practices tended to equalize wages by raising the earnings of the lowest paid, a group disproportionately female and minority.[31]

The escalating demands by women for equal pay at the bargaining table helped raise women's wages as well. During the war, labor women resorted to sit-downs and other direct action to adjust pay rates, and they joined with the Women's Bureau staff in pressuring unions to take advantage of the pay equity adjustments allowed under the War Labor Board (WLB).[32] A number of unions initiated WLB claims that resulted in back pay and wage adjustments for women and minority men; voluntary adjustments by employers affected another 60,000 women.[33] After the war, with the WLB dismantled, labor women sought permanent mechanisms for securing equal pay such as union contract clauses and legislative statutes that would require it.[34]

Women's demands for wage adjustments met resistance from employers and from their fellow male unionists. In the telephone industry, for example, women telephone operators gathered in 1941 prior to the NFTW convention to discuss the particular needs of women. Their grievances included the failure of the executive board to initiate "a definite program to obtain classification of operators as skilled instead of unskilled," and to address the "matter of securing equal pay for equal work."[35] Mary Gannon, national NFTW chairwoman for telephone operators, later editorialized in favor of equal pay for equal work in the NFTW newspaper, arguing that "rates must be established on the basis of the jobs being done [and] no other factor." Outraged to find in 1945 that "the highest rate for a woman in a clerk's job was lower than the lowest rate for a man, although the jobs were practically the same," NFTW Education Director Ruth Wiencek also made a fuss. When male unionists ignored "educational materials" on equal pay, she recalled, "our female workers . . . made it pretty embarrassing for them. [Being] 60 percent women [we] are able to do that. It depends on how vocal your women's groups are."[36]

Pressure on the union and on management continued into the 1950s, but success was limited, especially for the all-female category of telephone operator. At the founding convention of the CWA in 1947 as well as at subsequent conventions, delegates passed resolutions urging "an end to male and female job classifications" and the "elimination of the differential between men's and women's salaries."[37] In response to member concerns, in the 1950s CWA filed grievances alleging discriminatory pay rates based on sex, and pushed the Bell system to adopt broad equal pay provisions in its contracts. But the company generally refused such provisions, and without equal pay contract language, arbitrators ruled the union pay grievances baseless.[38]

Equal pay demands made greater headway outside of telecommunications. By the mid-1950s equal pay clauses appeared in nearly one-third of all union contracts, and in manufacturing shops the proportion was even higher.[39] The factory campaigns, often involving minority women leaders, included demands for an end to wage discrimination on the basis of race as well as sex. African-American women were strong supporters of equal pay contract language, even when narrowly constructed. They were more likely to be assigned the heavier, dirty jobs that resembled men's work, and thus stood to gain more from traditional equal pay clauses than did white women. In meatpacking, for example, an interracial equal pay movement emerged led by Jarutha Coleman, an African-American woman who chaired the women's committee at the Chicago Swift plant, 70 percent of whose employees were black, and Joan Kelley, a white woman on UPWA's international staff. UPWA secured new equal pay contract language in bargaining with Swift and other industry giants, and by some estimates discriminatory wage differentials in the industry were cut in half by 1952 and "wholly eliminated" by 1958.[40]

In the electrical industry, the equal pay movement was even more extensive and well organized, although less effective than in meatpacking, in part because raising women's pay was a more costly undertaking in an industry so dependent on low-wage female labor. Nevertheless, the UE, and later its anticommunist rival, the IUE, pushed hard to eliminate wage inequities at General Electric, Westinghouse, and other electrical companies. Beginning in the early 1940s, UE women filed grievances and organized conferences in pursuit of wage equity; they also picketed, struck, and filed lawsuits. In 1945, they won a landmark case before the WLB. In the brief, UE called for the expansion of "equal pay for equal work," the "elimination of sex differentials in wages, the abolition of so-called women's jobs, and their reevaluation from the minimum rate paid to common labor." Siding with the union, the WLB allowed wage adjustments because "the jobs customarily performed by women are paid less, on a comparative job content basis, than the jobs customarily performed by men."[41] Indeed, even when a woman's job received the *same* number of points as a man's under the job evaluation system, the female job was arbitrarily paid less. The GE Job Evaluation Manual, for example, specified for years that "For female operators the value shall be two-thirds of the value for adult male workers."[42]

After the WLB disbanded, GE and Westinghouse continued their discriminatory wage practices. In response, the UE made closing the gender wage gap a top priority in nationwide strikes against GE and Westinghouse in 1946. GE refused to alter its pay practices in regard to women, but the UE at least succeeded in narrowing the gap between the top (mostly men) and bottom (mostly women) of the wage scale by winning a flat wage increase rather than a percentage. At Westinghouse, after a 115-day strike of 75,000 workers, the UE gained a similar flat increase for all, plus a cent an hour "set aside" in a fund for "narrowing differentials between men's and women's rates." The UE turned inward in the late 1940s, buffeted by internal dissension and cold war accusations, but by the early 1950s the fight resumed. UE issued model contracts and pamphlets detailing how locals could "tackle rate discrimination." In 1951 and 1952, the 17,000-member GE-Schenectady local instigated noonday demonstrations in which some 800 women picketed, some with signs reading, "Jobs Paid On Content—Not Based on Sex." Eventually, they won rate increases on 373 job classifications.[43]

The IUE mirrored the UE's concern over wage inequities, especially after many of UE's larger locals shifted into the IUE in the early 1950s. In its 1953 and 1954 contract proposals with GE and Westinghouse, the IUE called for "equal pay for equal work," the elimination of "the special category of women's rates," and a "no discrimination clause which would include the word 'sex'." Individual locals struck over gender wage inequities in 1953 and 1954, and although GE and Westinghouse continued to balk at signing equal pay provisions, the IUE had secured equal pay coverage for a hundred thousand members by the mid-1950s. In June 1957, at the IUE's first National Women's Conference, the 175 women representatives named "equal pay" and "work and job advancement opportunities" as their top priorities. They urged GE and Westinghouse to grant "equal pay," explaining that "By this we mean not only equal pay for identical work but equal pay for work of equal value no matter where it is done."[44]

Given the resistance of major female-employing corporations such as GE, Westinghouse, and Bell, it was clear that collective bargaining alone could not solve the problem of women's low pay. In the late 1950s companies such as GE adopted a new sophisticated hard-line bargaining stance and successfully avoided wage hikes, and large and small employers alike invented all kinds of subterfuge to avoid equalizing wages even after bargaining equal pay provisions.[45] To make matters worse, many local union officers and stewards simply ignored gender wage injustices. As one female machine operator wrote in 1955, "our committee man (AFL) doesn't care one way or the other. He thinks women should stay at home."[46]

Fig. 4.1 UE strikers hold out against Westinghouse in Emeryville, California, during the 1946 strike. In their 1946 negotiations with GE and Westinghouse, the UE made ending pay discrimination against women a priority. Courtesy of the Labor Archives and Research Center, San Francisco State University.

Equally important, less than a fifth of wage-earning women belonged to unions, and the prospects for another major leap forward in membership among private sector workers appeared dim. Unionization had spread rapidly in the 1930s and 1940s, but growth slowed in the 1950s. Women in particular were affected because it was often their occupations and industries that remained nonunion. The huge and growing clerical sector as well as retail sales and many low-level service jobs remained unorganized. The union record with regard to organizing clerical workers was particularly abysmal. The CIO had a clerical union, but its "industrial model" of representation, with its assumption of homogeneity and clear divides between employees, and employers was ill-suited to many clerical workplaces. Moreover, many CIO leaders evidenced a kind of class struggle bias toward organizing factory workers in heavy industry—workers who they perceived had more political and economic power. The AFL clerical union had its problems as well, and ultimately never expanded much beyond its initial base: the office staff employed by unions.[47]

Unions did make valiant attempts to expand their membership, as the postwar campaigns among textile workers, hotel employees, airline workers, and others attest. Yet securing union recognition had become much harder by the late

Fig. 4.2 A cartoon by LeBaron Coakley from the *IUE News*, March 1, 1954, showing the IUE's support for equal pay for women. The caption "An Easter Bonnet She Deserves" was emblazoned across the orignal cartoon when it appeared. The cartoon relies on assumptions about women's desires for fine millinery coupled with an image evoking the unfair class nature of consumption. Credit: IUE Archives, Special Collections, Rutgers University Libraries.

1940s. Operation Dixie, the CIO's massive effort to organize Southern workers, was defeated by a combination of red-baiting, race-baiting, and wholesale violations of the constitutional rights of assembly and free speech. The unions' own internal political factionalism also drained energy from organizing. The 1947 Taft-Hartley Act, which placed restrictions on secondary boycotts, picketing for union recognition, mass picketing, and closed shop (union control over hiring), undercut labor's ability to gain members as well as its ability to secure favorable contract terms. Indeed, by the early 1950s, when it was clear that the 1947 Taft-Hartley restrictions would apply to the Teamsters and other unions that operated among small intrastate employers, organizing slowed almost to a standstill in the private sector. The few breakthroughs, such as HERE's success in organizing much of the Miami Beach hotel strip in the late 1950s, came only after enormous personal and political resources had been expended.[48]

Equal Pay By Law

Labor feminists realized that economic and political action had to be combined if women's wages were to be increased. By the end of the war, they endorsed a legislative strategy for raising female pay that complemented their economic strategy. At a series of meetings and conferences held by the Women's Bureau for women union leaders, they reached a "broad consensus" that equal pay statutes and "minimum wage by law" were the best "legislative means of underpinning the wages of low-paid workers."[49] The most significant milestones on the federal level for both of these initiatives would not occur until the 1960s. But those achievements would not have been possible without the incremental yet crucial state legislative advances of the 1940s and 1950s.

For many labor feminists, equal pay legislation trumped all other concerns. It was key to achieving first-class economic citizenship, and "equal pay" gave social feminists a rallying cry with the symbolic weight and resonance to match the NWP's call for the ERA. Breakthroughs on the state level occurred quickly. Before World War II, only two states had passed equal pay statutes. But during World War II momentum for state legislation began to build, and by the end of the war, state groups had pushed through four new statutes. In the 1943 Washington State campaign, "women's clubs, labor unions, and community groups" initiated the legislation. Eventually, some 250 organizations joined the petition drive that beat back the opposition of NAM and other business groups and resulted in the passage of a strong equal pay law covering almost all women workers.[50]

The Women's Bureau, relying largely on the members of LAC, provided national coordination for state equal pay efforts during Frieda Miller's tenure. The Women's Bureau would contact the appropriate women on the committee when they knew of work being done in a state for equal pay, and LAC women would mobilize union locals throughout the state. They would promote cooperation between the unions and the women's groups, since in many cases the union bills only covered manufacturing, and the bills from women's organizations, only professional women.[51]

In 1947 alone, women's organization and labor groups introduced bills in eight states, and LAC members reported active interest in equal pay in "34 out of the 48 states."[52] The state federations of labor were prominent in many of the campaigns, along with union locals affiliated with the major CIO unions and women's groups such as the Business and Professional Women, the AAUW, and the League of Women Voters. The Chamber of Commerce, NAM, and other business groups opposed the state laws. Nevertheless, between 1946 and 1952 six states approved new equal pay laws. By the end of the 1950s, eight more fell into line, bringing the total to twenty states.[53]

But many laws fell short of the expectations of their backers. Most covered only a fraction of the workforce and few, if any, met the standards prescribed in the Women's Bureau's 1947 model state law.[54] The ideal law, according to the Bureau, would have prevented the "payment of a lesser rate to women than men for work of comparable character," provided for "a re-evaluation of women's work," and established an aggressive enforcement mechanism with strong penalties for violators.[55] Given the inadequacies of the state laws, the campaign for a federal equal pay bill took on greater urgency as the postwar years advanced.

A coalition of labor and women's organizations introduced the first federal equal pay bill in 1945; similar measures were submitted each year for the next eighteen. Forty-two organizations banded together under the auspices of the Women's Bureau to push for federal equal pay legislation in 1945, including many of those who would support the Women's Status Bill a year later. The CIO unions with large female memberships joined, along with middle-class women's organizations such as the AAUW and the YWCA. In 1945, the AFL testified on behalf of equal pay as well.[56] True to its single-minded focus on the ERA, the NWP refused to join.[57] NAM, the U.S. Chamber of Commerce, and a variety of employer representatives lobbied against the bill. The constituencies on either side of the question would remain essentially the same over the course of the next decade and a half.[58]

Florida senator Claude Pepper introduced the first equal pay bill into the Senate. Modeled after the 1942 War Labor Board General Order 16, it specified that it would be "an unfair wage practice" to pay women less than men in jobs with "comparable quantity and quality" or in jobs with "comparable skills." Frieda Miller conceded that the bill could not remedy inter-plant or cross-industry gender inequities—"waitresses could not be compared with taxi drivers"—but many intra-plant inequities would be affected. The bill proposed the establishment of "industrial committees" that would consult with state equal pay administrators to "re-evaluate and adjust job evaluation systems" for fairness. The committees would identify situations where men and women had the same points or job ratings but women received less pay ("dual wage scales") and "where women's skills were underestimated."[59]

The equal pay proposals favored by labor feminists met strong opposition. In 1946, Senator Robert Taft defeated Pepper's attempt to have the bill considered on the Senate floor. In 1948, after four days of hearings, the Equal Pay bills sponsored by Helen Gahagan Douglas and Margaret Chase Smith were not reported out of committee.[60] Employers objected to government interference with the right of business to determine its own wage compensation methods; they also trotted out various rationales for why women should be paid less.[61] They were particularly afraid of the expansive definition of wage discrimination that the bills embraced. They claimed it would destroy their "scientific and equitable system of job analysis" and open up the whole question of wage evaluation.[62]

In hopes of passage, proponents revised their proposals. The 1950 Equal Pay Bill allowed differentials in pay for "seniority" and "merit," and it deleted the sections in earlier bills that called for "industry committees" to "re-evaluate" the gender bias in all wage ratings. Yet despite these compromises, the 1950 bill failed to get out of committee.[63] The "comparability" language of the earlier bills had been only slightly revised, and without its removal, the bill remained a threat to business practices and to gender wage structures. Over the course of the 1950s, "comparability" language would vary from bill to bill, but essentially it was retained.[64] The equal pay proponents held firm to their goal of raising wages in the majority of women's jobs. They *and* their opponents knew that the "comparability" language was crucial.[65]

After 1952, the leadership of the national equal pay movement parted ways with the Women's Bureau. When Alice Leopold replaced Frieda Miller as head of the Women's Bureau after the election of Eisenhower in 1952, she alienated labor women by withdrawing the Bureau's opposition to the ERA and shifting her focus to "publicizing equal employment opportunities to women." She also reconstituted the LAC as a general advisory group and added non-labor representatives.[66] The reconstituted LAC limped along until 1957, but it no longer served as the center of reform strategy on equal pay: that responsibility now rested with the National Committee for Equal Pay (NCEP).[67]

The NCEP grew out of a 1952 national conference on equal pay, organized as one of Frieda Miller's last activities as Women's Bureau director.[68] The 1952 National Equal Pay Conference drew over a hundred attendees from unions, government agencies, women's organizations, community groups, and business. Caroline Davis and Lillian Hatcher came from the UAW. Other labor delegates included Pauline Newman, Myra Wolfgang; UPWA president Ralph Helstein; Florence Thorne, the elderly stateswoman of the AFL's Research Department; and representatives of the National Education Association and the American Nurses Association.[69] Participants voiced concern about the lack of progress with the federal equal pay campaign and dismay that the Wage Stabilization Board, set up for the duration of the Korean War crisis, tolerated "discriminatory wage practices against women, Negroes, and other minorities." Its equal pay policies, reformers fumed, were less effective than those in existence a decade earlier under the War Labor Board.[70] At its close, the delegates passed a resolution calling for a "permanent committee on equal pay" that would seek, "through legislation, collective bargaining agreements, and voluntary action," to eliminate wage inequity.[71]

A small group of conference attendees, the majority union representatives, quickly formed a committee to carry out the conference mandate. David Lasser, IUE's research director, acted as chair of the committee, and Caroline Davis as vice chair. Lillian Hatcher and Dorothy Haener of the UAW, CWA's Helen Berthelot, Katherine Ellickson, now in the Research Department of the CIO, and the IUE's new staffer Gloria Johnson were among the most active. Johnson, an African-American who would be a prominent advocate for women's rights and social justice into the 1990s, had taught at Howard University, her alma mater, and served as an economist with the U.S. Department of Labor before accepting a position with the IUE.[72] Women's groups such as the AAUW and the YWCA also sent representatives. At one of their first meetings, no doubt driven by the animosity between the UE and its anticommunist rival, the IUE, the committee restricted membership "to non-Communist organizations interested in working for equal pay in the three areas of education, collective bargaining, and legislation."[73]

The NCEP and the Women's Bureau now disagreed over what kind of equal pay legislation to support. The Women's Bureau backed HR 7172, the 1954 Equal Pay Bill submitted by Frances Bolton of Ohio. Bolton's bill used "equal" rather than "comparable" in its text and, according to the NCEP, had little enforcement power and limited coverage. In 1955, the NCEP drafted an alternative equal pay bill that solved these problems and reinserted the comparability language.[74] They convinced Edith Green, Democratic congresswoman from Oregon, to submit it. Green, who started out as an elementary school teacher, had gotten involved in politics after working with the Oregon Education Association. Elected in 1954 with "Portland's labor vote," Green introduced the NCEP's equal pay bill the next year.[75]

The CIO remained a stalwart supporter of a federal equal pay bill, having endorsed and lobbied for the federal Equal Pay Act from its inception in 1945. Support from the AFL, however, waxed and waned. The AFL backed "the principle of equal pay" in its public pronouncements and had advocated equal pay in the NRA codes as well as under the FLSA.[76] The AFL's legislative representative Lewis G. Hines testified on behalf of the 1945 Equal Pay Act, and AFL convention resolutions on equal pay in 1948 and 1949 favored "enactment of appropriate Federal legislation." Yet the 1948 and 1949 resolutions also reflected the AFL's ambivalence toward federal wage regulation, adding that progress would *best* be made through "voluntary negotiation" rather than through federal intervention.[77]

By 1951, the AFL backed away from federal action altogether, citing problems with government intervention in the aftermath of the restrictive 1947 Taft-Hartley Act. For the first time, the AFL convention went on record opposing a federal equal pay act.[78] The Executive Council urged the abolition of discriminatory women's rates, but equal pay *legislation* was problematic because, in the opinion of the Executive Council, unlike minimum wage legislation, government administrators would be intimately involved in setting wages above the minimums, thus interfering with the operation of collective bargaining.[79] The AFL declined the NCEP's 1952 invitation to send a permanent representative to the committee and reiterated its skepticism about federal legislation in 1953 and 1954.[80]

With the merger of the two federations in 1955, the differences between the AFL and the CIO on equal pay had to be worked out. For the AFL-CIO Executive Committee's February 1956 meeting, the new joint Research Department summarized the pros and cons on equal pay legislation, with a heavy emphasis on the former. The Research Department noted potential objections to equal pay legislation: it might necessitate an analysis of the company's entire wage structure, and it didn't solve the problem of equal opportunity or the low wages of unorganized workers. But equal pay legislation would make it easier to bargain higher wages for women, they pointed out, and it was consistent with union efforts on behalf of ending race discrimination and of establishing a federal FEPC. In light of the widespread sentiment among women in favor of equal pay, AFL-CIO endorsement also would "have a favorable public relations effect."[81] Nonetheless, although the AFL-CIO endorsed FEPC legislation, it still was not ready to back equal pay legislation. Instead, it set up a "Committee on Equal Pay" to study the question.

Kitty Ellickson, who had moved from the CIO Research Department into the merged AFL-CIO, joined forces with Nancy Pratt, formerly of the AFL Research Department, to lobby inside the AFL-CIO on behalf of equal pay. As part of their efforts to "bridge the differences on equal pay" between the AFL and the CIO, they initiated a survey in 1956 of the State Federations of Labor and their positions on equal pay legislation. Their strategy paid off when they discovered that the New York State Federation of Labor, AFL-CIO president George Meany's home federation, had been a strong supporter of equal pay legislation. However, the New York State Federation had insisted upon a law that relied primarily upon an administrative enforcement procedure, like that of the National Labor Relations Board, rather than a judicial one, in which individual employees initiated civil suits as their first recourse. "We went to Meany with this," Ellickson remembered, and it appeared that a solution had been found. A month later, at its June 1956 meeting, the AFL-CIO Executive Council went on record endorsing the NCEP-backed Green-Rogers-Douglas Bill (HR 6503, S 2708), with the one caveat that enforcement be modeled on the New York State equal pay law. At its 1957 convention, the AFL-CIO reiterated the labor movement's support for "the achievement of equal pay for comparable work" and added its endorsement of "the principle of federal equal pay legislation to prevent second-class treatment of working women."[82]

By the end of the 1950s, momentum for equal pay was building. Although business groups still opposed a federal law, and the Women's Bureau under Leopold continued to support the Bolton equal pay statute, the NCEP's political effectiveness was increasing. For one, NCEP members were "in accord as to the nature of the equal pay bill" they desired. In 1957, the NCEP reaffirmed its commitment to a broad federal statute that would end wage differentials for "work of comparable character on jobs the performance of which requires comparable skills."[83] In addition, after the AFL-CIO endorsement, George Riley, from the AFL-CIO's Department of Legislation, joined the NCEP, becoming a vocal and effective advocate for equal pay legislation.[84] And, Esther Peterson, who would emerge as the pivotal player in the equal pay battles of the 1960s, had returned from abroad. In 1958, she took a job as a full-time lobbyist for the Industrial Union Department, the division within the new AFL-CIO for the manufacturing unions headed by Walter Reuther, and shortly thereafter, began to work closely with the NCEP. In 1959, three states— Hawaii, Wyoming, and Ohio—passed state equal pay laws, the first new laws since 1955.[85] On the eve of the 1960 presidential election, the prospects for an NCEP-backed broadly conceived federal equal pay act looked bright.

WAGE PROTECTIONS FOR ALL

A large measure of agreement existed among labor feminists that statutory labor standards should be improved, and that, in the case of the sex-based state laws, the objective was to move toward the coverage of men as well as women.[86] Failing that, however, social feminists agreed that woman-only state minimums should be *retained* until the FLSA could be amended to provide comparable protection. Many of the lowest-paid women worked in intrastate industries and only had wage protection through the state laws; in addition, in some cases, state wage standards, covering women in a variety of industries, were superior to the federal.

Efforts to amend the FLSA began almost immediately after its passage in 1938, but the first hearings did not occur until 1945. The National Consumer's League set up the Committee for a Fair Minimum Wage in Washington to coordinate the national campaign.[87] The garment unions, ACWA and the ILGWU, were among the most active participants, relying on the lobbying and expert testimony of Esther Peterson, Gladys Dickason, Maida Springer-Kemp, Dollie Lowther Robinson, and others.[88] The primary legislative goal for ACWA in the 1940s, Peterson remembered, was "raising the minimum wage." In 1946, as ACWA's first legislative representative, Peterson worked closely with the secretary of labor's "Minimum Wage Committee," which included representatives from the ILGWU, the Textile Workers, and other unions as well as from the AFL and CIO. Pregnant at the time with the last of her four children, Peterson worried about whether she could get the bill passed before the baby came. "As the debate dragged on, I got bigger and bigger," she remembered. Her fellow lobbyists and Congressional friends promised to set up a maternity room on the Hill in case the baby came while she was up there. Senator Claude Pepper joked, "If it's a girl we'll name her Mini for minimum wage and a boy, Max, for maximum hours."[89]

Opposition came from NAM and from industry-based trade associations like the American Hotel Association. Opponents feared the economic impact of higher wages on profit margins. Many also opposed the extension of state power into the market. And, as had been true in the Progressive Era minimum wage debates, some felt profoundly disturbed by the idea that higher wages for women might prompt women to abandon their domestic duties.[90] As Maida Springer-Kemp recalled: "My first lobbying experience was minimum wage. The minimum wage was 37 cents an hour. And I think we were asking for something like 50 cents an hour. Well the way those senators and congressmen talked about it, you would have thought we all had tails. This was my first exposure to what the government felt about the working man and woman. One senator read a statement about mother love and how changing the wage structure would destroy mother love and the family because, you know, the majority of the workers were women. Now what mother love had to do with wages, I don't know. Women still would have to go to work."[91]

Despite the persistence of the reform coalition, progress at the federal level was slow. Automatic increases written into the original FLSA bill raised the standard from 25 cents in 1938 to 40 cents by 1945. A concerted campaign in 1955, led by ACWA, the ILGWU, the textile workers, and others, helped win an increase to a dollar an hour.[92]

Reformers met even more frustration in their efforts to expand the scope of the law. Coverage broadened slightly after 1941 as the commerce clause basis for FLSA protection was reinterpreted to include many local businesses under "those engaged in interstate commerce." But the statutory language of the FLSA, which excluded the majority of workers, remained unchanged. After the flurry of hearings in the immediate postwar years, none occurred until 1959.[93]

In seeking to expand FLSA coverage, labor feminists were challenging conventional notions of who was a worker and who could lay claim to the entitlements of industrial citizenship.[94] The issue took on heightened significance because in the United States, unlike in many other industrialized countries, most protections and benefits derived from one's status in the workplace rather than one's status in society. Thus, gaining full "industrial citizenship" was crucial for securing the basic economic rights and benefits that in other countries came as a result of national citizenship. In this instance, labor feminists did not try to dislodge the workplace as a basis for social entitlements; instead, they sought to redefine the basis on which industrial citizenship would be granted. As Anne Murkovich of the American Federation of Hosiery Workers saw it, coverage should be extended to "all people who are working for a living, no matter what type of work they are doing—I don't care what category they come under, whom they work for—they should be covered so that they get the same benefits as the rest of us."[95]

In contrast, employers relied upon gendered definitions of work to limit industrial citizenship. Employer representatives from hotels, for example, argued that jobs in their industry resembled private household employment and hence should be exempt because of their nonindustrial character. Workers performed similar kinds of tasks to those in the home, and their working conditions should be the same. Hotel workers needed to be on call and available 24 hours as would a mother or a domestic servant; their compensation, as with household labor, should not be contractual or guaranteed but dependent on the largesse of customers through tip income.[96] When relied upon as the principal means of income, as was often the situation in jobs held predominantly by men and women of color, the tipping system preserved the hierarchical aspects of the servant-master relationship. Others claimed that small businesses should be exempt because of the family-like paternalistic employment relations in this sector. The home was viewed, in Vivien Hart's phrase, as a "rights-free enclave."[97]

Opposition to expanding coverage to minority-dominated sectors such as agriculture and domestic service was fierce.[98] The economics of these industries—they were labor-intensive, marginal enterprises—spurred employer resistance. But the resistance reflected cultural notions as well. In part, it was the work itself: domestic work, for example, was the prototypic "nonindustrial" labor. And in part, it was *who* was doing the work: men and women of color. Agricultural labor, after all, is manual work, and many farmworkers engage in industrial-type activities (packing and loading food, for example). Thus, despite the efforts of reformers, the basis for industrial citizenship at the federal level remained narrowly defined throughout the 1940s and 1950s in large part due to race and gender bias.

Labor feminists had more success in improving minimum wage statutes at the state level. In the 1940s, labor and women's organizations joined forces to raise wage standards, with labor typically taking the lead. In Rhode Island, observed the head of the state Division of Women and Children, "the unions carried the ball" in raising the statutory minimum, "whereas formerly, when we enacted the previous wage law, it was the voluntary organizations that did it."[99] In 1950, the Women's Bureau could announce that 23 new wage orders had been issued and 62 orders revised. In addition, "all but a few minimum wage jurisdictions had taken some steps to better the legal minimum-wage situation of women in drug stores, restaurants, department and clothing stores, and other businesses in which sizable numbers of women earn their living."[100]

Many of the old-line craft unions, however, were still skeptical about state "protection" for men. The first attempt to add men to the New York state law, for example, met defeat in 1941, explained WTUL and CIO activist Helen Blanchard, because "one group of labor said they didn't want minimum wage for men. It wasn't until we argued with the men folks that these were women-employing service industries, that it wasn't to cover plumbers, nor was it to cover electricians or printers that they finally agreed to support us." But eventually New York passed a law extending minimum wage coverage to men, as did a handful of other states in the 1940s.[101]

Laws protecting men and women spread in the 1950s as AFL hesitancy about state regulation of male wages lessened. In Washington State, longtime Seattle waitress union official Beulah Compton had been trying to get a minimum wage law passed for men and women since the 1940s. By the 1950s, she had succeeded and had also risen to state office, where as the head of the Women and Minor's Division she was in charge of enforcing the newly broadened minimum wage law and the new equal pay act. Not content with just reforming Washington's laws, Compton worked with the newly merged state AFL-CIO in Montana to extend minimum wages to men and others still left out. At the public hearings on the law, Compton found that support came from some unexpected corners. "I remember one testimony given in favor of minimum wage law by a man—he was so rough and tumble, sort of a diamond in the rough. Well, he said he wanted to include babysitters and there was just a wild guffaw at the very idea . . . and he says: 'Hell, you pay your sheep herders 3 times that amount, aren't your babies worth so much?' I thought it was a pretty good argument."[102]

By the end of the 1950s, then, reformers had made progress at the state level. Wage standards had been raised and coverage broadened, and state laws now offered wage protection to the *majority* of women in the retail and service sectors.[103] And, since 1946, some eleven states had added men to their coverage, bringing the total to fifteen.[104] Yet wage floors remained low, and state laws continued to exempt agricultural and domestic work, the occupations in which minorities were concentrated. Only in California did a successful movement arise to end what farmworker activists called the law's "exceptionalism" toward agricultural labor.

The California farmworker movement grew out of the activism of Mexican-Americans like Dolores Huerta and Cesar Chavez and the pioneering work of the Community Service Organization (CSO), a community-based advocacy group for workers and the poor modeled after Saul Alinsky's Chicago organization of the 1930s. By the late 1950s, Dolores Huerta, who would later become the vice president of the United Farm Workers, was lobbying full-time for minimum wage coverage for California farmworkers in her job with the CSO. Huerta had grown up in a farmworker family, but had trained as a teacher before turning to political activism. The movement also had the support of key labor organizations, particularly ACWA, and groups like the California Citizen's Committee for Agricultural Labor (CCCAL), whose agenda included ending the bracero farm labor program and extending minimum wage coverage to farm workers. The CCCAL's research director, Anne Draper, introduced in chapter 1, brought with her from New York years of experience as a business agent and legislative advocate for the United Hatters Union. A flamboyant figure noted for her oversized hats and dramatic rhetoric, Draper organized and spoke at numerous public rallies and governmental hearings focusing on the abuses in what she called the "blue-sky sweatshops." Finally, at a historic meeting in October 1959, the California Industrial Welfare Commission, the agency responsible for setting minimum wages for the state's workers, voted to fix a minimum wage of $1.25 an hour for agricultural workers, thus ending the long-standing policy of setting minimums in every industry except agriculture. Their decision followed the public testimonies of women like Maria Moreno, a mother of twelve and a field worker for thirty years. Moreno testified to the widespread practice of bringing babies to the field because of the lack of child care, the employment of children as young as five, and the impossibility of supporting a family on the wages paid to field hands. Please, "do something for my children," she insisted, "it's too late for me."[105]

DEBATING THE WAGE

The postwar campaigns to raise women's wages affected wage-earning women in concrete and palpable ways, securing equal pay for some, and for others a guaranteed minimum wage. But the movement must be judged not only by the actual contract clauses and legislative statutes it secured but also by the ways in which it affected the larger ideology surrounding gender and wages. Alice Kessler-Harris has observed that the struggle for equal pay "expanded notions of justice, encouraging perceptions of male/female equality that had previously been invisible."[106] And clearly, in the intense debates over defining an "equal" and a "just" wage, labor feminists helped transform gender ideology.

The campaign for equal pay stimulated women to rethink the ideology of sexual difference that undergirded differential wage payments by calling into question what had previously been thought of as natural gender differences and inequities. Employers often justified women's low wages by pointing to women's inferior skills and their supposed inability to equal men in "the quality and quantity" of work performed. At times, working men as well as women accepted these rationales. But as technological innovations lessened the need for strength in many jobs and women took on men's jobs in wartime and economic crisis, notions of female inferiority as "producers" eroded both among employers and the workforce at large.

In the 1940s and 1950s, advocates of equal pay further undermined these historic rationales for women's low pay. They dismissed employer allegations of women's inferior job performance and opened up the whole question of the invisibility and undervaluation of women's skill. They argued that the "quality and quantity" of women's work equaled that of men's and hence, so should their wage.[107] Yet they also carefully pointed out that "equal to" should not be confused with "same as." The machines women tended might be smaller, and the skills and responsibilities they possessed quite different. In short, women deserved equal pay based on "comparability," not just "identity."

Postwar reformers promoted equal pay as a way of protecting "general wage levels and sustaining consumer purchasing power," and they talked about women's wage as a contribution to family income. But the dominant theme of supporters was ending the "rank injustice" women suffered in the workplace. Few labor feminists spoke in the unrestrained language of individual rights used by Congresswoman Chase Going Woodhouse in her 1945 Senate testimony on behalf of equal rights. We "can't lump people together in categories," she insisted; rather, "we must look at each working woman as an individual American citizen entitled to reward on the basis of the work she does."[108] Yet many labor feminists relied on a rhetoric of rights that linked women's claims to wage equity with their rights as equal producers, citizens, and consumers. Reformers repeatedly stressed "the rights" of all citizens, women included, to "simple" or "fundamental justice" in the workplace.[109] "Women are citizens," Helen Blanchard of the CIO Congress of Women's Auxiliaries reminded her audience in 1945, and they "pay the same prices for food, lodging, and clothing." Indeed, she concluded, women "are seeking through this bill the establishment on a national scale of the inherent right of economic equality."[110]

Yet once women's claims to wage equality based on their equal rights as citizen consumers and producers were recognized as legitimate, how would an "equal" wage be determined? Historically, within-plant wage differentials had rested in part on obscure and highly subjective calculations (often made by foremen and lower-level managers) having to do with an individual worker's productivity or "the quality or quantity" of work performed on the job. By mid-

century, however, many employers embraced a new philosophy of wage setting: job analysis by experts. Like the older employer rationales that stressed
"productivity," the job evaluation approach was, employers claimed, gender-
neutral: jobs were to be rated based on an objective system measuring skill,
responsibility, and effort. Wages would be paid according to these job ratings
and on no other basis. They too used the "rate for the job" rhetoric.[111]

Labor feminists like Frieda Miller doubted the employer claims of scientific
neutrality and noted the ways gender and race bias could creep into job analysis.
At the same time, she and many others saw the new job evaluation approach as
preferable to earlier ad hoc systems of wage setting and compatible with feminist notions of wage equality. Job analysis lent a scientific underpinning to the
argument that wages should be based on the job and not the sex of the worker.
Most reformers did not object to job evaluations per se; they simply wanted
them to be applied fairly to both men and women.[112]

Moreover, while job evaluation might be an advance in determining *relative*
wages, it was a poor guide to determining *absolute* wage levels. Raising absolute
wage levels was as crucial in ending wage injustice for women as securing
internal equity of wages. Many employers simply paid as low a wage as the
market would bear—that is, the lowest that could be offered and still find employees. Others conducted "market or industry wage surveys" and set wages in
accordance with wage levels at other comparable firms. Still others claimed
that a "fair wage" reflected the "value" of the "service rendered" or the good
produced.[113] But wages have never been a construct solely of the market or of
"marginal productivity." Ideological concerns for family and social stability have
influenced how employers set wages as well as how the larger culture constructed notions of wage fairness.[114]

In contrast to employers, most labor feminists believed that "productivity"
or the market could not be the *sole* determiner of wages. Indeed, it was precisely the inadequacies of the so-called market wage that inspired their support
for collective bargaining and for state regulation of wages. Wage justice meant
recognizing human need as well as gender equity. They echoed the language
and ideas of nineteenth- and early-twentieth-century labor intellectuals who
asserted that workers had a right to a "living wage" and an "American standard
of living." Wages, they insisted, should be high enough to allow for the consumption of a certain level of goods—something every American had a right to
expect.[115] And, women's wages, like men's, should at the very minimum allow
for economic self-sufficiency and self-support.

In the context of postwar America, the call for a wage sufficient for *female*
self-support was not only a challenge to employer approaches to wage setting,
but destabilizing to the larger gender status quo.[116] After 1937, many state wage
laws had moved from a "service rendered" to a "cost-of-living" approach (which
acknowledged need as an aspect of wage setting) in calculating a "fair wage,"
but the minimum wage for women continued to be defined as *less* than what was
needed for self-maintenance. Men's cost of living was often calculated higher, in

part because, it was reasoned, single men needed to purchase household services; women were expected to do their own housework.[117]

In contrast, labor women agreed that "little net difference existed between the cost of living for a single man and for a single woman."[118] The highly subjective "cost of living" or "self-sufficiency standards" in most of the minimum wage laws had been used to disadvantage women. Labor feminists turned those same vague formulations to their advantage. Mary Anderson reasoned that the proper "standard of living" for women required a budget that included money "for movies, sports, reading, study, or other leisure-time activities." It must also recognize "the human craving for beauty, companionship, and fun." ACWA's Anne Draper interpreted California's requirement that the legal minimum allow for "a proper living" to mean a wage "that would permit a working woman, entirely dependent on her own resources, to maintain her health, her job, her self-respect, and the respect of her friends and fellow workers."[119]

But women and men not only needed a wage sufficient for self-support; they often required a wage sufficient for the support of dependents—what historians now refer to as a "family wage."[120] The family wage ideology was labor's oldest and most effective alternative to a market-oriented, "productionist" wage. But to what degree was that tradition still a useful one for labor women? Could there be both equal wages for women and the right to a family wage?

RETHINKING THE FAMILY WAGE

Some scholars condemn the family wage as a patriarchal wage-setting mechanism that functioned to raise men's wages and lower women's and that "explicitly entitled a man to a dependent, service-providing wife." Others defend it as a rational class strategy that controlled the labor supply and raised the overall income of working-class families. Not surprisingly, it appears that the family wage did both.[121]

In most instances, the family wage system boosted the wages of all men, single and married, and lowered those of all women regardless of their family responsibilities. As early feminist critics such as Sophonisba Breckinridge in the United States and Eleanor Rathbone in Britain pointed out, the family wage system not only disadvantaged working-class (and other) women but harmed children as well. Not every single man married, nor did all married men share their higher income with their families, and vast numbers of children lived in poverty with female heads of families. Furthermore, not all women welcomed the idea of spending more time in the domestic arena, and, to the degree that the family wage only went to men, women were denied a direct and autonomous route to higher wages and increased leisure.[122] Still further, the family wage ideology was often racialized: the higher wage jobs that could sustain a family were often the preserve of white men.

Yet many employers paid higher wages *in recognition* of family need, and in some instances, these payments were not strictly limited to men.[123] Moreover, family wage adherents included many married (as well as unmarried) working-class women who supported a higher wage for breadwinners (even when defined solely as a male prerogative) because they believed it would raise their overall family income and allow some women to reduce their long hours in wage work. For men as well as women, supporting a male breadwinner's demands for a family wage was not synonymous with belief in female exclusion from wage work or female subordination in the home.[124]

For all its problematic impact on women's wages and female autonomy, the family wage framework did recognize, even if only implicitly, the necessity and value of domestic labor. It was premised on the idea that wages were a payment for reproductive as well as productive labor. Capital owed labor a wage return great enough to compensate for the effort of the individual worker in the wage realm as well as those in the home whose labor helped "reproduce" and replenish the wage worker. As Henry Ford expressed it: "The man does the work in the shop, but his wife does the work in the home. The shop must pay them both."[125] The family wage ideology was thus a powerful alternative to the setting of wages simply on the basis of individual "productivity" on the job. It was also a sobering antidote to the giddy assertion that society consists of independent autonomous beings, each capable of continuous self-support. In the late nineteenth and early twentieth century, the insistence that wages should be high enough to sustain family life was one of the most culturally potent and effective arguments that workers used in raising wage levels.

Yet by the mid-twentieth century, the long-standing commitment to such family wage ideologies in many industrialized countries outside the United States was in decline, among workers as well as the population at large. In what Nancy Fraser and Linda Gordon call "the de-centering of the ideal of the family wage," more married women entered paid work, and wages were increasingly determined on an individual rather than a household basis.[126] Labor movements across Europe, in Canada, and elsewhere backed away from the family wage, as well, supporting state family allowances or state wage supplements based on the number of children.[127]

But the postwar U.S. labor movement retained its historic commitment to boosting family living standards primarily through raising wages at the point of production, and it continued to call for a "living wage," meaning a wage based upon *family* rather than *individual* need or productivity. In the 1940s and 1950s, for example, the CIO pushed for minimum wage levels that would allow for the "adequate living" of a family of four. "A standard budget for a workingman's family" should assume a family of four, the CIO advised the BLS. Moreover, "in setting standards of adequacy," government agencies should "consider including labor-saving devices, since our modern goal for family living includes not overworking the housewife but providing her with adequate leisure for civic activities."[128] Echoing nineteenth-century arguments made on behalf of shorter hours, the CIO saw the "family of four" standard as necessary for "family health, worker efficiency, nurture of children, and the social participation of all members of the family." Only when workers have "the emotional security that comes with financial security . . . can they be the confident, independent individuals that American citizens have a right to be."[129] Again, the possibility of women earning this higher wage was not explicitly foreclosed, but despite the disproportionate number of minimum wage workers who were female and the increasing number of female heads of households, the persistent suggestion in the minimum wage debates was that the family head was male.

Only a few male union officials made the case that "family wages" as a wage-setting mechanism for employers was a relic of the past. NFTW general counsel Al Kane argued in the 1945 equal pay hearings that "There can be no place for a rule" that links wages "with marital condition" or "number of dependents." "Women are politically free and have the right to strive for and obtain economic independence."[130] Similarly, in a pamphlet on equal pay produced by the Rubber Workers' Department of Research and Education in the early 1940s, union members were asked to think seriously about whether they really believed that the "industrial wage should be influenced by one's marital status (married or single) or upon one's dependence, or financial independence, or number of dependents." If so, the pamphlet added incredulously, then how could this belief be actualized? Should wages "be measured in proportion to the number of dependents, the amount of their accumulated indebtedness, and in proportion to their extravagance or thrift?"[131] Most working-class men, however, still justified their arguments for higher wages by pointing to their family status and their responsibility for supporting a wife and other dependents.

Women labor reformers were even more divided over wage arguments relying on family wage rhetoric. After all, implicit in calls for a family wage were images of men as breadwinners and women as non-waged wives and mothers— images that could be and were used to legitimize the preservation of high wage jobs for men. In addition, the "rate for the job" idea, now increasingly widespread, tied pay to work performance rather than one's sex, age, race, marital status, parenthood, or number of dependents. Indeed, for some, the growing commitment to the dual principles of equal pay and "rate for the job" undercut family wages for *male* as well as *women* providers. When Frieda Miller asked the Labor Advisory Committee in 1945 whether "family dependents" should be considered "now that the minimum has been extended to men," the committee demurred, unable to reach a consensus.[132]

Some labor feminists, however, wanted to de-gender family wages and extend them to women as well as men. For them, "equal pay" and "rate for the job" were compatible with arguments for higher wages that recognized need and the work of social reproduction. As Mary Anderson had insisted decades earlier wages "should be established on the basis of occupation," but should *also* "cover the cost of living for dependents and not merely for the individual."[133] For these labor feminists, a woman's wage was not just a "fair wage" or even a "man's wage," but a "provider wage." Women supported families too, and raising their wages was a crucial aspect of ensuring the support of dependents. Agnes Winn, Assistant Director of the Legislative and Federal Relations Division, National Education Association, made the case for a "provider wage" for men and women at the 1945 Senate hearings on the Equal Pay Bill. She decried the recent trend among school boards "to change from [higher wage] differentials to all men to dependency allowances for married men." The "only fair basis," in her view, "would be the one adopted by some school systems that grant such allowances to men and women on an equal footing."[134]

Working-class rank-and-file women often embraced this more egalitarian understanding of the family wage as a way of ensuring their own economic survival and that of their family. Theirs was a world in which dependency and interdependency could not be denied. A wage that allowed a decent living for a *single individual* was simply not enough: an adult wage had to be sufficient to support dependents. Their calls for a "provider" wage were an effort to maintain the moral framework of the family wage and its implicit recognition of the wage as a payment for reproductive as well as productive labor. Whether they supported children, elderly parents, or a spouse, many working-class women frequently pointed to their own status as family providers when engaged in disputes over the rights of women to employment or to higher wages. They called themselves "heads of household" and reminded their brother trade unionists as well as employers of their job rights based on their family obligations.[135]

Although the congressmen faced by Maida Springer-Kemp in the minimum wage hearings of the 1940s thought raising women's wages would "destroy mother love," many working-class women thought just the opposite. Providing economically for one's family was a crucial component of "mother love" and of being a good mother. Working-class women rejected the artificial and non-overlapping categories of "breadwinner" and "homemaker." They claimed the breadwinner role, often seen as exclusively the prerogative of the father in elite homes, as an aspect of motherhood.[136]

The provider wage demand was also part of the larger working-class project of ensuring that workers, men and women, not be treated as mere commodities of economic exchange, as machines without feelings or lives beyond the workplace. Maida Springer-Kemp captures part of this effort in a 1978 interview. The labor and women's movement in which she participated, Springer-Kemp explains, sought a society in which workers would "have wages commensurate with what they were doing, [and] have a decent standard of living." But these movements also had other goals: "government and the employers [needed] to see that the worker is not just a pair of hands, that the worker has a mind, the worker has a home, has a family."[137]

CONCLUSION

By the end of the 1950s, labor feminists could point to significant changes in attitudes and practices in regard to women's wages. Yet they were far from reaching their goals of achieving wage equity with men and of ensuring that all wage earners had an income that would support themselves and their dependents. As unionization, equal pay provisions, and minimum wage statutes spread, the real wages of some women increased substantially in this period. But the majority remained outside of union ranks and without union or state guarantees of minimum or equal wages.

The wage campaigns of labor feminists also left an ambiguous and unresolved intellectual legacy, particularly in relation to the perplexing problem of the recognition and valuing of unwaged work. Nancy Fraser sees U.S. feminists as embracing a "universal breadwinner" model of reform because their strategy for equality rested primarily on demanding inclusion in the wage arena and gaining the same benefits and wages as "male breadwinners." And, as Fraser and others have suggested, the drive to universalize the "breadwinner" model does little to challenge the "hegemony of wage labor" and the market as the measure of value. In such a society, "everyone is expected to work and be self-supporting," and the invisibility and devaluation of unwaged domestic and parenting labor sustains the myth of male independence.[138]

Yet even in the countries outside the United States that eschewed the "universal breadwinner" model and preferred a "caregiver parity" model premised on social democratic policies which directly compensated childbearing, child rearing, and elder care, the inequality between the waged and the unwaged realm remains. "A new vision of the worker—a person whose life includes breadwinning and caregiving" is far from being realized in any society.[139]

Moreover, the distinct perspectives of labor women are often lost in the depiction of American feminists as uncritically embracing the male model of wage work. Labor feminists sought recognition as breadwinners, but they also wanted to ensure that a breadwinner wage incorporated the support of dependents. An individualized notion of a wage remained abhorrent to many. Of equal importance, by putting support for collective bargaining and government wage regulation for men and women at the heart of their reform program, labor feminists argued for democratizing wage-setting and for linking women's rights to the rights of all wage earners. They wanted economic parity with men, but they saw the importance of joining with men to transform the value and distribution of wages. Gender equity was inseparable from ending class exploitation. And, as the next chapter details, they created a politics of work and family that refused to privilege breadwinning over caregiving and that rejected a gender equity based on assimilation to the male sphere.

CHAPTER FIVE

The Politics of the "Double Day"

> The whole question, it seems to me, comes down to this: Shall we let
> women continue working longer hours than men, for less pay than men,
> and continue doing two jobs to their husbands' one?
>
> —*Mary Anderson*, Good Housekeeping, *1925.*

> The slick magazine idea of the American woman in negligee kissing
> her husband goodbye as he goes off to work and she returns to her kitchen full of
> machines to do the work for her is hardly a true one . . . she is off to work too.
> She has climbed over the walls of her kitchen, has worked in the market place,
> and learned about the world beyond the doormat.
>
> —*Esther Peterson, c1955*[1]

IN 1942, KATHERINE ELLICKSON, who had recently joined the CIO Research Department and would be one of the staunchest advocates for working mothers in the postwar era, voiced her concerns about the burdens of the "double day" in a revealing essay, "Short-time Work for Women." Earlier generations of women, she began, solved the conflict between wage work and family obligations by embracing either one *or* the other. The current generation was the first to combine the two, she insisted, and their frustration with individual solutions to this problem was creating a new politics. "These statements will seem heresy to many of the older generation of feminists," Ellickson continued. "Their fight was for the right to follow in men's footsteps, to have a similar legal, political, and social status. It was natural that they should stress equality of the sexes and overlook differences, for if they acknowledged the latter, the former might be denied them." But now the problem was different. Rather than adjust to men, the issue was "adapting the man's world to women." This task "transcends the efforts of isolated individuals" and would involve the fundamental restructuring of the work world. Ellickson ended her essay with concrete social policy proposals. The six-hour day and child care facilities, she believed, would go a long way toward making it possible for women to combine mothering and wage work.

For Ellickson, these kinds of far-reaching changes were not impractical impossibilities but logical extensions of earlier reforms. Just as "legislation to protect women from too long hours paved the way for more widespread government action for the shorter work-week," she reasoned, "perhaps married women's special needs will now provide a stimulus to the development of still shorter shifts." Her hopes for "shorter shifts" were not to be fulfilled. Yet like many labor feminists in the postwar decades, Ellickson never stopped searching for policies that could ease the burden of the "double day"—the problem that, in her view, could no longer be ignored if "equal opportunity for women" was to be won.[2]

Labor feminists placed ending the "double day" at the core of their reform agenda in the postwar decades. Their analysis of the problem differed from what would dominate the women's movement by the late 1960s, but it was neither conservative nor timid. They questioned the dominant gender order, proposing policies that would help women *combine* wage work and family life and enhance their control in both spheres. The solution to the tension between the household and the market was not returning women to the home full-time, but neither was it offering women access to jobs designed for men. Winning first-class citizenship involved more than equal access to jobs or even the right to equal compensation. There could be no equality without a transformation in the work patterns, norms, and practices of the work world itself. New governmental and employer policies were needed that recognized women's lives off the job without sacrificing their claim to first-class citizenship on the job—policies that, in Ellickson's words, would adapt "the man's world to women."

LABOR WOMEN AND U.S. FAMILY POLICY

The United States did not adopt many of the state income supports available to mothers and children in other industrial countries. The United States, for example, has no universal paid maternity leave, no universally available, publicly funded infant care programs, and no universal system of family and child allowances (direct state income supplements to families with children). Some scholars have held the second wave feminist movement to blame for this situation, arguing that it did not push sufficiently for programs that would help mothers and children; other writers have defended these same feminists, claiming that family concerns were always part of their policy agenda.[3]

In fact, most of the state supports for mothers and children were in place decades before the rise of 1960s feminism. Moreover, recent scholarship suggests that many of these policies came not as a result of feminist pressure but in response to *conservative* forces such as strong pronatalist movements or politically active religious groups that saw children as a social rather than an individual charge. For example, British feminists fought vigorously for mother and child endowments; yet France instituted these policies long before Britain and in a more generous fashion, largely as a result of pressure from conservatives.[4]

The U.S. situation can be laid at the doorstep of forces beyond the women's movement as well. The United States was spared the devastation of World War II and the ensuing crisis over declining birth rates. The disproportionate number of nonwhite poor in the United States and the antipathy toward them set the United States apart from other countries with more racially homogeneous populations. Racial and ethnic prejudice in the United States heightened the resistance to universal income supports for children. In addition, U.S. business leaders opposed government income supports for those not in the labor force, whether in the form of unemployment insurance or maternity benefits. And conservative politicians and a sizable public constituency remained opposed to publicly funded child care, favoring maternal care or private family-based solutions instead.[5] Ironically, despite pervasive pro-family rhetoric, the United States lacked the conservative constituencies that mobilized *for* social programs on behalf of mothers and children as they did in other countries, and the resistance to universal state welfare programs rather than private and job-based was substantial in the United States.

But what kind of family policies did labor feminists pursue in the decisive decades of the postwar era? And how successful were they? As we shall see, their agenda fell squarely within many of the cultural parameters of their time and place. They rarely if ever questioned women's primary responsibility for caregiving and household labor, and they, like most other Americans, evidenced a considerable amount of ambivalence about the wisdom of having young children cared for by anyone other than their mother. And they pursued a family policy that took the household, not the individual, as the primary unit of analysis.

At the same time, they articulated a feminist position at odds with conservative public opinion and, on occasion, at odds with the positions embraced by the larger labor movement. By the 1940s they had embraced universal social benefits for working mothers, such as hospital insurance coverage for childbirth and paid maternity leave, and they rejected policies premised on the assumption that most mothers desired to return full-time to the home. They believed that employers and the government should help bear the costs of children, and they were among the few voices raised in this period supporting publicly funded child care and calling for work-time policies that would meet the needs of caregivers as well as breadwinners.

Their class politics distinguished them as well. Higher wages was a crucial plank in their work and family agenda because they knew that increased pay was necessary for lower-income women to reduce work time and take advantage of job leave. Their strategies for raising women's wages included, as detailed earlier, unionization, living wage ordinances, and equal pay for comparable work measures. In addition to raising women's pay, however, they embraced higher *family* income measures because they believed that raising family wages allowed women greater choice in how they allocated time between home and market. Like the labor movement at large, labor women in this period sought higher family income primarily through raising wages on the job. Yet as the next sections will detail, through tax policies and other means, labor feminists found ways of making income demands for family and child support on the state as well as on employers.

CONSIDERING FAMILY ALLOWANCES

After World War I, many industrialized countries began to consider *universal* mother and child allowances. France, Germany, Italy, and the Netherlands instituted universal state family allowances in the 1930s, and other countries followed suit in the 1940s: Ireland, Australia, Canada, Britain, New Zealand, Norway, and Sweden. Denmark adopted family allowances in 1952, leaving the United States as one of the few holdouts.[6]

The labor movements in most industrialized countries remained indifferent to family allowances when the policies were first proposed. They feared that employer subsidies based on family size would be divisive, since not every male worker would receive the supplement, and they were equally skeptical of government payments to those with dependents. Instead, most favored the family wage policy or a higher wage paid directly to *all* (usually male) workers at the work site. Yet during the interwar years, labor movements across Europe, in Canada, and elsewhere belatedly begin to support state family allowances, following the lead of government bureaucrats, child welfare reformers, women's and church groups, and industry executives.[7] In Canada, for example, the labor movement officially opposed family allowances in the 1920s and remained undecided in the 1930s. In 1944, however, a family allowance law passed, largely due to Prime Minister MacKenzie King's strong endorsement, and by the mid-1950s, the Canadian labor movement was enthusiastically endorsing the policy, touting its beneficial effect on children and on efforts to alleviate poverty.[8]

Belatedly, the U.S. labor movement wrestled with the question of family allowances as well. The CIO convention called for a study of the family allowance plans of Britain in 1948, but the issue was not seriously debated until the mid-1950s, shortly before the AFL-CIO merger. The push came from outside the AFL-CIO: from individuals such as Oregon senator Robert Neuberger and from child welfare organizations such as the Child Welfare League of America and the conservative National Catholic Welfare Conference. Given the CIO's endorsement of state action and income entitlements for the unemployed, the poor, and the elderly, family allowance advocates saw the AFL-CIO as a natural ally in their efforts to pass what Senator Neuberger called "social security for children."[9]

In 1955, Neuberger wrote Nelson Cruikshank, AFL Director of Social Insurance Activities, expressing his readiness to go ahead with a campaign for family allowance should there be "some measure of AFL support."[10] In response, Cruikshank agreed to bring the issue before the Social Security Committee. To prepare, he asked the Research Department, which included Kitty Ellickson, for a report.[11] The department prepared an illuminating memo on the subject, laying out the pros and cons of endorsing family allowances. The memo opened by enumerating a long list of potential benefits. Family allowances would have a positive impact on child health and welfare and, by boosting overall purchasing power, aid national prosperity. Moreover, family allowances would allow more mothers to stay home with their children, and it would not damage the work ethic because state income supplements could continue whether or not one was employed. Earlier U.S. precedents for dependency coverage—the servicemen's dependency allowances and the dependency exemptions allowed under tax law—enhanced the political feasibility of family proposals.[12]

Yet the list of "drawbacks" was equally lengthy. Heading the list was the statement that family allowances would "violate the principle of a living wage" and make it "more difficult for unions to negotiate wage increases." The United States, unlike other countries, "was prosperous enough to pay good wages to everyone, supplemented by special programs to low-income families." Indeed, the report continued, "more could be accomplished through collective bargaining, through extending and raising the minimum wages, through extending dependency tax exemptions, and through liberalizing social programs such as public assistance, child welfare, and free school lunches." In short, the high costs associated with family allowances could be better used in other programs. Family allowances, it was feared, might also encourage higher birth rates—an incentive not needed in the United States, the report concluded. This latter point was important since the lack of concern over declining birth rates distinguished the United States from the many countries where family allowances were welcomed precisely because of the perceived boon to fertility.

In the end, the issue came before the AFL-CIO executive council for resolution. The Executive Council showed no enthusiasm for family allowances. Instead, it recommended that the AFL-CIO launch a new study, one that included "other kinds of programs to aid children" than just family allowances.[13] The AFL-CIO convention later adopted a resolution favoring the achievement of a "family allowance-type system" through expanding income tax exemptions for dependents.[14] Income assistance from the state would not come in the form of cash transfers but in the form of tax relief.

That the AFL-CIO rejected the *form* family support took in most other countries did not mean it lacked a program to aid families with children. Because voluntarism remained a powerful and shaping ideology in the postwar era, collective bargaining and the "principle of the living wage" occupied a central place in their family strategy. Many in the labor movement endorsed state wage supplements only when they were limited to those who were ill, disabled, aged, or incapable of working. An "able-bodied working adult," it was reasoned, should be paid a wage sufficient to support a family: he (and sometimes she) should not have to rely on wage supplements from the state. There were some exceptions to this rule, of course: wage supplements to the poor or the unemployed, both instances involving able-bodied adults, were deemed emergency or special, and hopefully temporary, circumstances requiring state aid.

Yet labor did not reject all state aid to families and children. Instead of state aid in the form of family allowances, the labor movement argued for more money for education, for free school lunches, and for increasing public assistance to poor families. Labor also proposed expanding the tax exemptions for dependents as well as the personal exemptions allowed each adult.

Tax exemptions for dependents were in many ways the American version of a state family allowance. From its inception in 1913, the American system of income tax allowed a personal tax exemption for each adult and an additional exemption for each dependent, helping set a minimum income below which no tax payment was expected. These exemptions—although the amounts allowed had been altered dramatically since 1913—were still part of the tax code in the postwar period. In 1948, for example, the tax code gave a married couple with two children an overall tax exemption of $2,400 ($600 personal exemption for each adult and $600 dependency exemption for each child).[15] When compared to the small stipends often available under family allowance programs outside the United States—Canada averaged $72 dollars per child in 1948—they appear to have provided a considerable boost in overall family income, especially for low- and middle-income families.[16]

After the war, both the AFL and the CIO mounted a campaign to increase tax exemptions and return tax policy to its highly progressive pre–World War II character. From 1913 until 1942, income tax had been "an elite tax" paid largely by the wealthy. Personal exemptions were set initially at $3,000, with an additional $500 for each dependent. Personal exemptions had been gradually lowered since 1913, but the Revenue Act of 1942 cut them back dramatically, while leaving dependency exemptions untouched. As a result, large numbers of lower- and middle-income groups paid taxes *for the first time*. By one estimate, as a result of wartime tax policies, those paying taxes increased from less than ten percent in 1939 to almost two-thirds of the population by the war's end. The labor movement saw raising exemptions as one way of rescinding this new "mass tax," and in 1948, they helped boost *both* personal and dependency exemptions to $600 from their low of $500.[17]

After this small but meaningful victory—the number of low-income families who would pay no taxes at all increased—the labor movement continued to pursue tax reform, directing their primary efforts toward increasing personal exemptions rather than dependency exemptions.[18] Their focus on raising personal exemptions in part grew out of an expectation that the severely reduced personal exemptions of wartime were only temporary. But it was also consistent with the labor movement's general preference for raising the income of all needy households rather than *only* those households with dependents. After 1948, however, the labor proposals for a more progressive tax code made virtually no headway, and would not be seriously revisited until the 1960s.

Labor's tax proposals, like its adherence to a living wage, were primarily class policies linked to labor force participation and, as such, had their limitations. Tax policies did not help those without income, a reality the labor movement acknowledged. Other measures such as full employment, enhanced public assistance, and antidiscrimination statutes were needed. And although higher exemptions raised overall income for families, the gender distribution of income remained intact. The labor movement's tax proposals also benefited families with stay-at-home wives as well as families with working wives and thus could be criticized as reinforcing the traditional family. Yet female-headed families could claim the exemptions labor proposed, and increasing overall family income through upping exemptions allowed working-class wives more *choice* about their labor force participation.

U.S. labor feminists generally supported the labor movement's family policy. They too emphasized a mixed public/private welfare model that sought higher wages on the job, supplemented by state aid to lower- and middle-income families through tax reform and the expansion of other social programs. And, unlike their counterparts in Britain, Australia, and elsewhere,[19] labor feminists in the United States never mounted a campaign on behalf of family allowances. Yet they broke ranks with their union brothers on *other* issues affecting family policy in the postwar years. As we have seen in earlier chapters, they pushed the labor movement to ensure that living wages went to women as well as to men and that wage discrimination against women's work was remedied. They also wanted the labor movement to do more to address the "special" needs of women, including the right to social supports for childbirth and child rearing.

Transforming Maternity Policy

Postwar labor feminists wanted major changes in the treatment of pregnant workers. They saw pregnancy as a social rather than a purely private responsibility, and they believed that the needs of pregnant women should be recognized in enhanced job benefits and social wages. They viewed the typical maternity policies of employers and the state as inadequate and discriminatory. Pregnant women were ineligible for coverage under almost all the unemployment and government disability programs instituted in the New Deal and after. Employers often refused to hire pregnant women, and fired them once their pregnancy was evident. "Mandatory leave" for three to six months was standard; few of these leaves came with rehire rights, health insurance, or income support. Employer policies also differed depending on the class, race, or ethnicity of the women employed. The policies for white native-born women in white-collar jobs were paternalistic and controlling, whereas the pregnancies of blue-collar women and women of color received little if any "protection." African-American women in particular were rarely subject to mandatory leave policies, nor were they transferred to lighter, safer work.[20]

Labor feminists argued that pregnancy should not be grounds for dismissal, and that pregnant women of all races and job classifications should have the right to transfer to a different job if they desired, or be provided special clothes or equipment to function in their current job. Pregnant women and new mothers should have their lost wages replaced as well. Job-based benefits should include employer-paid leaves during pregnancy (with the timing controlled by the woman) followed by an additional year of paid leave (which could be funded from sick leave and vacation pay) to care for the newborn. At the same time, these special benefits should not jeopardize women's claim to full industrial citizenship. Women's income and job security were to be protected by requiring that seniority, health benefits, and other contractual privileges remain in place during maternity leave. Of utmost importance, one's right to return to work in "an equivalent job" should be guaranteed.[21]

A few prominent labor women had reservations about seeing pregnancy as a societal rather than a private responsibility. And some worried that demanding special accommodations for pregnancy would undermine women's claims for equality in other areas.[22] But these views were in the minority by the 1940s. At the April 1945 Women's Bureau conference for union women, an elderly Julia Parker, long-time organizer for the telephone operator's division of the IBEW, raised one of the few objections to the endorsement of paid maternity leave (with job guarantee upon return). Intoning that "inequality can come in the back door as well as the front," Parker feared that seeking "to impose upon industry a special payment for women" jeopardized claims for "equal pay and equal treatment of women as citizens and workers rather than as women." Pregnancy was simply "one of nature's discriminations. On what grounds do you ask for pay?" Her dissent was dealt with summarily. "We make no bones about the fact that there are certain things women need that men don't," one delegate countered. Pregnancy was an "involuntary unemployment," Frieda Miller pointed out, and hence deserving of income support. After all, pregnancy was not "developed by women for their entertainment," she remarked dryly. It was "a social function" and as such should be borne by the community.[23]

The union leaders attending the Washington summit then debated whether maternity benefits should be bargained or the "cost spread over the whole society through some form of social insurance." The United States was behind in providing social insurance, Frieda Miller argued. "The Beveridge plan [in England] provides assistance to young children, and even in Cuba, men [as well as women] pay a tax that supports maternity benefits. Every child [does] have two parents." Ruth Young struck a compromise that the group appeared to endorse. "Negotiate it [maternity benefits] in your contract," she advised, "then when the government passes a full social security program, we can renegotiate the clause. We can take it out of the contract so we can get it from the community, which is the place we think some of this responsibility lies. . . . You can use the same argument about severance pay."[24]

Labor women took up Young's advice. Indeed, even *before* labor feminists gathered in Washington at the war's end, progress had been made at the bargaining table, especially in locals with large numbers of active women members. Mary Callahan, who during the war headed up her UE local's negotiating team, reported that "when the War Labor Board held down the lid on money, we negotiated things that were fantastic, that nobody ever heard of before: all kinds of insurance, maternity leave, maternity benefits. When my son was born in 1946, I got 17 dollars a week. This was a fantastic amount of money. And full seniority and time off. We had negotiated it in 1942."[25] Addie Wyatt, as recounted earlier, also remembered how incredulous she was in 1942 to find out that she was eligible for a maternity leave and her old job back upon return—

benefits she soon learned that had been negotiated by her UPWA local.[26] By 1944, many of the industry-wide welfare plans sponsored by ACWA also included maternity benefits. To advertise its accomplishment, the union printed the news on the back of its membership cards.[27]

These kinds of improved maternity protections and benefits became common in unionized workplaces as the baby boom got underway after the war.[28] By the mid-1950s, the standard maternity protections in contracts negotiated by the large CIO industrial unions included leaves with job protection, transfer rights, no loss of seniority or health benefits, use of accrued sick pay during leave, and health insurance plans that covered maternity care.[29] Even AFL union contracts provided "pregnancy leave" or "accepted pregnancy as constituting one of the reasons for 'leave for good cause.'" In addition, maternity benefits were now "almost invariably included in union-negotiated health and welfare plans."[30] Some employers, of course, continued to resist giving women more control over how to manage their pregnancies. In 1955, for example, CWA regional director Selina Burch led a 72-day strike in New Orleans in part to secure "maternity leave in the contract and the right to arbitrate any suspension." Only after 10,000 people paraded in the streets did the CWA local emerge with the contract changes it desired.[31]

Yet maternity policies for the *majority* of employed women were far from adequate. Particularly galling was the fact that the majority of leaves, in union and nonunion settings, provided for only partial wage replacement.[32] Changing policy at the federal level provided one avenue of redress. Senator Robert Wagner, backed by both the AFL and the CIO, had introduced the Wagner-Murray-Dingell (WMD) Bill in 1943, sometimes referred to as "the American Beveridge Plan" after the British social security and health care legislation upon which it was modeled. The aim of the WMD Bill was to expand New Deal entitlements and remedy earlier defects, including the exclusion of maternity benefits. The bill died in committee, but was reintroduced in 1945, again with the strong endorsement of the AFL and the CIO. The 1945 version, referred to as "the new social security bill," called for national health insurance, the extension of old age insurance to farm workers and domestic employees, raising old-age, survivor, and unemployment benefits for those already covered, and adding benefits for temporary and permanent disability. "Married women workers" would be entitled to the maximum of twenty-six weeks of disability benefits and an additional twelve weeks of paid maternity leave.[33]

Labor feminists backed the proposals for state income supports for childbearing, testifying on behalf of the 1945 WMD Bill and its successor bills, introduced until the early 1950s. Frieda Miller, for example, testified in 1949 on behalf of HR 2893, which, among other things, proposed amending the Social Security Act to require an "insurance system for maternity protection" for eight weeks before and eight weeks after birth.[34] She continued her efforts in the early 1950s, working with the Children's Bureau to secure a federal law that would move the United States closer to the standards emerging in other industrial countries: a minimum three-month paid leave with job security. These efforts to bring a "full social security program" to the United States, to use Ruth Young's language, went down to defeat, opposed by the usual array of business groups, conservative Republicans, and southern Democrats as well as special interest groups such as the American Medical Association.[35]

Stymied at the federal level, labor women focused on changing discriminatory state policies.[36] Unemployment boards, for example, often assumed pregnant women were not "available for work" and thus ruled them ineligible for benefits. Refusal to accept full-time work for "domestic reasons" disqualified others. Many women fell through the cracks because as part-time or short-term workers they simply had not accumulated enough income to qualify for benefits. One delegate to the UAW Women's Advisory Board complained that "women were picked on more than anyone else. They disqualify you for unemployment insurance if you have a child. One worker had to go to the doctor to prove that she was not going to have a baby in order to collect unemployment insurance. We [in this local] are working hard to get that law revised."[37]

Some pregnant wage-earning women, excluded from unemployment benefits, sought income support from state disability systems, only to find they were ruled ineligible from these programs as well. Undoubtedly, underneath these contradictory rules lay the real reasons for excluding pregnant women. Many worried that including such a large class of recipients (all pregnant workers) would bankrupt these newly instituted income security systems. In addition, state policy was driven by gendered notions of who was a real worker (and hence deserving of state entitlements) and fears that paying state benefits directly to pregnant women would undermine female economic dependency on a male family head.[38]

Katherine Ellickson, executive secretary of the CIO's Social Security Committee in the early 1950s, frequently entered objections to "the hard and fast rule disqualifying pregnant women" from unemployment and disability payments when such legislation was up for review.[39] Labor feminists in California and elsewhere lobbied hard to amend the state social insurance laws to include disability payments during pregnancy.[40] Despite these efforts, only four states provided any cash benefits to pregnant women through their disability systems before the 1960s. By the 1950s most states settled on a uniform policy of granting unemployment benefits only for "involuntary quits," thus excluding women who stopped work for childbirth or any other family obligation, including dependency care.[41]

At the end of the 1950s, the United States had forged a path rejected by almost all other industrialized countries: it made no social provision for loss of income due to childbearing. "Women must not be penalized for carrying out their normal functions of motherhood," Esther Peterson told a convention of international government officials in 1958. But "we in the United States suffer a kind of cultural lag in our social awareness of this problem relative to that of some of our European brethren. The achievement of our real goal of adequate maternity leave with cash payment and medical and hospital insurance for all women workers is still ahead of us."[42]

Fig. 5.1 Kitty Ellickson confers with her counterpart in the AFL, Nelson Cruikshank, before speaking at a 1953 conference on social security. The document Ellickson
is holding is entitled, "For A Healthy America." Credit: George Meany Memorial
Archives.

ENSURING PROPER CARE FOR CHILDREN

Securing social support for the rearing of children proved as daunting as making
the case for changing maternity policies. Publicly funded day care has always
met opposition in the United States in part because policy makers and the
public at large were ambivalent toward the employment of mothers, especially
those with young children.[43] Suspicions about the state taking over welfare functions that once belonged to the family also remained strong in the post–New
Deal era, as did fears that having out-of-home care provided by nonrelatives
would be detrimental to children.

   Working-class women shared many of these concerns. Some also associated
public day care with well-meaning but condescending charity programs that all
too frequently had justified their existence by pointing to working-class mothers' neglect of their children. Not surprisingly, the majority of working-class
women, like the public at large, preferred family and informal arrangements to
public day care. Some got help from their own parents or from another relative.
Others found neighbors with whom they could exchange child care or other
services. Many working-class parents also chose shifts starting at different times
in order to cover the home front on a 24-hour basis.[44]

Fig 5.2 Esther Peterson teaches a 1958 ACWA class on labor's political goals. Credit: UNITE Archives, Kheel Center, Cornell University, Ithaca, New York.

Child care programs—regardless of whether government, community, or employer-run—were not always seen by working-class women as an adequate response to their problems. Many agreed with Mary Anderson's analysis that "as a social philosophy the establishment of day nurseries for the children of working mothers is only a stop gap"; it is "not a solution of anything"—particularly not to the problem of having two jobs as homemaker and wage earner.[45] Child care programs helped mothers *manage* their "double day" more easily and often meant less worry about their children's welfare. But such programs did little to make it possible for women to spend *more* time with their children and *less* time on the job. Long hours and compulsory overtime remained. Paying someone else to care for her children while the wage-earning mother labored in a 10-hour-a-day factory or service job was rarely a satisfactory solution. Many, as we shall see, expressed more enthusiasm for the historic labor demand for "more money and less work" than for day care as a strategy for lessening the burdens of the "double day."

Nevertheless, despite these reservations, working-class women were often among the most vocal in making a case for child care assistance from employers and the government. Family and community-based solutions to child care often proved inadequate. Neighbors and kin could be unavailable or unreliable, and few working-class families had the resources to employ full- or even part-time professional caregivers. Ensuring proper care for the children of working mothers often *required* the resources of employers and the state. As more women used child care programs in the 1940s and 1950s and as their union leaders pushed for the needs of working mothers to be recognized as a public, not just a private, responsibility, the sense of child care as a legitimate social entitlement increased among working-class women.

Indeed, women union leaders were among the most forceful and persistent proponents of child care programs in the 1940s and 1950s. As with maternity policy, they pursued a mixed welfare model, seeking to secure benefits in the private sector as well as through the state. They favored direct state subsidies to government day care centers as well as more indirect subsidies such as changes in tax policy or increased funding for public schooling.

STATE SUBSIDIES FOR CHILD CARE

The crisis of World War II put day care on the national agenda. By the end of 1942, federal funds flowed for the first time to public day care centers open to children of all working mothers. Yet even when national security appeared to depend on women leaving their homes for war work, a deep ambivalence about mothers working and children being cared for by nonrelatives outside the home persisted.[46] The initial policy of the War Manpower Commission was to recruit *only* women without children under fourteen. When some government funding for day care eventually became available under the 1942 Lanham Act, many communities hesitated to take advantage of the funds.[47] Public day care was still associated "with welfare and cruelty" in the minds of some, a last resort when neighborhood and kinship ties had broken down.[48] Lillian Herstein, a long-time official in the Chicago Teachers' Union, spent much of her time as a consultant to the War Production Board "encouraging employers and communities to apply for Lanham Act funds."[49] Some 3,102 centers eventually opened nationwide. At their peak they served a million and a half children, a fraction (some 3 percent) of the children of employed mothers. Nevertheless, fears of public day care lessened as people began using the centers, and by the end of the war, the stigma of group care of children had begun to fade.[50]

The Congress of Women's Auxiliaries, the national federation of CIO women's auxiliaries, made "solving the child care problem their major objective." At their third annual conference in 1943, they resolved that "adequate child care be available to every child of a working mother" and that "nurseries be set up in every community, administered by the boards of education located in public schools."[51] That same year, Eleanor Fowler, president of the Congress, and Catherine Gelles, its secretary-treasurer, gave impassioned testimony at congressional hearings on behalf of increasing government spending for child care. Gelles presented "the CIO position," which was that government should "assume full responsibility for nurseries" as in England and that all "employed mothers" should be eligible. The AFL joined the auxiliaries at the 1943 hearings, testifying for increased funding and urging that a labor representative be put on child care advisory committees to avoid the past "paternalistic approach" toward working women.[52]

Labor women outside the auxiliaries mobilized as well. UAW women held one of their first regional women's conferences in Detroit in 1943. They strongly backed the extension of the Lanham Act and called for more help with child care from their union. The UAW responded, urging its affiliates to take responsibility for "the care and solicitude of the children of soldiers and working mothers."[53] At the April 1945 Women's Bureau Conference, delegates from the FTA found a sympathetic response to their call for "nurseries for the little ones [and] after-school programs for the 8 to 12 year-olds." Child care aid, the FTA newspaper later editorialized, will "more and more be insisted upon because it is good for our children, as an extra facility in addition to good homes. It helps their education, it helps their health, and it helps their busy mothers."[54]

At the war's end, federal funding under the Lanham Act ended, despite the protests from labor women and the resistance of public officials like New Jersey congresswoman Mary Norton. Much of the public, including public officials, believed that day care was no longer needed, since most mothers would be leaving their wartime work and returning to the home. In October 1945, Congress approved only a four-month temporary extension.[55]

When the last bit of federal funding dried up in 1946, employed mothers in communities across the country banded together to seek alternative sources of government funding for the Lanham Act child care centers. In California, where the most successful campaign to preserve government support occurred, the child care movement attracted labor feminists from a wide range of political sympathies. HERE Waitresses' Local 48 in San Francisco, led by newly elected president Jackie Walsh, had helped instigate a Central Labor Council "Committee on the Care of Children of Working Mothers" in 1942. Walsh, who retained her power within the local for the next three decades, shored up her support by steering clear of radical politics.[56] The Labor Council Committee joined the postwar effort, along with the California State CIO Women's Auxiliary, the Los Angeles Central Labor Council, and other organizations. They created such a furor over the discontinuation of federal funding for child care that the state appropriated $3.5 million for child care for low-income parents in 1946, extending it every year until 1957, when it became a permanent part of the budget.[57]

Tillie Lerner Olsen, later to gain international acclaim as the author of *Tell Me a Riddle* (1961) and other fictional accounts of working-class life, was at the center of much of the California activity. Born in 1912 to poor Russian-Jewish immigrants who had settled in Omaha, Nebraska, Olsen joined the Young Communist League (YCL), the CP youth organization, as a teenager. She threw herself into the heady radical politics of the early 1930s, helping organize packinghouse workers and leading mass demonstrations on behalf of the unem-

ployed. Olsen's own life wasn't so far removed from the women she was defending. She already had a daughter, born in 1932, that she was struggling to
support as a single mother while she pursued her political activities and attended to her own fiction writing. Olsen completed much of her first novel in
this period, a work that would be published decades later as *Yonnondio: From
the Thirties* (1974). And by 1934, Olsen had achieved a measure of literary as
well as political notoriety. In 1934, her short story, "The Iron Throat," published
in *Partisan Review*, captured the attention of the New York literary establishment—a "work of young, uncertain but sensitive genius," Robert Cantwell of
the *New Republic* proclaimed. When Cantwell's review appeared, no one could
find her to give her the news: she was in jail, arrested once again for political
activities, this time in connection with the 1934 San Francisco Maritime strike.[58]

Olsen's activities on behalf of child care began soon after she joined the
Women's Auxiliary of the International Longshore and Warehouse Union
(ILWU) and married Jack Olsen, a former YCL comrade who later became
publicity and education director of ILWU Warehouse Local 6. By 1943, Tillie
Lerner Olsen was president of the California State CIO Women's Auxiliary, a
vice president of the CIO's Congress of Women's Auxiliaries, and in charge of
the CIO Council for Child Care.[59] After her third child was born, Olsen turned
her energies more to community politics, where she continued her focus on
child care, pursuing the CIO-Auxiliaries' 1943 goal of establishing child care
centers through local boards of education. At the war's end, Olsen was appointed a member of the San Francisco Board of Education Child Care Committee, a group she had helped start as president of her local elementary school
Parent Teacher's Association. In 1945, she proudly sent out a notice to "All
Mothers Working or Who Intend to Work" that the first child care center in
San Francisco administered by the City's Board of Education was "definitely
opening."[60] San Francisco had become one of the few cities in the country to
provide public funds for child care.

Working-class women led public demonstrations and lobbying efforts in
other communities in the immediate postwar years, but in only a few did they
secure concrete results.[61] In almost all instances, the government funding was
limited to low-income women—a situation that perpetuated the stigma of public day care. In Detroit, UAW's Millie Jeffrey recalled that "we fought hard . . .
to keep the Lanham Act nurseries," and obtained funding from the Board of
Education for three years. But "the steam was going out of the demand from
the consumer standpoint. When the Welfare Department took them over, the
usage just went down, down, down." The Michigan State Day Care Committee
fell apart by the end of the 1940s.[62] In New York, women succeeded in pressuring the state to pass a child care bill in 1946 and 1947. Governor Dewey vetoed
the 1947 bill, dismissing the women who picketed his home as communists, but
some state funding for child care was eventually leveraged, continuing into the
1950s and beyond.[63]

With little help forthcoming from the government, working-class women
turned to their unions for assistance. At women's conferences sponsored by the

UE in the early 1950s, as well as at other union forums, women raised the need for "day nurseries" and "help with juggling absenteeism and child care."[64] The UPWA women's committee, for example, urged local unions in 1954 and again in 1956 to sponsor "full-time nurseries for pre-school age children" in areas where there was concentrated membership and to provide child care at union meetings to help facilitate women's participation.[65]

In many cases, these requests went unattended. But in others, the local union stepped into the breach opened by lack of government services. Seattle waitress and union leader Beulah Compton, who raised her two daughters alone after her husband left her at age 23, won reelection in her 3700 member local in 1953 on a platform promising a union-sponsored nursery for children during afternoon and evening union meetings. Once elected, Compton also arranged for an older, former waitress to be on call through the union when working waitresses needed emergency child care.[66]

Unions such as the Seattle waitresses' local with their own resident caregiver were rare. But numerous locals had their own "community services" departments. These divisions, set up to help union members with problems outside the plant such as day care, credit, or housing, multiplied in the postwar era.[67] Some employed mothers also had recourse to enlightened union welfare departments like the one operating in New York's large hotel workers' local. In the late 1940s, the Women's Committee of that local pushed for "child care centers in their communities," and insisted that the union's welfare department be used to advise members about child adoption and offer members referrals to local child care providers.[68]

At the national level, women labor leaders applauded union efforts to meet the needs of working mothers, and they pressed for government assistance, now focusing on securing indirect state aid through changes in tax policies.[69] Yet even these more modest proposals for government assistance for child care, especially when aimed at benefiting *all* working mothers, met resistance—and even from within the women's reform community. When Gladys Dickason and Kitty Ellickson brought up the need for day care centers at a July 1949 LAC meeting and urged that someone look into the problem, the Women's Bureau representatives had to remind them of the continuing ambivalence of the Children's Bureau and its belief that "the welfare of children requires the retirement of women with young children." But Ellickson persisted. Day care centers were "still important for mothers who have no choice," she countered, and "mothers of school age children need help."[70]

At a Women's Bureau conference the following year, there continued to be a "divergence of opinion on the question of whether married women with young children should be encouraged to work." But after much urging from Ellickson and other labor women, it was agreed that "services for the care of children should be developed to enable women to work if they must."[71] Of equal import, the conference also favorably considered the CIO tax proposal, introduced by Ellickson, "that the expense of child care to working mothers be charged as a legitimate expense of industry and allowance made to the mother for this."[72]

In 1954, some four years later, Congress adopted a modified version of the CIO recommendation as part of a major overhaul of tax code provisions: they changed the federal tax code to allow employed mothers to itemize child care expenses as a business tax deduction. After all, as Julia Thompson, the Washington representative for the American Nurses Association, explained at the congressional hearings about the proposal, child care is a necessary expense associated with earning one's living and should be deductible like other business expenses. The present tax laws are "unfair to women generally," she concluded. "Men can deduct alimony payments—how is that related to earning their living?"[73]

Labor feminists had pushed for a tax provision without a "ceiling on the amount deductible or the total income."[74] The tax break, they argued, should be universal and provide greater financial relief. In 1953 and 1954, with various tax bills before Congress (and two state bills before Minnesota and Oregon legislatures that were both defeated), UAW women and others within the CIO initiated an "intensive letter campaign" in support of permitting *all* employed mothers a child care deduction.[75] The legislation enacted fell short of what labor feminists wanted: it limited the child care deduction to $600 ($900 for two or more children under 13), and only allowed employed mothers, widows, and widowers with incomes of $4500 or less to claim it.[76]

The 1954 legislation, some analysts observed at the time, reflected the "prevailing attitude" that there should be *some* use of public funds for child care, but only "where mothers have to work." Even among those backing the change, few argued that there was "a reason for expanding child care facilities in order to enable mothers who do not *have* to work to do so."[77] Indeed, Congressman Klein, who supported applying the child care deduction to all taxpayers, regardless of income, fretted that "some women might decide they do not like housework and want to get a job."[78]

The CIO, however, struck a somewhat different tone. Stanley Ruttenberg, CIO director of research, testified that "when a mother decides it is desirable for her to go to work, the Nation should provide a framework of tax policy which recognizes the importance of adequate care for her children." The bill, he continued, would help children, should be available to a "working wife, widow, or widower, *or parent*" (italics added), and would be "a long overdue acknowledgement of women's double contribution to society" as "mothers and breadwinners."[79]

The AFL, like the CIO, was "in sympathy with those who wish to relieve widows and mothers from taxation." Yet they had many reservations about the specifics of the childcare deduction, and unlike the CIO, they paid scant attention to the overall problem of women's equal access to paid employment. Working mothers, they acknowledged, had "particular problems," but they believed that the best way of solving these problems was to solve the "broader issues facing low-income groups overall." Consistent with their earlier emphasis on tax policy aimed at raising the income of all low-income families, they urged

Congress to raise the $600 personal exemptions allowed for adult taxpayers and decrease the tax rate on the first $2000 of income above the exemption level.[80]

The 1954 legislation was disappointing not just to labor feminists but to the labor movement as a whole. Not only was the child care tax deduction quite small, but a tax deduction was worth more the higher one's tax bracket, and did little to help those not paying taxes at all. Nevertheless, the passage of the bill marked a significant turn in federal policy toward child care: it legitimized the care of children by adults other than their mother and recognized the breadwinner role of mothers.

As the 1950s wore on, efforts to secure public support for child care gained momentum, helped in part by the burgeoning birth rate and by a society growing more amenable to the idea of wives and mothers in the labor force. The 1950s may have been experienced by some as the height of a vitriolic "feminine mystique" emphasizing stay-at-home moms and domesticity, but other cultural and economic forces tempered and even countered that ideology. As Elizabeth Rose observes, 1950s culture was full of "mixed messages," some of which gave new legitimacy to women's paid work as "a way of serving the family and the nation."[81] A 1955 article in the *American Federationist*, for example, lauded "the feminine invasion" because "today, when so much depends on our ability to out-produce the Russians, the fullest employment of trained womanpower has become a vital factor in the Cold War."[82] The widely read reports flowing from the Columbia University National Manpower Council (NMC) reflected a similar acceptance of female employment derived from a concern for a full-employment cold war economy.[83]

The idea of mothers—even mothers with younger children—taking jobs gained legitimacy in the 1950s as ideas about the needs of children changed. At the 1957 NMC Womanpower Conference, attended by women business and civic leaders, including AFL-CIO women, speakers debated the impact of maternal employment on children, with some pointing to the harmful effect of absent mothers while others ventured that "mother substitutes" and out-of-home child care could benefit children. Many attendees felt that small children did best when cared for by their own mothers, and hence they expressed reservations about mothers with "young children" working outside the home—but exactly how young was not clear. Some thought mothers with children under the age of six should refrain from employment. Others drew the line at mothers with children under three. Most, however, set the age at which a child no longer required full-time maternal care much lower than the officials during World War II, who urged mothers with children under age 14 to stay in the home.[84]

Working-class women viewed these issues through their own lens of economic imperatives. Whether mothers with young children should work was an issue that divided working-class women, just as it did the larger society. Yet few seemed to feel the psychological conflict experienced by elite women caught up in the "feminine mystique." When Mirra Komarovsky interviewed blue-collar women in the late 1950s for her study, *Blue-Collar Marriage*, she was astounded to discover their lack of guilt about working outside the home. It was as if she had entered a strange "pre-Freudian" world, she mused.[85] In many working-class communities, mothering had long included being a good provider as well as a good nurturer. Employment, rather than being incompatible with good mothering, was viewed as "a fulfillment of a mother's duty to her children."[86] In part because of this expanded definition of mothering, many working-class women experienced less guilt about working outside the home. Wage work was not about their own pleasure but about ensuring the well-being of their families.

Although labor feminists and their allies were not able to sustain the experiment in government support for child care that began during World War II, significant progress toward establishing child care as an entitlement had occurred by the end of the 1950s. During the 1940s and 1950s, Elizabeth Rose writes, "a new discourse" concerning day care emerged, one which "challenged but did not replace the older vision of day care as charity for poor single mothers."[87] Labor women were at the forefront of this new, more positive view of child care. They asserted a right to publicly provided day care in the 1940s. In the early 1950s, they fought for liberal tax breaks for all working mothers, and by the end of the decade, as we will see, they mounted yet another national campaign to secure publicly funded child care centers.

THE POLITICS OF TIME

Low-income women required more than maternity benefits and child care assistance to lighten the burden of the "double day". Domestic obligations were for many a lifelong affair, including the duties of long-term dependent care as well as the daily routine of cooking, laundry, cleaning, and shopping. Accommodating these realities required a fundamental restructuring of employment. Central to the required transformation was attention to what sociologist Carmen Sirianni has called "the politics of time." Labor women in the postwar era did not characterize their issues in this way, yet many of the policies they pursued can be grouped under this rubric.

World War II was a turning point in the history of workers' struggle over time. The movement for a shorter work*day* and a shorter work*week* receded after the FLSA set the forty-hour week as the national standard, and it never returned to a central place in the reform agenda. But the push to shorten work time and to gain more control over time found new expression in efforts to gain a shorter work *year* and a shorter work *life*. A crucial shift in the politics of time thus occurred in the postwar years which was as much a change in workers' strategy and language as in their desires or beliefs.[88]

Indeed, in the 1940s and 1950s, the labor movement invented a host of *new* approaches to reducing the overall time workers spent on the job. Beginning in World War II, with the War Labor Board restrictions on wage increases, unions turned to alternative means of enhancing the well-being of their members. Many pursued and won innovative fringe benefits that affected worker income as well as work time. After the war, additional unions adopted this expanded bargaining agenda, winning health insurance and retirement benefits as well as paid sick leave, paid vacations, and supplemental income during layoffs. Many of these benefits offered workers increased income *and* reduced work time. Like the historic demand for a shorter workday in the nineteenth and early twentieth century, these postwar work time policies were popular in part because they did not require that time be traded for money.[89]

The politics of time were as gendered as the politics of pay in the postwar era. Labor women supported efforts to reduce work time for *different* reasons than did men, and at times, they devised their own distinct counterproposals to those of the male-led labor movement. Working-class women desired leisure as did men, but finding ways of meeting their *dual* responsibilities as breadwinner and caretaker was of even greater concern.

The new approaches to time reduction that took center stage in the postwar era—paid vacations, predetermined paid holidays, and early retirement—were not designed to lighten women's double day. Having a month off in the summer or a three-day holiday weekend or the ability to retire earlier provided little relief for those trying to juggle household and wage labor. Housework necessitated a *daily* form of accommodation. Moreover, child-rearing responsibilities often were heaviest at the beginning of one's work life rather than at the end. Unfortunately, women's needs did not appear to influence union or employer policy to any great degree in this arena. As the UAW's Walter Reuther explained, most workers preferred time off in the form of large blocks—what he called "lumps of leisure." Employers were also more amenable to granting one more holiday or one more week of vacation than instituting a six-hour day or giving workers more control over their hours—policies that would have offered working women some relief.

In response, women sought alternatives to the "lumps of leisure" approach to reducing work time: for example, policies that would provide time off from work on a *daily* basis rather than time off in large continuous blocks. Indeed, after the war, the movement for a shorter work*day* feminized noticeably, becoming a demand supported primarily by women. Benjamin Hunnicutt's study of worker attitudes toward the six-hour day at Kellogg reveals the gendered nature of support on this issue. Kellogg instituted the six-hour day in the 1930s as a work-sharing measure, and it quickly became popular among both men and women. By the 1940s, however, enthusiasm among men waned, according to Hunnicutt, and longer hours and overtime pay gained appeal as consumer desires grew. Many working-class men, Hunnicutt concludes, felt uncomfortable spending so much time in the domestic sphere under the sway of women. They felt more powerful on the job than at home. Wage work reinforced their masculine identity and helped them fulfill their masculine duty as breadwinners. In contrast, women supported the six-hour day at Kellogg into the 1980s. Spending time in the home realm was not experienced as gender role conflict, nor did they feel shame at wanting time away from paid work. Time spent in the home realm bolstered their self-confidence and self-esteem, and the home was experienced as a space where they exercised power.

The politics of shorter hours at the national level reveals a similar kind of gender divide. While the shorter *hours* strategy had been eclipsed by other approaches to time reduction by the 1940s, it had not wholly disappeared from the national union agenda. In the 1930s and earlier, labor had argued for shorter hours as a way of solving unemployment, raising wages, and promoting "health, efficiency, home life, and citizenship."[90] In the postwar era, however, the shorter hours strategy reemerged in a limited number of industries primarily as a way of combating unemployment. In 1948, the AFL set up a "shorter workday committee," composed mainly of building tradesmen, with the principal impetus being "to maintain jobs" and "stave off mass unemployment."[91]

In the mid-1950s, interest in shorter hours returned on a wider scale, spurred by the increase in automation. Still, the gender divide persisted. In September of 1956, the AFL-CIO sponsored a conference on shorter hours to assess union and worker interest. Commentators noted little enthusiasm among men for lowering daily or weekly hours except in situations where the "threat of unemployment" loomed. Women, however, particularly working wives, desired a shorter workday "so that they had more time to manage their household duties," and they saw its achievement as a high priority. Women's support was "a notable factor" in the ILGWU's recent achievement of a 35-hour week for the majority of its members, one speaker commented, adding that the "strong desire for a 7-hour day" among CWA operators has sparked action by that union too.[92] CWA's 1955 bargaining program included reduction in the hours phone operators worked; the following year a shorter workweek with no reduction in pay was requested for all workers.[93] Yet even in the CWA where women predominated, men tended to set bargaining priorities, according to one high female officer. That meant more emphasis on "money items such as higher wages" and less attention to "women's aspirations, especially shorter hours."[94]

On the whole, postwar labor women had to be satisfied with a politics of time designed primarily with men in mind. Money took priority over shorter hours, and men's desire for leisure trumped women's desire for relief from the "double day." Firms with a majority of women did offer slightly different benefit packages to their employees than those with male-dominated workforces: women were more likely to get various forms of paid leave (sick leave and vacation) than were men. But even this small accommodation came with a price tag—making it one that may not have been worth the cost. Women in female-majority jobs and industries were also *less* likely to get benefits such as health insurance and pensions that directly supplemented their money earnings. Moreover, in high-wage, male-dominated industries, women received fewer benefits of all kinds than did men. Some contracts limited benefit coverage to full-status, full-time employees, thus excluding the many women holding part-time and temporary jobs. Others required continuity of service based on seniority to establish eligibility, as was true for the first employer-financed pension program set up in the auto industry in 1949. Women who took time off for childbirth and lost their seniority also lost their pension benefits.[95]

Legislating Work Time

By the postwar era, labor women held a wide range of opinions about whether there should be hour laws and just what precisely these laws should specify. The state woman-only laws were the most controversial. In contrast to the campaign for minimum wage coverage for women, the efforts to pass state hour laws had been far more successful. In 1957, some 43 states had laws regulating women's work hours. A few of these laws used overtime or premium payments as a disincentive to long hours, as did the FLSA, but the majority relied on the older paternalistic approach: they simply set mandatory limits on the number of hours a woman could work. In Oregon, for example, women could not work over 48 hours in a week, regardless of how much money employers were willing to pay. The law expressly forbade it.

Here, once again, was a policy that appeared to construct a trade-off between time and money. These state laws helped women limit the time demands of the wage sphere. Yet in exchange for that protection, women lost lucrative overtime payments. In addition, employers often refused to hire or promote women into higher-wage jobs, claiming that the legal restrictions on women's work hours made them unsuited for such jobs. The solution, as Frieda Miller recognized in 1945, was to construct the issue like "the old 8-hour fight . . . where we have reduction of hours without loss of [wage] standards," but a consensus was never reached among labor women on how precisely to achieve that aim.[96]

Many labor women now disagreed with Mary Anderson's assessment that "special hour restrictions" for women were never "any handicap" to them.[97] But most still believed that the advantages of the state hour laws overrode the disadvantages, in part because the federal wage and hour law had yet to be extended to the majority of women. They also believed that the state laws could be improved through amendments. Seattle union official Beulah Compton pronounced the eight-hour law "a constant headache that had outlived its usefulness in some respects" once she became state director of the Women and Minors Division in the late 1950s. But she opposed repeal. Instead, she favored a relaxation of the law so that in certain circumstances women, like men, would have access to the higher overtime payments.[98]

Support for retaining the woman-only hour laws was particularly strong among women in female-dominated occupations. HERE women in California, for example, tenaciously defended the woman-only state hour law with its mandatory limits on hours worked. When the Business and Professional Women (BPW) of California proposed liberalizing the eight-hour work limit for women in 1957 to allow for "voluntary overtime," HERE women objected. Overtime pay for them would be minimal, they pointed out, and few waitresses believed that allowing women to work overtime would open up the high-tip dinner and liquor service jobs. They also felt that their relatively weak bargaining power as blue-collar women meant that so-called *voluntary* overtime would become *involuntary*. Voluntary overtime was a fiction, explained one HERE female official. The BPW proposal appeared reasonable in principle, she continued, but for nonprofessional women, an employer "suggestion becomes an order." Without controls, "you are setting the stage for excessive compulsory overtime." Former hotel maid Bertha Metro, representing the primarily black Hotel and Club Service Workers in San Francisco, concurred, adding that many working women with children in day care would be forced to quit their jobs if required to work overtime. Elizabeth Kelley of the San Francisco Waitresses' Union joined the attack: "Who's going to pick up the kids, cook their dinner? We're happy that we have a little legislation, and we'll fight to keep it. We're not a bunch of college women, we're waitresses."[99]

Labor women's support for sex-based hour laws is often invoked as an example of gender conservatism. Yet there is little evidence that they backed hour laws because of a belief in restricting female autonomy or a desire to return women to the home. Rather, they wanted mechanisms that allowed women to combine caregiving and breadwinning and that prevented the intolerable oppression of compulsory long hours. The ability to leave work at a time the worker could predict, even if it meant less pay or fewer opportunities for promotion, was a benefit they valued.[100]

Labor women's attitudes toward sex-based hour laws also grew out of a reasoned assessment of how a specific law would affect the earnings and employment opportunities of a particular group of workers.[101] Women in service and retail sectors had little to gain from outright repeal and much to lose. They remained united in favor of sex-based hour laws into the 1960s. In contrast, women in industrial jobs such as automobile production and meatpacking functioned in a different labor market context, and as later chapters will detail, by the 1960s many reached a different conclusion about the desirability of such laws.[102]

The issues raised in the postwar debates over hour laws were many: who needed protection from "overwork" and how? Could a single law protect all employees equally? When was overtime voluntary? When was it mandatory? What policies could be devised that would meet the needs of those desiring higher wages as well as those desiring a real choice to work less? These issues were to appear in even starker form in the debates surrounding the enforcement of the Civil Rights Act in the 1960s. They are still on the agenda.

Conclusion

Labor women in this period devised a multifaceted and pragmatic politics of work and family. Achieving higher wages was a key element in their family policy. Without the ability to provide for their families, little else mattered. Yet linked intimately to higher wages was the age-old goal of shorter hours. Theirs was a work-family politics that was attempting to solve the particular problems of nonprofessional women. To them, that meant attention to the fundamental class problems of low wages and long hours.

Yet they rooted their class politics in the realities of women's lives. They pushed for unions, employers, and the state to recognize the particular needs of women and the particular discriminations suffered by women as a sex. Women's problems will never be solved, Mary Anderson once asserted, by "conforming to men's ways."[103] The world of work and the policies governing it needed to be transformed. Labor feminists wanted government and employer policies that would help women combine wage work and family life and would not penalize women for childbearing and child rearing. They wanted a sufficient standard of living for workers and a world in which caregiving was as important as wage earning.

Labor Feminism at High Tide

No matter how many humorous comments are made about the Equal Pay Bill
as a "sex bill," the fact is that an overwhelming proportion of
women feel that job and pay discrimination against them is a serious matter.

—*Esther Peterson, February 13, 1963*[1]

We do not want special privileges. We do not need special privileges. I believe
that we can hold our own. We are entitled to this little crumb of equality.

—*Congresswoman Katharine St. George, during the House debates over adding
the "sex" amendment to the Civil Rights Act, February 8, 1964*[2]

IN 1961, A NEWLY ELECTED President Kennedy announced the creation of the
President's Commission on the Status of Women, the first federal body devoted
to assessing women's status and needs. The next few years witnessed an explo-
sion of legislation affecting women's rights on the job, including the Equal Pay
Act, Title VII of the Civil Rights Act, and sweeping amendments to the Fair
Labor Standards Act. Scholars invariably recognize these dramatic federal initiatives as crucial to the rise of second wave feminism and the upending of
gender norms that followed in the late 1960s.[3] Yet the origins of these reforms
and the reasons for their passage remain obscure and at times puzzling, occurring as they did *before* the rise of a mass-based women's movement.

This chapter offers a missing piece of that puzzle by putting the legislative
battles of the early 1960s within the context of the ongoing efforts of labor
women to extend first-class economic citizenship to women. From the perspective of labor women, the federal initiatives of the early 1960s were the culmination of some twenty-five years of political activism, made possible in part by
the political ascendancy of labor liberalism and the increasing assertiveness of
women within that movement.[4] The establishment of the PCSW, long a goal of
labor feminists, unleashed a national debate over women's status, and labor
women's proposals for achieving women's equality, stymied for so long at the
federal level, received serious consideration in Congress. Yet the laws that
eventually passed, in the view of labor feminists, were often compromises, reflecting the agenda of equal rights feminists and conservative businessmen as
much as or more than their own. Labor women viewed the changes in federal

policy as crucial first steps toward women's equality. What they could not fore-
see, however, was where these first steps would lead.

During the Eisenhower years, Kitty Ellickson remembered, "proposals to overcome discrimination or to provide adequate community services had little
chance for implementation."[5] But as the 1960 election approached, progressive
New Dealers, labor feminists included, believed they now had a chance to
realize substantial gains in federal policy.

It was not only the possibility of returning the Democrats to the White House
that stirred these hopes. The chilling effect of McCarthyism on political thought
and experimentation had lessened by the end of the 1950s, as had the more
confining aspects of the postwar gender ideology. The powerful rhetoric of the
civil rights movement changed the political landscape of the late 1950s as well,
legitimizing the idea of the expansion of citizenship rights and calling into question long-established social and economic hierarchies. Gathering steam since
the 1940s, the civil rights movement burst onto the national stage in the mid-
1950s with the Montgomery, Alabama, bus boycotts and the highly publicized
racial confrontations on the steps of Central High School in Little Rock, Arkansas and at lunchroom counters throughout the South.[6] The civil rights movement sparked a public debate about equality and discrimination, one that challenged the notion of separate but equal and insisted upon equal treatment and
equal access for all citizens. Black women participated in great numbers, finding
new sources of personal strength and gaining valuable experience in political
organizing and strategy. The civil rights movement also strengthened the labor
movement and legitimized minority concerns within it. In the 1940s and 1950s
civil rights leaders often sided with those within the minority community advocating unionism and other collective solutions to the economic disenfranchise-
ment of African-Americans.

Changes within the labor movement added to the mix. To many, the merger
of the AFL and the CIO in 1955 signaled a new unified labor movement with
enhanced political and economic clout. Yet this new "labor monopoly," as some
called it, realized neither the exaggerated fears of its critics nor the hopes of
its adherents.[7] Union density—the proportion of the total labor force that is
unionized—peaked in 1954 at about 33 percent and then began a slow decline,
falling to 25 percent by 1970.[8] Labor's image also suffered under the harsh
spotlight of the Senate's 1957 McClellan Committee investigations into "labor
racketeering." The committee hearings, which featured Robert Kennedy, the
committee's chief counsel, locked in combat with Teamster president Jimmy
Hoffa and other labor leaders, exposed the public to sordid tales of union corruption and strong-arm tactics.[9]

Yet despite these and other problems, the labor movement remained a powerful institutional presence throughout the 1950s and 1960s. Union member-

ship, already standing at fourteen million in 1950, actually *increased* over the next two decades, reaching seventeen million by 1955 and nineteen million by 1970.[10] Of equal importance, although the merger did not reinvigorate union organizing, it did have a positive impact on labor's political programs. In the political arena at least, the AFL-CIO adopted many of the CIO's perspectives. The shift partially reflected the proclivities of the AFL-CIO's first president, George Meany, a heavyset, blunt-speaking former Bronx plumber and building trades official who, since 1952, had been president of the AFL. Earlier, as secretary-treasurer of the AFL, Meany had helped establish Labor's League for Political Education (LLPE) in 1947, and led its campaign to elect Truman in 1948. Truman's narrow victory underscored for Meany the necessity of labor's commitment to political mobilization. Meany emerged as an effective and unapologetic advocate of enhanced state benefits and entitlements.[11] He agreed, for example, that the passage of disability insurance should be a top legislative priority for the merged movement. And, in an unusual coup, Social Security Disability Insurance (SSDI) passed Congress in 1956 over the opposition of the American Medical Association, the Chamber of Commerce, NAM and the Eisenhower Administration. SSDI provided social security benefits to the disabled and marked the first major advance in social insurance programs since 1939.[12]

The labor feminist agenda made some headway in the merged movement too. Yet as was the case with African-Americans in the labor movement, the late 1950s saw an increase of tension between women activists and the labor movement's established leadership.[13] Women's rising expectations and desire for an independent voice simply outpaced the ability or willingness of the male-led movement to respond.

After the merger, as already recounted, the AFL-CIO adopted the CIO position on equal pay, and by the late 1950s, federal equal pay legislation moved to a prominent place in labor's legislative wish list.[14] But labor women wanted more than support for equal pay. Kitty Ellickson, among others, wanted the merged movement to set up a "Committee on Women Workers" that would "consider not only equal pay but social security affecting women, employment and training, and other questions of women's economic status." Carrying forward her proposal, Ellickson's former colleagues in the CIO Research Department, Stanley Ruttenberg and Peter Henle, recommended a "Committee on Women Workers" in a memo responding to queries from AFL-CIO Executive Board members concerning equal pay policy. Equal pay, they counseled, is but one part of "a larger problem of providing additional resources within the AFL-CIO to deal with the special needs of women workers."[15] At that point, in 1956, the AFL-CIO ignored the recommendation for a "Women's Committee," but labor feminists continued to raise it.

In 1958, Esther Peterson, now employed full-time as a lobbyist for the Industrial Union Department of the AFL-CIO, brought together a group of top women labor leaders, including Ellickson (assistant director of the AFL-CIO Social Security Department), Caroline Davis, still head of the UAW Women's

Department, and Gloria Johnson of the IUE Research Department, to discuss policy on state labor laws. The conversation veered off into a number of directions, including reviving Ellickson's notion of a national "Women's Committee" to promote the concerns of women within the AFL-CIO, before returning to the proposed topic. The group "felt it desirable to take a fresh look at women's protective legislation," in particular the "8-hour absolute maximums and the night work laws." Such laws "may be essential to women's welfare and safety," but at the same time, the group concluded, employers used them "to discriminate in pay and promotion against women." The group recommended the AFL-CIO sponsor a "trade union conference on women's problems." Such a conference would look at the need "for new legislation" and help spark "action" on securing unemployment pay for pregnant women, maternity leave guarantees, training programs, expanded minimum wage coverage, and better equal pay laws.[16] The planning committee for the conference, the group hoped, would become a permanent "women's committee" with a full-time staff person. The recommendations circulated among top male labor officials and planning meetings ensued, but whether the conference would materialize and in what form was left unresolved.

Pressure from women bubbled up within international unions as well. The overflow crowd at IUE's first national women's conference in 1957 called for "equal pay for work of equal value," "equal job and promotion opportunities," civil rights legislation, and more liberal tax exemptions for working mothers.[17] The UAW boasted a thriving Women's Department, and in the late 1950s, it experienced a resurgence of local women's committees and conferences, as did other unions. Resolutions from the women's committees and caucuses frequently made their way to union conventions. ACWA women's 1954 "Resolution on Women's Rights," for example, which called for child care tax deductions and "federal legislation prohibiting discrimination against women workers and guaranteeing equal pay," was reaffirmed at subsequent ACWA conventions. Later versions specified the necessity to end "unjust discrimination," implement "equal pay for work requiring comparable skill and training," and the speedy adoption of federal legislation which would "constitute a true bill of rights for working women and preserve existing protective state laws."[18]

UNION WOMEN AND DEMOCRATIC POLITICS

Labor women's influence within the labor movement and the Democratic Party expanded in the 1950s as labor's volunteer political army feminized. Prior to the merger, the majority of AFL women's auxiliaries, for example, were not politically engaged, and the AFL did not encourage such involvement from AFWAL or its affiliates. That situation began to change in 1956 when the CIO women joined the old AFL auxiliaries, giving them a new energy and rationale. The emphasis of the CIO on political mobilization and its willingness to incorporate women into its political programs now infused the AFL.

AFL and CIO auxiliaries had declined in the 1950s, but they were far from moribund. At the time of merger, the CIO National Auxiliary counted twelve thousand members and the AFL's AFWAL listed fifteen thousand. In addition, numerous local and national auxiliaries existed independently of the two federations. AFWAL, for example, estimated that close to *a million women* belonged to AFL auxiliaries that had not yet affiliated.[19] The hope of the AFL-CIO, a hope embraced by the new AFL-CIO National Auxiliary leadership, was to involve *all* auxiliaries, affiliates as well as independents, in the political work of returning the Democrats to power and electing more sympathetic politicians at every level.

To further this effort, in 1959 the AFL-CIO National Auxiliaries hired as its first full-time national director Marcella Beatty, whose background as an experienced political organizer affirmed the new emphasis on political mobilization. Beatty's involvement with unions began when she organized her fellow Boeing aircraft inspectors. She later became a shop steward and full-time union organizer. But Beatty's most recent position had been as the Kansas Women's Activities Director for the AFL-CIO's new political arm, the Committee on Political Education (COPE), where she had reinvigorated the women's division.[20] The AFL-CIO's campaign to shift auxiliary women's focus to politics found fertile ground. The majority of auxiliaries added political action committees, and hundreds of auxiliary women earned 100-hour volunteer pins for legislative work.[21]

The new AFL-CIO reached out to women outside the auxiliaries as well. The CIO, since the 1940s, had recognized the importance of women's vote and the difference the volunteer labor of union women, both members and wives, could make in determining election outcomes. But the AFL didn't evidence much interest in women's political citizenship until the early 1950s. Some AFL leaders blamed women for the Republican victory in 1952,[22] and in 1954, anxious about how women would vote, the AFL set up a "Women's Activities Division" (WAD) within Labor's League for Political Education (LLPE). WAD was charged with educating women who "have refused to vote or have voted for enemies of labor" and with instituting a "Women's Committee of the LLPE" in every local union.[23] Mrs. Margaret Thornburgh, the division's new director, pointed out that political work should appeal to women because it could boost self-confidence, offer "an opportunity to get away from the everyday routine of housework," and "help protect the family's standard of living." Women's right to jobs, equal pay, and accommodations for childbirth and child care, issues stressed by the CIO in its outreach to women, were conspicuously absent.[24]

With the merger, WAD changed its approach, especially after the AFL-CIO hired former CIO staffer Esther Murray to direct the Eastern Division. A friend of former Democratic congresswoman Helen Gahagan Douglas and a past candidate for Congress in California herself, Esther Murray launched an ambitious program of political *leadership* for women. Working with CWA's Helen Berthelot, UAW's Millie Jeffrey, and IUE's Mary Callahan, among others, WAD set up full-time organizations in at least fifteen states and held conferences

Fig. 6.1 The official logo of the AFL-CIO National Auxiliaries adopted in 1957. The phrase "Woman-Power" often accompanied the logo. On first glance, it is an image reinforcing traditional gender roles: graceful feminine hands lovingly
enfold the AFL-CIO insignia of two male hands clasped together. Yet the encircling female hands are holding up the
male hands, and they are larger. Credit: AFWAL Collection,
George Meany Memorial Archives.

across the country to "encourage citizenship participation" by women.[25] Once
involved, women asked for and received increased responsibility and authority.
"In the beginning," Mary Callahan recalled, "the woman's role in COPE was
very minor—changing addresses, making phone calls. We used to rebel and
raise Cain about how we should be at the polls and ringing doorbells too."[26]
By 1958, when COPE held regional political conferences to develop political
strategy and leadership, from a quarter to a half of the delegates were women.[27]

In 1960, COPE was operating in all fifty states, and WAD chapters existed
in four hundred and forty communities.[28] In addition to its financial contributions to Democratic candidates, COPE sponsored a national voter registration
drive, signing up over a million and a half new voters, and coordinated a massive

Fig 6.2 Women "man" the telephone lines at a local UAW hall in Milwaukee, Wisconsin, as part of labor's "get out the vote" campaign during the 1958 elections. Credit: James Conklin, Milwaukee Journal Sentinel Photo, November 5, 1958, George Meany Memorial Archives.

election-day voter drive. AFL-CIO women, auxiliary and union members alike, took the lead in telephone brigades, neighborhood canvassing, and election-day get-out-the-vote campaigns.[29]

The famed CWA phone bank operation Selina Burch coordinated in Louisiana is but one example. Rather than call only union members, Burch got a list of all registered voters in the county and had her operators call them one by one. "After all, who knows better how to talk to a voter over the telephone than a telephone operator?" one political observer mused. Commenting on the phone bank her local ran for Louisiana congressman and Democratic whip Hale Boggs and John F. Kennedy in 1960, Burch credited the skill of the operators. "There is nothing technical or mechanical about it. Our people were valuable to the candidate because of their ability to listen and understand how the voter is responding. And telephone operators know how to keep it simple. It's not mysterious." Boggs linked his subsequent victory to her efforts, later becoming "dear friends" with Burch and CWA president Joe Beirne.[30]

To complement the work of COPE, Esther Peterson convened a group of Washington labor women in May 1960 at the National Democratic Club. The group included newcomers Marcella Beatty and Esther Murray as well as long-time allies Kitty Ellickson, Helen Berthelot, and Gloria Johnson.[31] By October

Fig. 6.3 Lillian Hatcher with a group of UAW volunteers during the 1960 Presidential election. Credit: UAW Women's Department, Archives of Labor and Urban Affairs, Wayne State University.

the group had grown to two hundred labor women, representing the auxiliaries, AFL-CIO staff, and elected women officers from a wide range of national unions. They designated themselves "The Committee of Labor Women for Kennedy and Johnson" and sent out a national call inviting other women to join. Another hundred responded. Peterson had created a powerful new national organization—one whose members were deeply engaged in politics themselves and who also had ties to labor's volunteer army of women in communities across the country.[32] Peterson, now working full-time for Kennedy, toured the country, setting up labor rallies and speaking on behalf of the Democratic candidates. She also organized a "Speaker's Bureau" of leading women unionists, including Kitty Ellickson; Caroline Davis; Sylvia Gottlieb, Assistant to the President, CWA; and Evelyn Dubrow, Washington legislative lobbyist for the ILGWU.[33]

Kennedy's victory margin was slim in 1960, and he did not forget his loyal labor allies. Esther Peterson was an obvious choice for a government post. Kennedy knew she had been one of his earliest supporters and had been a moving force in mobilizing labor support at all levels, from the top brass in Washington to women's auxiliary chapters in the hinterlands. He also knew her personally, having worked with her in the late 1940s when he was a young congressman and she a fledgling ACWA lobbyist. Peterson delighted in telling how she got the assignment:

> When I first reported for my job, I walked into a meeting at the old CIO headquarters at Jefferson Square. The meeting included lobbyists from all the major industries, including the auto workers, the rubber workers, and the steel workers. A lot of the men weren't comfortable having a woman working with them on Capital Hill. Phil Murray, the wonderful president of the CIO, later told me that after the meeting a group of the lobbyists went to him and asked, "What are we going to do with Esther?" The practice at the time was to assign a lobbyist to a legislator to keep him informed on union issues and, in a way, to keep tabs on him. Someone said, "Give her to Kennedy; he won't amount to much." One of the best breaks I ever had.[34]

When the call came from the White House asking, "Esther, what do you want?" she turned down the caller's suggestion of a United Nation's appointment and settled on the Women's Bureau. Peterson remembered thinking that she could do her "best work" there, in part because of her strong "union base." Union women and Women's Bureau staff also lobbied her heavily, urging her to take the Women's Bureau job.[35] Her old friend Arthur J. Goldberg, a former labor counsel to the Steelworkers and the CIO, had been nominated for secretary of labor, and he too was eager for her services.[36] Only a few, such as NWP National Chair Emma Guffey Miller, opposed Peterson's appointment. Although a Democrat, Miller objected to Peterson, characterizing her as "antagonistic to the movement of the freedom of women" and "controlled by labor."[37] Less than a year after her confirmation, Goldberg secured legislation creating a new assistant secretary of labor position and promoted Peterson into it, making her the highest-ranking woman in the Kennedy administration. She was now responsible for the Bureau of Labor Statistics and all activities relating to working women.[38]

Peterson's influence during the Kennedy years, like her appointment itself, rested on more than her long-standing cordial relationship with the new president and her personal charisma. It also sprang from her close-knit network of labor women allies and her institutional ties to the millions of women in trade unions and auxiliaries. During her first year as Women's Bureau director, Peterson sought to recharge those connections and to reaffirm the 1940s policy agenda she had spent her life pursuing.

"When I took over the Women's Bureau," Peterson wrote in her memoirs, "I wanted to make some changes to bring back the spirit of the bureau in the days of Mary Anderson and her successor Frieda Miller, to revive it from its fallow years under Eisenhower."[39] In particular, Peterson wanted to shift the focus of Women's Bureau programs away from "the professional women approach" of Alice Leopold—"her emphasis as to women's employment had been completely opposite of what I wanted"—and back to solving the problems of lower-income women. "We wanted equality for women," she later recalled, "but we wanted bread for our low-income sisters first."[40] To aid her in this reorientation, she moved quickly to reestablish the Union Women's Labor Advisory Committee (LAC) to the Bureau that her Republican predecessor had allowed to lapse, calling an initial meeting of the group in February 1961.

The group eagerly assented to many of Peterson's proposals, including a national commission to examine the discriminations and problems faced by women, government support for child care services, federal equal pay legislation, the extension of the FLSA, and opposition to the ERA.[41] Yet the group divided over policy regarding women's work in the home, an issue close to Peterson's heart. When Peterson showed sympathy to a proposal from a Unitarian church group seeking "a $2500 tax exemption for women who stay home and care for children," noting it "would show that work at home is of economic value," the IUE's Gloria Johnson objected. "Such a law," she feared, "would make it seem that women don't have to work." Kitty Ellickson sided with Peterson, arguing that there should be some way of "establishing the value of the services women provide, some recognition on the part of government." The group eventually moved on, unable to reach a consensus on the proposal. No one, it seemed, could figure out a way of valuing women's work *inside* the home that didn't raise fears of jeopardizing women's status *outside* the home.[42]

Nevertheless, Peterson had long been passionate about the need to value "the things women do for their families," and she was not about to abandon that commitment now. Homemakers were still the largest single female occupational group in 1960, she was fond of pointing out, and their work "is just as skilled as the work men have always done." Indeed, Peterson believed that women's market work would never receive the pay and respect it deserved until household labor was valued.[43]

Although few top policy makers in government or labor shared Peterson's views, she did find support among housewives themselves. Peterson chose "Homemakers and Workers" as the theme around which to organize a series of regional Women's Bureau conferences during her first year in office. She was thrilled when housewives disrupted the Michigan conference. "A group of housewives came in," Peterson recalled. "They asked why there wasn't any economic value assigned to the work they did, staying home taking care of the house and kids. They ended up standing in the back of the room chanting, 'We want to be part of the GNP.' "[44]

Government policy toward housework was not the only issue that proved divisive. The group continued to find common ground in staunch opposition to the ERA, fearing it would erase all sex-based state laws, the good along with the bad, without putting new labor standards protections in place. They agreed that sex-based hour laws needed to be amended so that women did not have to choose between time and money or opportunity and protection. Yet how to translate these sentiments into public policy was *not* readily apparent in 1961, nor was it clear whether the group could cohere if forced to choose between these competing needs.

Added to these fissures were new strains. The group of labor women now gathered around Peterson had bonded in the 1930s and 1940s not just on the basis of their gender beliefs but also on the basis of their class solidarity. They had built the labor movement in their youth and saw it, despite its many flaws, as the best institutional vehicle for their social reform aspirations. Their loyalty to it and to what it stood for was not in question.

Yet the labor movement frustrated even as it inspired. As the 1960s dawned, many among this group of aging loyalists found increasing occasion to criticize the current union institutions and the men leading them. With their own years in the movement lengthening, women found that the "glass ceiling" blocking their advancement into the top decision-making positions within the AFL-CIO was becoming all too apparent. While the new AFL-CIO adopted elements of the more progressive CIO political agenda, the personnel policies toward women at the new Federation appeared worse, not better. Kitty Ellickson, now working in the AFL-CIO Washington headquarters, remembered her shock at being in an institutional culture less hospitable to women than the one she had left in the CIO. She warned her close friend Esther Peterson about this new, less woman-friendly climate at the AFL-CIO when Peterson interviewed for a job there in 1958. Other ALF-CIO women advised Peterson not to "let them undercut you" in salary negotiations. Both warnings proved prophetic. Eventually, Jim Carey, the secretary-treasurer of the Industrial Union Department of the AFL-CIO, agreed to pay Peterson a fair salary but only after Peterson's protests.

> When we discussed the terms of my employment, Carey asked me to accept a salary that was $2,000 less than that of the man who held the job before, even though the job was identical. He had the audacity to say, "Oh, Esther, you don't need the money. Oliver has a good job." I was appalled. I asked, "Is that the way you negotiate for all your people in the union?"[45]

Labor women's expectations for change were rising, and none more so than those of black women. Black trade unionists were increasingly critical of the AFL-CIO leadership and its policies on race in the 1950s. A few months before the testy public confrontation between A. Philip Randolph and George Meany at the 1959 AFL-CIO convention over the Federation's policy on racially segregated locals, seventy black union leaders met "to consider the problems confronting the 1,500,000 Negroes who are members of Organized Labor." In May 1960, they held the founding convention of a new national organization of black unionists, the Negro American Labor Council. The NALC operated as a pressure group within the labor movement, but it also linked itself to a black separatist tradition, one that rejected the paternalism of white liberals and argued for the need for black leadership on black problems.[46] A year later, women trade unionists began discussing similar actions.

"TAKE TO THE HILLS MEN. THE DAM HAS BUSTED"

The first national inter-union women's conference, held in June 1961, reflected a new, more tumultuous relationship between labor women and the established

male leadership. AFL-CIO women leaders had been pushing for a national
AFL-CIO women's conference since at least 1958. They never succeeded in
convincing the AFL-CIO to sponsor the event, but in early 1961, they finally
won backing from the Industrial Union Department (IUD). Led by Walter Reuther and Jim Carey, the IUD had been set up after the merger as a national
department within the Federation to represent the interests of the former CIO
unions. It also operated as an independent power base within the federation
for the Reutherite perspective on social and international affairs, one that emphasized state regulation and liberal internationalism.[47]

In a letter to IUD affiliates in April, Reuther and Carey characterized the
"central theme" of the conference as "how can women best contribute to the
growth and security of our IUD unions."[48] A conference planning committee,
consisting of Caroline Davis, Gloria Johnson, Sylvia Gottlieb, Evelyn Dubrow,
and others had, however, decided to pursue quite a different theme: "The Problems of Working Women." With the backing of Peterson, Ellickson, Dorothy
Haener from the UAW Women's Department, and Julia Maietta, an old friend
of Peterson's from the ACWA, all of whom offered "encouragement" and other
"special services," the committee moved ahead, energized by the response it
was receiving from the field.[49]

The conference theme hit home. Some 175 women from 21 different international unions gathered at the Mayflower Hotel in Washington for the three-day
affair. It was a remarkable national event.[50] The conference delegates laid out
in a systematic and straightforward way the issues that concerned them as
women and as workers. Uncannily prescient, these would be the issues that,
one by one, would become the subject of public policy debate over the course
of the next two decades. Of equal importance, the conference revealed a new
and growing alienation of women from their male union brothers, one that if
not addressed, would surely fester, crippling the social movement upon which
labor women so depended.

The political agenda of the assembled women delegates came through most
clearly when the conference broke into four discussion groups. What emerged,
duly recorded, transcribed, and published by the IUD, was both a culmination
of the feminism simmering since the 1940s and a harbinger of the shocks that
were to come.

The first group, led by Caroline Davis, focused on women's "Economic Problems: Job Opportunities" and what unions could do. The group reached "complete agreement" on a number of remedies for the discrimination women faced
in hiring, promotion, and wages. They wanted "no discrimination because of
sex, age, or marital status" language included in collective bargaining
agreements and in regulations for government contracts. They also wanted
"model maternity leave clauses in our contracts with guarantees for retaining
job rights, sick leave benefits, and disability insurance under state law." They
"of course" favored "equal pay for equal or comparable work" and urged
"greater benefits and job protection for part-time workers." Not all remedies,
however, were universally applicable, the group found. Separate seniority lists

for men and women might "result in wide discrimination against women" in some industries, while in others, combining such lists would cause "many women to lose their jobs."[51]

Discussion Group 2 on "Legislative Problems: Protective Legislation," facilitated by Gloria Johnson, chose to deal "largely with federal action, and action by the AFL-CIO, that would eventually sift down to the local level." They stressed the need for federal standards rather than local, and urged the revision of "outdated laws where this can be done without sacrificing basic protections." Their proposals for federal legislation forecast with amazing accuracy what was to unfold in the next decade. They recommended a federal law guaranteeing equal pay for equal work, an amendment to "the recent presidential order [prohibiting race discrimination] on government contracts to prohibit discrimination because of sex," and a new fair employment practices law prohibiting sex discrimination in the private sector. They also urged "support of the AFL-CIO recommendation to extend the minimum wage to the millions of women in service occupations—particularly in restaurant, laundry and hotel industries, and to agricultural and domestic workers not now covered." Eligibility for unemployment compensation during pregnancy was raised as another type of protective legislation "which should be discussed," but the group ran out of time. Following this group's recommendations, the entire conference discussed how these objectives could be achieved. The delegates settled on two mechanisms: the Women's Activities Division of COPE and the Labor Advisory Committee of the U.S. Women's Bureau.[52]

Group 3 on "Social Problems: The Working Mother" recommended increased government funding for child care centers and for "extra-curricular activities at public schools." They also urged changes in tax policies: a higher ceiling on the deductions allowed for child care costs and raising the present personal tax exemption of $600 to at least $800 or $1000. Group 4 on "Living Standards" reiterated many of the ideas already on the floor, noting the need for raising the minimum wage, extending FLSA coverage, and bargaining for maternity leave, equal pay, and a guaranteed annual wage.[53]

A new angry tone infused much of the conference. As the *IUD Bulletin* observed, "during the question and answer period delegates made it clear that while the working woman faces discrimination in industry, neither does she have equal rights within the labor movement."[54] The plenary speakers who struck these same chords resonated best with the crowd. Conference delegates sat stone-faced through much of Walter Reuther's keynote but cheered and clapped as social critic and acclaimed lecturer Agnes Meyer turned her barbs against labor's male establishment. Agnes Meyer's background differed dramatically from many of those in the audience. Raised in a wealthy Republican family, she had married Eugene Meyer, a government official under Hoover who eventually became the publisher of the *Washington Post*, before embarking on a career as a journalist. As a young college student, Meyer had imbibed John Dewey's pragmatist philosophy, his cooperative social democratic message, and his skepticism of top-down solutions, all of which gave her respect for working

Fig. 6.4 Noted journalist Agnes Meyer fields questions after her keynote address entitled, "A Call for Modern Liberalism," to the first national union women's conference
in 1961. Caroline Davis stands next to her. Credit: George Meany Memorial Archives.

people and the voluntary institutions they had created.[55] Her feminist sentiments helped her bridge the class gap as well.

"It weakens our democracy not only economically but morally when we make
distinctions in our treatment of labor either on the basis of sex or color," she
began. Then the bomb dropped. "Union leadership is, indeed, not without blame
for this injustice. Grateful as I am to our labor leaders for their magnificent contributions to the nation's progress and welfare, I feel that theirs is the *most exclusive
masculine world left on the American scene.*" She concluded that "something
radical" must be done "to wake up this country to the problems of the woman
worker." She recommended three crucial interventions. First, the female-dominated occupations—teachers, clericals, and women in the retail trades—must
organize. Second, women must be elected to high union positions. And, third,
given the "solidarity between women members of unions" revealed at this conference, "it might be valuable to have a *women's labor movement* without cutting
off your affiliation with your separate unions that now have male leadership."[56]

ACWA vice president Bessie Hillman spoke just as bluntly. "I have a great
bone to pick with the organized labor movement in this country," she began.
"In my opinion they are the greatest offenders as far as discrimination against
women is concerned." To back up her accusation, Hillman pointed to the all-

male AFL-CIO Executive Council and the dearth of women on national union executive boards. She ended on a rather contradictory note, however, telling women to go back to their unions and "assert yourself by being worthy and by standing up to all the tests in the labor movement—and then you're going to be recognized."[57]

Meyer's and Hillman's caustic comments met with enthusiastic applause from the largely female audience. A *Washington Star* reporter captured a different mood among the male delegates. After sitting through the impassioned remarks of the plenary speakers, Jacob Clayman, administrative director of the IUD, was heard to mutter to the few other beleaguered male attendees, "Take to the hills, men. The dam has busted."[58]

In 1961, Clayman's prediction was premature. Though the waters were rising, the dam had not yet given way. It would take some years before the flood he feared would sweep through the labor movement, upending deeply rooted practices and rearranging much in its path. Yet labor women had clearly sounded a challenge to the male leaders of their movement and to society at large. It was a challenge that later would be echoed by women in the civil rights movement and the student New Left. It also would spur the transformation of federal policy over the course of the next two decades.

THE TRANSFORMATION BEGINS: THE PRESIDENT'S COMMISSION

The first breakthroughs during these years occurred in government, not union, policy. During the three years of the Kennedy presidency, Congress did indeed consider many of "the problems of working women" that the AFL-CIO women had so forcefully articulated. Although the remedies that emerged from these debates would leave much to be desired, labor women believed a slumbering giant was awakening, and they were right.

Within two months after Kennedy's inaugural speech in January 1961, Peterson had met with trade union women to discuss reviving the commission idea and had convinced a small committee of labor women, including Helen Berthelot, Dollie Robinson, and Kitty Ellickson, to begin drafting a proposal.[59] What emerged from these discussions closely resembled what labor women had proposed in the 1940s. The commission's primary purpose would be to end "unfair discrimination against women." It would take a broad approach, examining the employment status of women as well as their political and civic accomplishments. Its policy recommendations would be flexible and pragmatic, evaluating legislation and employer practices on a case-by-case basis. As public policy, a single categorical intervention like the ERA, it was agreed, left much to be desired.[60]

Peterson proposed the President's Commission on the Status of Women to Goldberg in June. It would "help women move to full partnership and genuine equality of opportunity," she wrote in justification, and would "substitute constructive recommendation for the futile agitation about the ERA." The commission would make suggestions on "adopting protective laws to changing conditions," on "new and expanded services required for women as workers, wives, and mothers," and other topics.[61] Having secured Goldberg's blessing for the commission, Peterson now convinced Ellickson to take a leave from her job at the AFL-CIO and devote herself full-time to the commission.[62] Ellickson agreed, and in consultation with Peterson, Goldberg, trade union women, and Women's Bureau staff, she prepared a background paper detailing the rationale for the commission.[63]

In it, Ellickson foregrounds the conflict between home and employment, especially for working mothers, largely reiterating her analysis of the 1940s. Women, she begins, desire "a warm, secure home *and* a satisfying job." Yet these are difficult to achieve given the "prevailing institutions and work practices largely shaped by and for men" and the realities of motherhood that involve "special needs and responsibilities." She calls on the government to address women's dilemma as a *social* problem rather than leaving it to be borne by individual women in individual families. But she is also careful to put these policies in a context that respects individual rights and freedom of choice. "Women, like men," Ellickson reminds her audience, "have the right to life, liberty, and the pursuit of happiness. Each makes her own decisions on dividing her energies among her family, earning a living, and other pursuits."[64]

Peterson and Ellickson agreed on the need to address women's problems broadly and pragmatically. The commission, they believed, needed to advance the well-being of "both housewives and workers."[65] To secure these ends, Ellickson emphasized the necessity of changing employment norms and practices much as she had in the 1940s when she wrote about the need for a shorter workweek and negotiated it for herself at the CIO. Such structural changes in employment, she believed, would help women better combine their multiple commitments. Peterson was more enamored with the Swedish approach to women's double day: government-run agencies where women could hire well-trained and well-paid "mother substitutes" or "homewatchers."[66] She returned often to the need for reorganizing housework, upgrading labor standards for household employees, and securing increased government support for household services.

In early December, Secretary of Labor Goldberg wrote President Kennedy to secure his support for the commission, relying on language drawn almost word for word from Ellickson's draft proposal.[67] Kennedy agreed, signing Executive Order 10980 establishing the President's Commission on the Status of Women (PCSW) on December 14, 1961.[68] Eleanor Roosevelt agreed to serve as chair, Peterson acted as executive vice-chair, and Ellickson as the commission's executive secretary, coordinating its work. Peterson appointed 26 commissioners (11 men and 15 women) and involved dozens of others in committee and consultation assignments. She drew on many of her labor friends, and she reached out to business executives, government officials, community leaders, and academics. On the commission itself sat IUE Executive Board member

Fig. 6.5 Left to right: Katherine Ellickson, Eleanor Roosevelt, and Esther Peterson attend a press conference announcing the appointment of Ellickson as executive secretary of the President's Commission on the Status of Women, January 1962. Credit: Archives of Labor and Urban Affairs, Wayne State University.

Mary Callahan, AFL-CIO Secretary-Treasurer William Schnitzler, NCNW President Dorothy Height, Congresswoman Edith Green, Radcliffe College President Mary Bunting, Senator Maurine Neuberger, Attorney General Robert Kennedy, Princeton economics professor Richard Lester, historian Caroline F. Ware, and others. The technical committees advising the commission had a similar mix of appointees, including trade union women Caroline Davis, Addie Wyatt, and Bessie Hillman.[69]

Kennedy's executive order establishing the commission charged it with developing recommendations "for overcoming discriminations in government and private employment on the basis of sex" *and* "for services which will enable women to continue their role as wives and mothers while making a maximum contribution to the world around them."[70] Some, including perhaps Kennedy himself, hoped that the commission would allow women to fulfill new duties in the market without altering women's traditional family roles or changing what Frieda Miller had identified in the 1940s as the "masculine pattern" of employment. Yet this interpretation of the PCSW mandate was not what had inspired the labor women who proposed the commission, nor would it be the tone of the commission report when it finally emerged some two years later.

"Hold the Huzzahs, Girls"

The commission was one of many proposals Peterson pursued in 1961, and it provoked the least opposition. In contrast, Peterson's advocacy of government funding for child care found few, if any, Congressional allies. Labor women, among the foremost advocates of government-supported day care services in the 1940s and the early 1950s, were now hopeful of finally realizing their agenda, in part because of growing support from middle-class women reformers. The Children's Bureau had changed its attitude toward government day care after its 1958 survey of the nation's day care needs demonstrated the inadequacy of community-based day care. Several groups, including labor, social service agencies, and children's advocacy organizations, now coalesced to press for passage of the Day Care Assistance Act (S1286), introduced by Senator Javits on March 5, 1959. The bill authorized millions of dollars of federal funding for child care services, available to *all* working mothers.[71]

In testifying for the bill, Peterson, then still a lobbyist for the IUD, argued for child care services "available without regard to the motives of the consumer," in part because child care, in her view, benefited children as well as their mothers.[72] Her perspective did not prevail. Universally available day care was still seen by many as a threat to the traditional family and as a poor substitute for "mother-love." When a much-revised Javits Bill finally passed on July 25, 1962, it was a pale imitation of the universal benefit Peterson and others had envisioned. Limited funds were authorized, and *only* low-income women had access to them. Moreover, in sociologist Jill Quadagno's opinion, many in Congress signed onto the bill in the hopes of "putting stay-at-home welfare mothers to work" rather than "helping mothers already in the labor force." Nevertheless, the 1962 Javits Bill was the *first* appropriation of federal funds for day care since World War II; it was also the first such appropriation *not* in wartime or economic crisis.[73]

Labor women met equally formidable opposition in their efforts to pass improved wage standards. Amendments to the FLSA had been thwarted repeatedly since its passage in 1938, principally by an alliance of Southerners fearful of altering the racial order, and conservative Republicans protective of class privilege and the right of business to manage free of government intrusion. Overlaying these concerns were gendered notions of who deserved a "living wage" and anxiety about maintaining women's primary commitment to the home.[74] Nevertheless, during the first year of Kennedy's presidency, Secretary of Labor Goldberg and others in the administration put labor standards on the front burner, looking largely to the AFL-CIO for help.

The resulting legislation raised wage minimums to $1.25 an hour and for the *first* time since 1938 expanded *coverage* statutorily. Some 3.6 million workers gained federal wage and hour protection, including employees of large retail and service enterprises, most of whom were women and minority men. The amendments chipped away at the older restricted definition of which industries and which workers deserved federal government protection. Still, many non-white and female workers were unprotected either by federal or state statute. Employees of laundries, hotels, restaurants, hospitals, and other small retail and service enterprises fell outside the law; so did agricultural and domestic workers. It was these workers, numbering at least 17 million, whom labor feminists were determined to cover in the next set of amendments. The momentum, they felt, was on their side.[75]

No one among the labor women advising Esther Peterson denied the importance of the labor standards struggle. Still, for many, the campaign for equal pay was what inspired the greatest passion. It had occupied a central place in their economic agenda since at least World War II, and now, finally, after the passage of some twenty state equal pay laws, the possibility of a breakthrough on the federal level seemed at hand.[76]

In January 1961, Oregon congresswoman Edith Green introduced an Equal Pay Bill, and in March, at a meeting in Esther Peterson's office, representatives from the National Committee for Equal Pay (NCEP), the AFL-CIO, and various labor unions agreed that the bill, with "certain modifications," was acceptable. The group praised the Green bill for its use of language specifying equal pay for "work of comparable character." Their recommendations for modification included expanding the bill's coverage and revising the administrative mechanism for enforcement.[77] Notwithstanding this unusual show of unified support from equal pay proponents, Green's bill failed to gather steam, and by the summer, the AFL-CIO's George Riley was admonishing Secretary of Labor Goldberg not to let equal pay legislation "yield to other activities. We will have to drive our stakes and stand firmly for enactment in the foreseeable future if we are to have the legislation."[78]

The fight resumed in 1962 with delegations of union women descending on Washington to lobby their representatives and the usual array of labor and women's organizations defending the bill in committee hearings.[79] Caroline Davis's 1962 testimony was particularly eloquent, pointing to the "immorality of discrimination on the basis of sex" and the necessity for governmental regulation because voluntary organizations like her union, the UAW, could not solve the problem alone.[80] In 1962, and again in 1963, equal pay advocates stressed the degree to which equal pay made moral and economic sense: it was about ending a "rank injustice against women" and ensuring that "all Americans" were "first class economic and political citizens." As consumers, women paid the same prices as men for food and rent; on the job they also created "value" equal to men. Equal pay would stimulate the economy, boost morale and productivity, and protect the wage rates of both men and women, they argued.[81]

Advocates for passage remained firmly committed to comparability language. The bill itself required "equal wage rates for work of comparable character on jobs the performance of which requires comparable skills." Representative Herbert Zelenko, chair of the House hearings, speaking for the bill's proponents, defined equal pay as setting a "rate for the job without regard to sex—

Fig 6.6 The 1962 UAW delegation to Washington lobbying for the passage of the Equal Pay for Equal Work Bill. Dorothy Haener is second from the left; Caroline Davis is third from left. Credit: Archives of Labor and Urban Affairs, Wayne State University.

in the factory, in the school, in the office, in the store, and in all other places where men and women perform work of comparable character."[82]

Proponents believed that comparability language was necessary so that a *broad* range of women's jobs could be *reevaluated*, new rates set for the jobs, and pay raised. A majority of employers now relied on job evaluation specialists who specified a wage "rate for the job," but that didn't solve the problem. As Peterson pointed out, what was important was ensuring that these rates were set without sexual bias or regard for the sex of the worker. As Arthur Goldberg put it, behind the rate differential between men and women is "the false concept that a woman intrinsically deserves less money than a man. This outmoded concept, rooted in a psychological downgrading of women's skills, [is] false."[83]

NAM, the U.S. Chamber of Commerce, and other business representatives opposed the legislation. The "market will correct any inequities," they claimed; furthermore, the proposed bill was "unnecessary government intrusion" and would add costs to business.[84] Some employers defended their sex-based pay practices and complained of job loss for men: "We pay male secretaries more because there was the possible potential of their rising to more important jobs. If the law passes, we'll have to hire only women."[85] Others claimed to support the *principle* of equal pay, but offered amendments that, in the eyes of many, would damage the bill beyond repair. Business lobbyists repeatedly tried to limit the impact of the law by substituting the words "identical" or "equal" for "comparable" in the text of the bill and by inserting voluntary and private enforcement mechanisms for government regulation. The legislative representative of the National Federation of Business and Professional Women's Clubs portrayed government oversight as insulting and maternalistic. "I personally feel that if some woman feels she is being discriminated against by her employer in the rate of pay, then she should have the courage to stand on her own two feet and make the complaint. I don't think she should expect somebody to come in and play nursemaid for her."[86]

In 1962, those opposing a strong equal pay bill included women politicians as well as lobbyists, and their notions of gender equality proved crucial in determining the final shape of the bill. The defining moment occurred in the House debate. Katherine St. George, the Republican congresswoman from New York and a long-time advocate of the ERA, rose to amend the Equal Pay Bill, proposing to strike out "for work of comparable character" and substitute "for equal work." To St. George, differences between men and women, social or anatomical, were irrelevant. The path to equality lay through "equal treatment," and women could *only* lay claim to first-class citizenship based on being the same as men. As St. George explained, "Equal implies no difference . . . what we really want is equality. We do not want favors."[87]

Congressman Zelenko objected. "Equal may mean exactly alike," he cautioned, and the comparability language, standard since the National War Labor Board (NWLB) rulings of World War II, permitted "a reasonable and practical appraisal of two jobs to determine whether they have enough like characteristics and skill demands to warrant the same basic pay rate." But St. George countered that the NWLB was "rather old hat." Moreover, using "comparable" requires "making this differential which is the one thing I am not particularly anxious to see. You are going back to that good old adage that women are so weak and delicate that they need protection."[88] Others jumped into the fray at this point, including Democrat Edith Green of Oregon and Republican Catherine Dean May of Washington. For a few rare moments, unusual in congressional debates, the conversation became an exchange dominated by women. In the end, the majority sided with St. George, despite Zelenko's final plea: "If you put in the word 'equal' we will have no equal pay bill at all." St. George's amendment passed 138 to 104.[89]

The Equal Pay Bill, now with St. George's amendment, emerged from the House, and a similar one passed the Senate. Congress adjourned, however, before the two bodies could agree on a final version. The issue was rejoined in 1963, with the 1962 bill reintroduced with the St. George amendment intact. Congresswoman Florence Dwyer of New Jersey and others tried to offer alternative bills but to no avail.[90] Even the February 1963 unanimous endorsement by the President's Commission of the need for federal legislation implementing "equal pay for comparable work" made little difference.[91] Peterson later ruefully recalled, "We believed we had the votes to win equal pay for comparable worth but we lost."[92]

Additional amendments weakened the bill further. In the House hearings in 1963, Congresswoman Green called the bill a "bare minimum," regretting the concessions "we were forced to make." She later reminisced in a letter to Kitty Ellickson about those concessions: "I remember so vividly the fight for Equal Pay for Equal Work. We had to accept an amendment exempting women in administrative, executive, and professional positions. Otherwise, we could not get enough votes to get it out of [NJ Congressman] Frank Thompson's sub-committee. And I believe you—or some one on the Commission [PCSW] told me of Frank's filing system for Equal Pay Legislation: 'B' for Broads."[93]

Despite these setbacks, equal pay advocates reluctantly ended up endorsing the 1963 bill, agreeing with the NCEP's assessment that "while not exactly what was wanted [it] is better than nothing since it does establish a law that can possibly be improved later." Many also believed that although the St. George amendment was unfortunate, the government agency administering the law, the Wage and Hour Division of the Department of Labor, could partially counteract her amendment by issuing broad interpretations of the legislation in its regulations.[94]

In 1963, who the law would affect and in what way was not a foregone conclusion. Some predicted the law would cover a broad range of women's jobs and help change "the custom of not putting the same economic value on the work of women as on the work of men."[95] Others saw the bill as limited in its reach, but a "first step," one that might result eventually in many new training and promotional opportunities.[96] When asked her professional opinion of the scope of the bill in April 1963, Anne Draper of the Research Department of the AFL-CIO came down squarely in the middle. It would "probably almost never" call for a "comparison of the extreme type" such as comparing plant drill press operator and business office stenographer. Plant and office jobs, after all, come under different classification systems. "But neither would the bill restrict comparison only to the 'same' kind of work. If so," she concluded, "it would be totally ineffective in reaching the discriminatory job rating systems" such as exist in many plants "where women's jobs are slotted at the lowest labor grades."[97]

The AFL-CIO sought to send the bill to conference to get clarification on "what constitutes wage discrimination based on sex," since many Republican members of the House Labor Committee "left little doubt" that their interpretation was that there was "not very much that any employer needs to worry about." But such a conference never took place.[98] The Equal Pay Act passed the House on May 23, 1963, and the Senate concurred a few days later. The eighteen-year fight culminated in a signing ceremony in the president's office on June 10, 1963 with Mary Anderson, Esther Peterson, Frances Perkins, Caroline Davis, and others in attendance.[99]

In the aftermath of the campaign, many supporters defended the bill as firmly establishing "the [equal pay] principal as law," and as "the first step in a broad campaign." The *Wall Street Journal* cautioned, however, to "hold the huzzahs, girls": the Department of Labor interpretations of the law were a long way off; equal pay could mean job loss for women; and, as an amendment to the FLSA, most women managers and professionals fell outside its reach.[100] At its June meeting, the NCEP, recognizing some of these same problems, turned its attention to how the Wage and Hour Division would define "equal" and to lobbying for the "extension of the FLSA which would mean wider coverage of the EPA." Over the next year or so, the NCEP kept close watch over the Wage and Hour Division of the U.S. Labor Department, sponsoring a conference with them in June of 1964 to mark the date the EPA took effect, for example, and repeatedly calling for the broadest possible interpretation of what constituted sex-based wage discrimination. By the end of 1965, however, the committee was losing momentum, discouraged by the narrow interpretation of the EPA language and its members preoccupied, at least for the time being, by other more pressing issues.[101]

In hindsight, the Equal Pay Act must be judged both a victory and a defeat. As Peterson explained in her 1995 memoir: "It was one of our first victories and it was an important victory, even though it wasn't as strong a measure as we would have liked."[102] In its defense, it was the first federal law explicitly addressing the issue of discrimination on the basis of sex. Although the law failed to end sex bias in wage-setting in the jobs held by the *majority* of women, it did ultimately raise wage rates and secure back pay awards for those millions of women in situations where they were doing work deemed "substantially equal" to men.[103]

Yet the passage of the bill turned out to have consequences far different from those its supporters hoped or predicted. Eventually the EPA coverage included administrative and other high-level women, but the 1962 St. George amendment limiting the *definition* of wage discrimination held firm. The debate over "equal pay" may have stirred new ideas among many women workers, but it also hardened the long-standing divisions among women reformers. Equal pay supporters were furious with their old adversaries in the NWP. "The issue of comparable worth was hard fought at the time and the predominantly Republican women who supported the ERA in 1960 were not with us. They had a part in our losing the comparable worth provisions," Peterson explained. "I had no regard for some of these women," she told another interviewer, "They supported the equal rights amendment but not the equal pay bill."[104]

In an ironic twist of fate, the passage of the Equal Pay Act helped undermine the very movement toward comparable pay that had inspired it. After their long, grueling battle to pass an "equal pay for comparable work" bill, labor feminists ended up settling for an "equal pay for equal work" bill that, once the dust settled, furthered the goals of their opponents as much as their own. "It really wrecked us," Peterson admitted later. Coalitions like the NCEP lost steam, and the act itself and its subsequent conservative interpretation stymied efforts to revalue "women's work" and undermine gender bias in wage setting in women's jobs. Since the law inscribed and validated the idea that women deserved "equality," but *only* when they held "men's jobs," the drive to enter men's jobs took on greater urgency, since other routes to higher pay were now foreclosed.

Further, although some advocates of equal pay resisted linking wage setting too closely to "work performed," the final bill and the administrative interpretations that followed hewed closely to the notion that a "rate for the job" should reflect the worker's *individual* effort and productivity. Shortly after the act's passage, the U.S. Women's Bureau, now directed by Mary Dublin Keysling, worked with Department of Labor officials to devise a new kind of family wage policy, one compatible with equal pay. When the draft regulations appeared explaining that employers could set higher wages for "family breadwinners," Beatrice McConnell, deputy director of the Women's Bureau, complained because the term suggested "heads-of-households" and "the majority of 'heads of households' are men." New language stating that being "a parent" might justify a wage differential was briefly considered. But the old "head of household" phrases kept stubbornly reappearing. In exasperation, Keyserling objected once again to the phrase: "It suggests a means-test approach" which is "entirely foreign to our previous American thinking." The matter ended there, with the older notion of household dislodged as a unit, and individual wage earning enshrined.[105]

"The Art of the Possible"

With the battle over equal pay winding down, many labor women fastened their hopes on the release of the final report from the President's Commission on the Status of Women. The twenty-six members of the commission, after their first meeting in the White House on February 12, 1962, had spent a year and a half deliberating. Under the guidance of Peterson and Ellickson, they had waded through technical reports from seven appointed committees and held four consultations, including one on the "Problems of Negro Women," before reaching agreement on a final document in October 1963.[106] At what was to be one of his last public presentations, President Kennedy released the commission's report, *American Women*, at a White House ceremony the first week of November. It quickly became a best-seller, with 64,000 copies distributed the first year and a commercial version issued soon after.[107]

Later characterized by Peterson as an exercise in "the art of the possible," the report's recommendations provoked criticism when first released and continue to remain controversial.[108] Yet set in the context of its time, it was a far-reaching document that sought a balance between opportunity and protection for men and women and, in historian Judith Sealander words, repudiated "the Progressive canonization of motherhood."[109] Although it ended up concluding that constitutional changes such as the ERA "need not now be sought,"[110] it

Fig 6.7 Fulfilling a goal long sought by labor feminists, Esther Peterson presents President Kennedy with the PCSW report. Mary Callahan of the IUE is standing on Peterson's right, looking at the President. Credit: Schlesinger Library, Radcliffe Institute, Harvard University.

roundly condemned sex discrimination and offered a concrete set of recommendations aimed at achieving gender equality.

American Women reflected many of the assumptions of Peterson, Ellickson, and the labor feminists gathered around them. It assumed that there were problems women faced *because* they were women, a view not widely shared at the time. Its primary challenge, however, was *not* to the gender *division* of labor but to the secondary status of women, both at home and in the market. Taking its cue from Ellickson, it assumed that women desired self-realization in a multitude of ways, carefully acknowledging that "women work in home and out for income and self-fulfillment."[111] Its aim was dual: to open up opportunities for women in the market realm *and* to enhance women's satisfaction in non-market endeavors. The report held that these changes, "long overdue," would not come about without societal and government action.[112] The problems women faced were structural and social, not private or individual. "Full equality of rights" had been denied women: employers, unions, and the government had an obligation to rectify that situation.[113]

Ironically, the few contemporary commentators that took the report seriously—much of the popular media treatment was "humorous, condescending or tinged with sexual undertones,"[114]—often saw it as undermining the very behavior some later critics claimed it reinforced.[115] By affirming women's right to employment, contemporaries worried that the PCSW report encouraged women to abandon their home responsibilities. Even anthropologist Margaret Mead complained about the commission's emphasis on "the value of employment," although for a different reason than most. She shared the commission's assumptions that "the *right* to work at a paid job is an intrinsic condition of human dignity" and that "everyone should have the same rights and opportunities as privileged white males." But she upbraided the report for not fully facing the incompatibility between women's caregiving roles and the pursuit of a high-powered career.[116]

The PCSW, however, was optimistic that the long list of concrete interventions they urged to help reconcile market work and family life would make a difference. The commission sought greater respect for women's non-market work and "more attention to the services needed for home and community life." Recommendations also included income guarantees for pregnant and unemployed women, child care services for women "whether they were working outside the home or not," better tax policies for families raising children, and changes in the social security system that would allow housewives to build up equity as if they were earning wages. The system of paid household labor needed "re-organization" to improve training opportunities, wages, and working conditions for those employed. Lastly, training opportunities and job readiness programs should be redesigned to better suit women's different career and work patterns.[117]

Some of the PCSW proposals concerning sex discrimination received attention even before the report was released. The commission's desire for a presidential directive banning sex discrimination in hiring, promotion, and training in federal civil service, for example, was taken up by Kennedy soon after the commission began its deliberations.[118] The commission's advocacy of federal and state equal pay laws embodying the principle of equal pay for comparable work, as we have seen, met an early defeat. But most of its proposals awaited a public hearing.

The commission appealed, for example, for an executive order fostering "equal opportunity for women" among employers with federal contracts, some one-third of large companies. This order would parallel JFK's March 1961 Executive Order 10925 instituting voluntary affirmative action and equal opportunity among federal contractors in regard to race, creed, color, and national origin, but would be *separate* from it. Also recommended were new *voluntary* practices among all employers in the private sector to reduce sex discrimination in hiring and promotion and create new training and educational opportunities designed with women's lives in mind.[119]

On these issues and others, there was dissent. Some objected to government involvement of any sort in business decisions and were clearly uncomfortable with setting up even voluntary affirmative action goals. Others like Caroline Davis felt that the commission had been *too easy* on employers.[120] She and other labor women chafed at the commission's reluctance to recommend government regulation in the private sector and its willingness to allow "voluntary" compliance among federal contractors.[121] Caroline Davis also submitted the lone dissenting opinion to the commission's recommendation of a *separate* "equal opportunity for women" executive order. Instead, reflecting the sentiments of many labor women at the 1961 AFL-CIO national conference, she favored adding sex to the *already existing* 1961 executive order. The commission's rationale for a separate law was that "discrimination based on sex involves problems sufficiently different from discrimination based on other factors to make separate treatment preferable." Sex discrimination was different because, unlike other forms of discrimination, not all sex-based differential treatment constituted unjustified discrimination against women. Davis and others, however, believed that all forms of discrimination were essentially alike and should be linked in public policy. The UAW Women's Department had been making this argument at least as early as 1951, when it recommended adding sex to President Truman's antidiscrimination regulations for government contractors.[122]

Finally, the old issue of sex-based state protective laws reared its head. Some commissioners had hoped for a statement supporting the passage of the ERA as a way of addressing sex discrimination at work, but the majority felt otherwise. They believed that the sex-based state laws should be retained until they could be amended on a case-by-case basis. Many sex-based protective statutes were "obsolete," they agreed, but others provided important benefits to the millions of women who, excluded from the FLSA, relied solely on state laws for wage and hour protection. "I'm for eliminating [the laws] which are only a ruse to keep women from improving their economic status," Mary Callahan explained in 1961 in her union newspaper, but "I'm for retaining those which are definitely protective."[123]

One of the most difficult problems for the commission, it turned out, was not stopping the ERA or agreeing that protective laws needed amending, but finding a consensus on the shape the *new* protective laws would take, particularly hour laws. The PCSW's Committee on Protective Labor Legislation, which included Addie Wyatt, Bessie Hillman, Mary Dublin Keyserling, and Mary Callahan, agreed that sex-based statutes regulating weight lifting, health and safety, setting minimum wages, and discouraging night work and long hours should be made "more flexible" and "applicable to both men and women." Minimum job protections are the "labor essentials of an economic bill of rights," and extending the state laws to men would benefit women, they reasoned. Women's opportunities for employment would increase, and "adequate protection for all workers means more adequate protection for working women. In addition, failure to protect men wage-earners inevitably affects the status of women as wives."[124]

Yet how to devise new hour laws was not immediately apparent. Forty-three states and the District of Columbia currently had woman-only hour laws that covered the majority of women and set a maximum limit on work time. These laws, the committee felt, adversely affected "the opportunities of women for employment" because men had no such limitations, and in the few cases where women potentially fell under FLSA coverage, state laws kept them from receiving overtime. Yet state laws offered better protection against long hours than did the FLSA. The FLSA approach to limiting hours was, in their minds, an inadequate check on employer power and on the competitive market's relentless drive toward longer hours. The FLSA used the disincentive of premium pay for overtime to discourage long hours, but it did not forbid them.

In response, the committee proposed new federal *and* state hour laws that would apply to both men and women. FLSA coverage would be extended so that all workers would receive overtime pay after forty hours. Yet the maximum hour provisions of the state laws would be retained, extended to men, and exemptions for professionals and executives added. In their view, men needed the right not to work just as did women. The FLSA was "a complement not an alternative to maximum hour limitations."[125] The women's standard should not be sacrificed in the process of modernization; rather, the best of both should be preserved.

The commission agreed with the committee in that it too thought the woman-only state maximum hour laws should be "maintained, strengthened, and expanded" until other provisions were in place. There was a consensus that the laws benefited women, particularly mothers, and contributed "to the strengthening of family life and to the general welfare of the nation." But the commission *rejected* the committee's proposal that the maximum hour laws (the female model of hour regulation) be extended to men. Instead, they favored relying *only* on the FLSA model and extending it to all workers. The "best way to discourage excessive hours for all workers," they concluded," is by requiring overtime of at least time and a half" after 40 hours.[126]

In part, this debate was about how to design a policy that took into account class differences among women. Many wage-earning women welcomed limits on employer demands for more work; others, including many professional women, controlled their own work hours and saw work as self-expression, not drudgery. Premium pay proposals ignored the needs of many wage-earning women; maximum hour laws failed to recognize the reality of white-collar and professional work. Thus, neither the committee nor the commission found a work time policy that sufficiently addressed the realities of the diverse interests of women.[127]

Gender differences, both assumed and manifest, proved just as troubling. On the one hand, the commission challenged aspects of the masculine mystique: it argued that men too needed "protection" and that many of the state laws for women should be extended to men. In so doing it was unmasking the myth of male power in the marketplace, that is, the assumption that men, unlike women, did not need protection from market forces. Yet it balked at extending maximum hour laws to men, in part because no one challenged the masculine mystique in the home—the assumption that men, unlike women, had only a limited capacity to nurture and that their nature prevented them from taking a greater role in the home. Nor did anyone argue that men ought to have more domestic duties and that limiting men's work time would open up that possibility.[128] Such a wholesale assault on notions of masculinity was not yet possible. While the commission's proposals to extend many of the state protective laws to men had the potential to begin a redefinition of masculinity, they were fragile shoots that, as we shall see, were easily trampled. Even today, though the masculine mystique has come under scrutiny in the private sphere, it has so far remained invincible in the market.

On November 22, 1963, only a few weeks after the White House ceremony announcing the Commission Report, President Kennedy was assassinated in Texas, throwing the administration into the crisis of transition and dashing labor women's hopes that the proposed recommendations would get timely and careful scrutiny. The Civil Rights Bill, however, already occupying center stage politically, was now finally positioned for congressional passage. The suffocating grip of the Southern Democrats and conservative Republicans was about to be loosened.

RACE AND GENDER: AN OLD DILEMMA REVISITED

Labor women, especially African-American labor women such as Addie Wyatt, Maida Springer-Kemp, and Dorothy Lowther Robinson, had been leading campaigns to end race discrimination since the early 1940s. By the late 1950s, they and others had helped make civil rights a priority for the labor organizations and women's networks of which they were a part. After the merger in 1955, for example, the new AFL-CIO adopted much of the CIO's legislative agenda on race. It pledged to "promote and defend the civil rights of all Americans," calling for fair employment practices laws, nondiscrimination clauses in union contracts, the integration of public facilities, and the end of barriers to African-American participation in politics.[129] It also became one of the most powerful and consistent supporters of the Civil Rights Act.[130]

Esther Peterson insisted that race and civil rights be part of the women's reform efforts she led in the early 1960s. Early in her tenure at the Women's Bureau, Peterson established a "Special Projects Branch" to examine the low-income occupations dominated by African-American women and ensure their inclusion in wage legislation.[131] She reached out to Dorothy Height of the NCNW, the organization founded in 1935 by Mary McLeod Bethune as "the voice of Negro womanhood." A long-time friend and political ally of Peterson, Height had taken the reins of NCNW leadership in 1958 and helped return the organization to national prominence by shifting its focus toward civil rights and community economic development. The NCNW had long supported social feminist goals such as increasing job security and opportunity for women, equal pay and labor standards for women's jobs, and blocking the passage of the ERA.[132] Peterson appointed Height to the President's Commission on the Status of Women, and in 1962, Height helped Peterson set up a consultation on the

"Problems of Negro Women" as part of the PCSW deliberations. For Ellickson, the consultation was "memorable." The commissioners, she recalled some years laster, were stunned; many had never heard "such graphic accounts of the realities for black Americans."[133]

Soon after, two hundred "leaders of women's organizations" came to the White House at Peterson's behest to inaugurate a "National Women's Committee for Civil Rights." Height and Peterson worked together on this committee, as did leaders of the AFL-CIO Women's Auxiliaries and many other labor groups, all pledged to help implement "the President's civil rights program."[134] Later, Height and Peterson would join forces once again on the National Committee for Household Employment (NCHE), which originated at a Women's Bureau Conference held in June 1964 to improve the status and working conditions of private household workers.[135] For Peterson, the NCHE was the culmination of decades of writing and speaking on the concerns of low-wage workers and the need to value women's household labor, paid and unpaid. In 1950, for example, Peterson had authored a report arguing that Sweden's domestic labor law, which established wage and hour standards for domestic workers, could serve as a model for upgrading the working conditions of U.S. domestics.[136]

When Mary Dublin Keyserling replaced Peterson as head of the Women's Bureau in 1964, leaving the nonprofit economic research institute where she worked with her husband, she continued the emphasis on low-income women and on African-American women in particular.[137] As a college student Dublin had pursued an interest in economics, winning a fellowship to the Geneva School for International Studies in 1929. Once in Geneva, she immersed herself in the study of the British labor movement and learned Keynesian economics from John Maynard Keynes himself. She never forgot his lessons, insisting throughout her life that increasing labor's purchasing power was essential to a healthy economy.[138] Once confirmed as head of the Women's Bureau, Keyserling laid out a program that gave priority to extending labor standards to low-wage workers and securing government income supports for childbearing and child rearing. Keyserling's themes echoed those of her friends and colleagues in the labor movement, yet they also bore her own particular stamp. Her concerns extended beyond the ranks of union members to poor and unorganized women, allowing her to form strong ties with civil rights organizations and groups working to end female poverty.

Keyserling threw herself into the battle for the Civil Rights Act, as did Esther Peterson and other labor women, little realizing that its passage would undermine key elements of their own program for women's equality. In the wake of Kennedy's assassination, the Civil Rights Bill made rapid strides in both houses in early 1964, encountering few surprises. On February 8, however, Howard Smith, the influential Southern conservative from Virginia and long-time advocate of the ERA, introduced an amendment that threw the liberal camp, particularly the women within it, into turmoil. Smith proposed to add "sex" to Title VII of the Civil Rights Act, making it illegal to discriminate on the basis of sex as well as on the basis of race, ethnicity, religion, and national origin.[139] Although

Smith reiterated how "serious" he was about doing "some good" for the "minority sex," he mocked the very idea of women's rights by a dramatic reading of a letter showing "how some of the ladies feel about discrimination." The letter complained of the imbalance between the numbers of males and females in the general population, which denied "the right of every female to have a husband of her own."[140]

Those who had encouraged Smith's amendment to the Civil Rights Act had a variety of reasons, not all benevolent. Working either alone or in consultation with Emma Guffey Miller, Alice Paul "hatched the idea" and suggested that two of her "lieutenants" write Smith, a long-time friend of the NWP and a sponsor of the ERA since 1945, asking him to introduce the sex amendment. It is possible that Paul and others were sympathetic to the Civil Rights Bill and did not think the amendment would jeopardize its passage. It is also possible that they saw the defeat of the Civil Rights Bill as a risk worth taking if it helped promote the passage of the ERA. Introducing the sex amendment would allow their supporters to make the case for ending *all* sex-based discrimination and would help counter the arguments made against ERA passage in the recent PCSW's report.

Nonetheless, some within the NWP clearly hoped the amendment would delay if not derail the passage of the Civil Rights Act, a bill they objected to because it promoted government regulation and because they favored the racial status quo. Butler Franklin, one of the two NWP lieutenants who proposed the amendment to Smith, wrote in her letter: "This single word 'sex' would divert some of the high pressure which is being used to force this Bill through without proper attention to all the effects of it." The other NWP lieutenant proposing the amendment, Nina Horton Avery, had long been active in Southern segregationist politics, as had Howard Smith.[141] In January 8, 1964, she wrote Smith explaining that adding sex to the Civil Rights Bill (CRB) was "from the standpoint of the NWP . . . merely a tool of strategy to take the pressure off the passage of any CRB." Thank God for members of Congress, she concluded, "who will use their brains and energies to prevent a mongrel race in the US and who will fight for the rights of white citizens in order that discrimination against them may be stopped."[142]

In the debate on the House floor over the amendment, proponents of the sex amendment, even those sympathetic to the overall bill, relied unashamedly on race prejudice to boost their position. Former NWP member and Democratic congresswoman from Michigan Martha Griffiths, who was closely associated with originating the sex amendment and in all likelihood would have introduced it had not Smith moved first, spoke strongly in favor of its passage. "I feel as a white woman," she began, "that when this bill has passed this House and the Senate and has been signed by the President that white women will be last at the hiring gate." Her speech closed with a final racial appeal: "a vote against this amendment today by a white man is a vote against his wife, or his widow, or his daughter, or his sister."[143] Midway through the debate, Catherine Dean May read a letter from NWP Chair Miller expressing alarm that without "any reference to civil rights for women" in this bill, the "white native-born American women of Christian religion" would be "discriminated against."[144] Male congressmen from Alabama, South Carolina, and Arkansas now joined in, reinforcing the idea that the bill, left as is, put white women at a disadvantage relative to colored women. Without the Smith amendment, a white woman "would be drastically discriminated against in favor of a Negro woman," one proclaimed. Indeed, explained another, Title VII offered "preferential rights" to colored women.[145]

The only woman who spoke against the amendment was Edith Green, veteran Democratic congresswoman from Oregon and perpetual sponsor of equal pay legislation. She opposed the amendment not out of opposition to women's rights but because she believed it would "be used to help destroy the bill." Indeed, she had been prepared to introduce her own sex amendment had not the administration interceded, convincing her of the Civil Rights Act's vulnerability.[146] Green feared (rightly as it turned out) that "After I leave the floor today, I shall be called an 'uncle Tom'—or perhaps an 'aunt Jane,' but I do not believe this is the time or place for this amendment." As a "white woman" she had "been discriminated against," but "the Negro woman has suffered ten times that amount of discrimination." She concluded: "if I have to wait a few years to end this discrimination against me, [I am willing] if the rank discrimination against Negroes will be finally ended."[147]

When the vote on the "sex amendment" was called in the House, most of the support came from Southern Democrats and Republicans. Most liberal Democrats opposed it, fearful of the consequences for the passage of the overall bill. But once it passed (by a vote of 168 to 133), Democrats dropped their opposition, not wanting to jeopardize the bill by opening it up to further amendments. And many who had spoken on behalf of the sex provision ended up voting against final passage of the amended Civil Rights Act.[148]

Like most liberal Democrats, Esther Peterson and many other labor feminists initially argued against adding the "sex amendment." It "took us somewhat by surprise," Peterson recalled. The "primary" fear was that "the addition of the new provision would defeat the bill. I for one was not willing to risk advancing the rights of all women at the expense of the redress due black men and women."[149] For labor feminists, ending discrimination on the basis of sex did not *always* have priority over other injustices. As Congresswoman Green made clear, at least in 1964, securing a law banning race discrimination took precedence over legislation banning sex discrimination. In addition, many labor feminists feared that the Civil Rights Act, like the ERA, might jeopardize woman-only state laws. As Peterson put it, she and her cohorts feared that "some worthwhile state laws would be eliminated without being replaced by laws covering both sexes."[150] Finally, for many, race and sex discrimination were different phenomenon, and the best public policy would treat them as such. Sex, unlike race, was not *only* a cultural category. Because of that difference, reasonable distinctions on the basis of sex were much more imaginable than on the basis of race.

Despite continuing concerns about its impact on gender policy, once the Civil Rights Bill cleared the House, labor feminists lobbied for the sex amendment's retention, largely because they accepted the administration's position that it was best not to open the bill up for debate.[151] And as with the Equal Pay Act, some comforted themselves with the hope that the law would be interpreted in their favor—that is, that Title VII (the section forbidding employment discrimination) would be judged as not in conflict with sex-based state laws. Only a few, like Caroline Davis, welcomed Title VII as a means of opening up job and earning opportunities for women and agreed with its equation of race and sex discrimination.

What passed largely unnoticed, late in the debate in the Senate proceedings, was the addition of an amendment by Utah Senator Wallace Foster Bennett, which allowed employers to *continue* to *differentiate* in the payment of wages on the basis of sex if so allowed under the Equal Pay Act.[152] This amendment would prove crucial in limiting women's ability to challenge sex-based *wage* discrimination, since it tied the definition of wage discrimination to the narrow "equal pay" language of the Equal Pay Act. Title VII thus had strong language guaranteeing women's hiring and promotion rights, but much weaker language on wage discrimination. Like the Equal Pay Act, it too structured the possibilities of gender reform, offering greater support for women to compete for men's jobs than to transform female-majority jobs.

For the time being, however, other matters took priority. Title VII did not become effective until the summer of 1965. Even then it would be a long time before government agencies and courts would offer their interpretations of its scope and meaning. In the interim, the Voting Rights Act of 1965 passed, and labor feminists were confident that their efforts to democratize economic citizenship through labor standards legislation would finally come to fruition as well. Little did they realize that the FLSA campaign would be the last to call upon their unified efforts for some time.

FLSA COVERAGE FOR THE MAJORITY

In July of 1965, a week after Title VII took effect, the outlook for securing congressional reconsideration of the "divided citizenship" inscribed into the FLSA coverage looked promising.[153] Support for the Democratic Party program was at a high-water mark after Kennedy's assassination, and sympathy for ending the persistent poverty of minority communities was cresting. For those who had supported the Equal Pay Act and applauded the PCSW's recommendations, expanding the FLSA was the crucial next move. The EPA, as an amendment to the FLSA, had the same limited coverage as the FLSA. Broadening the FLSA was thus the logical next step in the equal pay campaign.[154] As the President's Commission noted, expanding FLSA coverage was urgent because of the growing restiveness with sex-based state labor standards.

The AFL-CIO, which had made FLSA extension one of its top priorities in the 1966 Congress, proposed sweeping changes, including a $2.00 hourly minimum, a statutory workweek of 35 hours with double pay for overtime, and the extension of coverage to the "full extent of Federal prerogative." As estimated by Andrew Biemiller, the former Wisconsin congressman who now directed the AFL-CIO's Legislative Department, this latter proposal would bring 5.4 million additional workers under the FLSA. Employees of hotels, motels, restaurants, laundries, and hospitals would be protected, as would agricultural workers on large farms.[155] The administration's proposals were somewhat less radical but generally along the same lines.

Much of the testimony put the proposals in the context of the "war on poverty," characterizing the amendments as "antipoverty legislation" and as a way of attacking "the poverty of the employed." Nevertheless, there was a new sensitivity to the "whole problem of inequalities of one kind of another," including the historical exclusion of women.[156] Secretary of Labor Willard Wirtz, who replaced Arthur Goldberg after President Kennedy appointed Goldberg to the Supreme Court, expressed this sentiment explicitly. "Under the glare of the Civil Rights Act," he began, with its "establishment of equal opportunity as a broad national policy," the FLSA exclusions assumed a greater prominence. Previously, "we had not looked to see how many of the covered workers are women or nonwhite. Somehow those seemed like improper questions. We have learned the hard way, however, that this apparent objectivity has tended not to insure equal treatment but to camouflage unequal treatment."[157]

When the bill passed in 1966, it was a major triumph for the civil rights movement as well as the labor and women's movement. For the first time, the federal statute included the majority of women and minorities. Agricultural workers were covered, as well as the bulk of retail and service workers. Following the FLSA model, many of the states extended the coverage of their laws as well. Estimates vary, but the more careful ones conclude that after the 1966 amendments, some 44 million workers, or 84 percent of the private sector nonsupervisory workforce, were covered by labor standards legislation.[158] The two and a half million domestic workers were the only major occupational group still wholly outside the federal law. This extension of labor standards legislation to the majority of women and minorities *before* the rise of second-wave feminism was a significant achievement and one that resulted primarily from a coalition of labor and civil rights groups.[159]

CONCLUSION

In the early 1960s, the postwar movement for women's equality mounted by labor women appeared to be gaining ground. Their long-standing goal of a President's Commission on the Status of Women had become a reality, marking the first governmental acknowledgment of federal responsibility to working women. Its report, released in 1963, reflected much of the labor feminist agenda, and it sparked the beginnings of a public debate over women's unequal status and what government could do about it.[160] Federal laws now provided government funding for child care services to poor women and established equal pay for equal work. Such policies, it was hoped, would be openings for further improvements. The struggles for fair employment legislation and for expanding labor standards coverage had achieved an even greater measure of success. The New Deal was finally being redefined and extended to nonwhites and women.

Of course, there were tensions among labor women and between labor men and women. But for the time being, they were under control, reigned in by a commitment to the larger class-based vision of economic security and justice for working people. Labor women reformers continued to believe in the agenda they had articulated in the 1940s, and of equal importance, they continued to agree on how to achieve their goals. Few if any realized that their leadership of the women's movement was in jeopardy and that the alliances they had built with each other and with men in the labor and civil rights movement were soon to unravel. Bruised from battle, they were still confident that the partial victories won were the beginning of a more fundamental rethinking of social policy. In that last prediction they were correct, but not in the way they had planned.

CHAPTER SEVEN

The Torch Passes

NOW is a new voice of the 46 percent of American adult women who now work outside the home. The voice of women who wish no special privileges or protections, but wish full equality in truly equal partnership with men. The voice of women who have no interest in serving tea at "ladies auxiliaries" but who aspire instead to service in the mainstream of America's political, professional, and economic life."

—*Betty Friedan and Kathryn F. Clarenbach, for NOW, April 9, 1967*[1]

Equality for some women should not entail misery for others. The woman executive who wants to work long hours is a far cry from the average working woman, for whom compulsory overtime can be both backbreaking and home wrecking. The woman who must choose between neglecting her home and family by working excessive overtime or quitting her job to go on welfare is certainly not "free" in any real sense of the word. It is such a choice the proponents of the so-called ERA will be obliging many of the lower paid women workers, who they so facetiously refer to as "sisters," to make.

—*Myra Wolfgang*[2]

IN 1968, THE Women's International Terrorist Conspiracy from Hell, better known as WITCH, helped disrupt the Miss America Pageant in Atlantic City, New Jersey. Along with some 200 other women activists, they picketed along the boardwalk and at one point crowned a live sheep Miss America to protest the judging of women like livestock at a county fair. They also stuffed bras, girdles, high-heeled shoes, and other articles of women's clothing into a "freedom trash can."[3] This act captured the media's imagination and subsequently was seared into the public mind as an iconic image of the new feminist movement of the 1960s. Although it's unclear whether bras were ever actually burned, the label "bra-burner" stuck. The bra as a symbol of women's oppression communicated what was so new about this movement: it was not only about civil and economic rights but also about the most personal and intimate kinds of psychological and bodily bondage.

Three thousand miles away in California and three years later, labor women also relied upon bras to make a political point. This event, however, was as far removed in its emphasis from the Atlantic City protest as it was in geographical distance. Anne Draper, ACWA's West Coast Union Label Coordinator, stood in front of the California Industrial Welfare Commission, the state body setting policy on labor standards, testifying on behalf of raising the minimum wage for women and extending it to all workers. Outside, over a hundred demonstrators milled around, including a large contingent of farmworkers. The current minimum wage was "shockingly low," Draper maintained before the commissioners, "with no provision for the costs of children." "This poverty wage, the so-called 'Minnie budget' [after 'Minnie, the minimum wage worker,' a recurring character in a newspaper column by Joyce Maupin, Draper's fellow activist] should be thrown into the garbage can."[4] To enliven her testimony, Draper held up a tattered bra purchased from Woolworth's for $1.19, the amount allowed in the state budget cost-of-living calculations. The bra had fallen apart after three washings.[5] In Draper's universe, the bra was the ugly undergarment of poverty, hidden beneath the government's minimum wage rhetoric.

Although the Woolworth's bra never achieved the fame of the bras that supposedly went up in smoke in the "freedom trash can," both were an integral part of the new feminist movement that arose in the late 1960s and early 1970s. The history of what is now called second wave feminism is still very much in process, but the extraordinary variety and vitality of the movement is clear. In the late 1960s and early 1970s, sex-specific job ads disappeared from newspapers, as did many of the male-only editorial staffs. Landmark lawsuits such as those against AT&T and US Steel attacked inequitable wages and the segregation of jobs by race and sex. Ideas and practices long thought to be natural and hence invulnerable to change came under scrutiny. It was a "world split open," in Ruth Rosen's apt phrase, and a new feminist sensibility emerged.[6] The new feminism resembled its predecessor at the most fundamental level: it too sought to end women's secondary status and to inaugurate a new day of equality and freedom. But, like the feminism it sought to replace, it too was both appropriate to its times and limited by them.

In late 1965, three years before the Atlantic City protests, the labor feminist network that had arisen at the end of World War II was still intact. Yet within months, it would begin breaking apart, its members unable to agree on either goals or tactics. Strained by continuing disputes over sex-based labor laws, Title VII of the Civil Rights Act, and the ERA, the threads of consensus binding labor feminists together finally snapped. Some like Caroline Davis and Dorothy Haener joined with Betty Friedan to found NOW. Others like Myra Wolfgang resisted the new feminism's goals, fiercely disputing its assumptions about women's desires and how to fulfill them. Still others like Esther Peterson and Kitty Ellickson tried to steer a middle course, identifying as neither friend nor foe of the new feminism.

Many of the postwar generation of labor feminists, now in their sixties and seventies, remained politically active into the late 1970s and beyond. Esther

Peterson, Kitty Ellickson, Addie Wyatt, and Gloria Johnson, for example, continued to lecture, write, lobby, and organize. Others, however, began to retire by the 1970s, and some would die prematurely. Caroline Davis, for example, suffered the loss of her mother and husband in 1973 and then stepped down as director of the UAW Women's Department in 1975. Soon thereafter, she withdrew almost wholly from public life due to ill health and complications following surgery.[7] Cancer struck down ACWA's Anne Draper at age 56 in 1973 and Myra Wolfgang at age 61 in 1976.[8]

A generation was passing from leadership, but the political impulse it embodied persisted. By the early 1970s, many of the notions labor feminists championed were now commonplace: the right to wage work for all women, the unfairness of discrimination based on race or sex, and the idea of wage rates set by the job, not by the sex of the worker. Other aspects of their reform agenda, particularly those aimed at reducing class injustices in women's lives or securing the social rights necessary for full citizenship, fared less well. Nonetheless, this unfinished agenda was never far from consciousness, even as a new generation of labor women reinvented labor feminism for their time and place.

LABOR WOMEN, TITLE VII, AND THE FOUNDING OF NOW

With the extension of federal labor standards imminent at the end of 1965, labor feminists turned their thoughts to other legislative initiatives. Women's Bureau chief Mary Keyserling's legislative plans for 1965 gave priority to amending the FLSA but listed other goals as well: improved equal pay laws, government-sponsored child care, and paid maternity benefits through a nationwide temporary disability insurance program.[9] Yet the coalition among Southern Democrats and conservative Republicans held strong in the late 1960s as it had earlier, frustrating left-liberal efforts, including those of labor feminists to end wage discrimination or pass social supports for pregnancy and child rearing. The GOP gained forty-seven seats in the House and four in the Senate in 1966, defeating Illinois Senator Paul Douglas and other labor supporters.[10] The looming crisis over sex-based laws demanded the attention of labor women as well. Once again, state labor standards were in jeopardy, threatened this time by Title VII of the Civil Rights Act.

Few government officials knew what to make of the odd sex discrimination prohibition that had made its way into the Civil Rights Act. Even Franklin Delano Roosevelt, Jr., who in 1965 became the first commissioner of the Equal Employment Opportunity Commission (EEOC), the government agency charged with enforcing the law, sidestepped the question. When asked at one of his first press conferences about the sex provision, he offered only that "the whole issue" was "terribly complicated." The *Wall Street Journal* simply dubbed the amendment a "fluke," and expected it to be ignored. The *New York Times* ridiculed the idea of opening jobs to applicants regardless of sex, referring to it as "the bunny problem." Surely Congress had not meant for

men to become Playboy bunnies, the editorial reasoned. It would be "revolution, chaos."[11]

In contrast, many women took the new prohibition on sex-based employment
discrimination quite seriously. Within its first year of operation, the agency was
inundated with claims of sex discrimination, often from working-class and union
women citing unfairness on the basis of sex and marital status in wages, job
assignment, fringe benefits, and layoffs. Women in the UAW sued under Title
VII, as did women in meatpacking, steel, and other industries.[12] Unionized
women, unlike other women workers, were often emboldened to file EEOC
charges in part because the union protected them from retaliation by employers. Filing a union grievance was not that different from filing an EEOC complaint, and in many unionized workplaces, a peer culture supported the notion
that all workers should be treated fairly and that they had the right and even
the obligation to complain of arbitrary and discriminatory treatment.

A second group of women was paying close attention to the new law as well.
Women from all walks of life had read the PCSW report, finding its delineation
of unfair treatment all too familiar and all too enraging. State commissions on
the status of women had been authorized by President Kennedy in 1962 to
update the PCSW recommendations, and by 1965, pressure from women had
resulted in the establishment of these state watchdogs across the country.[13]
Labor women were active in the state commissions and served on the national
Citizens' Advisory Council on the Status of Women, set up under President
Johnson to extend the work of the PCSW, but business and professional women
dominated in terms of numbers and policy.[14] As one Women's Bureau regional
director explained, "Even when wage-earning women were appointed they
often didn't serve because they couldn't get their lost time from their jobs paid
for or their travel costs to the cities where the commissions met."[15] The commissions ended up being particularly interested in issues of hiring and promotion,
and many reached the conclusion that an aggressive enforcement of Title VII,
even one that jeopardized sex-based state labor laws, was necessary.[16]

Leading labor feminists added their voices to those condemning sex discrimination in hiring and promotion, and they criticized public officials, including
those in the EEOC, for their inaction. In a 1965 talk, "Looking Ahead: Title
VII and EEO," Women's Bureau director Mary Keyserling stressed that "far
too many occupations today are regarded as either a 'man's job' or a 'woman's
job' without any justification. If equality of opportunity is to be assured, these
sex labels, with very few exceptions, must disappear." According to her,
"women had a great stake" in how the EEOC interpreted the "bona fide occupational qualification" (BFOQ) exception in Title VII which allowed employers
to hire only one sex for a job if they could show that *only* that sex could perform
the job. Like many other feminists, she feared that the EEOC would interpret
the BFOQ exception broadly, thus ensuring that large numbers of employers
would continue the sex labeling of jobs.[17]

Nonetheless, many labor feminists, including Keyserling, hesitated to urge
EEOC action that might result in the loss of labor standards. Labor feminists

had long ago reached the conclusion that some sex-based laws discriminated against women and should be either amended or repealed. Yet one of the core tenets of postwar labor feminism had been that because *some* sex-based statutes benefited large numbers of women, the laws needed to be preserved until they could be amended.[18] In late 1965 and 1966, that consensus came under increasing pressure. Amending the laws one by one appeared to be a painstakingly slow process, and after the FLSA amendments passed in 1966, fewer women were relying solely on state law for protection.[19] Still, state laws provided the *only* protection for millions of women, and in many cases state statutes offered *additional* protections to those mandated by federal law. Forty-five states had *maximum* daily and/or weekly hour laws for women, for example, and numerous sex-based state laws existed that provided superior protection regarding rest and lunch breaks, seating, rest room facilities, weightlifting, and health and safety.[20] Most believed that these beneficial sex-based laws ultimately should be amended and applied to both sexes. But in the interim, they needed to be retained. That meant the EEOC needed to move cautiously if at all.

Initially, the EEOC sided with the status quo, issuing guidelines in late 1965 advising employers that refusing to hire women due to sex-based labor laws would not necessarily violate Title VII.[21] As FDR, Jr. wrote Frieda Miller in December 1965, "we don't assume that Congress intended to strike down all state laws."[22] But the following April, the EEOC changed its mind and decided to hear cases alleging that state laws violated Title VII. Social feminists and labor women protested. Writing to the EEOC chair in July 1966 on behalf of a coalition comprised of the IUE, the ACWA, the NCL, the YWCA, the AAUW, and others, NCNW's Dorothy Height urged retention of the state labor standards until the laws could be improved and extended to all workers.[23] Keyserling, lobbyists from the AFL-CIO, and others made the same point in hearings before the EEOC that summer.[24] Yet in a move that outraged many of their labor sisters, UAW feminists Caroline Davis and Dorothy Haener disagreed with the coalition's position, and they aired their views publicly. They testified at the EEOC hearings and urged the EEOC to move decisively *against* discriminatory sex-based state laws.[25]

This defection by the UAW was not, however, the only or even the most shocking.[26] Earlier, galled by the EEOC's vacillation on whether or not to allow help-wanted newspaper ads to identify jobs as male or female (racial preferences could no longer be mentioned), they had convinced the UAW convention to go on record in favor of the EEOC's full compliance with the law. A month later, when the Third National Conference of Commissions on the Status of Women rolled around—a meeting called by the Department of Labor to share information about the activities of the state commissions—they were still boiling. In the ensuing acrimony that erupted over Title VII, they lined up against the majority of their longtime labor allies, taking the side of the professional women from the state commissions, including Betty Friedan, already famous as the author of the 1963 bestseller, *The Feminine Mystique*.

Chairing the conference, Keyserling kept a firm hand on the proceedings from the podium, frustrating those in the audience who wanted a fuller debate over the Johnson administration's EEOC policy. Keyserling, Peterson, and others were looking for a way of preserving the beneficial state laws. They also wanted to avoid a public attack on the policy of government officials in a Democratic administration. But that night a group of women jammed into Betty Friedan's hotel room, including lawyer and civil rights activist Pauli Murray, Caroline Davis, Dorothy Haener, and Catherine Conroy, CWA official and Wisconsin Commission on the Status of Women (CSW) member. They quickly concurred that the conference should pass a strong resolution denouncing the EEOC for its inaction on Title VII enforcement and demanding that it treat sex discrimination as seriously as race discrimination. When Wisconsin CSW Chair Kathryn Clarenbach proposed such a resolution the next morning, Keyserling ruled it and another resolution in support of the ERA out of order. The dissenters then gathered at a table during lunch and, under the nose of the luncheon speaker, formulated their plans for "an NAACP for women," a concept, Dorothy Haener remembered, that she had first heard discussed by Dollie Lowther Robinson. An active member of the Women's Bureau LAC inner circle during her stint as education director for the Laundry Worker Division of ACWA, Robinson had been recruited by Peterson to work at the Women's Bureau in the early 1960s. She had raised the idea with Haener after a talk she had given at a Milwaukee conference earlier in the year.[27]

The organization the dissidents formed, NOW, held its first formal meeting in October 1966, electing Betty Friedan as its president.[28] NOW called for, among other goals, "equal participation and treatment of women in employment, education, and government," including aggressive enforcement of Title VII and the addition of a sex provision to President Johnson's 1965 Executive Order 11246 prohibiting race and other forms of discrimination among federal contractors. Labor women took on top leadership roles in the fledgling organization. Caroline Davis was NOW's first secretary-treasurer. Dorothy Haener sat on the executive board, and Catherine Conroy, now working for the CWA in Chicago, founded the Chicago chapter of NOW and became its first president.[29] In addition, the UAW bowed to pressure from its women leaders and offered NOW office space and administrative support during its crucial first year.

A number of labor women withdrew their membership in late 1967 when NOW endorsed the ERA, many later to rejoin, but they left NOW on solid footing. In 1967, President Johnson, feeling pressure from NOW, heeded the advice of Esther Peterson and the Women's Bureau and added sex to his 1965 ban on discrimination by federal contractors, a goal long sought by the UAW and the subject of Davis's dissent to the PCSW report.[30] The EEOC also changed its 1966 policy on help-wanted advertising, and, in part due to NOW's prodding, began to apply the principles used in race and national origin discrimination cases to the problem of sex. NOW's visibility soared and its membership grew steadily, reflecting the new feminism's appeal.[31] Women also began participating in a dizzying array of other feminist activities. On college campuses and in communities across the country, women started the first "consciousness-raising" groups to rethink virtually every aspect of their lives and what it meant to be female. By 1968, the women's liberation movement was in full swing, with a growing contingent of self-proclaimed radical and socialist feminist groups in New York, Chicago, Boston, Washington, and elsewhere. A mass movement was underway.[32]

Those "Undesirable Relics of a Past Era"

More than likely, a majority of feminists of all stripes agreed with Esther Peterson when she wrote the EEOC chair in late 1967 reaffirming her position that the BFOQ exception not be used to allow employers such as the airlines to continue hiring only young, unmarried women.[33] Most feminists also concurred with many of the recommendations made by the 1968 Federal Task Force on Labor Standards, one of four task forces set up under the auspices of the Citizens' Advisory Council. The Task Force on Labor Standards urged the removal of night work and other restrictive laws and the extension to men of beneficial laws such as those setting higher minimum wages or requiring rest breaks.[34] But the problem remained of what to do until the laws could be changed. Over that issue, feminists divided, with the majority of labor and social feminists still believing that retaining the good state laws, particularly the hour laws, took priority over eliminating the outmoded ones.

At the 1967 EEOC hearings Mary Callahan spoke in favor of retaining some sex-based laws and against "a clean sweep." Kitty Ellickson agreed. Concerned about the conflict between long hours and "the proper care of children," she urged retention of the hour laws and condemned the so-called "voluntary overtime policy advocated by many professional and business women." Calling long hours "a disease not an opportunity," she claimed there was "no evidence that women generally prefer extended opportunity for overtime work to a clear hours limitation, though obviously a number do."[35] But the UAW's Dorothy Haener, representing NOW, called on the EEOC to move forward *immediately* against sex-based protective laws. Laws based on "real biological factors, such as maternity leaves, separate rest rooms, pregnancy and the like" were "compatible with Title VII" and not in danger. Those "based on stereotypes as to sex" such as hour laws were "undesirable," in conflict with Title VII, and should be repealed.[36]

Why did the UAW women and other labor feminists break with the majority? In part, their ideas reflected the nature of the industry with which they were connected. Women in heavy industry like auto or steel were more likely to be covered by federal law than women in low-paying women's jobs and hence were less concerned about the loss of state protections. Moreover, they were often in direct competition with men and daily experienced the disadvantages of protective laws that barred them from promotions and premium pay.[37] Dorothy Haener blamed the loss of her wartime inspector job on the hour laws. Management, she remembered, claimed that the reinstatement of the nine-hour law after the war prevented the hiring of women on jobs where ten-hour shifts might occur. Haener had never forgotten the adverse impact of this "protection" on her life and the lives of her coworkers.[38]

In 1968, the AFL-CIO's Anne Draper identified these labor market differences as a "significant factor" in the dissolving consensus among labor women. "Women working in industries dominated by men do find themselves at a disadvantage," but "removing minimum legal protections from women in 'women's industries' does nothing that I can see to improve their opportunities in competition with men." The segregation of women in these sectors, Draper thought, was not due to protective laws: "Women would be 'separate but not equal' with or without labor legislation. It is quite significant," she observed, "that the unions that have been most outspoken on maintaining existing protective legislation have been those in industries where large numbers and proportions of women are employed, for example, the ACWA, the ILGWU, the HERE, and the CWA."[39]

Although a labor market analysis like Draper's explains much, the reality was messier. Not all women in female-dominated workplaces judged "protection" as in their interest, nor did all women in heavy industry favor overturning the laws. Women often divided on these issues. Older women in particular expressed ambivalence about dismantling the sex segregation of jobs. Some valued job security over job opportunity and saw protective laws and the gender divide they reinforced as enhancing employment security. Others did not want access to male jobs. They saw their current jobs as preferable to what they perceived as the harder and more dangerous work performed by men. For some, the conviviality of all-female departments was among the most rewarding and pleasurable aspects of their employment. Moving into a male-dominated department meant the loss of that female work culture and the strain of survival in an unfamiliar and perhaps unfriendly emotional terrain.[40]

Thus, many women labor leaders in male-dominated industries continued to support sex-based practices despite the growing discomfort of *some* of their constituents, because *other* of their constituents saw the laws as benefiting them. To make matters more confusing, often both groups saw themselves as fighting for sexual equality and the end to sex discrimination. In 1968, for example, the UPWA Women's Committee censured the EEOC for its lack of attention to sex discrimination. At the same time, as Addie Wyatt explained, the EEOC needed to deal with "sex discrimination realistically." In our industry, she continued, that meant sometimes keeping sex-based seniority provisions to stem "the erosion of the jobs of female workers and preserve the employment rights and opportunities of women."[41]

Last but not least, some women leaders felt reluctant to push for repeal even when their own constituents favored it, because of their loyalty to "protecting" their low-paid sisters in other unions. Frieda Miller had pleaded with the UAW women at their first national women's conference in 1944 to consider those not as privileged as they, and for some twenty years that alliance across industry and occupation had held. Despite the disadvantages to their own members, retaining the laws was deemed important because of the benefits to *other* women. Shortly before the EEOC hearing in 1967, Kitty Ellickson wrote UAW leader Olga Madar, inviting her and others to talk "about possible ways of reconciling the desires of UAW members in regard to state labor standards legislation with those of persons less favorably situated." Her expressed fears of being "unduly optimistic about the possibility of compromise" turned out to be justified. The UAW women reached a different conclusion in 1967 than in 1944. Ending sex-based laws, they now believed, would benefit their own members *and* the majority of *other* women.[42]

One of the bitterest battles among labor feminists occurred over the repeal of Michigan's 54-hour law. Like many of the state battles fought over hour laws, it pitted unions representing female-dominated sectors against male-majority unions such as the UAW.[43] Myra Wolfgang led the charge to preserve the law. In 1963, after Kennedy signed the Equal Pay Act, Wolfgang had organized a dinner in honor Caroline Davis of the UAW and her work on behalf of pay equity. Now, four years later, as the organizer of the "Ad Hoc Committee Against Repeal of Protective Labor Legislation for Women Workers in Michigan," she was bent on derailing Davis's agenda. Many of the workers she represented, the largely female and minority service staff of hotels, restaurants, and motels, remained exempt from the premium pay provisions of the FLSA. Hence, they had nothing to gain from repealing the maximum hour law, she insisted, and much to lose. In a scathing letter to Representative James Del Rio, Wolfgang said: "I cannot understand how you can equate the possible return of the 12-hour, 7-day week for women with 'equality and equity' between the sexes. That kind of equality women neither need nor want." She continued: "If you are arriving at the conclusion that I 'want my cake and eat it too,' all I can say is 'you're right'. As long as women have to work for the ingredients, bake the cake, and dispense it, then they will figure out a way to have it and eat it."[44]

In the long run, Wolfgang wanted limitations on hours set for men and women, with overtime strictly voluntary. In the meantime, executive, administrative, and professional women could be exempted, she suggested, and a "right to petition for an exception" made available to others. Davis and other UAW feminists wanted hour protection for both sexes in the long run as well, but they felt that in the interim, economic opportunity for women should not be held hostage. In the 1950s, the UAW had chastised Caroline Davis for advising Ohio women to seek changes in their state's hour law, but now they backed her efforts, as did Congresswoman Martha Griffiths. UAW leaders were well aware of the increasing numbers of sex discrimination grievances and EEOC charges being filed and the growing clamor against state protective laws from below. Many agreed when UAW attorney Stephen Schlossberg urged the international to litigate a test case "all the way to the Supreme Court" if necessary and in the meantime work to repeal the state laws, those "undesirable relics of a past era."[45]

What the UAW Women's Department lacked in the late 1960s, however, was unanimity from UAW women. The "most concerted effort" to block repeal from within the UAW came from women at Chrysler's Hamtramck plant in UAW Local 3, a group renowned for their successful effort to integrate women into men's jobs in 1959 when 800 women had faced being laid off. Making what Nancy Gabin describes as "feminist and class arguments" on behalf of retaining hour laws, they reiterated the themes sounded by their allies in Wolfgang's committee. Without the hour laws, forced overtime would be widespread, creating havoc for women like Stephanie Prociuk, who later sued the state to stop repeal. Prociuk, a middle-aged single woman, was the sole support and nurse to her 81-year-old invalid father.[46]

Repealing the law, Local 3 women feared, would make it more difficult to pass *new* laws protecting both men and women from overwork. "How can we hope to realize our goal of a 30 hour week at 40 hours pay when we insist on repeal of the 54 hour limit in exchange for no limits—resulting in possibly 10 or 12 hour days, six to seven day weeks?" they asked. The laws limiting hours at least "offered a small measure of protection against inhuman work schedules." They recommended that limits on mandatory overtime for *all* workers be inscribed into legislation and bargained into UAW contracts, but until then, the sex-based laws should remain.[47]

UAW Local 3's recommendation for a ceiling on hours for all workers remained as controversial in 1968 as it had been five years earlier when the PCSW tackled the issue. The 1968 Citizens' Advisory Council on the Status of Women, like its predecessor, the PCSW, recommended *replacing* maximum hour laws with voluntary overtime and premium pay for both sexes.[48] Once again, some labor women objected, seeing these recommendations as inadequate. Anne Draper of the AFL-CIO, for example, a member of the Citizens' Advisory Council's Task Force on Labor Standards, formally dissented, pointing out that premium pay was "insufficient leverage against excessive hours" and that employers would make overtime "a condition of employment." Mary Callahan and historian Caroline Ware, also on the Task Force, favored stronger measures than existed under the FLSA as well, although they did not register formal dissents.[49] The old hour laws asked women to sacrifice money, but relying only on the FLSA would mean a sacrifice of time. Labor women sought a policy that would not require a trade-off between money and time; they wanted access to premium pay *and* access to lower hours. Or as Wolfgang put it: they wanted to have their cake and eat it too.

For this to happen, however, the belief that the work lives of men should look more like those of women needed to be more widespread. The AFL-CIO and many international unions were committed to ending "long hours" and "involuntary overtime," and to extending "where possible" the state hour laws to men. But neither they nor labor feminists argued that reducing hours was a useful way of encouraging men to spend more family time.[50] Labor feminists did not see household labor as exclusively women's responsibility, nor did they see the division of labor between men and women as an unchanging given. Keyserling observed, for example, that the second shift was "not yet equally shared," although men were "assuming more household duties." Still, their response to this inequality was not to change men but to change work structures and policy, in part because, as Wolfgang bluntly stated, men were not "prepared to assume a fair and equal share of domestic chores."[51]

In other words, in 1968 as in 1963, labor feminists did not mount an attack on the sexual division of labor in the home. Instead, they argued only that women needed help, men were not about to provide it, and so the state needed to act. No one should be compelled to work excessive overtime, Wolfgang declared, but for the working woman, to be forced to do so was a "disaster." Without hour laws, women would be working longer hours and "the average working mother will have little or no help at her second job at home, unjust as this may well be." The rising number of "divorced women, widowed mothers, abandoned wives, and unwed mothers" made protection urgent. Lastly, reversing the historic arguments on behalf of hour laws, Wolfgang warned that women would be forced to *leave* the labor force if the hour laws were repealed. It would "undermine our entire double breadwinner type of economy."[52] By the late 1960s, Wolfgang could justify the hour laws by claiming the breadwinner mantle for women but not yet the caregiving label for men.

Despite Wolfgang's efforts, the law was repealed—not only in Michigan, but also in many other states. On August 19, 1969, after numerous NOW-led demonstrations and lawsuits, and much media scrutiny, the EEOC finally issued an administrative guideline holding that state laws which "prohibit or limit" opportunity for women conflict with Title VII.[53] Subsequent federal court decisions underscored the EEOC reasoning, striking down specific laws and casting doubt on the constitutionality of any sex-based state laws. A few states rewrote their protective laws, extending many of the standards to men, but in the majority of cases, the hour laws were repealed. At least for the time being, the female model of work time was rejected for men and for women. Opportunities to enhance their income had been extended to women, but neither men nor women now enjoyed protections from overwork and involuntary overtime. It was the male standard in *wages and hours* under the FLSA that would be the policy for the future.[54]

How the ERA Became a Labor Demand

With protective laws now disappearing, some labor women hoped for an easing of tensions among feminists and even a regrouping of women labor leaders around a new politics of equal rights, equal opportunity, and support for the ERA. With only a few sex-based state laws remaining, the potential damage of an ERA seemed minimal.[55]

By the end of the 1960s, much else had changed as well. For some, the rising prosperity of the postwar decades and the blurring of class lines linked to lifestyle and culture had muted the old class antagonisms. A larger percent of women were now attending college, many even the daughters of the working class, and their expectations of what they deserved at work and what was possible for them as individuals was changing. Increasingly, women of all classes were feeling as distressed by the lack of economic *opportunity* as by the lack of economic *security*. As female wage-earning grew among the middle and elite classes and the numbers of female-headed families shot upward, a new generation of working women with different histories, class sensibilities, and family ties was emerging. Partly as a consequence of these changes, women of all ages, political affiliation, and marital status were beginning to endorse the ERA, making it difficult for its supporters to be characterized simply as a small bunch of aging, single, elite conservatives.[56]

Nonetheless, those hoping for an easing of tensions and a new politics had underestimated the tenacity of the opposition to the ERA. Before 1972, only a handful of labor women changed their position and embraced the ERA. At the 1970 UAW convention, labor women secured an ERA endorsement from the union, the first to do so. Olga Madar and other UAW women also testified in favor of the ERA in May 1970 before Congress.[57] "Rights not roses is the watchword for an increasing number of American women, and the UAW believes unequivocally and unreservedly that the ERA is essential," Madar began. Protective legislation was still needed, she pointed out, but "a new type of strategy" was now possible that would "get the whole loaf of bread rather than just a half loaf."[58] The American Federation of Teachers, the Newspaper Guild, and the International Brotherhood of Teamsters rounded out the short list of labor backers.[59] The Women's Bureau made the switch in 1970 as well under the leadership of Nixon-appointee Elizabeth (Libby) Koontz, an African-American who had taught public school in North Carolina for thirty years and served as a national officer of the National Education Association.[60]

In October 1971, Esther Peterson quietly changed her mind, writing in a letter to Representative Martha Griffiths that it pained her to break with her many friends who still held the opposite view. But few woman-only laws remain, Peterson reasoned, and "now I believe we should direct our efforts toward replacing discriminatory state laws with good labor standards that will protect both men and women." "History is moving in this direction," she added, and "women must move with it." Such a move, Peterson believed, "entails a shared responsibility of all citizens." She urged women like Griffiths "who have found changes in the laws to be to their advantage to make every effort to assist those who still may be exploited."[61]

Many labor feminists in 1970 and 1971, however, remained resolutely opposed. Fear of the impact of the ERA on labor laws persisted, as did lingering class resentments.[62] In the congressional wranglings over the ERA in 1970 and 1971, representatives from the ILGWU, HERE, CWA, IUE, ACWA and the NCL (represented by Kitty Ellickson) stood up to oppose the ERA in language uncannily unchanged from 1945. "The heart of the matter is really the hours limitations," began ACWA's president Potofsky. "Repealing the laws would discriminate against the many for a few." Potofsky's testimony reiterated the 1968 ACWA convention resolution that condemned the ERA as a campaign "led by organized business and professional women and supported by employer interests" that would bring "excessive hours" and end time off before and after child-birth.[63] Ruth Miller, ACWA's West Coast officer and the chair of California's Commission on the Status of Women called low-income women "the forgotten majority," and, like the AFL-CIO's Anne Draper, accused the women's movement of pursuing the interests of the middle class at the expense of the poor. Keyserling, Ellickson, and Wolfgang also testified against the amendment.[64]

As the ERA forces gathered momentum, the invective against the "middle-class women's movement" became shriller, especially from the AFL-CIO. Doris Hardesty, a former staff member of the AFL-CIO Department of Civil Rights, published an attack on "the ladies of the lib" in the January 1971 *American Federationist*. These women, mainly from "business and professional women's organizations and their new ally, N.O.W.," she explained, were the principal proponents of the ERA. Some of these women "scorn" those who are "happy in their roles as wives and mothers," branding them "as 'Aunt Toms' in the overblown rhetoric of the 'movement.' " Economic inequities between men and women existed, Hardesty concluded, but a constitutional amendment would not cure the problem. What was needed, in her view, were day care centers, strengthened antidiscrimination and equal pay laws, and enhanced labor standards for all workers, including domestics.[65]

Myra Wolfgang, too, made no bones of her disdain for the "equal righters" who supported the ERA. Her hostility sprang from multiple sources: a practical concern for her constituents, deep class resentments, and a rejection of the equal rights paradigm of the new feminism. "I speak for 'Tillie the Toiler,' " Wolfgang began her May 1970 Senate testimony. Discrimination against women exists, she insisted, but "the ERA is not the solution to the problem." For working-class women, the ERA would bring "an equality of mistreatment."[66] "Our opposition is fundamental," Wolfgang declared, repeating verbatim Peterson's 1960 statement before the Republican Platform Committee, which itself had echoed arguments made by Florence Kelley decades earlier. "The chief conflict between those who support the amendment and those who oppose it, is not whether women should or should not be discriminated against, but what constitutes a discrimination against women. We, who want equal opportunity and responsibility and equal status for women, know that it is frequently necessary to obtain real equality through a difference in treatment rather than an identity in treatment." She wound up her May testimony by accusing "the many feminists who contend that there are no real differences between men and women, other than those enforced by culture" of talking "nonsense." Remember, she concluded in her September statement, "We are different, and different does not mean deficient."[67]

Wolfgang resented women like Betty Friedan, whom she angrily described as a "middle class intellectual whose knowledge about real women's problems is as fictitious as her claim to represent the women of America." Friedan's testimony before the Senate had not endeared her to Wolfgang. On that occasion Friedan had conjured up the same insults that had been hurled at labor and labor women by NWP women in 1948. "I accuse the male labor establishment of gross neglect and blindness to the problems of working women," Friedan roared. She found the "Aunt Toms" who agree with them just as infuriating.[68] In October 1970, when Betty Friedan visited Detroit for a "Women's Teach-In" at Wayne State University and trotted out her "Aunt Tom" label once again, Wolfgang returned the insult. "Look who's calling who an Aunt Tom," Wolfgang retorted, "she's the real Aunt Tom, the Chamber of Commerce's Aunt Tom. Anyone who tries to have repealed women's protective legislative . . . is doing the bosses' work and the real women of America know it."[69]

A few months later, Wolfgang took aim at the new women's movement more generally in an address before the AAUW. "I disagree with the approach that calls for the unity of women under the nebulous slogan that 'Sisterhood is Powerful." With a nod to Rudyard Kipling, she continued, "The Colonel's Lady and Judy O'Grady may be sisters under the skin but their lives, concerns, and needs are radically different. Class conflict influences conduct in our society more than does race or sex distinctions." Those supporting the ERA, she predicted, "will end up gaining for women the same mistreatment that men now suffer."[70]

Union WAGE (Women's Alliance to Gain Equality), an organization of California labor union women founded in 1971, agreed with many of Wolfgang's criticisms of the new women's movement. They also shared her concern about the impact of the ERA on low-income women, particularly women farmworkers in California who, since 1959, had gained benefits under state labor laws such as minimum wage coverage, toilets in the fields, drinking water, and washing facilities. California had one of the most extensive set of state labor laws in the country, with some fifty standards covering wage minimums, overtime, rest and meal breaks, ventilation, seats, rest room facilities, and other working conditions.[71]

Yet the Union WAGE strategy for preserving these protections differed from the National Committee Against Repeal of Protective Laws, founded by Wolfgang.[72] WAGE activists put their energies into passing what they called a "Labor ERA." They promised support for the ERA, but only if a proviso or a "labor rider" could be added that extended beneficial labor standard legislation to all workers. One newspaper headline summed up their campaign as "Women ask for Men's Rights."[73] WAGE women hoped eventually to bring together "women's liberationists" and trade union women into a new national organization to advance the needs of low-wage women, a vision they never realized. But they did have a major impact on California politics and social policy in the early 1970s.[74]

WAGE combined the formidable talents of three California women: ACWA's Anne Draper (already familiar to readers), Joyce Maupin, and Jean Maddox. All were veteran activists who had spent decades in labor and left politics. In the 1950s Draper and her husband, Hal, had been active in the New York Liberal Party (a third-party movement backed by ACWA president David Dubinsky, among others), and the Independent Socialist League, which later merged with the Socialist Party. Leaving the Socialist Party in 1962, they became leaders in the Berkeley Independent Socialist Club. Their household attracted young socialists and free-speech radicals of all sorts in the 1960s and early 1970s, including a group working on labor legislation.[75] A high-school dropout and self-described "romantic whose favorite book was *Moby Dick*," Joyce Maupin was attracted to cultural and political radicalism early, gravitating first to the Communist Party and then later to the Socialist Workers Party (SWP). After the birth of a daughter and a brief marriage to a merchant marine, Maupin organized for the SWP and wrote columns for the *The Militant*, the SWP's newspaper, on "Minnie the minimum wage worker," that "mythic figure who could live on a mini budget." Draper remembered clipping Maupin's column religiously, savoring its humor and feminist perspective. In 1960, Maupin moved to California, left the SWP, and got involved in union politics, becoming a steward in Local 29 of the Office and Professional Employees International Union (OPEIU), which covered the East Bay (Oakland and Berkeley).[76] There she met Jean Maddox, a one-time member of the Communist Party and union organizer, who by 1970 was president of OPEIU 29. Maddox and Draper, in line at the women's bathroom at a March 1971 NOW-sponsored conference at the University of California at Berkeley called "Breaking the Shackles," began talking about the lack of panels focusing on working-class women. Within two weeks Union WAGE was born, with Maddox as president, Draper as vice president, and Joyce Maupin as resident writer and publicist.[77]

Union WAGE reached out to NOW and other women's organizations for help in implementing the "Labor ERA" and extending the labor laws to men. But their position met with "much hostility from the women's movement," Maupin remembered.[78] NOW was angry because they believed the "Labor ERA" would block the ERA's eventual ratification in California. WAGE also encountered hostility from UAW women who supported an ERA without the rider and were miffed by WAGE's refusal to join the Network for Economic Rights, the new national organization launched by UAW women in 1970 that, among other goals, favored ending sex discrimination in state policy.[79] When WAGE convinced the San Francisco City Council to pass an ordinance in August 1971 in support of the "Labor ERA," NOW complained vociferously. Relations between NOW and WAGE further disintegrated when NOW picketed the California Labor Federation offices because WAGE had convinced the federation to support the ERA only if labor laws were extended to men. With the state federation's backing and the endorsement of the United Farm Workers, the ILGWU, and others, such a bill actually passed, but Governor Ronald Reagan vetoed it.[80] Once California ratified the ERA, however, tensions between NOW and WAGE subsided. In 1973, with NOW, Union WAGE, and the California State Federation working in tandem, California extended some but not all of its former sex-based labor standards to men.[81]

After the congressional passage of the ERA in 1972, the last holdouts began to come around. By the end of 1972, the IUE, the CWA, and other groups endorsed the ERA.[82] The AFL-CIO changed its position at its October 1973 convention, and ACWA finally shifted course in 1974.[83] Despite its official endorsement, the AFL-CIO provided only lackluster backing to the campaign for state ratification of the ERA and declined to send representatives to key coalition meetings. But the national AFL-CIO's attitude no longer reflected the sentiment of its women members or of its affiliates.[84]

After 1973, many unionists worked hard for the two-thirds state ratification that was needed for the amendment to become law. Indeed, as the chance for ratification of the ERA dimmed after 1975, labor women and their unions refused to give up, becoming core defenders of the ERA. Many AFL-CIO unions now actively campaigned for ratification, turning out large numbers of supporters for ERA demonstrations and rallies.[85] To bring the political realignment full circle, those organizing against them were often conservative Southern Democrats and Republicans. Some conservatives had simply lost interest in supporting the ERA because it could no longer be used as a weapon against labor standard legislation. Others now opposed it because they saw it as linked to a new mass movement that threatened the family and traditional gender roles. For labor women, the ERA took on associations beyond its stated goal of affirming women's right to legal equality. When interviewed by a reporter covering a "Labor for ERA" rally in 1980, the demonstrators, largely labor women, invariably explained their presence by talking about equal pay. The ERA had been incorporated into the larger labor feminist reform agenda and turned into a symbol of economic equality and workplace rights.[86]

With the collapse of labor's opposition to the ERA, the old wounds between the labor feminists and the "equal righters" began to heal. In 1978, the *IUE News* could cheerily endorse a new book, *The Story of Alice Paul*, and describe her "long tough fight for the ERA," without once alluding to the historic hostility between the NWP and the IUE.[87] Just as remarkable was the way in which, within a few years, individual labor women begin to "remember" a history that had never taken place. When interviewed in the late 1970s for an oral history project on trade union women leaders, women who had spent their lives railing against the ERA identified themselves as longtime supporters of equal rights and of the ERA.[88] They had closed the ideological rupture by constructing a past politics that resembled their present. The ERA had become a labor demand.

WOMEN'S DOMESTIC LABOR

The battle over Title VII and the ERA absorbed the energy of labor women in the late 1960s and pushed many to identify as either allies or foes of the new feminism. Yet some labor women were neither enthusiasts of the new feminism nor hostile toward it. Women like Esther Peterson and Kitty Ellickson sought to rally the new women's movement around their *own* unfinished agenda and take labor feminism to its next stage legislatively. Since the 1940s, they had insisted that women's first-class economic citizenship could never be achieved without attention to women's work in the home and to the "double day". In the late 1960s and early 1970s, they raised these issues once again, hoping to pass governmental policies that would increase the value and lessen the burden of women's domestic labor.

By 1965, Peterson began to withdraw from what was to her an ever more frustrating debate over Title VII, the ERA, and state protective laws. She saw no good choice. She disdained the politics of the NWP women, judging them and many of the new feminists who supported the ERA as having abandoned the advocacy of "bread and butter equality" and the needs of low-income women. Yet she also had become disillusioned with the battle to save sex-based labor laws. In an uncharacteristic but frank moment, she criticized her closest labor allies and their devotion to protective statutes, clearly wishing for a new strategy. "Let us not be like Lot's wife," she began, "always looking backward. If state and federal labor protections are so important, why are there still so many poor and downtrodden wage-earning women?"[89]

In late 1965, Peterson acceded to President Johnson's urging that she become his special assistant for consumer affairs, a position she held until Nixon's election in 1968 and to which she returned under President Carter in 1977. Peterson continued as Assistant Secretary of Labor for Labor Standards, but she distanced herself from the battles over the ERA and Title VII.[90] In alliance with Ellickson and others, she turned to the pursuit of new policies that would adapt the wage realm to the realities of women's lives. "The chief problem before us now," she wrote her friend Jacob Potofsky, ACWA president, is "finding more effective ways than we have in the past of ensuring worker safety, health, and welfare without limiting the access of any group to suitable work opportunities. This means that we must search beyond the narrow limits of the past for ways of making adaptations in work arrangements and schedules . . . and of providing essential services, such as day care and other personal or household services, to make such participation possible."[91]

Like Peterson, Ellickson also opposed the ERA until the early 1970s. Yet she too saw the need for change and welcomed aspects of the new feminism, describing it in 1973 "as a different wave in the long struggle for women's equality." Although "more representative of professional and upper middle-class groups than the larger number of wage workers," it reflected "the desire of young women to find their identity, control over their own bodies, and overcome the many discriminations that the PCSW by its very nature could not handle." She listed these as "the psychological aspects of discrimination, abortion, and the sharing of household tasks."[92] Yet the PCSW agenda, she continued to believe, still best represented the needs of wage-earning women. As her writings over the years consistently made clear, Ellickson linked women's economic equality to changes in the way household labor was valued and distributed. Now in her sixties and in semi-retirement, Ellickson turned to writing policy papers on how housework and voluntary activities could be included in measures of national production, and the importance of changing tax policy, providing social wages for child and elder care, and funding day care programs.[93]

Both Ellickson and Peterson viewed government-funded child care as only a partial solution to the conflict between home and job faced by working mothers, particularly low-income mothers. Yet when child care reemerged as a national issue in the late 1960s, they entered the political fray. After the 1962 authorization of federal day care funds for low-income women, few proposals had gotten very far in Congress. By the late 1960s, however, a new coalition of child care advocates coalesced which attempted to define child care not as a welfare function but as a community service to all families. In 1969, both the Senate and House held hearings on child care bills introduced by Congresswoman Patsy Mink and others. Labor feminists like Peterson, Ellickson, and Keyserling supported the campaign, as did a variety of labor unions, churches, children's groups, and social service organizations. NOW and other new feminist groups called for free quality child care for all women but did not play a leading role in the legislative campaigns. Peterson joined New York Democratic congresswoman Shirley Chisholm, Women's Bureau head Elizabeth Koontz, the AFL-CIO, and representatives from both garment trades unions in testifying in 1969. The ACWA, who had started negotiating with clothing manufacturers for employer-financed child care centers for union members in 1963, contributed significant lobbying power and financial resources.[94] In 1970, Nixon's own Task Force on Women's Rights and Responsibilities published its report, *A Matter of Simple Justice*, which included a proposal for "better child care" for women on federal assistance, "federal aid for child care for families not covered," and increased tax deductions for child care.[95]

In 1971, the coalition poured its resources into passing an omnibus child care bill, which, among other things, provided child care services to the poor for free and to the lower and middle classes on a sliding scale basis. They faced opposition from groups on the left concerned with community control as well as groups on the right fearful of disrupting gender norms. But with the support of Chisholm, Congresswoman Bella Abzug, and others, the 1971 Comprehensive Child Development Act (Title V of S. 2007) squeaked through both Houses, only to have President Nixon, in a heartbreaking moment, veto the bill on December 9, 1971. Calling it "the most radical piece of legislation to emerge from the 92nd Congress," Nixon claimed that "it would commit the vast moral authority of the National Government to the side of communal approaches to child rearing over against the family-centered approach" and promised to turn children into wards of the state.[96]

The passage of tax amendments affecting child care and family income in 1971 and 1972 provided only slight consolation. The Revenue Act of 1971 increased the amount that could be deducted for child care expenses and lifted the income limits on who could claim such deductions: the $600 deductible, in place since 1954, was raised to $4,800, and the income ceiling, set at $6,000 in 1964, jumped to $18,000. This change helped working-class and middle-income families reduce their taxes, but provided little relief to the lowest income groups. Working-class and middle-income families also benefited from the increase in personal exemption from $600 to $750 in 1972.[97]

The lowest income groups were not forgotten by Peterson, however. Following in the footsteps of earlier Women's Bureau directors Mary Anderson and Frieda Miller, she too sought ways of improving conditions for household employees when she took over the directorship in 1961. The upheavals of the late 1960s and early 1970s only intensified her commitment.[98] Organizations representing low-income women of color kept their distance from the child care campaigns, in part because of their skepticism about whether the needs of low-income mothers and household employees were being considered.[99] In contrast, the campaign to raise the labor standards among household workers stirred great enthusiasm among civil rights groups and engendered support from prominent African-American women from all walks of life. The campaign also coincided with the emergence of a national protest movement among household employees themselves.

No Longer One of the Family

Local organizations of household employees—inspired by the civil rights and poor people's movements—began forming in the late 1960s.[100] Dorothy Bolden, a veteran community and civil-rights activist who started cleaning houses in 1935 at the age of twelve, founded a domestic-workers organization in Atlanta in 1968. Its aim was to improve working conditions and build "respect for the women in this low-income field of labor." Bolden wrote: "I have been a maid all my life, I have rocked cradles and given guidance to little boys. Now we're going to give them some guidance when they are grown."[101] Similar groups organized in some two dozen other cities across the country. In 1971, some six hundred mostly black and middle-aged women gathered for the first national conference of household employees, sponsored by the National Committee of Household Employees (NCHE). Under the banner "pay, protection, and professionalism," they applauded enthusiastically as Chisholm, Peterson, Michigan congressman John Conyers, and others spoke of a new day for domestics. The conference received extensive press coverage, encouraging hopes that a fundamental shift in the working conditions of paid household labor was underway.[102]

The NCHE, formed in 1965 under the auspices of the Women's Bureau, grew out of the long-standing commitment of labor feminists to "eliminate the stigma from household labor," as Frieda Miller explained in 1947, and to put it on a "similar footing with labor in other occupations." Esther Peterson had donated money in 1964 to set up the organization, hoping that it would improve the status, dignity, and income of household employees and make a contribution to the larger goal of "putting economic value on what we do in our homes." She served on the NCHE Executive Board along with Dorothy Height and Frieda Miller, who agreed to chair the NCHE in 1967. Women's Bureau head Keyserling supported their work through organizing a number of daylong "consultations on Private-Household Employment" and gathering together a group of volunteers, including Ellickson, to serve as policy and funding advisors. Securing a series of Ford Foundation grants, the NCHE initially focused on training household employees and on fostering minority contractors in the private household-services sector who would be intermediaries between the employer and employee. This approach, it was thought, would give minority businesses a boost, expand the availability of household services, and benefit domestic workers by putting their employment on a "businesslike" basis rather than one "of master and servant."[103]

In 1969, under the new leadership of Edith Sloan, a young African-American woman with legal training as well as experience as a domestic worker, the NCHE redefined its priorities. It didn't abandon its training programs or its belief in the need for "model contracts" and the advantages of employment agencies. Nevertheless, much to the approval of Frieda Miller, who earlier had worried about how "we generate the pressure that will command the acceptance [of new labor standards] by employers," the NCHE turned its energies to building a national movement of household workers. At the 1971 national conference, the NCHE sponsored a membership-based dues organization, the Household Technicians of America, and envisioned organizing and affiliating local chapters of household employees who could be mobilized in legislative campaigns and who could eventually form their own unions and employment agencies to negotiate with employers. "Unless there are some changes made," Edith Sloan promised to loud cheers at the 1971 conference, "Madam is going to have to clean her own house and cook and serve her own meals because everyone is going to quit." Within a year, they had 32 organizations in 15 states.[104]

Household workers wanted living wages and benefits such as sick leave, vacation time, and social security. Like the striking hospital workers in South Carolina who carried signs in 1969 proclaiming "We are somebody," they sought "the respect due any human being" and an end to what they experienced as the oppressive "family" nature of the employment relationship. "We want to be treated like an employee," Mrs. Ruth Benjamin of New York City told *Newsweek* at the 1971 conference. "Everybody tells you you're in the family, and then they won't even give you a holiday." As one NCHE officer explained: "In no other industry is the modern day worker so completely at the mercy of her employer." Wages and hours were arranged informally, and many household employees were expected to work long hours at low pay out of loyalty and love for the family that employed them.[105] Domestics also complained of "uninvited familiarities by employers" and the "common use of first names." They wanted the employment relationship to be a "two-way street" characterized by "promptness, integrity, and courtesy" from both parties.[106]

Domestic workers organizing unions and employment agencies at the grassroots level found feminist allies hard to come by. The male-dominated labor movement didn't offer much help either. Detroit's Mary Upshaw McClendon, for example, who had organized the Detroit Household Workers Organization in 1969 to create "an awareness of the value of their labor" and to upgrade household workers' skills and bargaining power, received most of her support from church groups, the local NAACP, and the Urban League. She also found an ally in Lillian Hatcher of the UAW's Civil Rights and Women's Department.[107]

At the national level, where the major issue involved extending labor standards to household workers, there was more support from white middle-class feminists as well as from men and women in the labor movement. Nevertheless, women of color took the lead in the campaign to extend the FLSA to domestics. They combined grassroots lobbying from domestic worker organizations with pressure from female legislators such as Shirley Chisholm and Patsy Mink. Women's Bureau director Libby Koontz also lectured frequently about the importance of extending the minimum wage and other labor protections to "low income and no-income women." During the congressional hearings, held in 1971 and 1973, Edith Sloan of the NCHE testified on behalf of extensions, as did the NCNW, the AFL-CIO, and other labor, women's, and civil rights groups. Peterson, Ellickson, and Keyserling lent their expertise, lobbying and offering testimony. For the first time, professional women's organizations stepped forward, motivated in part by their interest in extending the equal pay provision of the FLSA to professional women. In 1974, domestic workers finally were added to the FLSA, a battle that had taken 36 years. Following the federal breakthrough, states began adding household employees to their minimum wage, unemployment insurance, and workers' compensation coverage, benefits from which household employees had previously been excluded in all but a handful of states.[108]

By the end of the 1970s, the NCHE and most of its affiliates were in decline, but the movement could claim significant victories: new labor standards legislation, economic gains in some key regional labor markets, and a role in fostering a sense of entitlement and individual capacity among household workers. Yet changing the nature of the employee-employer relationship in the home had proved formidable indeed. Edith Sloan had envisioned the NCHE affiliates as some day becoming "the nucleus for local unions," and some did try to unionize. But formal collective bargaining never materialized among private household workers. Nor were the domestic worker organizations able to sustain the worker-run employment agencies or the training programs for household workers. With wages low and employer expectations of deference and devotion still lingering, many maids simply "quit," as Edith Sloan had predicted. African-American women in particular abandoned private household jobs, seeking employment in the clerical and retail sector and in the "public household" jobs of hotel maid, home care aide, janitor, day care, and kitchen worker. These jobs were for the most part low paid, but at least their problems were more those of "employees" than servants. Unlike their counterparts in the home, many of the blue-collar service workers did organize, laying the foundation for the rise of service-sector unions such as the Service Employees International Union (SEIU) and the American Federation of State, County, and Municipal Employees (AFSCME) in the 1980s.[109]

CLUW: A DREAM BELATEDLY REALIZED

In March of 1974, the same year household workers gained federal protection, over three thousand union women descended on Chicago and jubilantly celebrated what many saw as the beginnings of a major upheaval in the labor movement. They had come to found the Coalition of Labor Union Women (CLUW). "Thirty-two hundred women on their own!" Mary Callahan recalled with a laugh. "Gosh, I'll never get over it!"[110]

The group was remarkably diverse. The bitter feelings over Title VII and the ERA had subsided, allowing the older generation of labor feminists to find grounds for cooperation with each other and with younger feminists. Olga Madar, an ERA advocate and an international vice president of the UAW, was elected president, but former ERA adversaries such as Myra Wolfgang helped plan the conference and took a leading role at the convention. Indeed, Wolfgang's quip when acting as convention chair—"And you can call Mr. Meany and tell him there are three thousand women in Chicago, and they didn't come to swap recipes"—brought the convention to its feet cheering.[111] Young labor feminists joined the old. Women came from 58 different unions, blue-collar, white-collar, and pink. Mexican-American teacher and farmworker organizer Dolores Huerta and the contingent of women agricultural workers who accompanied her received a standing ovation, despite the carping of the rival Teamster group. Some 20 percent of those attending were African-American, and they were well represented among the first slate of national officers. Addie Wyatt, now Director of Women's Affairs for the Amalgamated Butcher Workmen (which had absorbed the UPWA), was elected CLUW's first vice president, and she, along with Gloria Johnson of the IUE and Chicago Teamster official Clara Day, also sat on CLUW's first executive board.[112]

The founding of CLUW is often described as an expansion of the feminist impulse to those beyond the founding mothers of the second wave, presumed to be college-educated white women.[113] Yet as has been argued, many labor women were in fact feminists in the pre–second wave era, albeit feminists of a different sort than the new feminists of the 1960s and 1970s. Indeed, labor women, leaders as well as rank and file, were among the *first* to embrace the struggle for equality under the law and insist upon the aggressive enforcement of Title VII. Rather than being latecomers to the new feminism, they were among its initiators. Labor women "were and are pioneer feminists," Olga Madar summed up in 1974.[114]

In short, the advent of CLUW does not represent the trickling down of feminist consciousness to working-class women. Rather, it was a realization of a long sought goal of labor feminists: the creation of a national organization for trade union women. Ellickson and others had raised the idea in the 1950s; it also hovered over the 1961 national trade union women's conference. In 1968, Peterson tried to breathe life back into the idea and called together Wolfgang, Hatcher, Haener, Conroy, Wyatt, Callahan, and others. As Ellickson wrote in

Teamster and farm worker representatives signal their unity at the founding convention of CLUW, Chicago, Illinois, 1974. Olga Madar, the first president of CLUW is behind them to the right. Credit: Archives of Labor and Urban Affairs, Wayne State University.

1970, a "national organization of trade union women, not unlike the old Women's Trade Union League," was still needed, in part because many men did not see issues like equal opportunity "as sufficiently important or are afraid of the results."[115]

In 1970 as in 1968, however, labor feminists were still divided. In 1970, Ellickson, Wolfgang, and others organized the short-lived "Federation for the Advancement of Women"; the UAW Women's Department started a different coalition, the Network for Economic Rights, whose goals included voluntary overtime, child care, maternity protection, welfare reform, improved labor standards, and enhanced civil and legal rights. Eventually Wolfgang threw in her lot with the Network for Economic Rights, co-chairing it with Olga Madar. But it was not until 1973, with the AFL-CIO endorsement of the ERA, that tensions among labor women subsided enough to make the launching of a new, inclusive national organization possible.[116]

The rising militancy and separatist sentiment of black trade unionists spurred women unionists to take action. After 1968, black caucuses proliferated among auto workers, steelworkers, bus drivers, and others, and in September 1972, 1200 black unionists met in Chicago to form the Coalition of Black Trade Unionists, a national alliance of black unionists dedicated to securing justice for black workers. Less than a year later, a handful of women, including Addie Wyatt,

Olga Madar, Catherine Conroy, and Ola Kennedy, a black activist in the Steel-workers, met to plan a Midwest Union Women's Conference for June 1973. Some two hundred women responded, and by the end of the conference they unanimously endorsed Olga Madar's call for a national conference the following year. California women had already adopted a similar resolution (initiated by Union WAGE) at a California State Labor Federation–sponsored women's conference in March. Over the next year, union women gathered at dozens of other meetings across the country. In New York, six hundred women attended a New York Trade Union Women's Conference on January 19, 1974. Like union women elsewhere, they responded with enthusiasm when keynote Addie Wyatt called for trade union women to "get together" and insist on "equal opportunity for jobs" and "for leadership roles in our unions." She acknowledged that "there are those who feel threatened rather than strengthened by our coming together," but she insisted that "our intent and our goals are to build a labor movement stronger than we ever had before."[117]

As women poured into Chicago, hopes about the future of the new organization soared. Yet the rainbow of union sisterhood faded even as the celebration wore on. The thousands of women gathered on the convention floor stared up at the dais where a CLUW Executive Board sat that was heavily weighted toward the World War II generation. As befitted their years of trench warfare in the labor movement, those who chaired the conference, almost all from the older generation, relied strictly on Roberts Rules of Order, a process unfamiliar to many younger women and experienced by some as undemocratic. Those at the podium, fearful of the disruptive influence of radicals, particularly those on the left who wanted CLUW to be more independent of the labor establishment, kept a tight rein on the agenda. Debate was held to a minimum. An attempt from the floor to add employment rights for sexual minorities to CLUW's statement of purpose, for example, was ruled out of order, and some of its advocates ejected from the convention.[118]

Used to the more freewheeling and egalitarian exchanges of their political groups at home, some younger women went home alienated by the "bureaucratic style" of the convention.[119] Others were disappointed because they wanted more attention to sexual politics and gender roles; they tired of the unrelenting focus on economics and on policy linked to jobs and unions. A few older women shared these concerns and worried too that the group would remain marginal as long as it limited membership to trade union women. Joyce Maupin and Jean Maddox of Union WAGE, for example, were horrified when CLUW restricted membership to those *already covered* by collective bargaining contracts at its constitutional convention in 1975, a policy that excluded women in organizing campaigns and others who desired union representation.[120] The membership policy CLUW chose also meant that unlike the earlier Women's Trade Union League, CLUW would *not* be open to elite "allies."[121]

The decision to limit membership to trade unionists stemmed in part from legitimate concerns that opening up membership to nonunion women would deflect CLUW from its initial goals. Many CLUW leaders were disturbed by the "disruptive behavior" of sectarian leftists and the destructive factional fighting that had torn apart local chapters in the first year.[122] Labor women's distrust of more elite women had not disappeared either. As Joyce Miller, CLUW's corresponding secretary, explained to a 1976 Washington conference on the future of the women's movement, working-class women believed in "equal employment, day care, and equal pay," but they "reject the label of the women's movement" because of many of the "vague concepts espoused by middle-class feminists."[123]

Mary Callahan saw the tension arising from differences over tactics as well as goals. "Union women are a little bit suspicious of women in other organizations that you would term 'feminist.' We don't see eye-to-eye yet on a lot of ways to reach a goal. Those women can't understand that a union contract is a benefit to a woman as well as to a man. They are of the opinion that you go in and you pick out certain things that are just for women and the men are something else. Union women don't see it that way." Callahan also objected to what she termed "a caste system" among some "feminist leaders" that "union people don't have. It doesn't make you a higher level because you have a higher job." In her view, some feminists leaders were "suspect" because they were "looking at 'How can I become the manager.' Not, 'How can we get along and improve our lot in life?' It's, 'How do I get up there?'"[124]

In the end, although CLUW remained a labor women's organization, its feminism was a mix of the old and the new. CLUW embraced many aspects of second wave feminism, but it gave them a distinct trade union twist. Ratification of the ERA was "a principal objective," as was ending sex discrimination and opening up job opportunities to women. Although CLUW eventually endorsed reproductive rights and would battle with the AFL-CIO Executive Council about its unwillingness to take a pro-choice stand, many within the organization viewed cultural and sexual issues as potentially divisive and as marginal to the more important business of transforming work. The older concerns of the double day, of revaluing the skill and pay of women's jobs, and of raising labor standards for all workers, remained priorities. CLUW also operated as a "loyal pressure group" within the AFL-CIO, pinning its hope for change on strengthening and remaking trade union institutions. Of its four principal goals, one was "organizing unorganized women" and another, "increasing participation of women within their unions."[125]

CLUW's defense of trade union institutions created perhaps the greatest gulf between it and the larger women's movement. Big labor had long been a favorite target of young radicals angry over the AFL-CIO's support of the Vietnam War and labor's "collaborationist" contracts with corporate capital. The labor movement's heated assault on the ERA until 1973 and the sometimes infuriatingly old-fashioned sexism of its leaders only added fuel to the fire. Class stereotyping and arrogance undergirded these philosophical disagreements. As Irving Howe lamented in 1972 in *Dissent*, "we believe there is an unusual amount of ignorance about American workers, as well as a considerable degree of contempt and ideological preconception floating through both intellectual and popular life." The New Left was not immune to these prejudices, Howe observed. Its writings were shot through with "nasty elitist notions" about the working class as well as anger at them for not fulfilling their historical mission as revolutionaries.[126] Anne Draper of the AFL-CIO expressed similar frustrations with the "hostility and condescension toward unions" of the "middle-class 'women's rights' types." Too often, they "see unions, not as the struggling working-class combining in its own behalf against great odds," but "as a powerful, wealthy, entrenched institution of the status quo."[127]

CLUW's membership surged briefly after its founding convention but soon fell back to a disappointingly low level. Some of the strongest women leaders felt they could have more impact within their own labor organizations, where they could influence bargaining and other bottom-line issues *directly*, than in inter-union CLUW chapters whose institutional role within the labor movement remained vague. There were other disappointments, too, in those first few years. Those who hoped for a separate women's department within the AFL-CIO or for the appointment of a woman to the AFL-CIO Executive Council had to settle for increased attention to women's issues by the Civil Rights Department, a "half-loaf" compromise that Myra Wolfgang prophesied might leave women "with only the crumbs."[128]

Yet after the battles of its first few years, CLUW's membership began to grow, reaching 18,000 by the 1980s. ACWA's Joyce Miller, who acceded to the CLUW presidency in 1979, became the first woman to sit on the AFL-CIO Executive Council in 1980.[129] Of equal importance, CLUW served as an inspiring symbol for the many labor women, members and nonmembers alike, who were hard at work feminizing their union's leadership and priorities in the 1970s and 1980s.[130] Erma Wiszmann, president of CWA Local 7117 in Davenport, Iowa, may not have turned up on CLUW's membership rosters after she attended the first CLUW convention in 1974. Nevertheless, as she detailed in a long and frank letter to one of CLUW's officers, a month after returning home from Chicago, she decided to run for district vice president and she won. Determined to gain recognition for "our labors and our worth," Wiszmann then joined CWA's new National Women's Committee, where she led a revolt that threw out the officially sanctioned report and instead called on the CWA to institute "proportionate representation of women in CWA until equality was achieved." The "appointed male chairman almost had apoplexy," Wiszmann added, but "all twenty ladies" on the committee signed the new report anyway.[131] Four years later, CWA held its first national women's conference.[132]

CHAPTER EIGHT

An Unfinished Agenda

> The UAW deplores the economic inequity which forces many women to work when they would prefer to stay home and take care of their families. However, we insist, without reservation or qualification, first on the right of every woman to work, if she so chooses; second, on the right of every woman who does work to be paid for her labors on the same scale as men doing the same or comparable work and third, on the right of equal opportunity for advancement.
>
> —*UAW Convention Resolution, April 20–25, 1970*

> Instead of nullifying protective legislation, we should be working for the enactment of legislation providing equal pay for equal work, equal employment opportunity, meaningful child-care centers, school lunch programs, improved hour limitation laws, mandatory rest periods, reasonable weight lifting limitations, and equal access to all educational facilities. By so doing, women would become part of a social movement dedicated to reforming our social structure to permit true equality between the sexes.
>
> —*Myra Wolfgang, May 1, 1971*[1]

WITH THE ADVENT of CLUW in 1974, a national network of labor feminists existed that embraced many of the tenets of second wave feminism and continued to articulate a dual vision of civil and social rights for women. Yet to focus solely on CLUW and the leadership of women at the national level is to miss some of the most creative and effective reform initiatives among working women in this period. Indeed, in the late 1960s and early 1970s, the transformation of women's work occurred as much in response to pressure from below as from above. In countless workplaces across the country, labor women, both organized and unorganized, relied on economic and political pressure to challenge their secondary status at work. Many also turned to the courts, testing the limits and language of the new antidiscrimination laws.

In some cases, these activists found a receptive climate for their ideas within the labor movement, and they worked with and through their unions. In other instances, however, they rejected the leadership and strategies of organized labor, seeking different allies and different ways of advancing their interests than had an earlier generation.[2] Some broke entirely with the labor movement, casting their lot with all-female associations defined as much by gender as class. These new associations, particularly those formed by flight attendants and clerical workers, organized around traditional labor issues: respect, higher wages, and greater workplace control. But they did not stop there. They made a public and political issue of the gendered construction of women's jobs and claimed that the personal interaction between men and women at work and the "sexploitation" of women's bodies were as much labor issues as wages and benefits. In doing so, they expanded the vocabulary of workplace rights and helped redefine once again the meaning of discrimination.

Yet by the late 1970s, this initial phase of second wave activism among working women was largely over. The tensions between activists and organized labor diminished somewhat, and many younger second wave labor feminists now looked to unions as vehicles for their reform aspirations. Of equal importance, by the late 1970s, the older unresolved issues of accommodating work and family and upgrading women's jobs regained their place of centrality in the reform agenda. The pendulum had swung once again. In the first years of second wave feminism, the old feminism had learned from the new. As second wave feminism broadened and transformed in the late 1970s and 1980s, however, the lines of influence pulled in the other direction as the new feminism began to learn from the old.

"Sex Objects in the Sky Unite"

Wage-earning women reached an ideological tipping point in the early 1970s. Not all women wanted to cross the sexual divide, but most came to believe that men and women should have the freedom to choose which jobs they wanted, whether for good or ill. Young women embraced the new paradigm most enthusiastically. Many had spent their formative years in an era of prosperity, an environment far removed from the crucible of economic crisis, hunger, and poverty that forged the depression generation. They had a different sense of what was possible and what they deserved at work. And increasingly, they began to express these sentiments in novel and militant ways.

Flight attendants were among the first to articulate a new and expanded definition of workplace discrimination in this period.[3] In the early 1960s, when the airlines began firing "aging" stewardesses en masse, the battle over age discrimination heated up. Under growing pressure from the flight attendants themselves and with the aid of the new antidiscrimination legislation, the unions belatedly stepped up to the plate. Female union leaders within the Transport Workers and the Pilots unions held press conferences, met with government officials, and pushed hard for their male-dominated internationals to take the issue seriously. Individual women also filed grievances against the airlines through union channels and discrimination complaints with the New York Human Rights Commission and the Equal Employment Opportunity Commission.[4] In the 1965 hearings before the New York Human Rights Commission, hearings that eventually produced a favorable opinion from the commissioner, the efforts of TWU local president Colleen Boland to spur a more aggressive union stance paid off when TWU representative Francis O'Connell declared that his union was "pledged to go to the wall" on the issue of age ceilings.[5]

In 1965 and 1967, union leaders testified before Congress in an attempt to get the pending age discrimination legislation applied to everyone, not just those under 45. The behavior of the airlines, Margie Cooper of the Pilots charged in 1967, violated "existing moral standards and our civil rights principles." Putting "sex and beauty above all other considerations," she continued, "is more consistent with show business theatrics than air transport." Cooper's testimony proceeded without incident, but at other points in the hearings the presence of attractive flight attendants reduced the male congressmen to schoolboy displays of horseplay and humor. At one session before the House Labor Subcommittee, Representative James Scheuer asked the attendants to "stand up so we can see the dimensions of the problem," bringing howls from his fellow representatives. In the end, the subcommittee members reprimanded the airlines, scolding them for "operating flying bunny clubs," and ruled in favor of the attendants. But when the Age Discrimination Act passed in 1967, it only covered workers over the age of forty.[6]

Through it all, many of the major airline companies held unashamedly to their hiring biases. American Airlines defended itself on the grounds that "the stewardess's job required enthusiasm that is lost with age, and women between the ages of 38 and 50 undergo changes of body, personality, and emotional reactions which interfere with their performance of the job." Airlines also insisted that businessmen preferred younger women and that their profit margins would suffer if they lost the lucrative male business traveler market. Female passengers, business and otherwise, were invisible, and men who desired something other than titillation or who had a more expansive notion of female attractiveness were also ignored.

Eventually a few carriers broke ranks. After acrimonious negotiations with their union, Northwest agreed in 1967 to end forced retirement. Other carriers such as TWA followed suit, ending their two-year battle with the union and the EEOC. Finally, on August 10, 1968, the EEOC ruled in favor of the 1965 discrimination charge lodged by June Dodd, an American flight attendant. They held that American had violated the prohibition against sex discrimination under Title VII in singling out female but not male employees for mandatory retirement. After the American ruling, virtually all the airlines relented and changed their policies.[7]

The battle to open up the occupation to married women and mothers was just as drawn out, and in order to prevail, the flight attendants had to organize as much against their unions as with them. The Stewards and Stewardesses (S&S) Division of the Pilots had won an important arbitration ruling in 1965 requiring the reinstatement of a married attendant fired by Braniff—a ruling that was later upheld in federal court. In announcing the victory, the male officers of the Pilots revealed their continuing discomfort at taking flight attendant job rights seriously. In a jaunty, paternalistic press release, the Pilots Union described how they (the pilots) had "gone to bat on behalf of the S&S Division who felt that the airborne careers of today's modern girls shouldn't be grounded because of an earthbound husband."[8]

But attendants no longer deferred to the traditional gender hierarchies still desired by some employers and pilots. Eastern stewardesses, "sore about the marriage bar," picketed mediation proceedings in 1965 after the company rejected their proposals in bargaining. Attendants at other carriers also intensified their campaign against the single-only rule. They raised the issue in collective bargaining, they filed grievances and lawsuits, and they organized demonstrations. By 1967, of the 25 carriers under contract with the S&S Division, only three had no-marriage rules. That same year, the EEOC ruled that marital restrictions violated Title VII, giving unions as well as individual claimants another weapon in their arsenal. Faced with this array of opposing forces, even United, perhaps the most recalcitrant airline, finally relented and changed its policies on marriage.[9]

In 1971, the U.S. Court of Appeals struck down the "female-only" hiring policy in the airlines, ending one of the last discriminatory hiring practices in that industry. By the early 1970s, flight attendants could be of any race or sex, could marry, and could work past age 32. But flight attendants were now pushing for more than an end to discrimination in hiring: they wanted job opportunities equal to men and the right to control and define their own sexuality and "personhood."[10] The emergence of these issues paralleled the new feminism's focus on opportunity and its sensitivity to male exploitation and control of female sexuality. Flight attendants were influenced by this new sensibility; they also helped pioneer it.[11]

By the early 1970s, increasing numbers of flight attendants were married, and they now expected to stay in their job longer than the earlier average of eighteen months. But their jobs were becoming less and less satisfying. Wages were declining, hours were lengthening, and most gallingly, the occupation "sexualized" as companies came to rely upon female sexuality to sell seats.[12] The fantasy image of flight attendants in the 1950s had been the fresh-faced girl next door—the kind you wanted to marry. Now the image shifted to the "playmate in the sky," available for sex, or the "flying geisha girl," there to entertain and please.[13] Airlines routinely required flight attendants to wear hot pants and other sexually alluring uniforms. Braniff promised a midair striptease-like fashion show. Air Jamaica's stewardesses would "make you feel good all over." National's rules called for all stewardesses to wear "Fly Me" buttons. The ad company responsible maintained with a straight face that no sexual innuendo was intended, despite their advertisements featuring stewardesses panting, "Hi, I'm Linda, and I'm going to FLY you like you've never been flown before." Continental learned from National's success. In 1972, they aired ads in which stewardesses promised that we "really move our tail for you."[14]

Flight attendants historically had taken pride in their appearance and in the company's celebration of their beauty, but the more crass approach now being taken by airlines was objectionable to many. The new sexy image encouraged harassment by male passengers; it also meant their job had become less respectable. As one explained, "It represents a lack of respect for hostesses. We have always projected pride, a class kind of image and this slogan is barroom talk. We're professional career women and mothers . . . not fly girls." Others objected to *any* gendered image being uniformly imposed. Why should stewardesses be asked to speak and look alike when other workers weren't treated this way? Former stewardess and popular author Paula Kane claimed the "new militancy" arose because stewardesses wanted "to free themselves from the prison of the female role" and assert their own individual identities.[15]

Beset by problems their male-led unions seemed incapable of understanding or accepting as "real," stewardesses launched the first all-female national organization of flight attendants, Stewardesses for Women's Rights (SFWR), in 1972. SFWR departed from the older labor feminism's close identity with the labor movement. Twenty-seven-year-old former Eastern flight attendant and University of Maryland Women's Studies student Sandra Jarrell, SFWR co-founder and first national coordinator, explained why at their founding convention: "The most obvious tool available for remedying the injustices we are subject to are [*sic*] the unions. Unfortunately, unions do not have the reputation of representing the interests of women." The male leadership, she continued, blame stewardesses, but the unions "will obtain rank and file support only if they stop limiting their representation to economic issues."[16] Instead of building cross-gender coalitions with working-class men, SFWR turned to closer partnerships with middle-class women, including airline women in managerial and supervisory positions. At least initially, they had friendlier relationships with organized feminism than with organized labor.[17]

SFWR aimed to end all forms of sex discrimination in the industry, but they turned first to "fight the policies of the airlines which strip us of our individuality and dignity" and "stigmatize us as sex objects."[18] They picketed films that depicted flight attendants as oversexed and empty-headed. They filed lawsuits against Continental and National, alleging that their airline ads created a hostile work environment. They distributed buttons reading "Go Fly Yourself" and sent out "National, Your Fly is Open" bumper stickers. Their media campaign culminated in the release of a "counter-commercial" aimed at ending "sexploitation." In it, they defined themselves as professionals responsible for passenger safety, not passenger sexual titillation. "The sex-pot stewardess image is unsafe at any altitude," the script proclaimed, because "people do not obey the safety orders of their sexual fantasies."[19] As one SFWR leader told *Time* magazine: "We're in the business of saving tails, not serving them. The airlines are asking for pecuniary returns with a part of my anatomy that is not for sale."[20]

Although SFWR took the initiative in the campaign against "sexploitation," the few female-led flight attendant unions joined them. The Association of Flight Attendants (AFA), the renamed S&S Division of the Pilots Union that had bargained a more autonomous relationship with the Pilots in 1973, was among the most involved. SFWR and the AFA worked to change the rules governing appearance, demanding that airlines change stewardesses' uniforms and abolish their archaic grooming and weight requirements. They also made progress in addressing other issues such as promotional opportunities for stewardesses, workplace health and safety, and the end of mandatory layoffs during pregnancy.[21] While SFWR kept up its flurry of lawsuits and media pressure, the unions threatened strikes, sick-ins, and the old Industrial Workers of the World tactic of slowdowns—what Kelly Rueck, the strong-willed AFA president, described as a "spontaneous loss of enthusiasm" for the job.[22]

SFWR folded in 1976, but it had made a splash despite its abbreviated organizational life. It captured media headlines. It also moved issues of control over one's body and personality into the center of airline union politics, ultimately reinvigorating unionism among flight attendants. By the end of the 1970s much had changed for flight attendants. New, more dignified uniforms appeared, and flight attendants no longer resembled mass-produced life-size Barbie dolls.

RAISES AND ROSES

The new feminist sensibility affected working women *outside* of unions as well as those within, but not in the way many in the labor movement hoped, at least not initially. In the 1960s, "union fever" swept through the public sector, bringing teachers, sanitation workers, clericals, hospital workers, and others into unions. The civil rights movement inspired many to collective action, and trade union representation became one way of fulfilling the new movement's aspirations for respect, dignity, and escape from poverty.[23] Some predicted that the success of public sector organizing and the rise of the new feminist movement would help inspire a new wave of union organizing among women, one that would reach the millions of still unorganized women in the private sector.

Yet one-third of these women held jobs as clericals, and the relation between female clerical workers and unions had always been problematic.[24] For much of the twentieth century, union leaders viewed female clerical workers as virtually "unorganizable." In many instances, their views were accurate. Not only did office workers tend to see themselves as "white-collar" or part of "management," but the occupation attracted a disproportionate number of married women, many of whom defined themselves as short-term and "secondary earners" regardless of their income or length of tenure. By the 1960s, however, the situation had changed. The working conditions of clericals declined as their needs and expectations rose. As larger, more bureaucratic organizations became the norm and the new office technologies spread, secretaries were increasingly treated more like production workers than administrative assistants. Some were reorganized into office clerical pools; others saw their jobs downgraded to a monotonous routine of typing and filing. Moreover, a growing number were single or were heading families without a partner. They spent more years at work and felt frustrated by their "secondary earner" wages and the lack of pro-motional opportunities.[25]

But would they join unions? Despite the union organizing occurring among white-collar government employees and among low-wage service workers in hotels and hospitals, many labor leaders remained skeptical about the potential among *private sector* office workers. After all, many secretaries had strong per-sonal loyalties to their bosses; moreover, the hostility to unions in insurance and banking—where close to a third of clerical work was concentrated—was legendary. And, indeed, the walls separating unions and clerical workers held firm in this period. Few unions pursued office workers, and when the new feminism inspired secretaries and other office workers to turn to collective ac-tion, they organized largely *apart* from the labor movement, forming their own independent clerical worker associations.

Rumblings among private sector clerical workers began in the early 1970s and continued unabated throughout the decade. Margie Albert, a 25-year office veteran and a steward for the Distributive Workers of America, spoke of a "new spirit" sweeping America's secretaries in a 1973 *New York Times* opinion edito-rial piece; New York congresswoman Bella Abzug read it into the *Congressional Record*.[26] Albert claimed the movement erupted in 1969 when employers im-posed a "no pants, dresses only" rule on office staff. Women rebelled, she re-ported, signing petitions, organizing delegations to the boss, and threatening mass walkouts.[27] Albert may have exaggerated the extent of the discontent, but within the next few years, at least a dozen independent office-worker organiza-tions sprang up, perhaps the most effective being 9to5.

Set up in 1973, 9to5 grew quickly from its origins as a luncheon gripe session for Harvard University secretaries to a community organization with hundreds of members. It was led by University of Chicago refugees Karen Nussbaum and Ellen Cassedy, who had both been active in the more radical women's liberation wing of second wave feminism.[28] Similar groups formed in Chicago, New York, San Francisco, and elsewhere. By the end of the decade, twelve local groups (with a total membership of some ten thousand) had united under the umbrella of the National Association of Working Women.[29] They cared about traditional labor issues such as low wages and job control, but they also ventured into new territory, defining job duties based on traditional notions of male and female roles as exploitation. Being a good "office wife" was no longer a source of pride but a "servant role" resented as demeaning and limiting. Secre-taries wanted to be promoted on the basis of their own efforts and skills rather than rise as appendages to their bosses. They resisted the non-job-related duties often required of them—duties, as activist and author Jean Tepperman ex-plained, "that have no purpose but to make the boss seem, and feel, important." They were required to attend to the bosses' personal needs, and like the wife at home, their labor was invisible, neither acknowledged nor respected. 9to5 and many of the other clerical worker organizations set out to change this state of affairs.[30]

Office-worker groups used lawsuits, petitions, pickets, as well as more unorthodox tactics—described by one reporter as a combination of "street theatre and Madison Avenue hype"—to draw attention to the plight of secretaries. Their attempt to "repossess" National Secretaries Day, perhaps their most infamous campaign, instigated a public debate over the working conditions of secretaries and the cultural norms governing boss and secretary interaction. Relying on the slogans "Respect, Rights, and Raises" and "Raises not Roses" (later changed to "Raises *and* Roses"), they called on secretaries to refuse participation in the widespread once-a-year ritual of luncheon and flower offerings that accompanied National Secretaries Day, begun in the early 1950s. They held "worst boss contests" to ridicule publicly the most outrageous requests that bosses made of secretaries, and they picketed individual bosses and companies whose office practices and pay policies they deemed egregious.[31]

Like SFWR, office-worker groups had an impact way beyond their small numbers. By the end of the 1970s, the movement had helped win millions of dollars in raises for office workers, had spurred the development of employer affirmative action plans, turned National Secretaries Day into a contested ritual, and inspired a hit "9to5" song, movie, and TV show. Ultimately, the office-worker movement helped transform the daily office encounters that had done so much to humiliate and demean secretaries. As *Business Week* noted in 1980, 9to5 changed public "notions of fairness," of "what a boss may fairly ask a[n] office worker to do." Personal errands, coffee-making, and numerous other requests were no longer acceptable business practice in most offices. Like their counterparts in the home, secretaries were no longer a perk of the powerful or an invisible appendage; they were emerging as individuals.[32]

Yet these gains, as significant as they were, left many problems unsolved. While some office workers got raises, promotions, and enhanced job control, many others, chiefly those who occupied the lower rungs of the occupation—typing, filing, and processing forms in huge, faceless offices—still faced low wages and poor working conditions. Indeed it was often the secretaries with the "preferred spots in small, private offices" who experienced the most dramatic improvements. The women relegated to the more impersonal, assembly-like conditions stayed put. Not surprisingly, women from the working class and women of color held a disproportionate number of these jobs.[33]

From the beginning, the leaders of many of the office-worker organizations had pushed for changes affecting "the entire class of women who are being discriminated against."[34] Unionization was one way of broadening the movement and pushing employers to address the needs of the mass of clerical workers, not just the elite. But few in the office-worker movement saw unions as their allies in the early 1970s, and unions returned the favor. "We came to the idea of unionizing women gradually," Nussbaum remembered. The first time she had ever thought about it was at a peace demonstration in 1972. "After the main march, a little group demonstrated in front of the Justice Department. They were chanting, 'What are unions for? General strike to end the war.' I thought to myself, 'Mmmm, unions as organizations for social change. What an idea.' " Later, 9to5 members approached different unions "with the proposal that they should fund us to organize clerical workers, even though we had no members to offer, or dues, or anything." Their responses confirmed her worst stereotypes. "One of the group went to the local Teamsters," Nussbaum recalled. "She was told, 'Well, you can't organize women workers because they think with their cunts, not their brains.' Not everyone was as bad, but everyone said no." It wasn't until years later that 9to5 worked out a deal with SEIU. They "offered us money—practically nothing, but money—*and* a charter, *and* a chance to organize workers. So we started our own union."[35]

THE RETURN OF THE REPRESSED

By the mid-1970s, second wave labor feminism entered a new phase. Younger labor feminists showed a new willingness to work in alliance with the male-led labor movement, and the movement as a whole shifted its focus and priorities. Labor women within a variety of unions had continued to pursue work and family reforms throughout the 1960s and early 1970s. Now these issues resurfaced and even asserted primacy. Moreover, by the late 1970s, a new comparable worth movement took hold, capturing the imagination of working women across the country.

SFWR worked more closely with unions in its last few years, and when it folded in 1976, many of its young leaders moved into full-time union work. A few became officers in the older already-established unions, joining pioneers like flight attendant Peggy McGuire, the New York-based TWU leader who raised wage and hiring discrimination issues in collective bargaining throughout the 1960s, and Kelly Rueck, the former vice president of the S&S Division who founded the AFA.[36] Others established and then led a bewildering array of new independent female-led flight attendant unions, almost all set up between 1976 and 1979.[37] Rather than reject unions per se, former SFWR members now argued that women should establish their own. "Whatever the failings of unionism, we would have few benefits or security without collective bargaining," one SFWR member explained. "Unions may not be very chic, but then neither is a substandard wage."[38]

Office workers and their organizations followed a similar trajectory. 9to5 chapters in Boston and Providence spun off union locals affiliated with SEIU in the late 1970s, and nationally, 9to5 negotiated a separate, autonomous clerical worker division within SEIU called District 925, with Karen Nussbaum as its new president. University clericals at Columbia, Harvard, Boston University, and other campuses started to organize unions, as did small groups of white-collar workers in the private sector. Eight women bank tellers formed the Willmar Bank Employees Association Local 1 in 1977 after their complaints about women being passed over for promotion were dismissed by the bank president with the explanation that "We are not all equal, you know." Their valiant picketing in the freezing Minnesota winter for the right to negotiate over the terms and conditions of their employment captured national media attention and inspired labor and women's activists to follow suit. In 1981, District 925 of the SEIU launched a national campaign to organize women clericals in insurance and banking.[39]

Many workplace activists turned to the labor movement as a vehicle for their feminist aspirations in the late 1970s because the labor movement now appeared more amenable to the interests of women. SEIU and AFSCME, for example, the unions that had organized low-wage public sector and service workers throughout the 1960s and early 1970s, were beginning to champion a whole host of feminist concerns. Initially, these new public sector unions had focused on solidifying collective bargaining and forging unity in the face of employers and a public wary of public servants (many of whom were minority) having power. In their union building stage (somewhat analogous to the 1930s for industrial unionism), the specific needs of women *as women* were not foremost on the agenda. But by the late 1970s the situation was changing. The new public sector unions had stabilized, and women were rising to important positions of power.[40]

WORK AND FAMILY ISSUES REDUX

The older industrial unions were declining in economic and political power by the 1970s. Nevertheless, they were crucial actors in the campaigns of this era to end discrimination against pregnant women and mothers and secure the benefits and social services necessary for women to balance household and market labor. Second wave labor feminists thus maintained the dual focus of the earlier generation of labor women on social as well as civil rights.[41]

Title VII lawsuits brought by flight attendants, telephone operators, and others in the late 1960s and early 1970s helped end, or at least diminish, the still widespread discriminatory practices against pregnant women and mothers. The most frequent complaints brought to the EEOC by women in its first year were of "loss of jobs due to marriage or pregnancy."[42] In 1970, the EEOC ruled that Western Airline's policy of "automatic and permanent termination of female employees during pregnancy" violated Title VII; they also ruled against the airline practice of not hiring mothers. In 1971, Southern Bell rescinded its longstanding ban against the hiring of unwed mothers, "a policy that had especially disadvantaged black women" according to historian Karen Anderson. And, in a 1974 case concerning women teachers, the Supreme Court found "forced pregnancy leaves unconstitutional."[43]

With these court cases involving the equal job rights of pregnant women and mothers gaining favorable hearings for the plaintiffs, attention shifted to the issue of maternity benefits. A few unions such as the UAW continued to speak out about the need for a national social insurance program that would "replace wages lost before and after childbirth," and the AFL-CIO routinely backed national health insurance legislation with its provisions for universal maternity benefits. Without political allies, however, there was little legislative progress on these issues.[44]

Indeed, by the end of the 1970s, it appeared harder, not easier, to make a case for state income support for mothers, including poor mothers. Conservatives had always opposed social wages of any sort. Their opposition to state maternal aid for the poor hardened as increasing numbers of needy single-parent families qualified for welfare and middle-income mothers left home for market work. Support for a guaranteed minimum income for all single-parent families with children (a group almost wholly comprised of mothers and children) waned among mainstream Democrats as well.[45] NOW had always been skeptical of programs that, in effect, offered social wages to mothers, arguing that they tended to reinforce traditional gender roles and strengthen the male breadwinner ideal. They wanted policy makers to focus on women as individuals, and they favored equal opportunity and other programs that helped increase women's individual income rather than those that focused on increasing family income. By the late 1970s, the majority of feminists and many liberals moved closer to that position. The emphasis had shifted toward enabling women to participate in market work, regardless of family or class status.[46] Yet women, like men, were not merely creatures of the market; nor were they unencumbered individuals. The right to a life apart from work and the economic value of reproductive labor needed acknowledgment.

Given the unfavorable political climate for social wages for childbirth and parenting, reformers turned to collective bargaining and lawsuits, pursuing the AFL-CIO goal of "pregnancy and maternity leave paid on the same basis as any other disability."[47] Lawsuits appeared to offer the most promise, especially after the EEOC issued pregnancy guidelines in 1972 stating that pregnancy was a "disability" and as such should be treated like any other disability.[48] Health insurance plans that excluded childbirth or temporary disability policies that made exceptions for pregnancy were now possibly illegal under Title VII. With the backing of the California State Federation of Labor and HERE Local 48, two pregnant San Francisco waitresses filed suit in federal court to collect lost wages through the state disability insurance, a system, they pointed out, that offered income to men for prostate and circumcision operations.[49]

Other union suits claimed discrimination in employer-based benefit provisions. Starting in 1950, the IUE had repeatedly sought sick leave for pregnant women in bargaining with GE and other employers, but to no avail. In 1973, IUE attorneys Ruth Weyand and Winn Newman filed charges with the EEOC; they also filed a nationwide class action suit in federal court charging GE, Westinghouse, and GM with "benefit discrimination," since women absent because of pregnancy were barred from using sick leave. To draw attention to the case, the IUE called for a one-day strike over the lack of benefits for mothers and children, pointing out that GE "pays disability benefits for such things as hair transplants but not for childbearing."[50] A few months earlier, the CWA had filed another class action suit against AT&T, claiming that their temporary disability plan, which also excluded pregnant women, violated Title VII.[51] The New York-based Women's Rights Project and the ACLU filed claims for "pregnancy-related disabilities" with the EEOC and the New York State Human Rights Commission on behalf of flight attendants who were forced to take unpaid leaves of absence when pregnant. Their lawsuits paralleled the class action suits filed against many of the airline carriers by flight attendant unions.[52]

The courts initially sided with many of the union-backed suits, but in 1976, the Supreme Court, in *Gilbert v GE*, reversed the lower court rulings in a 6 to 3 decision in favor of GE.[53] The majority opinion reasoned that employer disability plans excluding pregnancy or childbirth from coverage did *not* discriminate against women; rather, they were merely making a distinction between pregnant persons and non-pregnant persons. Indignant, labor women from the IUE, CWA, UE, ACWA, and other unions launched a campaign to seek *new* legislation that would once and for all ban discrimination against pregnant women. Joined by NOW, NAACP, the League of Women Voters, and other women's and civil liberties groups, the coalition, under the leadership of IUE counsel Ruth Weyand, was successful in passing the Pregnancy Discrimination Act of 1978. The Act, which amended Title VII, made it clear that policies governing disability could not provide lesser benefits for pregnancy than they did for other disabilities.[54] Only then did the Bell System finally agree with CWA to provide paid leave for childbirth and an optional non-paid leave for child care. United Airlines and other carriers also relented in 1978, permitting stewardesses to use accrued sick leave during their pregnancy.[55]

Labor women had picked up the mantra of equal treatment and asserted, in chorus with the larger women's movement, that pregnancy should be treated like any other disability. They also, however, continued to promote another approach to the pregnancy dilemma, one that took gender differences into account. A few states had retained or passed maternity statutes in the 1970s providing leave and some measure of job protection; a determined group of labor women had helped secure these protections. They applied to women *only*: men had no such guarantees of leave or job retention when a child was born. Nevertheless, according to Lisa Vogel, legislators and others believed the laws "consistent with the equality framework."[56] In California, one of the states with a maternity statute, pregnant women enjoyed a right other disabled workers did not: the right to return to their job. When Lillian Garland, a receptionist at the California Federal Savings and Loan Association, tried to exercise that right in 1982 and return to work after a disability leave for a difficult pregnancy, the bank said her job had been filled. Backed by the Chamber of Commerce and other employers' groups, the Savings and Loan Association sued under Title VII, claiming the state law discriminated against men by providing women "special benefits" and should be struck down. Such a ruling would leave employers free to deny or grant disability leave to all employees.[57]

The women's movement divided over the case. The Coalition for Reproductive Equality in the Workplace (CREW), a group that included Betty Friedan as well as the ILGWU, 9to5, and other labor organizations, defended the state law. NOW and the Women's Rights Project of the ACLU agreed with the bank that the law was discriminatory. CREW argued that the equal treatment paradigm was inadequate, since it left women but not men still having to choose between their job and having a child. They also justified "special benefits for pregnant women" as necessary to secure "the equal right to bear children." Consistent with the philosophy she espoused in 1981 in her new book, *The Second Stage*, Friedan now argued for "a new doctrine of equality," one that acknowledged that "women are different from men" and "are the ones who have the babies. We shouldn't be stuck with always using a male model, trying to twist pregnancy into something that's like a hernia." In contrast, NOW and the ACLU explained that "We don't think women are weak and in need of special assistance. The notion that pregnancy is a special disability is a stereotype, and stereotypes hurt us." They, like CREW, were strong advocates of proposed federal legislation guaranteeing parental leave for both parents, and in a friend-of-court brief, they encouraged the Supreme Court to consider requiring California employees to extend the same benefits to all disabled employees. But without such an extension, they recommended the state law be repealed. As with the battle over the ERA, the division was in part philosophical, in part strategic: did giving women special treatment, even if short-term, help or hurt them? Did such sex-based protections act as incentives or as barriers to broader more inclusive labor standards?

Finally, on January 13, 1987, the Supreme Court sided with the state in the suit brought by California Federal. In a vote of 6 to 3, they ruled that states *may* require employers to grant special job protections to pregnant employees even if similar protections are not granted for other disabilities. Justice Thurgood Marshall, writing for the majority, claimed that when Congress passed the Pregnancy Discrimination Act, it intended only to prohibit discrimination against pregnant workers and had not prohibited discrimination in their favor. The California law, he continued, "promotes equal employment opportunity" because it "allows women, as well as men, to have families without losing their jobs." The ruling opened up the possibility of creating social policy that moved beyond the male model, at least in regard to pregnancy. The women's movement remained divided, however, and passionately so, over the question of how and whether gender difference should be acknowledged in law and policy.[58]

In 1991 when the Supreme Court ruled in favor of the UAW under Title VII and agreed that Johnson Controls, a battery manufacturer, had to end its "paternalistic policies" that excluded all fertile women from jobs exposing them to lead toxins, feminists took a variety of positions. Some sided with the UAW, arguing that although in the long run neither men nor women should have to face exposure to deadly chemicals, the best interim policy was a gender-blind, equal treatment standard. Others disagreed, noting that adding women to the group now free to choose dangerous work was not an advance. Moreover, "equal treatment" policies would not result in gender equality. Since only women bore children and fetuses faced greater hazards than did adults from lead exposure, women faced a dilemma that men did not: having a healthy child could require the loss of wage work for the mother but not the father. Neither

Title VII nor the Occupational Safety and Health Act, passed in 1970 to protect men and women from unhealthy and unsafe jobs, had sufficiently dealt with the question of difference and how equitable standards could be devised that provided as much protection to women as to men.[59]

The women's movement, including labor women, remained less divided over child care. After the 1971 Nixon veto of the comprehensive child care bill, labor women stepped up their efforts on behalf of federally funded and union-negotiated child care. Prompted largely by ACWA, the AFL-CIO organized "labor's first major conference on day care" in Chicago in 1972, where Joyce Miller, the social services director of ACWA who had helped set up its child care centers in the early 1960s, exhorted delegates to action. CLUW put child care at the top of its agenda in 1975 and urged repeatedly, as did the AFL-CIO, "massive federal commitment to early childhood development and day care."[60] When Miller became president of CLUW in 1979, the pursuit of affordable and universally available child care continued.

Conservative opposition to government expenditures on child care was formidable, however, as was resistance to state income support for childbearing. Tax credits for child care did expand in 1976 and 1978. But even when CLUW and other women's groups scaled back their work and family agenda in the 1980s, settling on the passage of *unpaid* family leave as a feasible goal, President George Bush vetoed it twice before President Clinton signed the bill into law in 1993. The final law, the Family and Medical Leave Act (FMLA), required employers with over 50 employees to grant up to three months of unpaid leave for the birth or adoption of a child or for the care of a sick family member.[61] It was certainly a victory, just as the passage of Title VII and OSHA had been. But as with other gender-blind approaches to reproductive issues, women still confronted choices men didn't because only women faced involuntary leave because of childbirth.

The FMLA also left class inequities intact. Without income replacement available, few low-income workers could take advantage of these new rights. Involuntary wage work remained a problem for working-class women. As CLUW's 1977 report "A Commitment to Children" specified, a national policy on children and families that would meet the needs of working-class women included affordable child care, paid leave, and a "floor under family income and full employment."[62] It was also intimately linked to raising women's wages, a point not lost on the thousands of working women who rejuvenated the call for equal pay for comparable work in the 1980s.

COMPARABLE WORTH RESURFACES

In the 1980s, a comparable worth or pay equity movement burst onto the national scene, capturing the energy and imagination of working women across the country. It was a direct descendant of the postwar labor women's campaign for comparable worth and a "rate for the job without regard to sex," but few knew of this history. Many of the participants, even those in the unions most intimately involved such as SEIU and AFSCME, thought they had invented the idea. They were wrong; comparable worth had a long historical pedigree: one rooted in the labor movement itself.

In the late 1960s, Title VII had inspired advances in regard to job integration and affirmative action and had encouraged women to raise their income by seeking men's jobs. Women also used the Equal Pay Act for wage hikes when they could find men doing work that was "substantially similar" to theirs. Millions of women were still stuck in low-paying female-majority jobs, however, with little or no recourse, legal or otherwise. The Equal Pay Act had been amended in 1972 to cover executive, administrative, and professional women, but its limited applicability to women holding similar jobs to men remained intact.

A handful of unions, including AFSCME, the UAW and the IUE, kept alive the comparable worth idea. Women (and some men) within these unions persistently argued that helping individual women escape from the female job ghetto was not enough, that what was needed was lifting the pay for those women left behind. In the late 1960s and increasingly in the 1970s, they urged the women's movement to push both for upgrading women's jobs and "providing for equal pay for comparable worth under the Equal Pay Act." They also raised these same issues with employers, filing grievances and lawsuits against employers alleging sex bias in the way wages were set for women's jobs.[63] The IUE, for example, filed pioneering lawsuits under the Equal Pay Act and Title VII claiming sex bias in wage setting at Westinghouse plants in Ohio and New Jersey. At the company's lamp assembly plant in Trenton, New Jersey, where women comprised eighty percent of the workers, the company rated each job based on knowledge, training, and responsibility, but then instructed supervisors to pay women less than men for jobs receiving the same rating. This was necessary, they explained, because of the "more transient character of [women's] services, overtime limitations, and the general sociological factors not requiring discussion herein." Still, the *highest* women's rate in Trenton was *lower* than the *lowest* male rate.[64]

In the late 1970s the issue began to resonate more broadly. In 1976, Kitty Ellickson, Dorothy Haener, Gloria Johnson, and other women from labor as well as from women's groups such as NOW began meeting at the IUE headquarters in Washington as part of the National Women's Agenda Task Force on Women and Employment. They proposed a focus on the "elimination of artificially depressed wage rates for traditional female jobs, and the attainment of equal pay for work of equal value."[65] CWA, CLUW, and other labor groups passed resolutions endorsing comparable worth and urging Congress to make it a priority. Veteran civil rights attorney Eleanor Holmes Norton lent her considerable talents to the effort during her tenure as EEOC chair from 1977 to 1981. Norton spoke out in favor of comparable worth, and the EEOC initiated high profile lawsuits charging wage discrimination in women's jobs. In April 1980, when the EEOC held hearings on "comparable worth," labor and women's groups turned out to testify.[66]

A year later, when the Supreme Court in *County of Washington v. Gunther* held that female prison matrons who were paid seventy percent of male prison guards' salary could sue under Title VII, even though their jobs differed, siding with AFSCME, the issue hit the national airwaves. AFSCME had been negotiating for pay equity raises throughout the 1970s, but had made little headway. Eventually, they hired the IUE legal team of Winn Newman and Ruth Weyand to give them advice in pressing their comparable worth claims on behalf of public sector clerical workers, and the IUE attorneys had helped prepare the lawsuit that eventually made its way to the Supreme Court. In 1983, AFSCME finally won its Title VII lawsuit against the State of Washington, claiming over $500 million for underpaid state workers in female-dominated jobs.[67]

Now armed with the credible threat of legal action, thousands of clerical workers, nurses, food service workers, and others negotiated pay equity advances at the bargaining table; they also set up commissions to "cleanse job evaluations of sex bias," thus affecting wage structures permanently. A national debate ensued over the skill and value of women's jobs. As one participant in the Oregon comparable worth campaign among state workers recalled, "[we] asked why workers who take care of people consistently earn less than workers who take care of things. . . . Women who were formerly ashamed to admit they were clerical workers proudly asserted the value and importance of their work."[68] Although after 1985, the courts began to rule against the union plaintiffs, upholding employer rights and "free-market" ideology, many unions continued to win "pay equity" gains through collective bargaining. They negotiated "bias free" jobs evaluation schemes; they also proposed and won higher wage gains for those in the lowest wage categories, a practice known as "solidarity bargaining."[69]

LABOR WOMEN AT THE MARGINS

The labor feminist commitment to civil and social rights thus reasserted itself in the late 1970s and 1980s. Yet it now existed in quite a different environment than it had a generation earlier. The labor movement on which it depended was no longer a growing and vibrant social movement. New public sector unions arose in the 1960s that partially offset union declines in manufacturing and elsewhere, but the trends were unmistakable. In the 1970s, union density fell slowly and steadily, dropping from 26 to 22 percent of the labor force. In the 1980s, the decline continued, particularly among the large industrial unions beset with increased global competition and aging technology. Women were now a third of all union members, up from a fifth in 1968. But over the course of the 1980s, the labor movement lost millions of members, a situation it had not faced since the 1920s. Labor membership fell from 20 million in 1980 to less than 17 million in 1990. Unions were having enormous difficulty expanding their base, whether in manufacturing, construction, or service jobs.[70]

Organizing among clerical workers was no exception. Labor faced hostility from aggressive and powerful employers as always, and it now lacked the support of government officials who had once offered it some measure of protection and legitimacy. Employers fought with every weapon available, particularly in the insurance and banking sector. "We never knew what hit us," Nussbaum remembered some fifteen years later. "We got smashed over and over. These businesses had not traditionally been unionized, and they were damned if they were going to be the first ones in the new wave. We never had an easy election."[71] By the end of the 1980s, the banking industry had changed some of its most egregious discriminatory pay and promotion policies, but union density had actually fallen over the course of the decade.[72] The insurance industry was equally invincible. After a hard-fought organizing and contract victory for District 925 at the Syracuse offices of Equitable Life, the company closed its Syracuse branch and dismissed its unionized workers.[73]

Organizing fared somewhat better in the public sector and among university clericals. Although prestigious schools such as Harvard, Yale, Vassar, and Columbia balked at the notion of sharing control and wealth with their largely female clerical staff, some 70 percent of the campaigns conducted among university clericals in the 1970s and 1980s emerged with union contracts. Sizable clerical divisions now existed within SEIU, AFSCME, and the UAW. Still, the campaigns had been brutal. Harvard, for example, engaged its support staff in an exhausting fourteen-year ordeal before conceding defeat in 1988.[74]

Similarly, the pay equity movement fared quite differently in the private than in the public sector. Despite its initial success among state and county workers, it failed to spread to white-collar corporate offices and industrial parks. It remained limited and constrained, due in large part to the weakness of labor among private sector office workers. As later research revealed, pay equity statutes had passed, even in the public sector, due largely to the support of organized labor. It was simply an impossible task to transform salary structures in the absence of workers' collective power.[75] Labor feminists had increased their numbers and leadership in a class movement that was rapidly declining in power and prestige.

Just as significantly, labor women's other traditional allies seemed remote as best. New Deal liberalism had survived the 1960s, losing some key battles but winning others, particularly those having to do with expanding the civil rights of minorities and women. By the 1980s, though, a new conservatism reigned, and the Democrats, fearful of being marginalized and tarred with the Big Labor brush, pursued a politics that kept the trade unions at arm's length. The particular and pressing needs of working-class women were not a priority for the larger feminist movement either. Labor feminist allies like Frieda Miller, Kitty Ellickson, or Esther Peterson were few and far between. Second wave feminism had helped transform the climate for gender politics, opening up new opportunities and freedoms for all women, but the problems of how to realize those rights and how to make them a reality for the majority of women remained.

The Next Wave

I WROTE THIS book to give my mother's generation their due. I also wrote in hope that a history of labor feminism might inspire and inform the next women's movement. For I think that the feminism of the twenty-first century will look as much like the one my generation left behind as the one it invented.

Yet the next women's movement will be different from any of its predecessors. Social movements are successful because they speak to the needs of their time. They can learn from the past, but they can not succeed by imitating it. A reading of history that is useful to the future must be one that embraces as well as discards, that praises as well as criticizes. That means having a "double consciousness" about the labor feminism of the depression generation as well as the new feminism that came of age in the 1960s.

This book has emphasized the positive and forward-thinking aspects of the political philosophy of the postwar generation of labor feminists. It is worth restating those here. But it is also appropriate to concentrate on the failings of that movement and the ways in which their ideas must be transcended.

REVALUING LABOR FEMINISM

Many of the ideas of mid-century labor feminists no longer seem so wrong-headed, in part because their intellectual framework now appears to be one to which we are returning. Labor feminists recognized multiple sources of inequality and injustice. They understood that gender inequality is but one form of oppression and that it is not necessarily always the primary injustice bearing down on women. In some eras and for some people, class or race inequalities may emerge as more problematic or more in need of resolution than gender inequities.

The labor feminists whose stories are told in this book saw nothing contradictory in asking for "equal rights" and "special benefits." For them, equal treatment was insufficient to bring equality. They claimed the rights of men and more. They understood that equality was a relationship of difference, and that achieving rights equal to men was a place to begin, not end.

In part because of their embrace of difference *and* equality, they maintained a healthy skepticism toward the masculine standard, especially as it manifested itself in public policy. The work world of men, in the view of most labor feminists, was not necessarily better than the work world of women. Nor were the workplace norms to which men subscribed necessarily the ones to which women should aspire. Quite the contrary. Women needed to challenge ideologies that valued male activities over female or that granted rights and privileges only to men or those who acted like them.

Mid-century labor feminists articulated a vision of gender equality that, far from being conservative, demanded sweeping change, change geared not toward ending gender divides but destabilizing gender hierarchies. They were rethinking the gender spheres by revaluing those things deemed female. They wanted access to paid work and to the status, power, and monetary benefits it bestowed. Yet they refused to see it as the only realm that should offer such rewards. The work traditionally associated with women, whether paid or unpaid, was just as skilled, essential, and worthy of attribute as the work of men.

As the market economy spreads across the globe, the criticisms of the unalloyed benefits of labor market participation voiced by labor feminists take on renewed significance. Labor women sought employment, yet at the same time they sought to keep wage work from overwhelming the rest of life. They offered a powerful critique of the free market and the nature of competition within it. Individuals did not exist as autonomous unencumbered entities; nor were they rewarded equally when competing in the market. The market penalized those with outside commitments to family and community; it also offered an unfair advantage to those who entered it with accumulated capital. The removal of barriers to market entry thus was insufficient to achieve economic equality. Preexisting structures of difference and histories of appropriation affected the market performance of individuals and its economic rewards. Individual rights had to be supplemented with social.

Moreover, the vaunted "liberty of contract" so celebrated by many equal rights feminists was a myth. There was no "freedom" to contract without a viable choice of alternative work; in addition, the power of corporations and of combined capital vitiated individual bargaining, rendering it meaningless. The only real "liberty of contract" existed between parties of relatively equal power. Collective representation at the workplace—or some similar equalizing mechanism—was thus necessary if free labor and liberty of contract were to be realities.

Mid-century labor feminists articulated a labor politics and an economic analysis that differed substantially from the conservatives of their day. Like their liberal democratic allies, they favored state intervention and regulation of the market. Yet the labor wing of the Democratic Party, including labor feminists, had its own laborist version of the New Deal. Theirs was a more grassroots participatory vision than the elitist regulatory one embraced by many New Dealers; they mixed their liberalism with a healthy dose of populist egalitarianism. And, while they believed in state regulations, they tempered this endorsement with the need for voluntary decentralized institutions like unions.

Their penchant for blending state solutions with more bottom-up participatory intervention offers a way forward today. The state can not solve every problem. It imposes universal one-size-fits-all solutions that often are not solutions at all. Government policy is a top-down, externally generated solution as well, one that relies on experts and abstract knowledge rather than local and particularistic know-how. Labor feminists advocated a *mix* of public and private interventions, of state regulations and labor-management enforcement. The state could set regulations, but working people and communities had to participate in defining and enforcing those rules.

REFASHIONING LABOR FEMINISM

Still, there is much about mid-century labor feminism that should be rethought, including certain intellectual rigidities that kept labor feminists from leading the social movements of the 1960s and 1970s. These rigidities, if not identified and dissolved, will likely have the same dampening effect today.

The new feminists of the 1960s and 1970s had many complaints about the politics of their mothers, and their criticisms were often well taken. They demanded that sexual divisions give way as well as sexual hierarchies, that the political be redefined to include the personal and the sexual, that men be confronted *directly* about their behavior at home as well as at work, and that new forms of worker representation be invented. They also challenged the masculine mystique in new ways, exposing the myth of male incompetence in the home and shattering the notion that masculinity was incompatible with changing diapers or consoling a crying child.

Labor feminism had helped create the new movement; it also was transformed by it. Inspired by the new feminism, labor women worked harder than ever to build a new, more woman-friendly labor movement in the 1970s and 1980s. But while the jolt of feminist energy the labor movement got from working women's turn to unions reconnected it briefly to its old crusading spirit, it did little to stem labor's loss of membership and influence. As the twentieth-first century dawns, 40 percent of union members in the U.S. are now women, but the labor movement represents only 14 percent of the workforce (10 percent of the private sector and 37 percent of the public sector).[1] Moreover, organized labor's decline will continue unless the labor movement creates a new class politics that is more in step with the aspirations and realities of the twenty-first century workforce.

Unfortunately, mid-century labor feminists provide less help in reconceiving a class politics than they do in rethinking gender politics. Like the labor movement of which they were a part, labor feminists failed to fully recognize the changing nature of work and of workers—a failure that must be rectified by any movement whose goals include the transformation of work and of economic relationships. This narrowness of focus was problematic then, as it precluded effective representation for many non-factory workers, but in the twenty-first century it is a recipe for permanent marginality and continuing decline.

The industrial working class has declined in the United States; in its place has arisen a workforce that is increasingly in white-collar and service jobs. A new class politics will need to recognize the changing realities and aspirations of this new working class.

Workers now have more education and higher expectations about what they will gain from work and how much responsibility they will be asked to assume. They are interested in self-representation and in organizations that empower them individually as well as collectively. A labor movement seeking to be the vehicle for such aspirations will need to move beyond the older factory-style unionism that treated all workers the same and that bargained only for job security rather than for work redesign and increased possibilities for learning and worker self-management. Relying on the factory as the prototypic work-place, the unions that arose in the 1930s assumed a rigid and non-overlapping demarcation between employee and employer, an adversarial relation between worker and boss, and a homogeneous, semiskilled workforce with little interest in career advancement or workplace governance.[2]

The postwar labor feminists were tied too closely to this particular form of unionism. They offered little in the way of a critique of it, and hence found it difficult to transform unions to meet the needs of the growing ranks of white-collar and service women. These workers, as the new organizations among flight attendants and clericals in the 1970s made clear, have different issues than do factory workers. Their problems are psychological as well as economic; they need organizations that can regulate interactions with customers and clients not just with the boss. Indeed, for many service and white-collar workers, the qual-ity of the service they provide and the amount of control they exert over the service interaction or the provider-client exchange is as central to their financial security and job satisfaction as the employer-employee relationship. Just as new industrial unions arose that reflected the longings and fears of the New Deal generation, new unions must be born that express those of today's workforce.

There are signs that such a transformation is underway. Although not yet widespread, new independent forms of worker representation and collective power are emerging outside of organized labor.[3] Other experiments are under-way within AFL-CIO unions. SEIU broke with traditional models of both or-ganizing and representation in its successful efforts to unionize home care work-ers, predominantly African-American and Latina women. By 1995, some 45,000 home care workers had signed up in California alone; flourishing union locals also existed in Chicago, New York, New Orleans, and other cities. In 1999, after a twelve-year campaign, an additional 75,000 home care workers in Los Angeles County voted for union representation, making it one of the largest single union victories since the massive organizing campaigns of the 1930s.[4]

The Harvard Union of Clerical and Technical Workers, which secured its first contract with Harvard in 1988, has also been consistently innovative in representing the new working class. The union reflects its female-dominated service-worker constituency in its bargaining agenda and in the actual institu-tional structures it has built. Kris Rondeau, one of the lead organizers, proclaims the approach "a feminine style of organizing." Its goals, she explains, are simply "self-representation, power, and participation." In collective bargaining negoti-ations with Harvard, the sessions took place in the style of the Polish Solidarity negotiations, with large numbers of small teams grouped around tables, working out compromises on specific issues. Collective bargaining also involved, according to Rondeau, "many initial days where our people simply told their life stories. You see, management needed to know the realities of our lives and to know that our lives were as important as theirs."[5]

By creating structures that encouraged involvement, the union forged a powerful organization in which commitment and creativity flourished. In their negotiations in the early 1990s, for example, HUCTW won a 30 percent wage increase, improved benefits allowing more paid leave for family and community time, and in one of their hardest-fought battles, finally achieved raises, enhanced job security, and benefit parity for part-time employees. HUCTW also insisted on its own skills training classes for clerical workers in how to negotiate relationships with intemperate and demanding students, faculty (the worst), and other university personnel. Their goal was to end the "customer is always right" rule and develop more humane norms for clerical-customer interactions.[6] In her 1983 book, *The Managed Heart*, Arlie Hochschild argued that many service jobs involve "emotional labor" or forced emotional effort. She called for a new workplace movement that recognized workers' right to control their emotions (their "heart") in much the same way that factory workers insisted that their bodies be protected from unwarranted abuse. Her call is being heard by an increasing number of unions.[7]

CLASS AND THE WOMEN'S MOVEMENT

Yet meeting the needs of working-class women will depend on a new class politics emerging within the larger women's movement as well as within organized labor. Working-class women have always needed allies outside their class, but creating a revitalized cross-class coalition seems achievable today in a way it hasn't for decades. The current women's movement has now embraced much of the labor feminist agenda as its own. The burdens that once bore down largely on working-class women—long hours, the incompatibility of parenting and employment, the lack of societal support for caring labor—are increasingly the problems of everyone, and the women's movement has given these issues top priority. It is a movement that intervened in crucial ways in the debate over welfare policy and that continues to push employers, unions, and the state for better approaches to balancing work and family, including enhanced child care options, paid family leave, and job redesign.[8]

Still, the women's movement, like the labor movement, has a "class" problem. Theirs is not so much an inability to discard an outmoded class framework, however, as a failure to incorporate "class" as a continuing and central category of analysis. What is needed is a more class-*conscious* approach, one that acknowledges class as a still-salient, lived experience that shapes the needs and perspectives of *all* women. For left unaddressed, class reproduces itself in social relations and in social policy. And without such a class-conscious approach, the problems of one group of women end up being solved at the expense of another.

A more class-conscious feminism would define itself as about the removal of class and race injustice as well as gender, and policies that protect working-class institutions such as unions would be understood as important to the progress of women. In other words, the decline of organized labor would be seen as a feminist issue. Most women do not have sufficient power as individuals to effectuate change in employer practices; they must rely on collective power. Where such power exists, women have enjoyed higher wages, better benefits, and the beginnings of some control over their working conditions and work environment.

The history of labor feminism makes it clear, for example, that a work and family policy for low-income women is intimately linked to increasing worker economic and political power. Only then can nonprofessional workers secure the higher wages, paid leaves, and other kinds of income that will allow them to shorten their hours. Only then can the arbitrary power of supervisors in low-wage jobs be curbed enough to allow workers the flexibility and control over work time a healthy family life requires.

The women's movement must not abandon its long-standing call for the right to economic freedom and opportunity. Yet the question of the quality of jobs and the distribution of income needs to be inseparable from the quest for access. Raising the wages of those at the bottom must be as important as opening up jobs for those near the top.

The next women's movement, if it is to succeed, must tackle the economic and class issues that still lie at the heart of women's second-class citizenship. It must continue to believe, as labor feminists did, that workplace justice is only achievable in tandem with social rights, and that the life and labors of the home and community are as much to be valued as those of the market.

AD-CHS	Anne Draper Collection, CHS
AD-GMMA	Anne Draper Files 1913–96, Economic Research Department Record Group 13, GMMA
AD-SUL	Anne Draper Papers, 1938–73, SUL
AF	*American Federationist*
AFA-ALUA	Association of Flight Attendants, Dallas Collection, 1952–80, ALUA
AFWAL-GMMA	American Federation of Women's Auxiliaries of Labor, Record Group 52, 1935–77, GMMA
AL-SL	Alice Leopold Papers, SL
ALUA	Archives of Labor and Urban Affairs, Walter P. Reuther Library, Wayne State University, Detroit, Michigan
BL-UCB	Bancroft Library, University of California, Berkeley, California
CFL-LARC	California Federation of Labor Collection, LARC
CHS	California Historical Society, San Francisco, California
CK-TL	Connie Kopelov Papers, 1974–87, TL
CLUW-ALUA	Coalition of Labor Union Women Collection, ALUA
DH-ALUA	UAW Women's Department: Dorothy Haener Papers, 1932–82, ALUA
EP-SL	Esther Peterson Papers, 1884–1998, SL
FM-SL	Frieda Miller Papers, 1909–73, SL
FPD-ALUA	UAW Fair Practices and Anti-Discrimination Department, Women's Bureau Papers, 1946–53, ALUA
FTWP-UP	Federation of Telephone Workers of Pennsylvania, Western Region, Pittsburgh, 1945–83, UP
GMMA	George Meany Memorial Archives, Silver Spring, Maryland
HB-ALUA	Helen W. Berthelot Collection, 1946–88, ALUA
IUE-RU	International Union of Electrical Workers Records, RU
JAH	*Journal of American History*
KPE-ALUA	Katherine Pollak Ellickson Papers, Parts 1–3, 1921–78, ALUA
LARC	Labor Archives and Research Center, San Francisco State University, San Francisco, California
LD-GMMA	Legislative Department Records, AFL, AFL-CIO, 1906–78, GMMA
LH-ALUA	UAW Women's Department: Lillian Hatcher Papers, 1942–79, ALUA
LS-ALUA	Lillian Sherwood Collection, 1938–66, ALUA
MDK-SL	Mary Dublin Keyserling Papers, 1924–88, SL
MJ-ALUA	Millie Jeffrey Collection Papers, 1930–84, ALUA

MM-ALUA	Mary Upshaw McClendon Collection, ALUA
MN-RU	Mary Norton Papers, RU
MW-ALUA	Myra Wolfgang Papers, 1963–76, ALUA
NCEP-GMMA	National Committee for Equal Pay Files, 1953–74, Unprocessed, GMMA
NDWU-SLA	National Domestic Workers Union Records, 1965–79, SLA
NFTW-TL	National Federation of Telephone Workers, TL
NYT	*New York Times*
RU	Special Collections and University Archives, Rutgers University, New Brunswick, New Jersey
SFWR-TL	Stewardesses for Women's Rights Records, 1963–87, TL
SHSW	State Historical Society of Wisconsin, Madison, Wisconsin
SL	Schlesinger Library, Radcliffe Institute, Harvard University, Cambridge, Massachusetts
SLA	Southern Labor Archives, Special Collections Department, Pullen Library, Georgia State University, Atlanta, Georgia
SUL	Department of Special Collections, Stanford University Libraries, Stanford, California
TL	Tamiment Institute Library, Robert F. Wagner Labor Archives, New York University, New York
TO-SUL	Tillie Olsen Collection, SUL
TUWOHP	The 20th Century Trade Union Woman: Vehicle for Social Change, Oral History Project, Institute of Industrial Relations, University of Michigan, Ann Arbor, Michigan
TWU-TL	Transport Workers Union of America Collection, TL
UE-UP	United Electrical Workers, National Headquarters Records, 1935–80, 1986 Red Dot Accession, UP
UIOHP	University of Iowa Oral History Project, Iowa City, Iowa
UP	Archives of Industrial Society, University of Pittsburgh Libraries, Pittsburgh, Pennsylvania
UPWA-OHP	United Packinghouse Workers of America Oral History Project, State Historical Society of Wisconsin, Madison, Wisconsin
VF-ALUA	Vertical Files, ALUA
WAC-ALUA	Women's Auxiliaries Collection, UAW, 1941–76, ALUA
WB-RG86	Women's Bureau, U.S. Department of Labor, Record Group 86, National Archives and Record Center, Washington, DC
WD-ALUA	Women's Department Papers, UAW, 1919–82, ALUA

NOTES

INTRODUCTION
THE MISSING WAVE

1. Neil MacFarquhar, "What's a Soccer Mom Anyway?" *NYT*, Oct. 20, 1996.

2. "Pink-collar" is a term coined by Louise Kapp Howe in *Pink Collar Workers: Inside the World of Women's Work* (New York: G.P. Putnam's Sons, 1977) to refer to female-majority jobs such as secretary, waitress, beautician, or salesclerk because they don't fit comfortably into either the blue-collar or white-collar category. Pink-collar jobs are typically low paid, dead-end, offer few benefits, and involve a service or emotional expectation.

3. Carey Goldberg, "Suburbs' Soccer Moms: Fleeing the GOP and Much Sought," *NYT*, Oct. 6, 1996; Ruy Teixeira, "Finding the Real Center: Lessons of the 1996 Elections," *Dissent* (Spring 1997): 51–59.

4. Nancy Seifer, *Absent from the Majority* (New York: American Jewish Committee, 1973).

5. In my view, class is a cultural as well as an economic category. It can best be understood as an elastic concept that inflects values and identity rather than as a social fact that *produces* a particular consciousness. For elaboration, see E. P. Thompson, *The Making of the English Working Class* (New York: Penguin Books, 1963), preface; Patrick Joyce, "Narratives of Class," in *Class*, ed. Patrick Joyce (Oxford: Oxford University Press, 1995), 322–32; and Beverly Skeggs, *Formations of Class and Gender: Becoming Respectable* (London: Sage Publications, 1997), introduction. When I use the term "working-class" in this book, I do not mean to suggest a rigid dichotomous class categorization of society. I am simply referring to that majority group in society whose income, whether from their own market work or that of family members, derives primarily from non-supervisory wages or salary.

6. On Wolfgang, see box 1, files 1–5, MW-ALUA; "Myra Wolfgang," VF-ALUA; Edwin Lahey, "Myra, the Battling Belle of the Working-Man's Café Society," *Detroit Free Press*, July 24, 1966; Jean Maddern Pitrone, *Myra: The Life and Times of Myra Wolfgang, Trade Union Leader* (Wyandotte, MI: Calibre Books, 1980); Dorothy Sue Cobble, *Dishing It Out: Waitresses and Their Unions in the Twentieth Century* (Urbana: University of Illinois, 1991), 97–99, 128–30; Dana Frank, "Girl Strikers Occupy Chain Store, Win Big: The Detroit Woolworth's Strike of 1937," in Howard Zinn, Dana Frank, and Robin D. G. Kelley, *Three Strikes: Miners, Musicians, Salesgirls, and the Fighting Spirit of Labor's Last Century* (Boston: Beacon Press, 2001), 57–118; Daniel Katz, "Myra Wolfgang," in *Notable American Women*, vol. 5, ed. Susan Ware (Cambridge, MA: Harvard University Press, 2004).

7. Cobble, *Dishing It Out*, 128–30; "Myra Wolfgang," VF-ALUA .

8. Cobble, *Dishing It Out*, 128–30. Quote from Pitrone, *Myra*, 122–24.

9. Cobble, *Dishing It Out*, 12, 199–200; press release, "Wolfgang Routs Friedan," Oct. 22, 1970 (box 1, file 6, MW-ALUA).

10. The term "feminist" also seems appropriate because the labor women leaders I am writing about used it to describe themselves.

11. I began this book thinking I was recovering a feminism created solely by working-class women, and I used the term "working-class feminism" to describe it. Yet as the research progressed and it became clear that the women reformers I was documenting were a *multi*-class group of women closely associated with the labor movement, I decided to call them "labor feminists." Jacquelyn Dowd Hall also uses the term "labor feminist" in "O. Delight Smith's Progressive Era: Labor, Feminism, and Reform in the Urban South," in *Visible Women: New Essays on American Activism*, ed. Nancy Hewitt and Suzanne Lebsock (Urbana: University of Illinois, 1993), 166–98. Annelise Orleck uses the term "industrial feminists" to refer to the working-class women whose lives she unfolds in her evocative study, *Common Sense and a Little Fire: Women and Working-Class Politics in the United States, 1900–1965* (Chapel Hill: University of North Carolina Press, 1995), 6–7.

12. Historian William O'Neill coined the term "social feminist." See O'Neill, "Feminism as a Radical Ideology," in *Dissent: Explorations in the History of American Radicalism*, ed. Alfred F. Young (DeKalb: Northern Illinois University Press, 1968), 275–77, and O'Neill, *Feminism in America: A History*, 2nd rev. ed. (New Brunswick, NJ: Transaction Publishers, 1989), xiv. I consider labor feminism a strand within a broader social feminist movement. Not every social feminist, however, was a labor feminist. Labor feminists stressed unions as vehicles for lifting women's status, for example, an emphasis not shared by all social feminists. The differences and commonalities among women reformers will be further elaborated in chapter 2.

13. Much of the recent scholarship on social rights is indebted to T. H. Marshall. He stressed the need to move from civil and political rights to a consideration of social rights, which he defined in 1950 as the right "to economic welfare and security" and the social provisions needed "to live the life of a civilized being according to the standards prevailing in the society." See *Citizenship and Social Class* (Cambridge: Cambridge University Press, 1950), 11. The labor feminists whose stories are told here would have agreed. At the same time, their movement is not fully captured within Marshall's framework. They emphasized the need to revalue women's labor and the importance of redesigning jobs to better suit homemakers. Increasing state provisions was one among many goals. For illuminating work expanding upon Marshall, see Nancy Fraser and Linda Gordon, "Contract versus Charity: Why Is There No Social Citizenship in the U.S.?" *Socialist Review* 22 (July–Sept. 1992): 45–67; Ann Shola Orloff, "Gender and the Social Rights of Citizenship: The Comparative Analysis of Gender Relations and Welfare States," *American Sociological Review* 58 (June 1993): 303–28; and Eileen Boris and Sonya Michel, "Social Citizenship and Women's Right to Work in Postwar America," in *Women's Rights and Human Rights: International Historical Perspectives*, ed. Patricia Grimshaw et al. (New York: Palgrave, 2001), 199–219.

14. I am particularly in debt to the following: Nancy Gabin, *Feminism in the Labor Movement: Women and the United Auto Workers, 1935–1976* (Ithaca, NY: Cornell University Press, 1990); Ruth Milkman, *Gender at Work: The Dynamics of Job Segregation by Sex during World War II* (Urbana, University of Illinois Press, 1987); Dennis Deslippe, *Rights, Not Roses: Unions and the Rise of Working-Class Feminism, 1945–1980* (Urbana, University of Illinois Press, 2000); Alice Kessler-Harris, *Out to Work: A History of Wage-Earning Women in the United States* (New York, Oxford University Press, 1982); Susan M. Hartmann, *The Other Feminists: Activists in the Liberal Establishment* (New Haven: Yale University Press, 1998); Venus Green, *Race on the Line: Gender, Labor, and Technology in the Bell System, 1880–1980* (Durham, NC: Duke University Press, 2001); Georgia Nielsen, *From Sky Girl to Flight Attendant: Women and the Making of a*

Union (Ithaca, NY: Cornell University Press, 1982); Vicki Ruiz, *Cannery Women, Cannery Lives: Mexican Women, Unionization, and the California Food Processing Industry, 1939–1950* (Albuquerque: University of New Mexico Press, 1987); Diane Balser, *Sisterhood and Solidarity: Feminism and Labor in Modern Times* (Boston: South End Press, 1987); Melinda Chateauvert, *Marching Together: Women of the Brotherhood of Sleeping Car Porters* (Urbana: University of Illinois Press, 1998); Bruce Fehn, "African-American Women and the Struggle for Equality in the Meatpacking Industry, 1940–1960," *Journal of Women's History* 10 (Spring 1998): 45–69; and Lisa Kannenberg, "From World War to Cold War: Women Electrical Workers and Their Union, 1940–1955" (master's thesis, University of North Carolina, Charlotte, 1990). For powerful and imaginative recreations of working-class women's politics, family, community life, and job experiences in the nineteenth and early twentieth century that have influenced this study, see Christine Stansell, *City of Women: Sex and Class in New York, 1789–1869* (Urbana: University of Illinois, 1987); Ardis Cameron, *Radicals of the Worst Sort: Laboring Women in Lawrence, Massachusetts, 1860–1912* (Urbana: University of Illinois, 1993); Orleck, *Common Sense and a Little Fire*; Carole Turbin, *Working Women of Collar City: Gender, Class and Community in Troy, New York, 1864–86* (Urbana: University of Illinois Press, 1992); Dana Frank, *Purchasing Power: Consumer Organizing, Gender, and the Seattle Labor Movement, 1919–1929* (Cambridge: Cambridge University Press, 1994); and Elizabeth Faue, *Community of Suffering and Struggle: Women, Men, and the Labor Movement in Minneapolis, 1915–1945* (Chapel Hill: University of North Carolina, 1991).

15. Long-standing gender biases, still operative in the field of labor history, perpetuate working women's absence from the story as well. For elaboration, consult Ava Baron, "Gender and Labor History: Learning from the Past, Looking to the Future," in *Work Engendered: Toward a New History of American Labor*, ed. Ava Baron (Ithaca, NY: Cornell University Press, 1991), 1–46, and Alice Kessler-Harris, "Treating the Male as Other: Redefining the Parameters of Labor History," *Labor History* 34:2–3 (Winter 1993): 190–204.

16. Consult Hewitt and Lebsock, introduction to *Visible Women*, 1–13, as well as the essays by William Chafe and Sara Evans in that same volume for the ways middle-class women's activism has transformed notions of the political. See Theda Skocpol, *Protecting Soldiers and Mothers: The Political Origins of Social Policy in the United States* (Cambridge: Cambridge University Press, 1992) for how women's clubs wielded considerable political power through nontraditional means. See also Paula Baker, "The Domestication of Politics: Women and American Political Society, 1780–1920," *American Historical Review* 89 (June 1984): 620–47.

17. For example, Robert H. Zieger, *The CIO, 1935–1955* (Chapel Hill: University of North Carolina Press, 1995), 349–51. Unlike Zieger, Nelson Lichtenstein, in his recent overview of twentieth-century labor history, offers an unusually full discussion of the problems women faced in the labor movement and the role women played in building the new CIO. But he concludes that after the 1930s, "Except for the most left-wing of the unions, women's issues remained marginal to laborite ideology until the second wave of feminism arrived late in the 1960s." Nelson Lichtenstein, *The State of the Union: A Century of American Labor* (Princeton, NJ: Princeton University Press, 2002), 90.

18. Women in auxiliaries rarely if ever are counted when women's membership in unions is tallied. But I would argue that they should not be excised from the membership count simply because the nature of their membership diverged from the male standard. Nor should it be assumed that they exercised little influence in union affairs because they lacked formal routes to power.

19. Karen Sacks, *Caring by the Hour: Women, Work, and Organizing at Duke Medical Center* (Urbana: University of Illinois, 1988).

20. In this, the old labor history and the new converge. See, for example, Philip Taft, *The A.F. of L.: From the Death of Gompers to the Merger* (New York: Harper and Brothers, 1959), or Melvyn Dubofsky, *The State and Labor in Modern America* (Chapel Hill: University of North Carolina Press, 1994).

21. For the term "labor liberalism," see Kevin Boyle's pioneering work, *The UAW and the Heyday of American Liberalism, 1945–1968* (Ithaca, NY: Cornell University Press, 1995), preface and introduction. The political ideas of working people confound many of the categories in common usage to describe political groupings in the U.S. For the eighteenth and nineteenth centuries, historians have offered a class-nuanced understanding of republicanism that recognizes a more egalitarian tradition rooted in the working classes. For the twentieth century, however, liberalism is as yet largely uncomplicated by class variants.

22. The literature is immense. Comparative studies include Susan Pedersen, *Family, Dependence, and the Origins of the Welfare State: Britain and France, 1914–45* (Cambridge: Cambridge University Press, 1993); Seth Koven and Sonya Michel, eds., *Mothers of a New World: Maternalist Politics and the Origins of Welfare States* (New York: Routledge, 1993); Gisela Bock and Pat Thane, eds., *Maternity and Gender Policies: Women and the Rise of the European Welfare States, 1880s–1950s* (London: Routledge, 1991); and Ulla Wikander, Alice Kessler-Harris, and Jane Lewis, eds., *Protecting Women: Labor Legislation in Europe, the United States, and Australia, 1880–1920* (Urbana: University of Illinois, 1995). Illuminating studies focusing primarily on the U.S. include Alice Kessler-Harris, *In Pursuit of Equity: Women, Men, and the Quest for Economic Citizenship in 20th-Century America* (New York: Oxford University Press, 2001); Linda Gordon, *Pitied But Not Entitled: Single Mothers and the History of Welfare 1890–1935* (New York: The Free Press, 1994); Skocpol, *Protecting Soldiers and Mothers*; Gwendolyn Mink, *The Wages of Motherhood* (Ithaca, NY: Cornell University Press, 1995); Jill Quadagno, *The Color of Welfare: How Racism Undermined the War on Poverty* (New York: Oxford University Press, 1994); and Robert Lieberman, *Shifting the Color Line: Race and the American Welfare State* (Cambridge, MA: Harvard University Press, 1998).

23. Studies of the *private* welfare system or the "public/private welfare state" that have aided me include Sonya Michel, "Motherhood and Social Citizenship in the U.S. Public/Private Welfare State," paper presented at the Organization of American Historians Annual Convention, Apr. 18, 1997, San Francisco, CA; Jennifer Klein, *For All These Rights: Business, Labor, and the Shaping of America's Public-Private Welfare State* (Princeton, NJ: Princeton University Press, 2003); Sanford Jacoby, *Modern Manors: Welfare Capitalism Since the New Deal* (Princeton, NJ: Princeton University Press, 1997); Alice Kessler-Harris, *A Woman's Wage: Historical Meanings and Social Consequences* (Lexington: University Press of Kentucky, 1990); Benjamin Hunnicutt, *Kellogg's Six-Hour Day* (Philadelphia: Temple University Press, 1996); Lise Vogel, *Mothers on the Job: Maternity Policy in the U.S. Workplace* (New Brunswick, NJ: Rutgers University Press, 1993); Jill Quadagno, "Women's Access to Pensions and the Structure of Eligibility Rules: Systems of Production and Reproduction," *The Sociological Quarterly* 29 (Winter 1988): 541–58; and Lauri Perman and Beth Stevens, "Industrial Segregation and the Gender Distribution of Fringe Benefits," *Gender and Society* 3 (Sept. 1989): 388–404.

24. For an early criticism of the "declension trope" that dominates postwar labor history, see Judith Stein, "The Ins and Outs of the CIO," *International Labor and Working-Class History* 44 (Fall 1993): 53–63.

25. Boyle, *The UAW and the Heyday of American Liberalism*, 2, 4. See Ira Katznelson, Kim Geiger, and Daniel Kryder, "Limiting Liberalism: The Southern Veto in Congress, 1933–1950," *Political Science Quarterly* 108 (Summer 1993): 283–306, for a compatible study concluding that the power of the "southern veto on labor issues" was a prime impediment to labor's continuing reform efforts.

26. Lichtenstein, *State of the Union*, ch. 3, quote on p. 136; Judith Stein, *Running Steel, Running America: Race, Economic Policy, and the Decline of Liberalism* (Chapel Hill: University of North Carolina, 1998); Jack Metzgar, *Striking Steel: Solidarity Remembered* (Philadelphia: Temple University Press, 2000). For other accounts emphasizing the continuance of labor reform impulses, see Zieger, *The CIO, 1935–1955*, 374, 376, and Alan Derickson, "Health Security for All? Social Unionism and Universal Health Insurance, 1935–1958," *JAH* 81 (Mar. 1994): 1333–56.

27. Leila Rupp and Verta Taylor used the term "doldrums" to describe the postwar decades. They focused on the National Woman's Party as the predominant carrier of feminism in those years. See *Survival in the Doldrums: The American Women's Rights Movement, 1945 to the 1960s* (New York: Oxford University, 1987).

28. For the extension of feminism into the 1920s and 1930s, see Nancy Cott, *The Grounding of Modern Feminism* (New Haven: Yale University Press, 1987); Landon R. Y. Storrs, *Civilizing Capitalism: The National Consumers' League, Women's Activism, and Labor Standards in the New Deal Era* (Chapel Hill: University of North Carolina Press, 2000); Wendy Sarvasy, "Beyond the Difference versus Equality Debate: Post-Suffrage Feminism, Citizenship, and the Quest for a Feminist Welfare State," *Signs* 17 (Winter 1992): 329–62; Sybil Lipschultz, "Hours and Wages: The Gendering of Labor Standards in America," *Journal of Women's History* 8 (Spring 1996) 114–36; J. Stanley Lemons, *The Woman Citizen: Social Feminism in the 1920s* (Urbana: University of Illinois Press, 1973); and Amy Butler, *Two Paths to Equality: Alice Paul and Ethel M. Smith in the ERA Debate,1921–1929* (Albany: State University of New York Press, 2002). On feminism after 1930, see Cynthia Harrison, *On Account of Sex: The Politics of Women's Issues, 1945–1968* (Berkeley, University of California Press, 1988); Susan M. Hartmann, *From Margin to Mainstream: American Women and Politics since 1960* (New York: Knopf, 1989); Daniel Horowitz, *Betty Friedan and the Making of the Feminine Mystique: The American Left, The Cold War, and Modern Feminism* (Amherst: University of Massachusetts Press, 1998); Kathleen Laughlin, *Women's Work and Public Policy: A History of the Women's Bureau, U.S. Department of Labor, 1945–1970* (Boston: Northeastern University Press, 2000); Paula Giddings, *When and Where I Enter: The Impact of Black Women on Race and Sex in America* (New York: Quill William Morrow, 1984); Jacqueline Jones, *Labor of Love, Labor of Sorrow: Black Women, Work and the Family, From Slavery to the Present* (New York: Vintage, 1986), chs. 7 and 8; and Kate Weigand, *Red Feminism: American Communism and the Making of Women's Liberation* (Baltimore, Johns Hopkins University Press, 2001). A few accounts pay close attention to the contributions of labor women to feminism: Gerda Lerner, "Midwestern Leaders of the Modern Women's Movement: An Oral History Project," *Wisconsin Academy Review* (Winter 1994–95): 11–15; Susan Hartmann, *The Other Feminists*; Deslippe, *Rights, Not Roses*; and Gabin, *Feminism in the Labor Movement*.

29. The term "re-wave" is from a panel at the Organization of American Historians, Apr. 11–14, 2002, Washington, DC, entitled "Origin Stories, Origin Myths: Rewaving the History of Feminism." Chaired by Linda Gordon, the panel included papers by Nancy Hewitt, Lisa Tetrault, and Barbara Winslow.

30. For a recent discussion of the continuing scholarly bias toward ERA feminists as "forward-looking" and ERA opponents as conservative defenders of motherhood and the family, see Butler, *Two Paths to Equality*, 2–5.

31. For other work on the lives and ideas of working-class women and women of color that suggests the need for new measures of "feminist consciousness," see Evelyn Nakano Glenn, "From Servitude to Service Work: Historical Continuities in the Racial Division of Paid Reproductive Labor," in *Unequal Sisters: A Multicultural Reader in U.S. Women's History*, 3rd edition, ed. Vicki L. Ruiz and Ellen Carol DuBois (New York: Routledge, 2000), 436–65; Patricia Hill Collins, "Black Women and Motherhood," in *Rethinking the Family: Some Feminist Questions*, ed. Barrie Thorne and Marilyn Yalom (Boston: Northeastern University Press, 1992), 219–22; Deborah King, "Multiple Jeopardy, Multiple Consciousness: The Context of a Black Feminist Ideology," *Signs* 14 (Autumn 1988): 42–72; Deborah Gray White, *Too Heavy a Load: Black Women in Defense of Themselves 1894–1994* (New York: W.W. Norton, 1998); Myra Marx Ferree, "Working-Class Feminism: A Consideration of the Consequences of Employment," *Sociological Quarterly* (Spring 1980): 173–84; and Bock and Thane, "Editor's Introduction," in *Maternity and Gender Policies*, 1–20.

32. Lenore Weitzman, *The Divorce Revolution: The Unexpected Social and Economic Consequences for Women and Children in America* (New York: Free Press, 1985) was one of the first to make this point. For later work in this vein, see Mary Lyndon Shanley, "Spousal Equality and the Law: Beyond an 'Equal Rights' Approach," in *Writing a National Identity*, ed. Vivian Hart and Shannon Stimson (New York: St. Martin's Press, 1993), 89–105.

33. For calls to rethink the "equality" vs. "difference" dichotomy, see, among others, Joan Scott, "Deconstructing Equality-versus-Difference: Or, the Uses of Post-structuralist Theory for Feminism," *Feminist Studies* 14 (Spring 1985): 157–211; Joan Scott, *Only Paradoxes to Offer: French Feminists and the Rights of Man* (Cambridge: Cambridge University Press, 1996); Vogel, *Mothers on the Job*; Cynthia Daniels, "Competing Gender Paradigms: Gender Difference, Fetal Rights, and the Case of Johnson Control," *Policy Studies Review* 10:4 (Winter 1991): 51–68; and Butler, *Two Paths to Equality*.

34. Here I am building on arguments advanced in my earlier work. See Cobble, *Dishing It Out*; "Recapturing Working-Class Feminism," in *Not June Cleaver: Women and Gender in Postwar America*, ed. Joanne Meyerowitz (Philadelphia: Temple University Press, 1994), 57–83; and "Remaking Unions for the New Majority," in *Women and Unions: Forging a Partnership*, ed. Dorothy Sue Cobble (Ithaca, NY: Cornell University Press, 1993), 3–23.

35. For the proliferating body of scholarship that is writing women of color back into feminist history, see Beverly Guy-Sheftall's preface to *Words of Fire: An Anthology of African-American Feminist Thought* (New York: New Press, 1995) and the works cited in note 31. For an early call to recognize the way class and race shape feminism, see Gerda Lerner, "Women's Rights and American Feminism," *American Scholar* 40 (Spring 1971): 244–46.

36. Denise Riley, *Am I That Name? Feminism and the Category of "Women" in History* (Minneapolis: University of Minnesota Press, 1988).

37. William Julius Wilson, *The Declining Significance of Race: Blacks and Changing American Institutions* (Chicago: University of Chicago, 1978), and *Bridge over the Racial Divide: Rising Inequality and Coalition Politics* (Berkeley: University of California Press, 1999).

38. Nancy Fraser, "After the Family Wage: What Do Women Want in Social Welfare?" *Social Justice* 21 (Spring 1994): 80–86.

39. Melanie Phillips, "Home Truths: A Review of Midge Decter's *An Old Wife's Tale*," *Wall Street Journal*, Aug. 28, 2001.

CHAPTER 1
THE OTHER LABOR MOVEMENT

1. Gladys Dickason, "Women in Labor Unions," *Annals of the American Academy of Political and Social Science* 251 (May 1947): 71.

2. Esther Peterson, "The World Beyond the Valley," *Sunstone* 15: 5, issue 85 (Nov. 1991): 21–26.

3. William Chafe, *The Paradox of Change: American Women in the Twentieth Century* (New York: Oxford, 1991), 161–62; Alan Clive, "Women Workers in World War II: Michigan as a Test Case," *Labor History* 20 (Winter 1979): 44–72.

4. "Series D 29–41. Labor Force by Age and Sex: 1890 to 1970," 131–32, and "Series D 49–62. Marital Status of Women in the Civilian Labor Force: 1890 to 1970," 133–34, in *Historical Statistics of the United States, Colonial Times to 1970* (White Plains, NY: International Publications, 1989).

5. Gertrude Bancroft, *The American Labor Force: Its Growth and Changing Composition*, Census Monograph Series (New York: John Wiley and Sons, 1958), 45; "Series D 49–62. Marital Status of Women in the Civilian Labor Force: 1890 to 1970," 133; Carl Degler, *At Odds: Women and the Family in America from the Revolution to the Present* (New York: Oxford University Press, 1980), 418–35; Frieda Miller, "Women in the Labor Force," *Annals of the American Academy* 251 (May 1947): 35–43; Frieda Miller, "What's Become of Rosie the Riveter?" *NYT Magazine*, May 5, 1946, 40. For a fuller discussion of the class and racial-ethnic differences affecting female labor force participation, see Teresa L. Amott and Julie A. Matthaei, *Race, Gender and Work: A Multicultural Economic History of Women in the United States* (Boston: South End Press, 1991).

6. Miller, "What's Become of Rosie the Riveter?" 40; Sherna Gluck, *Rosie the Riveter Revisited* (Boston: Twayne, 1987).

7. Oral histories of women war workers attest to this change most persuasively. See, in particular, Gluck, *Rose the Riveter Revisited*, but also Brigid O'Farrell and Joyce Kornbluh, *Rocking the Boat: Union Women's Voices, 1915–1975* (New Brunswick, NJ: Rutgers University Press, 1996).

8. Carmen R. Chavez, "Coming of Age during the War: Reminiscences of an Albuquerque Hispana," *New Mexico Historical Review* 70:4 (Oct. 1995): 396–97, as quoted in Vicki Ruiz, *From Out of the Shadows: Mexican Women in Twentieth-Century America* (New York: Oxford University Press, 1998), 82.

9. Chafe, *The Paradox of Change*, 129–31; National Manpower Council, *Womanpower* (New York: Columbia University Press, 1957), 322.

10. Joanne Meyerowitz, "Beyond the Feminine Mystique: A Reassessment of Postwar Mass Culture 1946–1958," in *Not June Cleaver*, 239–62.

11. Lynn Weiner, *From Working Girl to Working Mother: The Female Labor Force in the US, 1820–1980* (Chapel Hill: University of North Carolina Press, 1985); 85–90.

12. Karen Tucker Anderson, "Last Hired, First Fired: Black Women Workers During World War II," *JAH* 69 (June 1982): 83–86; Karen Tucker Anderson, *Changing Woman: A History of Racial Ethnic Women in Modern America* (New York: Oxford University Press, 1996), 185–95.

13. Mary S. Bedell, "Employment and Income of Negro Workers, 1942–52," *Monthly Labor Review* 76 (1953): 599, table 2. Persons of Mexican ancestry had been excluded from the white category in 1930 but included in 1940 and 1950. See U.S. Bureau of Census, *Census of Population: 1950*, vol. II, *Characteristics of Population* (Washington, DC: GPO, 1953), 35–36.

14. Karen Tucker Anderson, "Last Hired, First Fired," 89; Bedell, "Employment and Income of Negro Workers," 600.

15. Paul Burstein, *Discrimination, Jobs, and Politics: The Struggle for Equal Employment Opportunity in the United States since the New Deal* (Chicago: University of Chicago, 1985), 8–9.

16. On Randolph, see Jervis Anderson, *A. Philip Randolph: A Biographical Portrait* (Berkeley: University of California Press, 1972); on the NAACP, Patricia Sullivan, *Days of Hope: Race and Democracy in the New Deal Era* (Chapel Hill: University of North Carolina Press, 1996), especially 141–42. The phrase "within the Veil" is from "The Forethought" in W.E.B. Du Bois, *The Souls of Black Folk* (New York: Fawcett Publications, Inc., 1961).

17. Marten Estey, *The Unions: Structure, Development, and Management*, 2nd ed. (New York: Harcourt Brace Jovanovich, Inc., 1976), 2–13.

18. Gabin, *Feminism in the Labor Movement*, 232; Sara Evans, *Personal Politics* (New York: Vintage, 1979), 212–32.

19. Faue, *Community of Suffering*, chs. 4–5; David Brody, *Workers in Industrial America: Essays on the 20th Century Struggle* (New York: Oxford University Press, 1993), chs. 3–4; Christopher Tomlins, "AFL Unions in the 1930s: Their Performance in Historical Perspective," *JAH* 4 (Mar. 1979):1021–42; Cobble, *Dishing It Out*, chs. 3–4.

20. Dickason, "Women in Labor Unions," 71–73.

21. Ibid., table 2, 71.

22. Milkman, *Gender at Work*, ch. 3; Frank, *Purchasing Power*; Faue, *Community of Suffering*.

23. The early assessments of women's relationship to unions during wartime and re-conversion were quite negative. See, for example, Sheila Tobias and Lisa Anderson, "What Really Happened to Rosie the Riveter? Demobilization and the Female Labor Force, 1944–47," in *Women's America: Refocusing the Past*, ed. Linda Kerber and Jane deHart (New York: Oxford University Press, 1982), 354–73. Ruth Milkman offers a more balanced analysis in "Rosie the Riveter Revisited: Management's Postwar Purge of Women Automobile Workers," in *On the Line: Essays in the History of Auto Work*, ed. Nelson Lichtenstein and Stephen Meyer (Urbana: University of Illinois, 1989), 129–47.

24. Dickason, "Women in Labor Unions," table 2, 71; Estey, *The Unions*, 8; Ruth Milkman, "Union Responses to Workforce Feminization in the United States," in *The Challenge of Restructuring: North American Labor Movements Respond*, ed. Jane Jenson and Rianne Mahon (Philadelphia: Temple University Press, 1993), 226–50.

25. Kannenberg, "From World War to Cold War," 12, 69, 73 and "The Impact of the Cold War on Women's Trade Union Activism: The UE Experience," *Labor History* 34 (Winter 1993): 309–23; Milkman, *Gender at Work*, 113.

26. Bruce Fehn, *Striking Women: Gender, Race, and Class in the UPWA, 1938–68* (unpublished manuscript in possession of the author, July 1999), 105, 155.

27. Milkman, *Gender at Work*, 113.

28. For ILGWU and ACWA figures, see Dickason, "Women in Labor Unions," 72. For national figures, see "Report, Conference of Trade Union Women, April 19–20, 1945," 32 (box 1544, file "1945 Union Conference," WB-RG86).

29. See box 36, file 8, and box 1, file 9, AD-GMMA, for ACWA membership in the 1950s and 1960s.

30. For FTA membership figures, see "Statement by FTA," in U.S. Senate, *Equal Pay for Equal Work for Women: Hearings before a Subcommittee of the Committee on Education and Labor, US Senate, 79th Congress on S. 1178, October 29–31, 1945* (Washington, DC: GPO, 1946), 184–85.

31. Cobble, *Dishing It Out*, tables 5A–5C, 6, 7, 8; Jack Barbash, *Unions and Telephones: The Story of the Communications Workers of America* (New York: Harper & Brothers, 1952), chs. 1, 9; Thomas R. Brooks, *Communications Workers of America: Story of a Union* (New York: Mason/Charter, 1977), 63, 238; John Schacht, *The Making of Telephone Unionism, 1920–1947* (New Brunswick, NJ: Rutgers University Press, 1985), 26–27, 166; George Kirstein, *Store and Unions: A Study of the Growth of Unionism in Dry Goods and Department Stores* (New York: Fairchild Publications, 1950), 217. For a comparison with earlier figures, see "Report, Conference of Trade Union Women, April 19–20, 1945."

32. Estey, *The Unions*, 5–6.

33. Fehn, *Striking Women*, 100–110, 152–60, and Fehn, "African-American Women and the Struggle for Equality," 45–69; *CIO News*, June 1, 1953.

34. Ruiz, *Cannery Women, Cannery Lives*; Robert Korstad and Nelson Lichtenstein, "Opportunities Found and Lost: Labor, Radicals, and the Early Civil Rights Movement," *JAH* 75 (Dec. 1988): 786–811.

35. Clive, "Women Workers in World War II," 44–72; Gabin, *Feminism in the Labor Movement*, 141; Milkman, *Gender at Work*, 84–98; "Guide"and box 7, file 12, LH-ALUA; "Guides" and other materials in FPD-ALUA and WD-ALUA.

36. Kannenberg, "The Impact of the Cold War," 310–11; Gerald Zahavi, "Passionate Commitments: Race, Sex, and Communism at Schenectady General Electric, 1932–1954," *JAH* 83 (Sept. 1996): 514–50. In 1944, the *CIO News* (Oct. 2, pp. 2, 8) reported that women held some 295 positions as local union officers; Zahavi (528–32) also notes women's increasing representation among union staff.

37. Philip S. Foner, *Women and the American Labor Movement: From World War I to the Present* (New York: The Free Press, 1980), 399–400.

38. Kannenberg, "The Impact of the Cold War," 310–19; box 2396, file "Women's Conferences, 1953–62," UE-UP; boxes 63, 186, and 2186, IUE-RU.

39. Figures from "Statement of Al Philip Kane, General Counsel, NFTW," In U.S. Senate, *Equal Pay for Equal Work Hearings, October 29–31, 1945*, 129–45.

40. For the pre-1930s history of telephone operator unionism, see Stephen Norwood, *Labor's Flaming Youth: Telephone Operators and Workers' Militancy, 1887–1923* (Urbana: University of Illinois, 1990). For the 1930s and early 1940s, see Schacht, *The Making of Telephone Unionism*, ch. 8; interviews with Ruth Wiencek and Catherine Conroy, TUWOHP; interview with Helen Berthelot by John Schacht, UIOHP; Green, *Race on the Line*, 70–182. Also see the *Federation Voice* (newspaper of the NFTW), TL; Eva Keith, Gen'l. Sec.-Treas., Federation of Women Telephone Workers of So. California, to C.W. Werkau, Sec.-Treas., NFTW, letter, Aug. 31, 1943, NFTW-TL; and box 416, file "Alliance of Independent Trade Unions 1972–76," FTWP-UP.

41. Dorothy Sue Cobble, "Telephone Strike of 1947," in Ronald Filippelli, ed., *Labor Conflict in the United States: An Encyclopedia* (New York: Garland, 1990), 521–23; Green, *Race on the Line*, 177–82; *Telephone Worker*, Jan. 1946, 4.

42. Schacht, *The Making of Telephone Unionism*, ch. 8; box 416, file "Alliance of Independent Trade Unions, 1972–76," FTWP-UP; Philip Foner, *Women and the American Labor Movement*, 400–402; *Telephone Worker*, Dec. 1945 and Mar. 1947; Cobble, "Telephone Strike of 1947," interview with Ruth Wiencek by Carol Bowie, June 2, 1976, TUWOHP, 17.

43. John Shaughnessy, Jr., "Report on Alliance Reorganization and Structure," Apr. 9, 1975 (box 416, file "Alliance of Independent Trade Unions, 1972–76," FTWP-UP).

44. Cobble, *Dishing It Out*, ch. 4, table 8.

45. For retail union history, see George Lipsitz, *Class and Culture in Cold War America: 'A Rainbow at Midnight'* (South Hadley, MA: J.F. Bergin Publishers, 1982), 81–84; Kirstein, *Stores and Unions*, 102; interview with Marion Sills, conducted by author, 1977, Women in California Oral History Collection, CHS. For office worker unionization, see Sharon Strom, "'We're No Kitty Foyles': Organizing Office Workers for the Congress of Industrial Organizations, 1937–50," in *Women, Work and Protest*, ed. Ruth Milkman (London: Routledge & Kegan Paul, 1985); for flight attendants, Nielsen, *From Sky Girl to Flight Attendant*; for teachers, Marjorie Murphy, *Blackboard Unions: the AFT and the NEA, 1900–1980* (Ithaca, NY: Cornell University Press, 1990); on nurses, Patrica D'Antonio, "Nurses' Unions," and "Nursing Profession," in *The Reader's Companion to U.S. Women's History*, ed. Wilma Mankiller et al. (Boston: Houghton Mifflin Company, 1998), 310, 434–36; Darline Clark Hine, *Black Women in White: Racial Conflict and Cooperation in the Nursing Profession, 1890–1950* (Bloomington: Indiana University Press, 1989); Susan Reverby, *Ordered to Care: The Dilemma of American Nursing, 1850–1945* (Cambridge: Cambridge University Press, 1987).

46. The body of literature on women's auxiliaries is surprisingly small. For examples, see Marjorie Penn Lasky, " 'Where I Was a Person': The Ladies Auxiliary in the 1934 Minneapolis Teamsters' Strikes," in *Women, Work, and Protest*, 181–205; Susan Levine, "Workers' Wives: Gender, Class, and Consumerism in the 1920s US," *Gender and History* 3 (Spring 1991): 44–64; Chateauvert, *Marching Together*; and Teresa Poor, "Married to the Union: The Woman's International Typographical Auxiliary and the Duty to Consume, 1900–1942" (master's thesis, Labor Studies and Employment Relations Department, Rutgers University, 2000).

47. Frank, *Purchasing Power*; Mary E. Ryder, "'Purchasing Power' and Those Who Use It," *AF* 35 (July 1928): 820–23; Mrs. R. J. Lowther, "The Typographical Woman's International Auxiliary," *AF* 36 (Aug. 1929): 971–72.

48. See, for example, Paula Pfeffer, "The Women behind the Union: Halena Wilson, Rosina Tucker, and the Ladies Auxiliary to the Brotherhood of Sleeping Car Porters," *Labor History* 36 (Fall 1995): 557–78; Lasky, " 'Where I Was a Person,' "181–205; ILWU Auxiliary Papers (ILWU Archives, San Francisco); "Socialist Women and Labor Struggles, 1934–1945: A Report by Participants," *International Socialist Review* 36 (Mar. 1975): 20–25, 36–38; "Retirement Ends 35 Years' Service to UAW Causes," *UAW Solidarity*, Apr. 1972.

49. Information on the AFL auxiliaries is based primarily on the AFWAL Collection, GMMA, in particular box 11, file 66, and "The History Book" in box 20. Material related to the Congress of Women's Auxiliaries is in LS-ALUA and WAC-ALUA.

50. "History Scrapbook," box 20, and material in box 11, file 66, AFWAL-GMMA; *History of the American Federation of Women's Auxiliaries of Labor*, pamphlet published by AFWAL, Washington, DC, n.d. [c.1945] (State Historical Society of Wisconsin); I. M. Ornburn, "Women's Auxiliaries Federate," *AF* 43 (May 1936): 486–87; I. M. Ornburn, "The Women Pitch In: Auxiliaries Actively Promote Label Drive," *AF* 52 (Sept. 1945): 630–31. For a claim of two million members by 1994, see box 11, file 68, AFWAL-GMMA.

51. "History Scrapbook," box 20; AFWAL *Bulletins*, 1943–47 (box 17, files 23–25); *Women's Auxiliary News*, 1944–50 (box 17, files 26–29); *Proceedings of the AFWAL*, Sixth Annual Convention, April 17–19, 1953 (box 12, file 11), all in AFWAL-GMMA. See also Philip Foner, *Women and the American Labor Movement*, 368–74, and Anna R. Kelsey, "No Substitute for Auxiliaries," *AF* 60 (Aug. 1953): 13.

52. See, for example, *CIO News*, July 30, 1938, 6; Aug. 8, 1938, 8; May 1, 1939, 7; interview with Catherine Gelles by Jack W. Skeels, University of Michigan–Wayne State University, July 7, 1961, ALUA.

53. *CIO News*, Sept. 25, 1939, 5; Apr. 8, 1940, 5; June 17, 1940, 2; Nov. 25, 1940, 1; Nov. 3, 1941, 6; Nov. 24, 1941, 12; Dec. 8, 1941, 3; Philip Foner, *Women and the American Labor Movement*, 329.

54. Faye Stephenson, VF-ALUA. On the value auxiliary women placed on wage-earning experience as a background for leadership, see "Two UAW Groups Ask Martin to 'Undo' Union Acts," *Detroit Times*, Oct. 8, 1937, 12.

55. "Catherine Gelles," VF-ALUA.

56. CIO-CWA, *How to Build a Better Life: CWA Manual* (CIO Education and Research Department, pamphlet no. 155, 1947), 25–28, in the audio-visual files, LS-ALUA.

57. *CIO News*, July 6, 1942, 6, and Nov. 27, 1944, 9; Committee Reports and CIO-CWA Convention Proceedings (boxes 3–5, LS-ALUA); "Official Report to the Fifth Annual Conference, CIO-CWA, Atlantic City, NJ, November 18, 1946" (box 3, file 6, LS-ALUA); Philip Foner, *Women and the American Labor Movement*, 368–74.

58. Karen Sacks revised her initial estimates of female power upward as she came to reject the correlation of power with formal leadership titles. See Sacks, *Caring by the Hour*, 1–4. C. Wright Mills referred to the new generation of labor leaders emerging in the 1940s as the new men of power. Mills, *The New Men of Power: America's Labor Leaders* (New York: A.M. Kelley, 1948).

59. Gary Fink, "Introduction: The American Labor Leader in the Twentieth Century: Quantitative and Qualitative Portraits," in Fink, *Biographical Dictionary of American Labor* (Westport, CT: Greenwood Press, 1984), 29, table 8. Systematic data comparing changes in the percentage of leadership positions held by women and men does not exist. However, my point is based on an *absolute* increase in the numbers of women in leadership positions and the emergence of a critical mass of women leaders. For further information about women's leadership, see Dickason, "Women in Labor Unions," 77; "Trade Union Positions Held by Women in 13 International Unions with 50,000 or more Women Members," memo, July 1957 (box 9, file 11), and "Memo," Jan. 1958 (box 9, file 1, AD-GMMA).

60. Fink, *Biographical Dictionary of American Labor*, 108, 159, 295–96, 435, 459, 505; Orleck, *Common Sense and a Little Fire*; prologue; Ann Schofield, *'To Do and to Be': Portraits of Four Women Activists, 1893–1986* (Boston: Northeastern University Press, 1997); Ann Schofield, introduction to Rose Pesotta, *Bread upon the Waters* (Ithaca, NY: Cornell University Press, 1987), v–xix.

61. On Parker, see Norwood, *Labor's Flaming Youth*, 302–3; on Herstein, see O'Farrell and Kornbluh, *Rocking the Boat*, 10–33; on Anderson, see Mary Anderson, *Woman at Work: The Autobiography of Mary Anderson as Told to Mary N. Winslow* (Minneapolis: University of Minnesota Press, 1951).

62. Alice Kessler-Harris, "Rose Schneiderman and the Limits of Women's Trade Unionism," In *Labor Leaders in America*, ed. Melvyn Dubofsky and Warren Van Tine (Urbana: University of Illinois Press, 1987), 160–84; Pesotta, *Bread upon the Waters*; Orleck, *Common Sense and a Little Fire* and her article, "Rose Schneiderman (1882–1972)," in *Portraits of American Women from Settlement to the Present*, ed. G. J. Barker-Benfield and Catherine Clinton (New York: Oxford University Press, 1998), 379–402; Schofield, *To Do and to Be*; Norwood, *Labor's Flaming Youth*, 216–303; Mary Anderson, *Woman at Work*; Eileen Boris, "The Quest for Labor Standards in the Era of Eleanor Roosevelt: The Case of Industrial Homework," *Wisconsin Women's Law Journal* 2 (1986): 53–74.

63. Anderson, *Woman at Work*; Edward T. James, "Mary Anderson," in *Notable American Woman: The Modern Period*, ed. Barbara Sicherman and Carol Hurd Green (Cambridge: Harvard University Press, 1980), 23–25. On the Chicago WTUL, Elizabeth Anne Payne, *Reform, Labor, and Feminism: Margaret Dreier Robins and the Women's Trade Union League* (Urbana: University of Illinois Press, 1988), ch. 2.

64. Schofield, *To Do and to Be*, 82–112; Orleck, *Common Sense and a Little Fire*, prologue, chs. 1–4; Lillian Faderman, *To Believe in Women: What Lesbians Have Done for America—A History* (Boston: Houghton Mifflin Company, 1999), 109–113; 369–70n; Interview with Pauline Newman by Barbara Wertheimer, November 1976, TUWOHP.

65. Schofield, *To Do and to Be*, 50–81; Orleck, *Common Sense and a Little Fire* chs. 4 and 6; Orleck, "Rose Schneiderman and Working-Class Women," in *Women and Power in American History: A Reader* (vol. II from 1870), 2nd ed., ed. Kathryn Kish Sklar and Thomas Dublin (Upper Saddle River, NJ: Prentice-Hall, 2002), 80–95; and Orleck, "Rose Schneiderman (1882–1972)", 379–402.

66. On Bessie Hillman, see Karen Pastorello and N. Sue Weiler, "Bessie Abramowitz Hillman," in *Women Building Chicago, 1790–1990: A Biographical Dictionary*, ed. Rima L. Schultz and Adele Hast (Bloomington: Indiana University Press, 2001), 391–93; Jane Julianell, "Lost Women: Bessie Hillman: Up from the Sweatshop," *Ms.* 1 (May 1973): 16–20, and Fink, *Biographical Dictionary of American Labor*, 295–96.

67. See Fink, *Biographical Dictionary of American Labor*, 31–33, for a comparison of the family status of women labor leaders with the female population at large.

68. Ruth Milkman, "Ruth Young," in *American National Biography*, ed. John A. Garraty and Mark C. Carnes (New York: Oxford University Press, 1999), 181–83; Ruth Young Collection, TL; Milkman, *Gender at Work*, 92; Zahavi, "Passionate Commitments," 544–48.

69. Constance Coiner, *Better Red: The Writing and Resistance of Tillie Olsen and Meridel Le Sueur* (New York: Oxford University Press, 1995), chs. 5–7; Guide to the Collection and unidentified clippings (box 18, file 1), TO-SUL.

70. Ruiz, *Cannery Women, Cannery Lives*, 41–57, 69–85, 116; Ruiz, *From out of the Shadows*, 72–82.

71. Ruiz, *Cannery Women, Cannery Lives*, 99–101; interview with Elizabeth Sasuly by Robert Korstad, n.d., in possession of the author; e-mail correspondence from Vicki Ruiz, July 7, 2002 and Aug. 4, 2002, in possession of the author.

72. Ruth Feldstein, "The Labor Movement," in *Black Women in America: An Historical Encyclopedia*, ed. Darlene Clark Hine, Elsa B. Brown, and Rosalyn Terborg-Penn (Bloomington: Indiana University Press, 1993), 685–89; Gerda Lerner, ed., *Black Women in White America: A Documentary History* (New York: Vintage, 1973), 265–74.

73. O'Farrell and Kornbluh, *Rocking the Boat*, 114; interview with Mary Callahan by Alice Hoffman and Karen Budd, May 7, 1976, TUWOHP; *IUE News*, Oct. 1979, 8, and May 11, 1959, 5; *AFL-CIO News*, May 9, 1959; Fink, *Biographical Dictionary of American Labor*, 144–45; James P. Quigel, *Union in a Hurry: The 50th Anniversary of the IUE* (New Brunswick, NJ: Exhibition Catalog, Rutgers University Libraries, 2000), 3.

74. O'Farrell and Kornbluh, *Rocking the Boat*, 121–22, 134.

75. Interview with Addie Wyatt by Rick Halpern and Roger Horowitz, Jan. 30, 1986, UPWA-OHP, tape 54, side 1. Addie Wyatt, " 'An Injury to one is an injury to all': Addie Wyatt Remembers the Packinghouse Workers Union," *Labor's Heritage* (Winter/Spring 2003), 26–27.

76. Interview with Addie Wyatt, UPWA-OHP, tapes 54 and 55; Fehn, *Striking Women*, 128–298; Wyatt, "An Injury to one is an injury to all."

77. Pitrone, *Myra*, chs. 1-8; box 1, files 1 and 3, MW-ALUA; *Detroit News*, Feb. 4, 1953; "Myra K. Wolfgang, Feminist Leader, 61," *NYT*, Apr. 13, 1976; Katz, "Biographical Sketch of Myra Komaroff Wolfgang."

78. The class background of many of the individual women is ambiguous because full biographical information is lacking and because there is no consensus among social scientists about how to determine class categorization. The significant point is that this was a multi-class coalition of women reformers.

79. U.S. Dept. of Labor (USDL), Women's Bureau, *Status of Women in the US, 1953*, Bulletin 249 (Washington, DC: GPO, 1953), 23–25.

80. Quotes from Esther Peterson (with Winifred Conkling), *Restless: The Memoirs of Labor and Consumer Activist Esther Peterson* (Washington, DC: Caring Publishing, 1995), 17, and Peterson, "The World beyond the Valley," 23. See also Marie Tedesco, "Esther Peterson," in *Biographical Dictionary of American Labor*, 461, and O'Farrell and Kornbluh, *Rocking the Boat*, 58–83.

81. Peterson, *Restless*, chs. 3–4. Quotes on pages 40 and 56.

82. Ibid., chs. 5–6, quote on p. 87.

83. Quotes from interviews with Katherine Ellickson by Philip Mason, Dec. 15, 1974, 20–22, and by Dennis East, 1976, ALUA. See also box 1, file 30, KPE-ALUA pt. 2; "E. P. Ellickson, 91, A Labor Economist," *NYT*, Jan. 13, 1997; Reminiscences of Katherine Pollak Ellickson, 1966–67, Peter A. Corning, interviewer, pp. 1–14, in the Columbia University Oral History Research Office Collection.

84. Interview with Ellickson by East, 8–9, ALUA.

85. David Brody, "Gladys Marie Dickason," in *Notable American Women: The Modern Period*, 192–94; Dickason, "Women in Labor Unions," 78; "Ten Who Deliver," *Fortune*, Nov. 1946, 141–53; Fink, *Biographical Dictionary of American Labor*, 186–87; "Gladys Dickason, Ex-Union Official," *NYT*, Sept. 1, 1971; "Gladys Dickason Made Asst. Director of CIO So. Drive," *The Advance*, Aug. 15, 1946, p. 3.

86. "Ten Who Deliver," 143; "Gladys Dickason Made Asst. Director of CIO So. Drive," 3.

87. Interview with Millie Jeffrey by the author, Oct. 19, 2001, Detroit, MI; interview with Millie Jeffrey by Ruth Meyerowitz, August 13, 1976, TUWOHP; Fink, *Biographical*

Dictionary of American Labor, 316–17; Gabin, *Feminism in the Labor Movement*, 93, 99, 143; "Guide," MJ-ALUA. See also the extensive set of clippings in Millie Jeffrey, VF-ALUA.

88. Interview with Millie Jeffrey by the author; interview with Millie Jeffrey, TUWOHP; Christopher Cook, "Millie Jeffrey: Worth More Than Her Weight in Justice," *Michigan Woman*, Jan.–Feb. 1991; Sheryl James, "Thoroughly Modest Millie," *Detroit Free Press Magazine*, Jan. 23, 1994, 8–10; Neila Pomerantz, "Union Women," *Metropolitan Detroit*, Nov. 1984 (vol. 1, no. 9), 66.

89. Interview with Millie Jeffrey, TUWOHP.

90. Interview with Caroline Davis by Ruth Meyerowitz, July 23, 1976, TUWOHP, quotes on 83, 112–14, 2; "Lady Labor Leader: To Keep Labor Peace and Prosperity in an Indiana Factory, the Boss of Local 764 Just Acts Like a Woman," *Life*, June 30, 1947, 83–85; see also Gabin, *Feminism in the Labor Movement*, 143; "Caroline Davis," VF-ALUA; box 4, file 1, and box 3, file 18, WD-ALUA.

91. Interview with Caroline Davis, TUWOHP, 47–48, 117–18; long quote from 94–95; interview with Millie Jeffrey by the author.

92. Marie Teasley, "Hatcher Retirement Marks New Beginning," *Michigan Chronicle*, June 21, 1980; "Lillian Hatcher," VF-ALUA; Hatcher, "Descriptive Guide," LH-ALUA; "Dinner Event to Honor UAW's Lillian Hatcher," *Detroit News*, June 15, 1980; "Descriptive Guide," FPD-ALUA.

93. "Olga Madar," VF-ALUA; Jerry Hartford, "He-Man UAW Has a Girl Sports Director," *Wage Earner*, December 6, 1946, 9; Pomerantz, "Union Women," 66.

94. Interview with Dorothy Haener by Lyn Goldfarb, Lydia Kleiner, and Christine Miller, July, 1978, TUWOHP; the quotes are from Tom Brokaw, *The Greatest Generation* (New York: Random House, 1998), 96, 97, 98.

95. James, "Thoroughly Modest Millie," 10; interview with Caroline Davis, TUWOHP; "Guide," LH-ALUA; box 3, file 17, WD-ALUA; "Guide," DH-ALUA.

96. No systematic surveys exist for this period on the race and ethnic background of women labor leaders. The U.S. Civil Rights Commission conducted the first major comprehensive survey of African-American women's leadership in unions in the late 1970s. They concluded that African-American women were severely underrepresented in top union posts, but that a greater proportion of African-American union women held *local* leadership positions than did white women union members. U.S. Commission on Civil Rights, *Non-Referral Unions and Equal Employment Opportunity* (Washington, DC: GPO, March 1982).

97. *IUE News*, March 18, 1971, 3.

98. Susan Hartmann, *The Other Feminists*, 14–52.

99. Karen Tucker Anderson, "Last Hired, First Fired," 97; Yevette Richards, *Maida Springer: Pan-Africanist and International Labor Leader* (Pittsburgh: University of Pittsburgh Press, 2000), 38–43.

100. Richards, *Maida Springer*, chs. 1–8; O'Farrell and Kornbluh, *Rocking the Boat*, 84–109; interview with Maida Springer-Kemp by Elizabeth Balanoff, Chicago, IL, June 27, 1977, TUWOHP, 62–63.

101. Interview with Dollie Robinson by Bette Craig, July 1976, New York City, TUWOHP; files 358 and 425, unprocessed, EP-SL; Richards, *Maida Springer*, chs. 2–4; Julianell, "Lost Women: Bessie Hillman,"16–20. On the laundry division, Hyman Bookbinder et al., *To Promote the General Welfare: The Story of the Amalgamated* (New York: ACWA, 1950), and Frederick DeArmond, *The Laundry Industry* (New York: Harper and Brothers, 1950), 149–51. For other black women activists within ACWA,

see Sabina Martinez, "A Black Union Organizer," in *Black Women in White America*, 263–65, and interview with Fannie Neal, by Marlene Rikard, May 27, 1977, TUWOHP; O'Farrell and Kornbluh, *Rocking the Boat*, 184–207.

102. "Guide," AD-SUL; Biographical Materials, box 1, files 1–3, AD-CHS; interview by the author with Joe White, Professor of History, University of Pittsburgh, Pittsburgh, PA, Mar. 23, 2001.

103. On Pesotta's resignation, see "Introduction" by Ann Schofield to Rose Pesotta, *Bread Upon the Waters* (Ithaca, NY: Cornell University ILR Press, 1987), v–xix.

104. "Memo, Jan 1958," box 9, file 1, AD-GMMA; interview with Evelyn Dubrow by Lydia Kleiner, Washington, DC, Aug. 21, 1976, TUWOHP; Fink, *Biographical Dictionary of American Labor*, 196; *Who's Who in American Labor* (New York: Arno Press, 1976), 162.

105. Cobble, *Dishing It Out*, ch. 8.

106. For a discussion of the advantages of sex segregation and craft unionism for female leadership in HERE, see Dorothy Sue Cobble, "Rethinking Troubled Relations Between Women and Unions: Craft Unionism and Female Activism," *Feminist Studies* 16 (Fall 1990): 519–48; for telephone women, Norwood, *Labor's Flaming Youth* and O'Farrell and Kornbluh, *Rocking the Boat*, 242–43.

107. Interview with Catherine Conroy by Elizabeth Balanoff, Aug–Dec., 1976, TUWOHP, 90–91. Women held more leadership positions in the NFTW than in the CWA. The NFTW had seven men and two women on the executive board in 1941 (*Federation Voice*, June 1941, 7); twenty-two men and seven women sat on the National Council (*Federation Voice*, June 1941, 1). The Long Lines Division of the NFTW also had a "Traffic Council," to which all the traffic (telephone operator) locals belonged (*Federation Voice*, Feb. 1941, 3 and Mar. 1941, 7). For female participation in bargaining, see *Federation Voice*, June 1941, 7. For the decline in the numbers of women telephone operators and discrimination against African-American women by the Bell System see Venus Green, "Race and Technology: African-American Women in the Bell System, 1945–1980," *Technology and Culture* 36 (Apr. 1995): S101–43; Green, *Race on the Line*.

108. Tony Carideo, "Stepping Forward with Catherine Conroy: Or How to Mix Unions and Feminism—and Survive," *The Milwaukee Journal*, July 9,1978, 6–15; Sean Devereux, "The Rebel in Me: An Interview with Selina Burch," in *Working Lives: The Southern Exposure History of Labor in the South*, ed. Marc S. Miller (New York: Pantheon Books, 1980), 271–90; O'Farrell and Kornbluh, *Rocking the Boat*, 231–56; interview with Ruth Wiencek, TUWOHP, 48–56.

109. Carideo, "Stepping forward with Catherine Conroy"; O'Farrell and Kornbluh, *Rocking the Boat*, 231–56; interview with Catherine Conroy, TUWOHP.

110. Devereau, "The Rebel in Me," 271–90; *(New Orleans) Times-Picayune*, Mar. 14, 1955, 3; May 14, 1955, 3; May 21, 1955, 12.

111. "Guide," HB-ALUA; background materials on Women's Bureau 1955 Women Power Conference, box 1, file 9, AL-SL; Helen Berthelot interview by John Schacht, May 6, 1969, 11–12, 18–19, UIOHP; Helen Berthelot, VF-ALUA.

CHAPTER 2
SOCIAL FEMINISM REMADE

1. Mary Anderson, "Should There Be Labor Laws for Women? Yes, Says Mary Anderson," *Good Housekeeping*, Sept. 1925, 52.

2. On the "Women's Bureau network," see Harrison, *On Account of Sex*. On the other organizations mentioned, see White, *Too Heavy a Load*, chs. 5, 6; Susan Levine, *Degrees of Equality: The American Association of University Women and the Challenge of Twentieth Century Feminism* (Philadelphia: Temple University Press, 1995); Susan Lynn, *Progressive Women in Conservative Times* (New Brunswick, NJ: Rutgers University Press, 1992).

3. Harrison, *On Account of Sex*; Judith Sealander, *As Minority Becomes Majority: Federal Reaction to the Phenomenon of Women in the Work Force, 1920–1963* (Westport, CT: Greenwood Press, 1983), 2–5; Laughlin, *Women's Work and Public Policy*.

4. Quotes from Susan Estabrook Kennedy, *If All We Did Was to Weep at Home: A History of White Working-Class Women in America* (Bloomington: Indiana University Press, 1979), 160–62; 185–87. See also Mary Anderson, *Woman at Work*; Lemons, *The Woman Citizen*, 3–40; Sealander, *As Minority Becomes Majority*.

5. "Statement of Mary Anderson, Chair of Special Committee for Federal Equal Pay Bill," in U.S. Senate, *Equal Pay for Equal Work for Women Hearings, October 29–31, 1945*, 181–82.

6. Press release, "Conference on American Women: Her Changing Role as Worker, Homemaker, and Citizen," Feb. 17–19, 1948 (box 8, file 169, FM-SL); "Women's Bureau Conferences, Fall 1944 through Spring 1947" (box 6, file 133, FM-SL); and box 1544, file "Women's Bureau Conferences 1945," WB-RG86.

7. Box 6, files 131–33, 140–41, and box 7, files 142, 146–48, all in FM-SL; box 9, file 1, AD-GMMA; box 1, file 2, LH-ALUA; Kathleen A. Laughlin, "Backstage Activism: The Policy Initiatives of the Women's Bureau of the U.S. Department of Labor in the Postwar Era, 1945–1970" (Ph.D. dissertation, Ohio State University, 1993), 117–54.

8. Anderson, *Woman at Work*, 18.

9. Interview with Miller by Mary Keyserling (box 14, file 277, FM-SL); Dee Ann Montgomery, "Frieda Segelke Miller," in *Notable American Women: The Modern Period*, 478–79; Lillian Faderman, *To Believe in Women*, 110–11, 369–70n; Schofield, *To Do and to Be*, 82–112, 166; Orleck, *Common Sense and a Little Fire*, 136–37, 144–47, 282–85; Newman interview, TUWOHP.

10. "Guide" and box 1, file 1, AL-SL.

11. "Biographical Sketch" and box 1, files 1–31, MDK-SL; Storrs, *Civilizing Capitalism*, 190–94; Storrs, "The Cold War and Historical Sources: A Policymaker Recasts Her Past," paper presented at the Organization of American Historians Annual Convention, St. Louis, MO, Apr. 1, 2000.

12. Sealander, *As Minority Becomes Majority*, 134.

13. Orleck, *Common Sense and a Little Fire*, 6. For more on the ideas of working-class women in the WTUL, see Butler, *Two Paths to Equality*, chs. 1, 4, and 5, and Elizabeth Payne, *Reform, Labor, and Feminism: Margaret Dreier Robins and the Women's Trade Union League* (Urbana: University of Illinois, 1988). On the maternalist feminists, see Seth Koven and Sonya Michel, "Womanly Duties: Maternalist Politics and The Origins of Welfare States in France, Germany, Great Britain, and the United States, 1880–1920," *American Historical Review* 95 (Oct. 1990): 1076–1108; Gwendolyn Mink, *The Wages of Motherhood: Inequality in the Welfare State, 1917–42* (Ithaca, NY: Cornell University Press, 1995); Molly Ladd-Taylor, *Mother-Work: Women, Child Welfare, and the State, 1890–1930* (Urbana: University of Illinois Press, 1994). For the "race, class, and ethnic meanings of maternalism," see Eileen Boris, "What About the Working of the Working Mother?" *Journal of Women's History* 5 (Fall 1993): 104–9, and Boris, "Gender, Race, and Rights," *Journal of Women's History* 6 (Summer 1994): 111–24.

14. See Mary Anderson, "Speech file #341-S-250," May 18, 1942, Commonwealth Club, San Francisco, WB-RG86, quoted in Sealander, *As Minority Becomes Majority*, 35.

15. UAW pamphlet, n.d. [c1945] (pamphlet files, CFL-LARC).

16. Press release, "Statement of the Women's Advisory Committee of the War Manpower Commission," Dec. 2, 1943 (box 13, file 266, FM-SL).

17. Quote from "National Conference Speaks for 300,000," *United Auto Worker*, Jan. 1, 1945, in "UAW-Women Members and Auxiliaries," VF-ALUA.

18. Peterson, *Restless*, 184.

19. Dickason, "Women in Labor Unions," 72–73.

20. Mary Anderson, "Women in War Industry," *AF* 49 (Mar. 1942): 18–19, 32; italics added.

21. *CIO News*, Jan. 24, 1944, 1.

22. "Conference of Women Representatives of Labor Unions," Apr. 19–20, 1945 (box 6, file 131, FM-SL); "Report, Conference of Trade Union Women, April 19–20, 1954" (box 1544, file "WB Conference, 1945," WB-RG86); "Summary, Oct 46 Conference" (box 897, file "WB Conference, 1946," WB-RG86). See also "Suggested Standards for Union Contracts" (box 901, file "Union Conference, 2/44," WB-RG86); *CIO News*, Feb. 23, 1948.

23. ACWA, *Proceedings*, 1948, 246–48; UPWA, *Proceedings*, 1947, 91–92, 203–7.

24. For example, "Transcript, April 1945 Conference," 103–4 (box 898, file "WB Conference, 1945," WB-RG86). See Boris, "Gender, Race, and Rights," for a similar depiction of the arguments used by African-American women during World War II. Mink, whose focus is more on middle-class maternalists, also suggests that after the war, a new generation came of age who "subordinated the politics of motherhood to the new politics of opportunity.'" See Mink, *The Wages of Motherhood*, viii–ix.

25. Sybil Lipschultz argues that even in the 1920s social feminists relied upon the language of "rights" and sought to "value difference without compromising equal rights." See "Hours and Wages," 125–27. See also Cott, *The Grounding of Modern Feminism*, and Boris, "What About the Working of the Working Mother?"

26. "Transcript, April 1945 Conference,"106 (box 898, file "WB Conf, 1945," WB-RG86).

27. On the increasing emphasis on the private provision of benefits and the changing political and cultural climate of the postwar decades, see Lichtenstein, "From Corporatism to Collective Bargaining," 122–52. For a discussion of various political tendencies within left-liberalism, see David Stebenne, *Arthur J. Goldberg: New Deal Liberal* (New York: Oxford University Press, 1996), 45–77.

28. The term "moral capitalism" is from Liz Cohen, *Making a New Deal: Industrial Workers in Chicago, 1919–1939* (Cambridge: Cambridge University Press, 1990), 209.

29. "National Conference Speaks for 300,000," *United Auto Worker*, Jan. 1, 1945, "UAW-Women Members and Auxiliaries," VF-ALUA. Statement of Frieda Miller, in U.S. House of Representatives, *Equal Rights Amendment to the Constitution and Commission on the Legal Status of Women Hearings before the Subcommittee No. 1 before the Committee on the Judiciary, March 10 and 12, 1948* (Washington, DC: GPO, 1948), 101.

30. For a similar point, see Sarvasy, "Beyond the Difference versus Equality Debate."

31. On the history of the term "feminist," see Estelle B. Freedman, *No Turning Back: The History of Feminism and the Future of Women* (New York: Ballantine, 2002), 3–6.

32. See, among others, Cott, *The Grounding of Modern Feminism*, ch. 4; Lemons, *The Woman Citizen*; Kathryn Kish Sklar, "Why Were Most Politically Active Women Opposed to the ERA in the 1920s?" in *Women and Power in American History*, vol. 2, 154–73; Sarvasy, "Beyond the Difference versus Equality Debate," 329–62; Butler, *Two Paths to Equality*.

33. From *Protective Legislation in Danger*, report of the Conference of Trade Union Women, Feb. 26, 1922, Pauline Newman Papers, SL, as quoted in Schofield, *To Do and to Be*, 104.

34. Cott, *The Grounding of Modern Feminism*; Sklar, "Why Were Most Politically Active Women Opposed to the ERA in the 1920s?"; Butler, *Two Paths To Equality*; Rupp and Taylor, *Survival In the Doldrums*; Jo Freeman, "How 'Sex' Got Into Title VII: Persistent Opportunism as a Maker of Public Policy," *Law and Inequality: A Journal of Theory and Practice* (Mar. 1991): 165–67.

35. "Transcript, October 46 Conference," 204–5 (box 897, file "Women's Bureau Conference, 1946," WB-RG86).

36. Alice Hamilton, "Why I Am against the ERA," *Ladies Home Journal*, July 1945 (box 92, file 3, KPE-ALUA pt. 1).

37. Carl Brauer, "Women Activists, Southern Conservatives and the Prohibition of Sex Discrimination in Title VII of the 1964 CRA," *Journal of Southern History* 49 (Feb. 1983): 40. It is important to clarify here that Brauer is talking about the predominant characteristics of each group. Not all NWP women were wealthy Republicans, nor were all opponents of the ERA non-elite Democrats. Moreover, as Kathryn Kish Sklar notes, regardless of the specific class backgrounds of individuals, the debate was "fueled by fundamental class distinctions in goals." Sklar, "Why the Majority of Women Opposed the ERA in the 1920s," 154. For more on the class dimensions of the ERA debate, see Butler, *Two Paths to Equality*, and Jane Mansbridge, *Why We Lost the ERA* (Chicago: University of Chicago Press, 1986).

38. Butler, *Two Paths to Equality*, 11, 72. For an earlier nuanced discussion of the "class-bound perspective" of the NWP, see Rupp and Taylor, *Survival in the Doldrums*, 144–53.

39. Dubrow interview, TUWOHP, 43–44. See also *CIO News*, Feb. 21, 1944, 4; NFTW, *Proceedings*, June 11–16, 1945 and Apr. 2–6, 1952, 457.

40. For descriptions of NWP members before the late 1960s, see Brauer, "Women Activists," 36–40; Leila Rupp, "Imagine My Surprise: Women's Relationships in Mid-Twentieth Century America," in *Hidden From History*, ed. Martin Duberman et al. (New York: New American Library, 1989), 395–410; Rupp and Taylor, *Survival in the Doldrums*, 25–26.

41. *FTA News*, Dec. 1, 1946; See also Elizabeth Sasuly's statement, FTA, *Proceedings* 1944: 88.

42. As quoted in Laughlin, *Women's Work and Public Policy*, 35.

43. Ibid., 35.

44. See, for example, Ethel Ernest Murrell, ed., *ERA: Questions and Answers on the ERA Prepared by the Research Department of the NWP* (Washington, DC: GPO, 1951), 6–7, 17–23. See also Freeman, "How 'Sex' Got into Title VII," 182.

45. As Brauer notes, although the sources of congressional support for and opposition to the ERA from the 1920s through the mid-1960s have not been systematically studied, it is "probably safe to say that most pro-union representatives were anti-ERA and most anti-union representatives were pro-ERA." Brauer, "Women Activists," 40.

46. See Mary Anderson, "Should There Be Labor Laws for Women?" 52–53, 156–64, 166–80, for an early statement of this view.

47. Butler, *Two Paths To Equality*, 4, 33–71, 92, 107.

48. Quotes from Laughlin, *Women's Work and Public Policy*, 93, and Mary Anderson, "Should There Be Labor Laws for Women?" 52.

49. Mary Anderson, "Postwar Role of American Women," *American Economic Review, Proceedings* 34 (Mar. 1944): 243.

50. Statements of Ruth Young, UE, and Elizabeth Sasuly, FTA, in U.S. House of Representatives, *ERA Hearings, 1948*, 209–10 and 211–12.

51. *Congressional Record*, vol. 93, pt.10, Jan. 3, 1947—Apr. 1947, A634–35.

52. Carmela Karnoutsos, "Mary Teresa Hopkins Norton," in *Notable American Women*, 511–12; Kessler-Harris, *In Pursuit of Equity*, 103–6; boxes 1–6, MN-RU.

53. Marilyn Elizabeth Perry, "Helen Gahagan Douglas," http://www.anb.org, *American National Biography Online*, Feb. 2000.

54. *Congressional Record*, vol. 93, pt.10, Jan. 3, 1947—Apr. 1947, A634–35; box 55, file 19, LD-GMMA; LAC minutes, Jan. 9, 1947 (box 6, file 140, FM-SL); copy of bill, HR 2396, in (box 92, files 3–4, KPE-ALUA pt. 1); LAC minutes, May 11–12, 1950 (box 7, file 142, FM-SL); "Reasons for Opposing the ERA," memo, Jan. 22, 1953 (box 9, file 1, AD-GMMA).

55. U.S. House, *ERA Hearings 1948*, 91, 113–14. See also U.S. Senate, *Equal Rights Amendment Hearings before a Subcommittee of the Committee on the Judiciary, September 28, 1945* (Washington, DC: GPO, 1945), iii–v. Most of those testifying in opposition were from labor organizations.

56. Harrison, *On Account of Sex*, 26. Laughlin, *Women's Work and Public Policy*, 37–38, describes the Women's Status Bill as "a positive alternative to the ERA."

57. U.S. Senate, *ERA Hearings, 1945*, iii–v, 52.

58. The Women's Status Bill had important continuities with the "Women's Charter" campaign launched in 1936 by Mary Van Kleeck, Mary Anderson, and other social feminists. The charter demands included "full political and civil rights for women, full opportunity for work according to their individual abilities, with safeguards against physically harmful conditions of employment and economic exploitation, compensation without discrimination based on sex, safeguards for motherhood through legal enactment of maternity insurance, and the right of united action towards the attainment of these aims." See Sealander, *As Minority Becomes Majority*, 155–56; Margaret Cowl, "Women's Struggles for Equality," *Political Affairs* 53 (May 1974): 40–44; Mary Anderson, *Women at Work*, 159–72, 210–14; Philip Foner, *Women and the American Labor Movement*, 331.

59. Minutes, Jan. 9, 1947 and Feb. 3, 1947, LAC (box 6, file 140, FM-SL); statement by Frieda Miller, Apr. 15, 1949 (box 8, file 168, FM-SL); box 91, file 12, KPE-ALUA pt. 1; "Agenda-Labor Advisory Committee Meeting," June 3–4, 1948 (box 6, file 141, FM-SL); box 55, file 19, LD-GMMA; box 92, file 3, KPE-ALUA pt. 1; Peterson, *Restless*, 102–14.

60. See, for example, "Report, Conference of Trade Union Women, April 19–20, 1945" (box 1544, file "WB Conference, 1945," WB-RG86); "Transcript, Oct 1946 Conference" (box 897, file "WB Conference, 1946," WB-RG86).

61. Minutes, LAC meeting, Jan. 9, 1947, box 6, file 140, FM-SL.

62. See U.S. House, *ERA Hearings, 1948*.

63. Statement of Helen Gahagan Douglas, U.S. House, *ERA Hearings, 1948*, 196.

64. Statement of Katharine St. George, U.S. House, *ERA Hearings, 1948*, 6–8. On St. George's background, see "Katharine St. George," in *Current Biography: Who's New and Why, 1947*, ed. Anna Rothe (New York: W.H. Wilson Company, 1948), 559–61.

65. Statement of Nina Horton Avery, U.S. House, *ERA Hearings, 1948*, 26.

66. Statement of Frieda Miller, U.S. House, *ERA Hearings, 1948*, 100–101.

67. Statement of Selma Borchardt, U.S. House, *ERA Hearings, 1948*, 143. For biographical information, consult Marie Tedesco, "Selma Munter Borchardt," in *Biographical Dictionary of American Labor*, 120–21.

68. Statement of Katharine St. George, U.S. House, *ERA Hearings, 1948*, 6–8.

69. Statement of Frieda Miller, U.S. House, *ERA Hearings, 1948*, 100.

70. Statements of Mrs. Emma Guffey Miller (10–13), Mary Murray (44–47), Mrs. Burnita Shelton Matthews (186–88), Nina Horton Avery; all in U.S. House, *ERA Hearings, 1948*.

71. Statement of Pauline Newman, U.S. House, *ERA Hearings, 1948*, 215.

72. Statement by Mrs. Ralph A. Young, Vice-Chair, NCSW, U.S. House, *ERA Hearings*, 1948, 118; Chafe, *The Paradox of Change*, 60.

73. U.S. Senate, *Equal Rights Hearings before a Subcommittee of the Committee on the Judiciary US Senate, 84th Congress, April 11 and 13, 1956* (Washington, DC: GPO, 1956), iii–iv, for a list of those testifying; "Statement of Mrs. Emma Guffey Miller," 25–27; "Statement of Katharine St. George," 17.

74. "Congress and the ERA," *Congressional Record*, vol. 50; Freeman, "How 'Sex' Got into Title VII," 167.

75. Dickason, "Women in Labor Unions," 74–75; minutes, LAC, Jan. 9, 1947 (box 6, file 140, FM-SL).

76. Statement by Frieda Miller in support of HR 2893, Apr. 15, 1949 (box 8, file 168, FM-SL).

77. Box 55, file 19, LD-GMMA.

78. Minutes of the Status of Women Committee, Feb. 9, 1949 (box 55, file 20, LD-GMMA).

79. Quote from Dickason, "Women in Labor Unions," 72–73.

80. Olya Margolin to KPE, letter, Aug. 18, 1954 (box 92, file 6, KPE-ALUA pt. 1).

81. National Manpower Council, *Womanpower*, 343–44.

82. On the Hayden amendment, see Carl Hayden to George Meany, letter, Nov. 4, 1957 (box 17, file 3); Andrew Biemiller to Senator Anderson, Feb. 12, 1957 (box 17, file 2); Hyman Bookbinder to Boris Shishkin, memo, Nov. 6, 1957 (box 17, file 3); all in LD-GMMA.

CHAPTER 3
WOMEN'S JOB RIGHTS

1. "Notes for a talk? Article? 1945," handwritten notes (box 16, file 17, TO-SUL).

2. Caroline Davis, undated speech, in box 9, file 15, "Speeches, 1948–1961," WD-ALUA.

3. Thomas Dublin, *Women at Work: The Transformation of Work and Community in Lowell, Massachusetts, 1826–1860* (New York: Columbia University Press, 1979), ch. 5; Kessler-Harris, *Out to Work*, chs. 3–4.

4. Few in the larger culture shared Olsen's sentiments. As Alice Kessler-Harris writes, "for generations, American women lacked not merely the practice but frequently the idea of individual economic freedom. Neither most men nor most women . . . could

imagine a right to work that was not conditioned by gender. See Kessler-Harris, *In Pursuit of Equity*, 18.

5. Miller, "What's Become of Rosie the Riveter?" 21.

6. For an excellent discussion of workplace contractualism, see Brody, *Workers in Industrial America*, ch. 5.

7. Glenn, "From Servitude to Service Work"; Amott and Matthaei, *Race, Gender, and Work*, chs. 2 and 4–8; Gloria Joseph and Jill Lewis, *Common Differences: Conflicts in Black and White Feminist Perspectives* (New York: Anchor Press, 1981), 27–28.

8. Weiner, *From Working Girl to Working Mother*, 108–9; Sealander, *As Minority Becomes Majority*, 58–60; Alice Kessler-Harris, "Gender Ideology in Historical Reconstruction: A Case Study from the 1930s," *Gender and History* 1 (Spring 1989): 31–37, and Kessler-Harris, *In Pursuit of Equity*, ch. 1.

9. For the divisions within the working class in the World War I era, see Maurine Greenwald, "Working-Class Feminism and the Family Wage Ideal," *JAH* 76 (June 1989): 118–49; for quotes: ACWA, *Proceedings*, 1936, Resolution no. 82; Lillian Herstein, "Women Discuss Wages," *AF* 36 (Aug. 1929): 949–59; Ethel Johnson, "Married Women Workers," *AF* 38 (Feb. 1931): 165–69; Mary Campbell, "Women Workers: A Challenge," *AF* 51 (Nov. 1944): 31.

10. Women's Bureau, *Preview as to the Transition from War to Peace*, Bulletin 18 (Washington, DC, 1944); "Women Securing Equal Seniority Rights," press release, Aug. 29, 1945 (General Correspondence, box 42, WB-RG86).

11. As Ruth Milkman has argued, in most industries, managerial control over hiring was unconstrained by union contract in the immediate postwar years, and even in highly unionized industries, employers retained the power to choose whom to hire and rehire regardless of seniority or any other union criteria. Milkman, *Gender at Work*, ch. 7.

12. "Transcript—April 20 1945," 130–31 (box 898, file "WB Conf. 1945," WB-RG86).

13. Resolution 36, "Protection of Women's Rights in the Auto Industry," UAW, *Proceedings*, 1946 (box 17, file 15, DH-ALUA); Gabin, *Feminism in the Labor Movement*, 37, 47–110, 143–87 (Emil Mazey quote on 163); Nancy Gabin, "Time out of Mind: The UAW's Response to Female Labor Laws and Mandatory Overtime in the 1960s," in *Work Engendered*, 353–54; Jeffrey interview, TUWOHP; Haener interview, TUWOHP, 33–34, 59–61. See also Boris and Michel, "Social Citizenship and Women's Right to Work," 203–4.

14. See citations in note 13 and Hatcher's report to the Labor Advisory Committee, LAC Minutes, July 22, 1948 (box 6, file 141, FM-SL); Lillian Hatcher to William Oliver, "Summary of Activities from November 1947 through June 1949," typed memo, June 10, 1949 (box 1, file 1, LH-ALUA).

15. *IUE News*, Oct 8, 1951, 2; *IUE News*, Feb. 16, 1953, 3. See also Callahan interview, TUWOHP; Susan Hartmann, *The Other Feminists*, 23, on the IUE. For other actions in defense of married women's jobs rights, see Dickason, "Women in Labor Unions," 74; Philip Foner, *Women in the American Labor Movement*, 377; Julia Kirk Blackwelder, *Now Hiring: The Feminization of Work in the U.S., 1900–1995* (College Station: Texas A&M University Press, 1997), 136–40; Green, *Race on the Line*, 177; *Telephone Worker*, Jan. 1945, 7.

16. "Advisory Council Minutes, 1954" (box 1, file 1, WD-ALUA). See also Caroline Davis to L. Earle Davidson, May 17, 1949 (box 3, file 18, WD-ALUA).

17. "Women Workers Win 'Battle of the Sexes' at UAW Convention," unidentified clipping, Mar. 31, 1955, in "UAW Women and Auxiliaries," VF-ALUA; UAW, *Proceedings*, 1955, 16; "Job Security for Women Workers Resolution, 1955," in *UAW Policy*

Established by Convention Resolutions Relative to Women Workers' Rights, 17 (box 17, file 15, DH-ALUA).

18. Claudia Goldin, *Understanding the Gender Gap: An Economic History of American Women* (New York: Oxford University Press, 1990), 161. On female employment in the 1950s, see, among others, National Manpower Council, *Womanpower*; National Manpower Council, *Work in the Lives of Married Women: Proceedings of a Conference on Womanpower* (New York: Columbia University Press, 1958); Weiner, *From Working Girl to Working Mother*, 98–99; Blackwelder, *Now Hiring*, 159–66; Eugenia Kaledin, *American Women in the 1950s: Mothers and More* (Boston: Twayne, 1984); Robert Smuts, *Women and Work in America* (New York: Columbia University Press. 1959), 145–50.

19. On hiring bars in teaching, see Chafe, *The Paradox of Change*, 116; Goldin, *Understanding the Gender Gap*, 161–63; Murphy, *Blackboard Unions*, 177–81, 209–31. For quip, see *Labor Review*, Mar. 8, 1961 (box 1, file 3, AD-SUL); for quotations from school districts, see *Memo on Behalf of Braniff*, 13 (box 3, file 22, AFA-ALUA); *Betty Green Bateman and ALPA v Braniff*, Case no. 394 (box 3, file 23, AFA-ALUA).

20. *Memo on Behalf of Braniff*, 13–16 (box 3, file 22) and Companies' Defense, Exhibit 20, Decision of System Board in Southern Airways, Inc., Atlanta, *Georgia v TWU*, Sept. 1966, 7 (box 3, file 24, AFA-ALUA).

21. Kathy Lukas, "The Evolution of the Flight Attendant in the United States," n.d. [c.1980] (box 2, file 59, SFWR-TL); *SFWR Newsletter*, 4:2 (Feb. 29, 1976): 3–4 (box 2, file 54, SFWR-TL); box 33, file "June–Dec 1972," TWU-TL; box 3, file 33, AFA-ALUA; "Our History: First in a Series," *Skyword: The Official Publication of the Professional Flight Attendants*, May–June 1997, 16.

22. Flora Davis, *Moving the Mountain: The Women's Movement in America Since 1960* (New York: Simon & Shuster, 1991), 16–25, estimates some 30–40 percent secretly married by early 1960s; for a lower estimate, see "Club Takes Poll on Stews," *NYT*, Mar. 29, 1966.

23. Lindsy Van Gelder, "Coffee, Tea, or Fly Me," *Ms*, Jan. 1973, 105; Nielsen, *From Sky Girl to Flight Attendant*, 92–96; box 3, files 20–24, in particular "Exhibit 23, Statement of Margie Cooper" (box 3, file 24, AFA-ALUA).

24. "One Union for Airline Line Employees," pamphlet, n.d. [c.1946], box 24, file "Local 500," TWU-TL; Frieda S. Rozen, "Turbulence in the Air: The Autonomy Movement in the Flight Attendant Unions" (Ph.D. dissertation, Sociology, Pennsylvania State University, 1988), 46–49; Nielsen, *From Sky Girl to Flight Attendant*, ch. 2.

25. Nielsen, *From Sky Girl to Flight Attendant*, 52–80; "Our History: First in a Series," 18, 21; Lukas, "The Evolution of the Flight Attendant in the United States," 1–10;

26. Nielsen, *From Sky Girl to Flight Attendant*, 84–87; "Exhibit 23, Statement of Margie Cooper," "*TWU v Pan Am*, Denied 5-12-48," "*ALSSA v TWA*, Denied 1952," and "*ALSSA v Eastern*, Denied 1959," all in box 3, file 24, AFA-ALUA. See also box 3, file 22, AFA-ALUA.

27. Memo on behalf of Braniff, 4, 8 (box 3, file 22, AFA-ALUA); Nielsen, *From Sky Girl to Flight Attendant*, 18–20.

28. "Airline Union Planned—Flight Attendants to Assemble in Chicago to Form Group," *NYT*, June 2, 1951; "Airline Stewardesses to Strike," *NYT*, Nov. 15, 1958; "Stewardesses Map T.W.A. Jet Walkout," *NYT*, Oct. 10, 1959; "T.W.A. Strike Date Set—Hostesses Plan Step Nov. 18 in Dispute over Hours," *NYT*, Oct. 22, 1959; *Intercom* (newsletter of ALSSA, Local 550, TWU), June 30, 1960 (box 31, TWU-TL).

29. Rozen, "Turbulence in the Air," 70; Nielsen, *From Sky Girl to Flight Attendant*, 60–79; box 27, TWU-TL; "Our History," 20–21; Lukas, "The Evolution of the Flight Attendant in the United States," 11–28.

30. Of course, older women had always worked in some sectors of the economy, and older African-American women may have even been the preferred service and agricultural workforce, particularly in the South.

31. *Service Aloft*, Nov. 1953, quoted in *Intercom*, 1967 (TL); "Our History: First in a Series," 20–21; Kane, *Sex Objects in the Sky*, 102; Gelder, "Coffee, Tea, or Fly Me," 89.

32. As quoted in Davis, *Moving the Mountain*, 21. See also Frank Prial, "The Great Girl Shortage in the Sky" (part 1), *NYT Telegram*, Aug. 25, 1965, 2:25.

33. "Our History: First in a Series," 20–21; Lukas, "The Evolution of the Flight Attendant in the United States," 11–15.

34. Nielsen, *From Sky Girl to Flight Attendant*, 56–60.

35. See, for example, Burstein, *Discrimination, Jobs, and Politics*, preface, chs. 1–5.

36. Karen Anderson, *Changing Woman*, 195.

37. For overviews of the history of minority women's employment, see Glenn, "From Servitude to Service Work"; Karen Anderson, *Changing Woman*; Jones, *Labor of Love, Labor of Sorrow*; Amott and Matthaei, *Race, Gender, and Work*. On teaching and nursing, see Murphy, *Blackboard Unions*, 146, 196–208; Hine, *Black Women in White*.

38. For a discussion of the transition to "free" or "at will" employment for white workers, see Robert J. Steinfeld, *The Invention of Free Labor: The Employment Relation in English and American Law and Culture, 1350–1870* (Chapel Hill: University of North Carolina Press, 1991).

39. Eric Foner, *A Short History of Reconstruction* (New York: Harper & Row, 1990); Jacqueline Jones, *The Dispossessed: America's Underclasses From the Civil War to the Present* (New York: Basic Books, 1992); Jacqueline Jones, *A Short History of the Laboring Classes: From Colonial Times to the Present* (Malden, MA: Blackwell Publishers, 1999), chs 4–7; Tera Hunter, *To 'Joy My Freedom: Southern Black Women's Lives and Labors after the Civil War* (Boston: Harvard University Press, 1997).

40. The standard narrative has been one of reform possibilities in the 1930s and wartime (due to the rise of industrial unions and the economic and political restructuring of war) that are dashed in the postwar gloom of rising business power, anticommunism, and union bureaucratization. By the 1950s, it is argued, most unions abandoned their reform vision and accommodated themselves to the values of the larger society— in race relations as in other areas. The general story is found in Nelson Lichtenstein, "From Corporatism to Collective Bargaining," 122–52, and Lichtenstein, "Labor in the Truman Era," in *The Truman Presidency*, ed. Michael Lacey (Cambridge: Cambridge University Press, 1989), 128–55. The declension view in regard to race is most compellingly put forward by Robert Korstad and Nelson Lichtenstein, "Opportunities Found and Lost." For an introduction to the immense literature on race and unions in the postwar era, see Bruce Nelson, *Divided We Stand: American Workers and the Struggle for Black Equality* (Princeton, NJ: Princeton University Press, 2001). See also Ray Marshall, *The Negro and Organized Labor* (New York: Wiley, 1965); Michel Honey, *Southern Labor and Black Civil Rights: Organizing Memphis Workers* (Urbana: University of Illinois, 1993); Alan Draper, *Conflict of Interests: Organized Labor and the Civil Rights Movement in the South, 1954–1968* (Ithaca, NY: Cornell University Press, 1994); Boyle, *The UAW and the Heyday of American Liberalism*; and many of the essays in *The CIO's Left-Led Unions*, ed. Steve Rosswurm (New Brunswick, NJ: Rutgers University Press, 1992).

41. The historical record is replete with instances in which white women resisted working side by side with women of color, as well as examples in which white women

formed coalitions to help open up jobs for minorities. See, for example, Dolores Janiewski, *Sisterhood Denied: Race, Class, and Gender in a New Southern Community* (Philadelphia: Temple University Press, 1985); Cobble, *Dishing It Out*; Green, *Race on the Line*; Bruce Fehn, "African-American Women and the Struggle for Equality in the Meatpacking Industry," 45–69; Ruiz, *Cannery Women, Cannery Lives*.

42. *New Republic*, Sept. 15, 1947. Other unions, such as the FTA, also had large minority memberships, but their economic and political power was less than that of the UPWA.

43. On the peculiarities of the UPWA, see Bruce Fehn, " 'The Only Hope We Had': United Packinghouse Workers Local 46 and the Struggle for Racial Equality in Waterloo, Iowa, 1948–1960," *Annals of Iowa* 54 (Summer 1995): 185–216. On the packinghouse industry and its union, see also Rick Halpern, *Down on the Killing Floor: Black and White Workers in Chicago's Packinghouses, 1904–54* (Urbana: University of Illinois, 1997); Roger Horowitz, *'Negro and White, Unite and Fight': A Social History of Industrial Unionism in Meatpacking, 1930–1990* (Urbana: University of Illinois, 1997); Deslippe, *Rights, Not Roses*, chs. 3 and 6.

44. Fehn, "African-American Women and the Struggle for Equality in the Meatpacking Industry," 45–69; Fehn, *Striking Women*; Deslippe, *Rights, Not Roses*, chs. 3 and 6. Deslippe is more critical of the gender politics of the UPWA than is Fehn, in part because he focuses on the tensions over layoffs in the late 1950s, while Fehn focuses on the breakthroughs in hiring in the early 1950s.

45. Wyatt interview, UPWA-OHP, tape 54, side 1.

46. For descriptions of the race- and sex-based job hiring practices in the stockyards, see Mary Anderson, "With Women Workers in the Stockyards," *AF* 39 (May 1932): 556–60; and Fehn, *Striking Women*, ch. 1.

47. "Interview with Mary Hammond," 54, and, "Interview with Anna Novak," 64, in *First-Person America*, ed. Ann Banks (New York: Vintage Books, 1980).

48. UPWA, *Proceedings*, 1947, 91–92, 203–7, and UPWA, *Proceedings*, 1949, 155–60.

49. For estimates of membership, UPWA, *Proceedings*, 1950, 165; reply from Charles Fischer, May 1, 1951 to Research Department Questionnaire (box 8, file 36, AD-GMMA); Fehn, "African-American Women and the Struggle for Equality in the Meatpacking Industry," 45–69.

50. UPWA, *Proceedings*, 1950, 169.

51. Fehn, "African-American Women and the Struggle for Equality in the Meatpacking Industry," 53–57; Fehn, *Striking Women*, 133–34.

52. Fehn, "The Only Hope We Had," 185–216; UPWA, *Proceedings*, 1952, 102, 119 for quote from Coleman; UPWA, *Proceedings*, 1954, 125.

53. Fehn, "The Only Hope We Had," 204–5; Fehn, *Striking Women*, 134–40; Fehn, "African-American Women and the Struggle for Equality in the Meatpacking Industry," 50–51; "Interview with Marian Simmons by Rick Halpern and Roger Horowitz, January 30, 1986," 17, 57–60, UPWA-OHP; telephone interview with Marian Simmons by the author, April 30, 2003.

54. Fehn, *Striking Women*, 134–40; Fehn, "African-American Women and the Struggle for Equality in the Meatpacking Industry," 50–51; UPWA, *Proceedings* 1952: 110, 120.

55. See UPWA, *Proceedings* 1954: 69; UPWA, *Proceedings* 1956: 83, 158–59.

56. UPWA, *Proceedings* 1954: 72–73.

57. Fehn, "African-American Women and the Struggle for Equality in the Meatpacking Industry," 52, 62.

58. For the increased legitimacy of women's job rights in the postwar era, see Gabin, *Feminism in the Labor Movement*, 143–87, and such archival collections as FPD-ALUA, WD-ALUA, and LH-ALUA. For an introduction to the intense debate over the ILGWU's racial record, see Richards, *Maida Springer*, 50–51, 88–91, 268–71. For efforts to integrate women's jobs in ACWA, see for example, interview with Fannie Allen Neal, TUWOHP.

59. On the CIO's record in regard to race, see Ray Marshall, "Unions and the Negro Community," *Industrial and Labor Relations Review* 27 (Jan. 1964): 181–87; Zieger, *The CIO*, 156–61, 345–49, 375; Boyle, *The UAW and the Heyday of American Liberalism, 1945–1968*, chs. 1–8. For the importance of the FEPC as a "legal/administrative template" for the Civil Rights Act, see Lichtenstein, *State of the Union*, 192–93.

60. Interview with Marian Simmons, UPWA-OHP, 57–60. See also Philip Foner, *Women and the American Labor Movement*, 413–15; Ruth Feldstein, "Labor Movement," in *Black Women in America*, 685–89.

61. Boyle, *The UAW and the Heyday of American Liberalism*, 120–22; Jeffrey interview, TUWHOP; Lisa Ann Phillips, "The Labor Movement and Black Economic Equality in NYC: District 65, 1934–1954" (Ph.D. dissertation, Rutgers University History Department, 2002); Richards, *Maida Springer*, chs. 1–4.

62. Wyatt interview, UPWA-OHP.

63. Richards, *Maida Springer*, 88–91.

64. For the struggle to integrate teaching, see for example, Earl Lewis, *In Their Own Interests: Race, Class, and Power in Twentieth Century Norfolk, Virginia* (Berkeley: University of California Press, 1991), 155–65; Murphy, *Blackboard Unions*, 146, 196–208; Earl Lewis and Victoria Wolcott, "American Teachers Association," in *Black Women in America*, 26–28. On nurses, see Hine, *Black Women in White*.

65. Cobble, *Dishing It Out*, ch. 1 and tables 1 and 2A.

66. Venus Green, "Race and Technology: African-American Women in the Bell System, 1945–1980," *Technology and Culture* 36 (Apr. 1995): S112–18; Green, *Race on the Line*, chs. 7–8, especially 202–4, 209–11, 322, and 42n.

67. Green, "Race and Technology," S112–18; Green, *Race on the Line*, ch. 2; Springer-Kemp interview, TUWOHP, 141–42; Rose Norwood interview, TUWOHP; Anderson, *Changing Woman*, 194.

68. "Aviation: A Chiding," *NYT*, Oct. 7, 1956, 31:4, and "First Negro Girl to Obtain a Position," *NYT*, Dec. 29, 1957, 25:2.

69. "Bias Inquiry Begun," *NYT*, May 10, 1956, 33; "Court Refuses Job Bias Review," *NYT*, May 8, 1957; "Racial Barriers Aloft," *NYT*, Feb. 11, 1958, 30; "T.W.A. Hires a Negro Student to Become Flight Stewardess," *NYT*, May 12, 1958, 49.

70. "Northwest Is Cited," *NYT*, Jan. 14, 1962, 86; "Airline Ordered to Hire a Negro," *NYT*, Mar. 10, 1960, 25.

71. Venus Green, "The 'Lady' Telephone Operator: Gendering Whiteness in the Bell System, 1900–1970," in *Racializing Class, Classifying Race: Labour and Difference in Britain, the USA, and Africa*, ed. Peter Alexander and Rick Halpern (London, Macmillan, 2000), 57–86.

72. "T.W.A. Hires a Negro Hostess," *NYT*, Feb. 10, 1958, 44; "T.W.A. Hires a Negro Student to Become Flight Stewardess," *NYT*, May 12, 1958, 49.

73. See CWA, *Proceedings*, June 22–26, 1953, 419, for quote. See also *NFTW News* 1941–47; *CWA News*, 1947–53; and CWA, *Proceedings*, 1949–60; Green, *Race on the Line*; and Schacht, *The Making of Telephone Unionism*.

74. Devereaux, "The Rebel in Me," 274–75; Joshua Freeman, et al., *Who Built America? Working People and the Nation's Economy* (New York: Pantheon Books, 1992), 623. See Wiencek interview, TUWOHP, for other examples of local attempts to support racial integration by the CWA.

75. Only a few unions still advocated work-sharing arrangements in which available work was shared equally among all union members. In these situations, usually involving workers with strong craft or occupational ties to their work and to each other, the union often operated a hiring hall or labor exchange, or simply kept a roster of union members. Employers would contact the union and union members would be matched to appropriate jobs. It was often the case that work was divided by sex and then shared, that is, all women would share "women's jobs" but would not share the work of men.

76. Green, "Race and Technology," S107–11; Women's Bureau, USDL, *Women Telephone Workers and Changing Technology*, Bulletin 286 (Washington, DC: GPO, 1963); Green, *Race on the Line*, 127, 160–64, 187. Here is the racial analogue to the gender revolving door image presented by Barbara Reskin and Patricia Roos in *Job Queues, Gender Queues: Explaining Women's Inroads into Male Occupations* (Philadelphia: Temple University Press, 1990). In their analysis, women integrate the very jobs that men are abandoning because of deteriorating wages and working conditions.

77. Fehn, " 'The Only Hope We Had,' " 185–216; UPWA, *Proceedings*, 1954–64; Fehn, *Striking Women*, 201; Deslippe, " 'We Had an Awful Time with Our Women,' " 15.

78. UPWA, *Proceedings*, 1956, 119–20. See also discussion in Roger Horowitz, *'Negro and White: Unite and Fight,'* 237–40.

79. UPWA, *Proceedings*, 1956, 121–28; Simmons interview, UPWA-OHP, 24–25. Simmons's proposal is not unlike the ABC System fashioned by the UPWA at Swift and Co. and later adopted by Local 1 in Ottumwa, Iowa in the mid-1960s. See Deslippe, "We Had An Awful Time With Our Women"; Wyatt interview, UPWA-OHP, tape 54, side 1; *CIO News*, Feb. 21, 1955, p. 10.

80. UPWA, *Proceedings*, 1956, 18–139, quote on 125.

81. UPWA, *Proceedings*, 1958, 224.

82. Ibid., 1958, 225; UPWA, *Proceedings*, 1960, 104–5, 120.

83. UPWA, *Proceedings*, 1962, 88–89; 92–93; UPWA, *Proceedings*, 1964, 37. Local 15 reported an unusual response to the ongoing layoffs: in 1964 the local struck to convince Armour to hire women, and they won. UPWA, *Proceedings*, 1964, 39.

84. See report from Discussion Group 1, IUD Conference, 1961 (box 9, file 11, AD-GMMA).

85. Dorothy Sue Cobble, "'Drawing the Line': The Construction of a Gendered Work Force in the Food Service Industry," in *Work Engendered*, 216–42.

86. Nancy Gabin, for example, finds divisions among auto women over seniority. See Gabin, *Feminism in the Labor Movement*, 143–87. For examples of women's preference for female jobs, see Neal interview, TUWOHP, 99, 107–8, and Pamela Sugiman, *'Labour's Dilemma': The Gender Politics of Auto Workers in Canada, 1937–1979* (Toronto: University of Toronto Press, 1994), ch. 5.

87. Callahan interview, TUWOHP. See also Wiencek interview, TUWOHP, 77.

88. "Transcript, April 1945 Conference," 126–27 (box 898, file "WB Conf.1945," WB-RG86).

89. Joseph Gaer, *The First Round: The Story of the CIO Political Action Committee* (New York: Duell, Sloan, & Pearce, 1944), 426–27; Resolution 24 on Women Workers, CIO, 1951 (box 7, file 142, FM-SL); UAW pamphlet, n.d. [c.1945–46], CFL-LARC.

90. "Report, Conf. of Trade Union Women, April 19–20, 1945" (box 1544, file "WB Conf. 1945"), and "Transcript, April 1945 Conference," 244–45 (box 898, file "WB Conf. 1945," WB-RG86). On the UE, see "Women in the UE, Dec 14, 1949," and "Report on Women in Our Industry Submitted by Ruth Young to the GEB, March 16–17, 1944," both temporarily in UE 2396, file "Survey of Women's Jobs v Men's Jobs"; conference summaries and resolutions, temporarily in UE 2396, file "Working Women Conferences 1953–62"; all in UE-UP. For Lowther's attempts to get nondiscrimination clauses (both on sex and race) in ACWA laundry worker clauses, see Minutes, LAC Women's Bureau, July 22, 1948 (box 6, file 141, FM-SL).

91. For changes in bargaining provisions by IUE, see *IUE News*, Sept. 8, 1952; Feb. 2, 1953; Aug. 27, 1956, 12; Sept. 1975, 5; Susan Hartmann, *The Other Feminists*, 1–13, 23–24.

92. See, for example, "Summary—October 1946 Conference" (box 897, file "WB Conf," WB-RG86); LAC Minutes, May 11–12, 1950 (box 7, file 142, FM-SL); "Advisory Council Reports" (box 1, files 1 and 11, and box 3, file 18, WD-ALUA).

93. On IUE, see *IUE News*, Oct. 22, 1970, 2; Susan Hartmann, *The Other Feminists*, 1–13.

94. Randolph quotes from Richards, *Maida Springer*, 89–90. The 1950 FEP Bill is discussed in Freeman, "How 'Sex' Got into Title VII," 169–71.

95. Burstein, *Discrimination, Jobs, and Politics*, 8, 21–23; Freeman, "How 'Sex' Got into Title VII," 169–71; US Department of Labor, Citizens Advisory Council, Task Force on Labor Standards, *Report of the Task Force on Labor Standards to the Citizens' Advisory Council on the Status of Women* (Washington, DC: GPO, Apr. 1968), 37. The New Jersey law, passed in 1945, was one of the exceptions.

96. Jeffrey interview, TUWOHP, 75.

97. See Fehn, "African-American Women and the Struggle for Equality in the Meat-packing Industry," 50–51; UPWA, *Proceedings*, 1952, 109–10; UPWA, *Proceedings*, 1956, 158–59; UPWA, *Proceedings*, 1947, 72, 81–82.

98. UPWA, *Proceedings*, 1964, 173–74; UPWA, *Proceedings*, 1956, 131–32.

99. Gabin, *Feminism in the Labor Movement*, 157; "The Woman in Society Resolution," adopted by the UAW Convention, April 20–25, 1970, Atlantic City, NJ (box 9, file 10, AD-GMMA).

100. Caroline Davis to Pat Whelan, May 31, 1973 (box 4, file 9, WD-ALUA).

101. For a fuller discussion, see Cobble, " 'Drawing the Line,' " 216–42, and *Dishing It Out*, ch. 7.

102. Gabin, *Feminism in the Labor Movement*, 143–87.

103. Gabin, *Feminism in the Labor Movement*, 204; *Women in the UAW* (no author, Detroit, UAW Women's Department, 1963), 3. See also Patricia Cayo Sexton's account of her tenure as chief steward in the 1940s and 1950s, "A Feminist Union Perspective," in *Auto Work and Its Discontents*, ed. B. J. Widick (Baltimore: Johns Hopkins University Press, 1976), 20.

104. Cobble, "Drawing the Line," 233–39, and *Dishing It Out*, ch. 7.

105. Fehn, *Striking Women*, ch. 4; Susan Hartmann, *The Other Feminists*, chs. 2 and 6.

106. Gordon, *Pitied but Not Entitled*, 113.

107. Once the invidious divisions among women by family status, race, ethnicity, and age lessened over the course of the postwar decades, women as a whole were better positioned to challenge inequities based on gender. As Bruce Fehn observes for the meatpacking industry, the "racial integration of women's work spaces" strengthened the

interracial coalitions of women seeking an end to sex-based wage differentials and other kinds of gender inequities. Fehn, "African-American Women and the Struggle for Equality in the Meatpacking Industry," 45–69.

CHAPTER 4
WAGE JUSTICE

1. U.S. Senate, *Equal Pay for Equal Work Hearing, 1945*, 1–12.

2. "Transcript, October 1946 Conference" (box 897, file "WB Conf, 1946," WB-RG86).

3. "National Conference Speaks for 300,000," *United Auto Worker*, Jan. 1, 1945 (file "UAW Women Members and Auxiliaries," VF-ALUA).

4. Although the reform vision of Progressive Era social feminists included raising women's wages through unionization and through laws regulating wages, ending *gender wage discrimination* had not been a central concern.

5. For the diversity of opinion within the AFL over protective legislation, see Skocpol, *Protecting Soldiers and Mothers*, ch. 4, and Vivien Hart, *Bound by Our Constitution: Women, Workers, and the Minimum Wage* (Princeton, NJ: Princeton University Press, 1994), chs. 4–7.

6. For accounts of the early history of protective laws, see Susan Lehrer, *Origins of Protective Labor Legislation for Women, 1905–1925* (Albany, State University of New York, 1987); Elizabeth Baker, *Protective Labor Legislation with Special Reference to Women in the State of New York* (New York: Columbia University Press, 1925); Kessler-Harris, *Out to Work*, ch. 7; Ronnie Steinberg, *Wages and Hours: Labor and Reform in Twentieth Century America* (New Brunswick, NJ: Rutgers University Press, 1982); Amy Dru Stanley, "Protective Labor Legislation," in *The Reader's Companion to U.S. Women's History*, 482–83; Kessler-Harris, *In Pursuit of Equity*, 30–33.

7. Hart, *Bound by Our Constitution*, chs. 4–6, quote on p. 66; Suzanne Mettler, *Dividing Citizens: Gender and Federalism in New Deal Public Policy* (Ithaca, NY: Cornell University Press, 1998), 34–40.

8. Hart, *Bound by Our Constitution*, preface, 6–8; Sklar, "Why Were Most Politically Active Women Opposed to the ERA?" 156–59. For more on the FLSA and the battle for its passage, consult Mettler, *Dividing Citizens*, 188–95; Kessler-Harris, *In Pursuit of Equity*, ch. 2; U.S. Congress, *Fair Labor Standards Act of 1937: Joint Hearings on S. 2475 and H.R. 7200*, pt. 1, June 2–5, 1937, and pt. 2, June 7–9, 1937 (Washington, DC: GPO, 1937).

9. Phyllis Palmer, "Outside the Law: Agricultural and Domestic Workers under the Fair Labor Standards Act," *Journal of Policy History* 7 (1995): 419–20.

10. Estimates of federal coverage vary. See Palmer, "Outside the Law," 419–20; Hart, "The Right to a Fair Wage,"106–24; Kessler-Harris, *In Pursuit of Equity*, 101–5; Mettler, *Dividing Citizens*, 199–201. Estimates also vary widely as to the number of women outside both federal and state statutes. Frieda Miller estimated in 1954 that some 47% of working women were not covered by *any* minimum wage legislation. Transcript, Miller interview by Keyserling (box 14, file 277, FM-SL).

11. Hart, "The Right to a Fair Wage," 108–17; Mettler, *Dividing Citizens*, 185–87. Mettler notes that "scholars have often assumed the law covered a far lower percentage of women than men," but her data analysis reveal that the FLSA minimum wage provisions covered "nearly equal proportions of the male and female work force." 200–201.

12. For an analysis of the differing perspectives of working-class men and women concerning equal pay before World War II, see Cobble, *Dishing It Out*, 152–56.

13. On the limitations of equal pay, see Kessler-Harris, *A Woman's Wage*, 83–112, and Kim Blankenship, "Bringing Gender and Race In: US Employment Discrimination Policy," *Gender and Society* 7 (June 1993): 204–26.

14. Blankenship, "Bringing Gender and Race In," 204–66, argues otherwise.

15. Alice Kessler-Harris suggests a similar range of motivations in her unraveling of the multiple meanings inherent in the equal pay slogan in *A Woman's Wage* (84–92).

16. Marguerite Fisher, "Equal Pay for Equal Work Legislation," *Industrial and Labor Relations Review* 2 (Oct. 1948): 50–51; Milkman, *Gender at Work*, 74–83; Tobias and Anderson, "What Really Happened to Rosie the Riveter?" 367–68.

17. The food service sector offers one of the clearest examples of how the rise in the demand for female labor, combined with other historical trends, transformed equal pay from a male to a female demand. See Cobble, *Dishing It Out*, 152–56, table 1. Kannenberg, "From World War to Cold War," 4, 11–42, also provides an extended case study of how pay equity shifted from an issue motivated by the desire to protect male wage rates to an issue of gender equality.

18. Mary Anderson, "Postwar Role of American Women," 237–44; Wyatt interview, UPWA-OHP, tape 54, side 1, and tape 55, side 1.

19. For the use of the "rate for the job" idea by employers, see Deborah Figart, Ellen Mutari, and Marylin Power, *Living Wages, Equal Wages* (Toronto: Taylor and Francis, 2002), ch. 7.

20. Mary Anderson, "The Postwar Role of American Women," 240.

21. On early advocacy of "rate for the job" in the United States, see Robert Moran, "A Rate for the Job Regardless of Sex: The Mandate of the EPA of 1963," 1–10 (unpublished typescript by the Administrator of the Wage and Hour Division, USDL, n.d. [c.1970], in box 11, file 7, KPE-ALUA pt. 1); Kennedy, *If All We Did Was to Weep at Home*, 160–61. See also Sophonisba Breckinridge, "The Home Responsibilities of Women Workers and the 'Equal Wage'," *Journal of Political Economy* 31 (Aug. 1923): 523–43. The International Labor Organization (ILO) promulgated a comparable worth standard in its official founding documents in 1919. See Heidi Hartmann and Stephanie Aaronson, "Pay Equity and Women's Wage Increases: Success in the States, A Model for the Nation," *Duke Journal of Gender Law and Policy* 1 (1994): 72–73.

22. Anderson, *Woman at Work*, 149.

23. "Transcript, April 45 Conf," 56 (box 898, file "WB Conf, 45," WB-RG86).

24. "Transcript October 46 Conf.," 66. This radical decoupling of gender and job construction foreshadows the work of feminist sociologists in the 1980s on how "gender creates the job." See, for example, Arlie Hochschild, *Managed Heart: The Commercialization of Human Feeling* (Berkeley: University of California Press, 1983).

25. LAC minutes, Sept. 21, 1945 (box 6, file 140, FM-SL); transcript, April 1945 Conference, 92 (box 898, file "WB Conf. 45," WB-RG86).

26. Alice Angus to Frieda Miller, Aug. 21, 1944 (box 901, WB-RG86); Mary Anderson to Blanch Freedman, Exec.-Sec., New York WTUL, June 7, 1944 (box 852, file "WTUL," WB-RG86); transcript, "Conference of Trade Union Women," Apr. 1945, 69 (box 1544, file "1945 Conference," WB-RG86).

27. In WB-RG86: "Transcript, April 1945 Conference," 56, 67, 180–81 (box 898, file "1945 Conference"); "Summary, October 1946 Conference," 2, and "Transcript, October 1946 Conference," 24–25, 66 (both in box 897, file "WB Conference, 1946"); "Report,

Conference of Trade Union Women, April 19–20 1945," 19 (box 1544, file "WB Conference, 1945").

28. Sheet entitled "March 17, 1945 Conference," and transcript, "Women's Bureau Conference for Women Trade Union Leaders, October 1946," 13 (both in box 897, file "WB Conference, 1946," WB-RG86).

29. Frank Levy, *The New Dollars and Dreams: American Incomes and Economic Change* (New York: Russell Sage Foundation, 1998).

30. The gap between union and nonunion women's wages also reflects the fact that the organized sectors of the economy have traditionally been the higher paid sectors, at least for nonprofessional workers. Nevertheless, intra-occupational and industrial comparisons reveal a union wage effect. For estimates of the effect on women, see Roberta Spalter-Roth, Heidi Hartmann, and Nancy Collins, "What Do Unions Do for Women?" in *Restoring the Promise of American Labor Law*, ed. Sheldon Friedman et al. (Ithaca, NY: Cornell University Press, 1994), 193–206.

31. For a study of "pattern bargaining" and the industrial union commitment to wage solidarity, see Jonathan Rosenblum, *Copper Crucible: How the Arizona Miners' Strike of 1983 Recast Labor-Management Relations in America* (Ithaca, NY: Cornell ILR Press, 1995), chs. 1, 2.

32. Fisher, "Equal Pay for Equal Work Legislation," 50–51; Fehn, *Striking Women*, 100–110; *CIO News*, Nov. 30, 1942.

33. For estimates of impact, see Statement of Frieda Miller, in U.S. Senate, *Equal Pay Hearings, 1945*, 10. For discussion of specific cases and limits of WLB policy, see Milkman, *Gender at Work*, 74–83; Tobias and Anderson, "What Really Happened to Rosie the Riveter?" 367–68; Clive, "Women Workers in World War II," 44–72; Fisher, "Equal Pay for Equal Work Legislation," 55–56.

34. Cobble, *Dishing It Out*, 154–55.

35. NFTW, *Proceedings*, 1941.

36. Transcript, "Women's Bureau Conference for Women Union Leaders, October 1946 Conference," 18, 35 (box 897, file "WB Conference, 1946," WB-RG86); *Telephone Worker*, June 1942, Apr. 1944, Aug. 1944, and Sept. 1944; U.S. Senate, *Equal Pay Hearings, 1945*, 134–36; *Telephone Flash*, Nov. 1946, 3.

37. NFTW, *Proceedings*, 1945; CWA, *Proceedings*, 1947, 43; CWA, *Proceedings*, 1953, 156.

38. The 1954 convention adopted an "equal pay for equal work policy" that called for no discrimination in wage payments to male or female workers who do the "same kind of work or work requiring equal effort and skill." CWA, *Proceedings*, 1954, 339; *NCEP Bulletin* 1:1 (Mar. 16, 1953) (NCEP-GMMA).

39. For various estimates, see John Earner, "Equal Pay for Equal Work," Women's Bureau reprint, in box 8, file 35, AD-GMMA; James C. Nix, "Equal Pay for Equal Work," *Monthly Labor Review* 74 (Jan. 1952): 41–45; National Manpower Council, *Womanpower*, 348.

40. Fehn, "African-American Women and the Struggle for Equality," 45–64; Fehn, *Striking Women*, 166–67; USDL, "Equal Pay Primer," leaflet no. 20, revised Jan. 1963 (box 8, file 32, AD-GMMA); Nancy Pratt, "When Women Work," *AF* 64 (Aug. 1957): 9; Wyatt interview, UPWU-OHP, tape 54, side 1. On the FTA efforts to establish "rate for the job regardless of sex, race, or any other consideration," see *FTA News* 5:12 (July 15, 1945): 6; *FTA News* 7:2: 3.

41. *CIO News*, Oct. 27, 1941, 2; Milkman, *Gender at Work*, 79–83; Kannenberg, "From World War to Cold War," 16–19, 31–38, 101, quote from pp. 95 and 103; Kannenberg, "The Impact of the Cold War," *Labor History* 34 (Winter 1993): 312.

42. Statement of Clifford McAvoy, Washington representative, UE, in U.S. Senate, *Equal Pay Hearings, 1945*, 162; Mary Dresser, "Rosie's Daughters: Still Underpaid," *IUE News*, March 1980, 6.

43. *CIO News*, May 13, 1946; Clifford McAvoy, in U.S. Senate, *Equal Pay Hearings, 1945*, 161–72; Kannenberg, "From World War to Cold War," 7, 43–44, 81–90; Zahavi, "Passionate Commitments," 531–32; Susan Hartmann, *The Other Feminists*, 19–24; telephone interview with Professor David Montgomery, former UE chief steward, Local 475, New York City, by author, Apr. 15, 2002.

44. *IUE News*, July 16, 1951, Aug. 13, 1951, Apr. 7, 1952, May 19, 1952, Aug. 25, 1952, Dec. 21, 1953, Jan. 18, 1954, May 10, 1954, June 6, 1955, May 13, 1957, June 24, 1957, and June 9, 1958. See also box 2186, file "1957 Women's Conference," IUE-RU, and Susan Hartmann, *The Other Feminists*, 19–24.

45. Statement of James Carey, US House, *Equal Pay Act Hearings before the Special Subcommittee on Labor of the Committee on Education and Labor, 88th Congress, March 15, 25–27, 1963* (Washington, DC: GPO, 1963), 112–15; *IUE News*, Jan. 18, 1954, June 9, 1958; Lisa Kannenberg, "The Product of GE's Progress: Labor, Management, and Community Relations in Schenectady, NY 1930–1960" (Ph.D. dissertation, Rutgers University History Department, 1999).

46. Nellie E. Lied to Mrs. Louella Miller Berg, chair, NCEP, Sept. 15, 1955 (file "Correspondence, 1954–1959," NCEP-GMMA).

47. For the ways in which the industrial model of unionism is unsuited for women's service and white-collar jobs, see Dorothy Sue Cobble, "The Prospects for Unionism in a Service Society," in *Working in the Service Society*, ed. Cameron Lynne MacDonald and Carmen Sirianni (Philadelphia: Temple University Press, 1996), 333–58; Sharon Strom, " 'We're No Kitty Foyles': Organizing Office Workers for the Congress of Industrial Organization," in *Women, Work, and Protest*, 206–34.

48. On Operation Dixie, see Barbara S. Griffith, *The Crisis in American Labor: Operation Dixie and the Defeat of the CIO* (Philadelphia: Temple University Press, 1988). On Miami Beach, see Cobble, *Dishing It Out*, 109.

49. "Report, Conference of Trade Union Women, April 19–20 1945," 2, 5, 18 (box 1544, file "WB Conference, 1945," WB-RG86); "Summary, October 1946 Conference" (box 897, file "WB Conf-1946," WB-RG86); "Transcript, April 1945 Conference," 244–45 (box 898, file "WB Conf, 1945," WB-RG86).

50. *CIO News*, April 4, 1943, 2; Fisher, "Equal Pay for Equal Work Legislation," 50–51.

51. "Transcript, October 1946 Conference," 13, and "Summary, Oct. 46 Conference," 1, both in box 897, file "WB Conf., 1946," WB-RG86.

52. Box 6, file 133, FM-SL; "Transcript, October 1946 Conference," box 897, file "WB Conf., 1946, WB-RG86.

53. For the support of the state federations of labor, see the Apr. 11, 1956 survey conducted by William Schnitzler, Sec.-Treas., AFL-CIO (box 8, files 33 and 35, AD-GMMA); "Memo on Responses from State Bodies on Equal Pay Legislation," May 24, 1956 from AFL-CIO Staff Committee on Equal Pay (Katherine Ellickson, Nancy Pratt, Stanley Ruttenberg) to William Schnitzler (box 17, file 1, LD-GMMA). See "Transcript, October 1946 Conference," 40 (box 897, file "WB Conf. 1946," WB-RG86) for a discussion of the organizations active in the equal pay campaigns. See also Fisher, "Equal Pay

for Equal Work Legislation," 50–51; Patricia Zelman, *Women, Work, and National Policy: The Kennedy-Johnson Years* (Ann Arbor: University of Michigan Research Press, 1980), 13–14; Raymond Munts and David C. Rice, "Women Workers: Protection or Equality?" *Industrial and Labor Relations Review* 24 (Oct. 1970): 6; Susan M. Hartmann, *American Women in the 1940s: The Home Front and Beyond* (Boston: Twayne Publishers, 1982), 134; Leopold, "Federal Equal Pay Legislation," 21; Laughlin, *Women's Work and Public Policy*, 40.

54. USDL, Women's Bureau, *National Consumers' League/Women's Bureau Joint Conference on State Labor Law Legislation Affecting Women, Washington, D.C., December 4–5, 1958* (Washington, DC: GPO, 1959), 39–41 and the voluminous correspondence related to equal pay state laws in box 8, file 33, AD-GMMA.

55. "Equal Pay for Women Means a Rate Based on the Job Not the Sex of the Worker," leaflet no. 2, 1947, USDL, Women's Bureau (box 8, file 35, AD-GMMA); Zelman, *Women, Work, and National Policy*, 13–14.

56. Harrison, *On Account of Sex*, 39–51. For a list of the organizations pushing for equal pay, see U.S. Senate, *Equal Pay Hearings, 1945*, 181–82.

57. Zelman, *Women, Work, and National Policy*, 9.

58. "Transcript, Oct 1946 Conference," 27–30 (box 897, file "WB Conf. 1946," WB-RG86); USDL Women's Bureau, "Equal Pay Primer," leaflet no. 20, revised Jan. 1963 (box 8, file 32, AD-GMMA). NAM testified against equal pay in 1948, 1950, and 1962, for example. National Manpower Council, *Womanpower*, 345–49; Laughlin, *Women's Work and Public Policy*, 55–56.

59. U.S. Senate, *Equal Pay Act Hearings, 1945*, 1–28; statement of Frieda Miller in U.S. House, *Equal Pay for Equal Work for Women Hearings before a Special Subcommittee on Education and Labor, 81st Congress, 2nd Session, May 17–19, 1950* (Washington, DC: GPO, 1950), 85–103. See also Fisher, "Equal Work for Equal Pay Legislation," 50–51.

60. Figart, Mutari, and Power, *Living Wages, Equal Wages*, ch. 8.

61. For example, statement of George Kohn, National Association of Manufacturers, in U.S. House, *Equal Pay for Equal Work for Women: Hearings before Subcommittee No. 4 of the Committee on Education and Labor, House of Representatives, Eightieth Congress, 2nd Session on HR 4273 and HR 4408, February 9–10–11, 13, 1948* (Washington, DC: GPO, 1948), 252–71; debate following statement by David Ziskind, representing the Committee for the Promotion of Equal Pay for Women, in U.S. House, *Equal Pay for Equal Work Hearings, 1948*, 47–51; statement of Leo Teplow in U.S. House, *Equal Pay for Equal Work Hearings, 1950*, 55–75; Chamber of Commerce Statement, U.S. House, *Equal Pay for Equal Work Hearings, 1950*, 135.

62. Statement of Kohn, U.S. House, *Equal Pay for Equal Work Hearings, 1948*, 258; statement of James W. Grove, chief industrial engineer, Armstrong Cork Co., U.S. House, *Equal Pay for Equal Work Hearings, 1948*, 283–84.

63. Statement of Frieda Miller, in U.S. House, *Equal Pay for Equal Work Hearings, 1950* (box 8, file 168, FM-SL).

64. See U.S. House, *Equal Pay for Equal Work Hearings, 1948* and *1950*; U.S. House, *Equal Pay for Equal Work for Women: Hearings before the Select Subcommittee on Labor of the Committee on Education and Labor, House of Representatives, 87th Congress, 22nd Session, Pt. 1 and Pt. 2, March 26–28, 1962* (Washington, DC: GPO, 1962).

65. See, for example, statement of David Ziskind, U.S. House, *Equal Pay for Equal Work Hearings, 1948*, 32–61; statement of Helen Blanchard, representing the CIO, and statement of Frieda Miller, U.S. House, *Equal Pay for Equal Work Hearings, 1950*,

26–40, 85–112, respectively; Herbert Zelenko in U.S. House, *Equal Pay for Equal Work Hearings, Pt. 1, March 26–28, 1962*, 1–2; statement by Caroline Davis, Director, UAW Women's Department, and formal statement by Esther Peterson, U.S. House, *Equal Pay for Equal Work Hearings, Pt. 2, 1962*, 337–40 and 215–21, respectively.

66. Laughlin, "Backstage Activism," 117–54; quote on 117. See also NCEP minutes and letter, Winifred Helmes to Helen Low, Oct. 1954 (box 1, file 8, AL-SL).

67. Testimony of David Ziskind, U.S. House, *Equal Pay for Equal Work, 1948*, 32–61; minutes of the Labor Advisory Committee, May 1950–May 1952 (box 7, file 142, FM-SL); "Labor Advisory Committee Meeting of the Women's Bureau, May 11–12, 1950" (box 1, file 2, LH-ALUA).

68. Kloak to Miller, memo, Dec. 10, 1951 (box 6, file 138, FM-SL).

69. Box 6, file 138, FM-SL; file "Membership Lists," NCEP-GMMA.

70. Kloak to Miller, memo, Dec. 10, 1951; "Statement for Women's Bureau Equal Pay Conference, March 1952: Equal Pay Policy for Women under the Wage Stabilization Board Compared with War Labor Board Policy" (box 6, file 138, FM-SL); "Resolution # 10" (box 7, file 142, FM-SL).

71. Press release, Mar. 18, 1953 (file "Correspondence 1954–59," NCEP-GMMA); files "Minutes, 1953–62" and "Background," NCEP-GMMA; National Manpower Council, *Womanpower*, 346.

72. Notes on contributors in Cobble, ed., *Women and Unions*, 433.

73. Minutes, Nov. 21, 1952 (file "Minutes 1953–62," NCEP-GMMA).

74. Box 8, file 35, AD-GMMA.

75. Laughlin, "Backstage Activism," 117–54; "Memo, NCEP Summation of Minutes and Bulletins to April 1, 1955" (unprocessed, NCEP-GMMA); *IUE News*, June 6, 1955, 9; *Current Biography*, May 1956, 225–26: Dennis Hevesi, "Ex-Rep Edith Green, 77, Is Dead: Early Opponent of Vietnam War," *NYT*, Apr. 23, 1987, D31.

76. In response to a question in the 1937 FLSA hearings about whether there should be differentials in pay by sex, AFL president Green responded: "Under no circumstances. The minimum rates of pay for women should be no lower than the minimum rates of pay for men. They are entitled to that." See U.S. Congress, *FLSA Joint Hearings*, 233.

77. Statement of Lewis G. Hines, AFL legislative representative in U.S. Senate, *Equal Pay for Equal Work Hearings, 1945*, 122–24.

78. AFL-CIO Research Dept., "Federal Legislation to Provide Equal Pay for Women for Equal Work," internal report, Feb. 1956 (box 17, file 1, LD-GMMA).

79. Box 9, file 7, AD-GMMA; AFL, *Proceedings*, 1951, 212–13, 541; Peter Henle and Nancy Pratt, "The Woman Who Works," *AF* 62 (July 1955): 22.

80. AFL, *Proceedings*, 1954, 161–62; George Riley to Edna Kelly, June 16, 1955 (box 16, file 55, LD-GMMA).

81. AFL-CIO Research Dept., "Federal Legislation to Provide Equal Pay"; "AFL-CIO Research Dept Memo on Equal Pay Submitted to Executive Council, Feb 1956" (box 9, file 7, AD-GMMA).

82. Comments on Federal Equal Pay Legislation, May 18, 1956, from Nancy Pratt and Katherine Ellickson to Stanley Ruttenberg (box 8, file 35, AD-GMMA); AFL-CIO Research Dept., "Fed Legislation to Provide Equal Pay"; Schnitzler to Rep. Edna Kelly, Jan. 15, 1957 (box 17, file 2, LD-GMMA); "Memo, Women Workers, Oct 10, 1955" (box 47, file 15), and "Draft Resolution" (box 92, file 9, KPE-ALUA pt. 1); K. P. Ellickson interview with Philip Mason, Dec. 15, 1974, 26, ALUA; "AFL-CIO and Women Work-

ers," pamphlet no. 44 (Washington, DC: AFL-CIO, December 1956, GMMA); AFL-CIO, *Proceedings*, 1955, 75–76; AFL-CIO, *Proceedings*, 1957, 492–93.

83. NCEP minutes, Feb. 28, 1957; Mary Anderson, "The Meaning of Comparable in Equal Pay Legislation"; *NCEP Bulletin*, July 1957 (NCEP-GMMA). See also AFL, *Proceedings*, 1957, 269.

84. He also advocated for equal pay within the AFL-CIO, suggesting in 1959 that the AFL-CIO set up a standing subcommittee on equal pay in the Legislative Department. George Riley to Andrew Biemiller, memo, Feb. 27, 1959 (box 17, file 6, LD-GMMA).

85. Peterson, *Restless*, chs. 5–6; AFL-CIO, *Proceedings*, 1959, 243.

86. "Summary, Oct 1946 Conference," 4–5 (box 897, file "F-WB Conf, 1946," WB-RG86; Mettler, *Dividing Citizens*, 205–7.

87. For the participation of women's organizations at the federal level, see Laughlin, "Backstage Activism," 83–116; Storrs, *Civilizing Capitalism*, 248–50; and Mettler, *Dividing Citizens*, 205–10. On state and local campaigns and the role of the NCL locally, see USDL, Women's Bureau, *National Consumers' League/Women's Bureau Joint Conference*, 1–17.

88. Statement of Gladys Dickason, U.S. House, *Hearings on Proposed Amendments to the Fair Labor Standards Act, 1945* (Washington, DC: GPO, 1946), 807–12; statements of Esther Peterson, Gladys Dickason, and Dollie Lowther, U.S. Senate, *Fair Labor Standards Act Amendments: Hearings, April 19–May 4, 1948, parts 1–2* (Washington, DC: GPO, 1948), 458, 480–502, 646–62.

89. Peterson, *Restless*, 64–67 (quote on p. 67). See also Dubrow interview, 39–40, TUWOHP; Springer-Kemp interview, TUWOHP, 58–59; Brody, "Gladys Marie Dickason," 192–94; Esther Peterson interview with Ronald J. Grele, Feb. 15, 1979 (box 2, file 28, EP-SL); Elizabeth Brandeis, "Organized Labor and Protective Labor Legislation," in *Labor and the New Deal*, ed. Milton Derber and Edwin Young (Madison: University of Wisconsin Press, 1957), 231–33; Peterson interview, TUWOHP, 16–18.

90. See, for example, statement of Reuben S. Haslam, associate counsel, NAM, U.S. House, *Hearings on Proposed Amendments to the Fair Labor Standards Act, 1945*, 213–49; statement of M. O. Ryan, American Hotel Association, U.S. Senate, *Fair Labor Standards Act Amendments: Hearings, April 19–May 4, 1948, parts 1–2*, 950–99.

91. Springer-Kemp interview, TUWOHP, 58–59.

92. Storrs, *Civilizing Capitalism*, 248–50; Brandeis, "Organized Labor," 232–33.

93. Hart, "The Right to a Fair Wage," 110–11; Brandeis, "Organized Labor," 233.

94. Much of the New Deal legislation reflected deeply gendered notions of who was a worker, and what constituted work or a workplace. On the gender biases of the Wagner Act, see Dorothy Sue Cobble, "Making Post-industrial Unions Possible,"in *Restoring the Promise of American Labor Law*, ed. Sheldon Friedman et al. (Ithaca, NY: Cornell University Press, 1994), 285–302. On the biases of the FLSA, see Hart, "The Right to a Fair Wage," 106–14, among others.

95. "Transcript, April 1945 Conference" (box 898, file "WB Conf 1945," WB-RG86).

96. Statement of M. O. Ryan, American Hotel Association, U.S. House, *Hearings on Proposed Amendments to the Fair Labor Standards Act, 1945*, 565–68; statement of Arthur J. Packard, on behalf of the American Hotel Assoc., U.S. Senate, *Fair Labor Standards Hearings, 1948*, 945–53.

97. Hart, "The Right to a Fair Wage," 111.

98. Minority-dominated occupations and industries were routinely excluded from Progressive Era sex-based protective statutes as well as from the labor laws of the 1930s.

Only Wisconsin included domestic workers in their minimum wage protection. See Hart, *Bound by Our Constitution*, 240 n80.

99. USDL, Women's Bureau, *"National Consumer's League-Women's Bureau Joint Conference*, 13.

100. "Summary, Oct 46 Conference" (box 897, file "WB Conf, 10/46," WB-RG86); "Transcript, Oct 46 Conference" (box 897, file "WB Conf. 1946," WB-RG86); "Report, Conference of Trade Union Women, April 19–20 1945" (box 1544, file "WB Conference 1945," WB-RG86); "Transcript April 1945 Conference," 55 (box 898, file "WB Conf. 1945," WB-RG86); *Catering Industry Employee*, Sept. 1940; USDL release, "Survey Material for Bulletin 227," Jan. 11, 1950 (box 991, WB-RG86); Barbara Babcock et al., *Sex Discrimination and the Law: Causes and Remedies* (Boston and Toronto: Little, Brown and Company, 1975).

101. Transcript, "Oct 1946 Conf," 173 (box 897, file "WB Conf., 1946," WB-RG86); Brandeis, "Organized Labor," 233.

102. Interview with Beulah Compton by Elizabeth Case, Oct. 19, 1977, TUWOHP, 48–58.

103. USDL, Women's Bureau, *National Consumers' League/Women's Bureau Joint Conference*, 18–19.

104. "Summary Oct 1946 Conference," 4 (box 897, file "WB Conf," WB-RG86); AFL, *Proceedings*, 1952, 285; President's Commission on the Status of Women, *Report on Protective Labor Legislation* (Washington, DC: GPO, 1963), 3–4.

105. On Huerta, see Blanche Linden-Ward and Carol Hurd Green, *Changing the Future: American Women in the 1960s* (New York: Twayne Publishers, 1993), 105–7; on Draper and the minimum wage hearings, see *Tucson Daily Citizen*, Mar. 30, 1961 (box 1, file 3, AD-SUL); *Labor Review*, Mar. 8, 1961 (box 1, file 3, AD-SUL).

106. Kessler-Harris, *A Woman's Wage*, 112.

107. For instance, testimony of Ruth Roemer, UE representative, 194–210, testimony of David Ziskind, 47–51, and testimony of Elizabeth Christman, 67–75, all in U.S. House, *Equal Pay for Equal Work Hearings, 1948*; statement of Caroline Davis, U.S. House, *Equal Pay for Equal Work Hearings, 1962*, 337–40.

108. U.S. Senate, *Equal Pay Act Hearings, 1945*, 154.

109. Statements by Ruth Roemer (194–210) and Helen Gahagan Douglas (11–12) in U.S. House, *Equal Pay for Equal Work, 1948*; testimony of Philip Kane, General Counsel, U.S. Senate, *Equal Pay Act Hearings, 1945*, 131; statement of Helen Blanchard, U.S. House, *Equal Pay for Equal Work, 1950*, 25–40; statement of Frieda Miller, *Equal Pay Act Hearings*, 1945, 9–11 (box 8, file 168, FM-SL); "NCEP Summation of Minutes and Bulletins to April 1, 1955: Reasons for Interest in Equal Pay," memo (file "Minutes," NCEP-GMMA); National Manpower Council, *Womanpower*, 345–49; Lillian Hatcher, "On the Labor Line," *Michigan Chronicle*, Aug. 11, 1953 (box 1, file 4, LH-ALUA).

110. Blanchard testimony, U.S. Senate, *Equal Pay Act Hearings, 1945*, 191–92; see also Elizabeth Christman, WTUL, in U.S. House, *Equal Pay for Equal Work Hearings, 1948*, 67–75.

111. Employer notions of "rate for the job" and "equal pay" differed substantially from those of labor feminists. Job evaluation may have helped phase out separate pay scales where men and women were in the same job in a single plant, but it did little to raise the overall wages in women's jobs or to challenge gender-based ideas of skill and productivity. See Deborah Figart, "Equal Pay for Equal Work: The Role of Job Evalua-

tion in an Evolving Social Norm," *Journal of Economic Issues* 34:1 (March 2000): 3–9; Figart, Mutari and Power, *Living Wages, Equal Wages*, ch. 7.

112. For example, statement of Frieda Miller, U.S. House, *Equal Pay for Equal Work Hearings, 1948*, 30–31.

113. Hart, *Bound by Our Constitution*, ch. 7.

114. Kessler-Harris, *A Woman's Wage*.

115. Lawrence Glickman, *A Living Wage: American Workers and the Making of Consumer Society* (Ithaca, NY: Cornell University Press, 1997).

116. The seeming obsession of the Women's Bureau in the 1940s and 1950s with establishing that most women worked out of economic need did underplay the liberatory role of employment in many women's lives, as critics have noted. Nevertheless, their emphasis is understandable, given the persistence of the myth of women as secondary or "pin-money" earners and the deeply embedded practice of setting wages according to the *desired* family form (male head and dependent women and children) rather than the *actual* household forms that existed.

117. On the shift in state laws, see Mary Anderson, "A Year of the Minimum Wage," *AF* 45 (Apr. 1938): 369–75. On how cost-of-living needs were calculated see, for example, New York State Department of Labor, "Cost of Living for Women Workers, NY State," 1948, 1950, 1956 (box 10, file 2, AD-GMMA). See also FTA statement, U.S. Senate, *Equal Pay for Equal Work Hearings, 1945*, 184–85.

118. Minutes, LAC, Sept. 21, 1945 (box 6 file 140, FM-SL).

119. Mary Anderson, "A Year of the Minimum Wage," 371–72; "IWC-1961," 7 (box 10, file 4, AD-SUL).

120. Larry Glickman makes an important and often overlooked point about terminology in his study, *A Living Wage*. He notes that the term "family wage" was not used by labor unionists in the nineteenth and early twentieth century; rather, they relied on the term "living wage"—a more gender-neutral term. "Family wage" was first used in the Progressive Era largely by middle-class reformers and later adopted by historians in the 1970s and 1980s to refer to the "living wage" traditions of labor union reformers.

121. Quote from Gordon, *Pitied But Not Entitled*, 53. See Heidi Hartmann's classic article, "Capitalism, Patriarchy, and Job Segregation by Sex," *Signs* 1 (1976): 137–69, for the case that the family wage reinforced male dominance at home and in employment. For the family wage in the American context, see Martha May, "The Historical Problem of the Family Wage: The Ford Motor Company and the Five Dollar Day," *Feminist Studies* 8 (Summer 1982); 399–424; Ron Rothbart, " 'Homes Are What Any Strike Is About': Immigrant Labor and the Family Wage," *Journal of Social History* 32 (Winter 1989): 267–84. European and British historians are deeply divided over the family wage. For a defense of the family wage as a rational class strategy, see Jane Humphries, "Class Struggle and the Persistence of the Working-Class Family," *Cambridge Journal of Economics* 1 (Sept. 1977): 241–58, and Humphries, "The Working-Class Family, Women's Liberation and Class Struggle: The Case of Nineteenth-Century British History," *Review of Radical Political Economics* 9 (Fall 1977): 25–41. For a critique, see Michele Barrett and Mary McIntosh, "The Family Wage: Some Problems for Socialists," *Capital and Class* 11 (Summer 1980): 51–73; Harold Benenson, "The 'Family Wage' and Working Women's Consciousness in Britain, 1880–1914," *Politics and Society* 19 (Mar. 1991): 71–108. For an excellent overview, see Laura Frader, "Engendering Work and Wages: The French Labor Movement and the Family Wage," in *Gender and Class in Modern Europe*, ed. Laura Frader and Sonya Rose (Ithaca, NY: Cornell University Press, 1996), 142–64.

122. Breckinridge was also critical of equal pay for ignoring "the differences in family obligations." She proposed a wage paid to both men and women sufficient for self-support and "one adult dependent." State supplements could be paid on the basis of the number of children. Breckinridge, "The Home Responsibilities of Women Workers and the 'Equal Wage.' " On Rathbone, see Barrett and McIntosh, "The 'Family Wage' "; Jane Lewis, "Models of Equality for Women: The Case of State Support for Children in Twentieth-Century Britain," in *Maternity and Gender Policies*, 73–92; Hilary Land, "The Family Wage," *Feminist Review* 6 (1980): 55–77; Pamela Graves, *Labour Women: Women in British Working-Class Politics, 1918–1939* (New York: Cambridge University Press, 1994). On the Australian feminist challenge, see Marilyn Lake, "A Revolution in the Family: The Challenge and Contradictions of Maternal Citizenship in Australia," in *Mothers of a New World*, ed. Seth Koven and Sonya Michel (New York: Routledge, 1993), 378–95.

123. "Eligibility for the Five Dollar Day," Ford Employee Manual, 1913. See also May, "The Historical Problem of the Family Wage," and Beulah Compton's discussion of restaurant owners who would pay her more because she had kids, TUWOHP interview, 32.

124. See, in particular, Rothbart, "Homes Are What Any Strike Is About"; Greenwald, "Working-Class Feminism and the Family Wage Ideal"; Colin Creighton, "The 'Family Wage' as a Class-Rational Strategy," *Sociological Review* 44 (May 1996): 204–24.

125. As quoted in May, "The Historical Problem of the Family Wage," 415.

126. Nancy Fraser and Linda Gordon, "A Genealogy of 'Dependency': Tracing a Keyword of the U.S. Welfare State," *Signs* 19 (Winter 1994): 324–33.

127. In France, for example, Frader notes that the "family wage disappeared as a demand of French male workers between the World Wars" (Frader, "Engendering Work and Wages," 145). See also Pedersen, *Family, Dependence, and the Origins of the Welfare State*; Pat Thane, "Visions of Gender in the Making of the British Welfare State: The Case of Women in the British Labour Party and Social Policy, 1906–1945," in Bock and Thane, eds., *Maternity and Gender Policies*, 93–118; Janine Bush, "Shaping an Identity: Women, Policy, and Family Allowances, 1920–1941" (Research School of Social Sciences, Australian National University, Nov. 1994; unpublished paper in author's possession).

128. "Statement on Behalf of the CIO on the BLS Study of a Standard Budget for a Workingman's Family" (box 36, file 19, KPE-ALUA pt. 1).

129. CIO Dept. of Education and Research, *Economic Outlook* 9:3 (Mar. 1948) (box 36, file 23, KPE-ALUA pt. 1).

130. U.S. Senate, *Equal Pay Act Hearings, 1945*, 131–32.

131. Rubber Workers, *Equal Pay for Equal Work* (pamphlet authored by Dr. A. L. Lewis, URWA Director of Research and Education), n.d. [c.1943] (box 9, file 7, AD-GMMA).

132. Minutes, LAC, Sept. 21, 1945 (box 6, file 140, FM-SL).

133. Mary Anderson, *Woman at Work*, 98, and "Women in Industry," *AF* 32 (May 1925): 333–35.

134. Statement by Winn in U.S. Senate, *Equal Pay Act Hearings, 1945*, 118.

135. For examples of this rhetoric, see Cobble, *Dishing It Out*, 162–70; FTA, *Proceedings*, 1944, 34; UPWA, *Proceedings*, 1952, 115–16; UPWA, *Proceedings*, 1958, 223–28.

136. Emphasizing the rights and needs of mothers did not imply that only women in the category "mother" could claim entitlements. It did mean, however, that seeing women only as individuals was not enough.

137. Springer-Kemp interview, TUWOHP, 82.

138. Fraser and Gordon, "A Genealogy of 'Dependency,'" 324–33. See Eva Feder Kittay, *Love's Labor: Essays on Women, Equality, and Dependency* (New York: Routledge, 1999) for an argument about the dependency of men and the interdependency of all human life.

139. Nancy Fraser, "After the Family Wage: What Do Women Want in Social Welfare?" *Social Justice* 21 (Spring 1994): 80–86.

CHAPTER 5
THE POLITICS OF THE "DOUBLE DAY"

1. Mary Anderson, "Should There Be Labor Laws for Women?" 52–53, 56–64, 166–80; Esther Peterson, "Women at Work in the United States" [c.1955], 1 (box 117, file 2345, EP-SL).

2. Katherine Ellickson, "Short-Time Work for Women" (dated Feb. 24, 1942), 6–7, and "Short-Time Work for Mothers or Children" (revised, Mar. 5, 1942), 2–4, 9 (box 92, file 1, KPE-ALUA pt. 1).

3. Sylvia Hewitt, *A Lesser Life: The Myth of Women's Liberation in America* (New York: William Morrow & Co., 1986); Lauri Umansky, *Motherhood Reconceived: Feminism and the Legacies of the Sixties* (New York: New York University Press, 1996).

4. Pedersen, *Family, Dependence, and the Origins of the Welfare State*; Frader, "Engendering Work and Wages," 142–64.

5. On attitudes toward child care, see Sonya Michel, *Children's Interests, Mothers' Rights: The Shaping of America's Child Care Policy* (New Haven, CT: Yale University Press, 1999); Elizabeth Rose, *A Mother's Job: The History of Day Care, 1890–1960* (New York, Oxford University Press, 1999).

6. Gordon, *Pitied But Not Entitled*; Skocpol, *Protecting Soldiers and Mothers*; Pedersen, *Family, Dependency, and the Origins of the Welfare State*; Jane Lewis, "Models of Equality for Women," 73–92; Bush, "Shaping an Identity."

7. Frader, "Engendering Work and Wages"; "Family Allowances," pamphlet, National Catholic Welfare Conference, Washington, DC, n.d. [1950–56] (box 49, file 16, KPE-ALUA pt. 1); Pedersen, *Family, Dependency, and the Origins of the Welfare State*; Jane Lewis, "Models of Equality for Women," 73–92; Gisela Bock and Pat Thane, "Editor's Introduction," in *Maternity and Gender Policies*, 1–20; Bush, "Shaping an Identity."

8. Gordon Cushing to Pat Conroy, Jan. 9, 1956, and other documents in box 49, files 12 and 15; Richard Neuberger, "Social Security for Children," *Eagle*, Mar. 1954, 7–9 (box 49, file 17), all in KPE-ALUA pt. 1.

9. Robert Kinney to Ellickson, memo, Oct. 10, 1950 (box 49, file 11, KPE-ALUA pt. 1); Neuberger, "Social Security for Children." Robert Kinney was chair of the Legislative Committee of the Child Welfare League of America and also served as assistant to the director, CIO Community Services Department.

10. Neuberger to Cruikshank, Feb. 22, 1955 (box 49, file 11, KPE-ALUA pt. 1).

11. Cruikshank to Neuberger, Mar. 10, 1955 (box 49, file 12, KPE-ALUA pt. 1).

12. Interestingly, an earlier memo included this additional reason: "AFL-CIO advocacy of such a study or of family allowances might be helpful politically by winning the friendship and cooperation of low-income people, especially in the South." The statement was not in the final memo. See "First draft, Jan 4, 1956, Proposed Memo on Family

Allowance," and revised draft, "Info and Arguments on Family Allowance, Jan 13, 1956" (box 49, files 12–13, KPE-ALUA pt. 1).

13. Cruikshank to Ellickson, memo, Mar. 30, 1956 (box 49, file 12, KPE-ALUA pt. 1).

14. Cruikshank to J. J. Morris, Apr. 6, 1956 (box 49, file 12, KPE-ALUA pt. 1).

15. John F. Witte, *The Politics and Development of the Federal Income Tax* (Madison: University of Wisconsin Press, 1985), 75–77, 137, 131–75.

16. The Canadian figure is from *Congressional Record*, Senate, vol. 94, part 3 (Mar. 16, 1948—Apr. 8, 1948) (Washington, DC: GPO, 1948), March 22, 1948, 3206.

17. On the history of tax coverage, see Witte, *The Politics and the Development of the Federal Income Tax*, 75–77, 83–87, 108–27, quotes from 110, 115, 125. For the impact of taxation policies on women, particularly employed women in two-earner families, see Edward J. McCaffery, *Taxing Women* (Chicago: University of Chicago Press, 1997) and Kessler-Harris, *In Pursuit of Equity*, ch. 4.

18. Statements of Russ Nixon and Stanley Ruttenberg, U.S. Senate, *Reduction of Individual Income Taxes: Hearings on HR 4790, March 1948* (Washington, DC: GPO, 1948), 367–87 and 388–408 respectively; "Statement of American Federation of Labor Re Dependency Care Allowance for Working Wives and Widows," and "Statement in Support of Permitting Employed Taxpayers to Deduct Expenses of Child Care from Their Federal Income Tax, Presented by Stanley Ruttenberg, CIO," U.S. House, *General Revenue Revision: Hearings before the U.S. House Committee on Ways and Means, Pt. 1, June/July 1953* (Washington, DC: GPO, 1953), 24, 71, and 69–70 respectively.

19. Barrett and McIntosh, "The Family Wage," 51–73; Lewis, "Models of Equality for Women," 73–92; Lake, "A Revolution in the Family," 378–95.

20. For a description of the typical maternity policies in place from the 1930s to the 1970s, see Vogel, *Mothers on the Job*, 36–43. For a summary of the alternatives proposed by labor feminists, see *CIO News*, Apr. 17, 1944, 6.

21. WB, "Suggested Standards for Union Contract Provisions Affecting Women," March 1944 (box 9, file 11, AD-GMMA); See also box 901, file "Union Conference, 2/44," WB-RG86.

22. Mary Anderson, for example, worried about mandating maternity benefits in private industry, fearing such special benefits "would work against women" and "would curtail opportunity for women." Anderson, *Woman at Work*, 157.

23. "Transcript April 1945 Conference," 103–6 (box 898, file "WB Conf. 1945," WB-RG86).

24. Ibid.

25. Callahan interview, TUWOHP.

26. Wyatt interview, UPWA-OHP, tape 55, side 1.

27. Howard Samuel and Lynne Rhodes, *Profile of a Union: The Amalgamated Clothing Workers of America* (New York: Comet Press, 1958), 35, 46–47; Hyman H. Bookbinder et al., *To Promote the General Welfare*, 82; ACWA, *Proceedings*, 1948, 216. For a list of unions and their maternity policies in 1945, see "Report, Conf. of TU Women, April 19–20, 1945," 21–22 (box 1544, file "WB Conf. 1945," WB-RG86).

28. Box 2396, file "Women, Contract Provisions Affecting," 1986 Accession, Red Dot no. 125, and "UE Fights for Women Workers, June 1952," UE pamphlet no. 290 (UE-UP); *IUE News*, Feb. 11, 1952, 10; Aug. 25, 1952, 12; Sept. 8, 1952, 7; Dec. 22, 1952; Jan. 5, 1953, 9; Dec. 21, 1953, 11; Jan. 1956–Jan. 1957; Apr. 11, 1960; Susan Hartmann,

The Other Feminists, 43–44; Winn Newman and Carole Wilson, "The Union Role in Affirmative Action," *Labor Law Journal* 32 (June 1981): 325–27.

29. See, for example, Dickason, "Women in Labor Unions," 74–75; *Catering Industry Employee*, Dec. 1951, 14; *Cafeteria Call*, New York, Feb. 1952, 6; *CWA News*, Mar. 1951, 3; Aug. 1958, 3; June 1969, 9. See also Oct. 3, 1947 LAC minutes (box 6, file 140), July 22, 1948 LAC minutes (box 6, file 141), May 10–11, 1951 LAC minutes (box 7, file 142), all in FM-SL; "Summary of First Meeting of UAW-CIO Women's Bureau Advisory Committee, July 13–14, 1950" (box 1, file 2, LH-ALUA); UPWA, *Proceedings*, 1952, 148–49; UPWA, *Proceedings*, 1954, 68–69; UPWA, *Proceedings*, 1956, 118–39; Bernice B. Heffner, "Women in Trade Unionism," *AF* 57 (Feb. 1950): 22.

30. Peter Henle and Nancy Pratt, "The Woman Who Works," *AF* 62 (July 1955): 20–22.

31. Devereux, "The Rebel in Me," 276–77; Stebenne, *Arthur J. Goldberg*, 145–46.

32. National Manpower Council, *Womanpower*, 339; Vogel, *Mothers on the Job*; Margaret Ann Sipser, "Maternity Leave: Judicial and Arbitral Interpretation, 1970–1972," *Labor Law Journal* 24 (Mar. 1973): 182–83; Anne Draper to Bert Seidman, memo, May 22, 1959 (box 9, file 11, AD-GMMA); President's Commission on the Status of Women, *Report of the Committee on Protective Labor Legislation* (Washington, DC: GPO, Oct. 1963), 15.

33. Box 9, file 22, KPE-ALUA pt. 2; *Congressional Record*, 79th Congress, 1st Session, vol. 91, pt. 12, June 11, 1945–Oct. 11, 1945, A3154, and vol. 91, pt. 4, May 7, 1945–June 6, 1945, 4920–27; vol. 91, pt. 11, Mar. 3, 1945–June 8, 1945, A2613–14.

34. Hearings, *Health Plan Senate, April 1946*; statement of Frieda Miller in support of HR 2893, Apr. 7, 1949 and Apr. 15, 1949, U.S. House, *Hearings before the Committee on Ways and Means*, 81st Congress, 1st Session on HR 2893, Social Security Act Amendments of 1949 (Washington, DC: GPO, 1949), 1587–93; box 8, file 168, FM-SL.

35. Kessler-Harris, *In Pursuit of Equity*, 210–11; Alice M. Hoffman and Howard S. Hoffman, eds., *The Cruikshank Chronicles: Anecdotes, Stories, and Memoirs of a New Deal Liberal* (Hamden, CT: Archon Books, 1989), 121–32; Arthur Altmeyer, "Temporary Disability Insurance Coordinated with Unemployment Insurance," *Social Security Bulletin*, March 1947, 4–5; box 9, file 24, KPE-ALUA pt. 2; "Plans for Pamphlet on Labor's Social Goals, Nov. 5, 1958" (box 49, file 10, KPE-ALUA pt. 1).

36. Cobble, "Recapturing Working-Class Feminism," 54–83; UPWA, *Proceedings*, 1944, 187; UPWA, *Proceedings*, 1954, 68–83; UPWA, *Proceedings*, 1965, 130–31; interview with Addie Wyatt, UPWA-OHP; interview with Maida Springer-Kemp, TU-WOHP; prepared statement, David J. Fitzmaurice, President, IUE, in U.S. House, *Legislation to Prohibit Sex Discrimination on the Basis of Pregnancy Hearing before the Subcommittee on Employment Opportunities of the Committee on Education and Labor, 95th Congress, June 29, 1977* (Washington, DC: GPO, 1977), 97–130.

37. Grace Sturk, minutes of UAW Women's Bureau National Advisory Committee Meeting (box 1, file 1, WD-ALUA); Mettler, *Dividing Citizens*, 119–28, 143–57.

38. Summary of April 1945 Conference (box 1544, file "WB Conf. 1945," WB-RG86); statement of Frieda Miller in support of HR 2893, Apr. 7, 1949 and Apr. 15, 1949 (box 8, file 168, FM-SL); Nancy Pratt, "When Women Work," *AF* 64 (August 1957): 25.

39. "CIO Statement in Support of Improvements in DC Unemployment Insurance Law Presented by KPE, Executive Secretary CIO Social Security Committee to Senate District Sub-Committee," press release, May 4, 1955 (box 9, file 28, KPE-ALUA pt. 1);

Report of Federal Advisory Council of Bureau of Employment Security on Unemployment Insurance (box 9, file 27, KPE-ALUA pt. 2).

40. See, for example, HERE Local Joint Executive Board Minutes, Sept. 5, 1950 and July 17, 1952, HERE Local 2 files, San Francisco. In 1957, the New Jersey Superior Court granted unemployment compensation to a woman on mandatory pregnancy leave. The case was brought by the IUE, Local 447. See *IUE News*, March 4, 1957, 7. See also *CWA News*, April 1958, p. 3; April 1959, p. 6; June 1960, p. 9.

41. California, New Jersey, Rhode Island, and New York allowed some cash benefits for pregnant workers. President's Commission on the Status of Women, *Report of the Committee on Protective Labor Legislation*, 14–16; Mettler, *Dividing Citizens*, 150–57; Kessler-Harris, *In Pursuit of Equity*, 349, 48n.

42. Esther Peterson, "The Changing Position of Women in the Labor Force; Labor Laws as They Affect Them; and the Role of Labor Departments in Future Developments," in *Labor Laws and Their Administration: Proceedings of the 41ˢᵗ Convention of the International Association of Governmental Labor Officials, Augusta, Ga, August 24– 28, 1958*, Bulletin 199, U.S. Department of Labor, 22–23 (box 116, file 2327, EP-SL).

43. On child care policy and attitudes in the U.S., see Michel, *Children's Interests, Mothers' Rights*; Rose, *A Mother's Job*; and Geraldine Youcha, *Minding the Children: Child Care in America* (New York: Scribner's, 1995).

44. For discussions of the child care arrangements preferred by wage-earning women, see Clive, "Women Workers in World War II," 66–67; Rose, *A Mother's Job*; Michel, *Children's Interests, Mothers' Rights*.

45. Mary Anderson, *Woman at Work*, 157–58.

46. See, for example, Robert Smuts, *Women and Work in America* (New York: Columbia University Press, 1959), 145–50; Youcha, *Minding the Children*, 332–34.

47. *CIO News*, Sept. 27, 1943, 6.

48. Youcha, *Minding the Children*, 307–35, quote 314.

49. Lillian Herstein interview by Elizabeth Balanoff, 1970–71, TUWOHP, 77–82.

50. Youcha, *Minding the Children*, 307–35, quote 334; Rose, *A Mother's Job*, 153–80; see Elizabeth Hawes, *Why Women Cry or Wenches with Wrenches* (Cornwall, NY: Cornwall Press, 1943), 185–92 for a rather remarkable account of how the war changed women's attitudes toward public child care.

51. Rose, *A Mother's Job*, 165–66.

52. *CIO News*, Mar. 9, 1942, May 4, 1942, June 22, 1942, Nov. 16, 1942, Dec. 14 and 21, 1942; Michel, *Children's Interests, Mothers' Rights*, 147–48. Statements of Eleanor Fowler, Catherine Gelles, and Lewis G. Hines in U.S. House, *Thomas Bill Hearings, June 8, 1943, 78th Congress*, 105–8, 91–93, and 93 respectively; Howard Dratch, "The Politics of Child Care in the 1940s," *Science and Society* 38 (Summer 1974): 184.

53. Gabin, *Feminism in the Labor Movement*, 75–77.

54. Report, "1945 Women's Bureau Conference on War and Postwar Problems for Trade Union Women," 26–27 (box 1544, file "Women's Conf, 1945," WB-RG86); *FTA News*, June 1, 1945, 4. For other examples, see Rose, *A Mother's* Job, 164–66; FTA, *Proceedings*, 1944, 88–90; *CIO News*, March 29, 1943.

55. Karnoutsos, "Mary Teresa Hopkins Norton," 511–12; Mary Norton to "Mr. President," Sept. 28, 1945 (box 6, file "H. Truman, 1945–58," MN-RU); Dratch, "The Politics of Child Care in the 1940s," 167–204.

56. Cobble, *Dishing It Out*, 161, 178; interview with Jackie Walsh by Lucy Kendall, CHS.

57. By the end of the 1950s, some California centers were open to middle- as well as low-income women. State funding was obtained in only three other states: New York, Washington, and Massachusetts. Youcha, *Minding the Children*, 332–34; National Manpower Council, *Womanpower*, 340–41; Women's Bureau, *Employed Mothers and Child Care* (Washington, DC: GPO, 1953); Ellen Reese, "Maternalism and Political Mobilization: How California's Postwar Child Care Campaign was Won," *Gender and Society* 10 (Oct. 1996): 566–89; John Shelley to San Francisco Labor Council, Aug. 28, 1942 (box 41, file "Committee on Care of Children of Working Mothers, 1942"), Helen Wheeler to John O'Connell, Apr. 2, 1943 (box 46, file "Local 110, 1943"), minutes and letters (box 44, file "Committee on Care of Working Mothers, 1943"), and box 65, file "LJEB, 1951," all in San Francisco Labor Council Records, BL-UCB; Waitresses' Local 48 minutes, Aug. 10, 1949, July 26, 1950, Sept. 5, 1950, Jan. 16, 1951, HERE Local 2 files; Herstein interview, 77–82, 92, TUWOHP.

58. For biographical information, consult TO-SUL; in particular see, FBI files (box 18, file 12); *Who's Who in Labor*, 1946 (box 18, file 12), *Omaha Herald*, c. 1932 (box 18, file 1), unidentified newspaper clippings (box 18, file 1). See also Coiner, *Better Red: The Writing and Resistance of Tillie Olsen and Meridel Le Sueur*, 141–73.

59. *People's World*, April 18, 1946.

60. *ILWU Auxiliary Bulletin # 16*, June 1943 and *McKinley [School] Newsletter #4*, June 1945 (box 18, file 8, TO-SUL).

61. Dratch, "The Politics of Child Care in the 1940s," 193–95.

62. Jeffrey interview, TUWOHP, 56–57; Clive, "Women Workers in World War II," 67; Sara Fredgant interview by Alice Hoffman and Karen Budd, June 2, 1976, TUWOHP, 72.

63. Reese, "Maternalism and Mobilization," 583; *Hotel and Club Voice*, Feb. 14, 1948, and June 25, 1949, 4; National Manpower Council, *Womanpower*, 340–41; Michel, *Children's Interests, Women's Rights*, 193–201. On activities in Philadelphia, where "unions were among the strongest consistent voices supporting the idea of day care," see Rose, *A Mother's Job*, 3–9, 164. On the involvement of union women in Detroit, see Jeffrey interview, TUWOHP.

64. Philip Foner, *Women and the American Labor Movement*, 411–13; "UE Fights for Women Workers, June 1952," UE pamphlet no. 290, UE-UP.

65. UPWA, *Proceedings*, 1954, 83; UPWA, *Proceedings*, 1956, 131; UPWA, *Proceedings*, 1965, 130–13; Bruce Fehn, *Striking Women*, 168–69.

66. "HERE Local 240 Records, 1951–54," and *240 News*, Feb. 1954, both on reel 342, Local Union Records Collection, HERE Archives, Washington, DC; interview with Beulah Compton, TUWOHP.

67. On "community services" within labor institutions at the local, state, and national level, see B. G. "Pete" Culver, *Leo Perlis, An Angel with the Union Label: A History of the AFL-CIO Community Service Program* (Farmersburg, IN: Jewett Publications, 1966). For the availability of day care through these departments, see Jeffrey interview, TUWOHP; Wiencek interview, TUWOHP; Conroy interview, TUWOHP.

68. *Hotel and Club Voice*, Sept. 7, 1940, 8; Mar. 23, 1946, 2; June 25, 1949, 4.

69. Minutes, LAC Meeting, Dec. 8, 1950 (box 7, file 142, FM-SL); A. Kloak to Miller, memo, May 13, 1952 (box 7, file 142, FM-SL).

70. Adelia Kloak to Frieda Miller, memo re "Follow-up on LAC Meeting," July 20, 1949 (box 6, file 141, FM-SL).

71. Report, Women's Bureau Conference, Nov. 10, 1950 (box 6, file 136, FM-SL). To advance the agenda of child care services for low-income mothers, the Women's Bureau

published two studies in the 1950s documenting the needs of low-income women for child care: Women's Bureau, *Employed Mothers and Child Care* (Washington, DC: GPO, 1953), and Women's Bureau, *Child Care Arrangements of Full-Time Working Mothers* (Washington, DC: GPO, 1959). See also Michel, *Children's Interests, Mothers' Rights*, 176–83.

72. Minutes, LAC Meeting, Dec. 8, 1950 (box 7, file 142, FM-SL); Elizabeth Koontz, "The Women's Bureau Looks to the Future," *Monthly Labor Review* 93 (June 1970): 7–8.

73. Statement of Miss Julia Thompson, ANA Washington representative, 49–51, U.S. House, *General Revenue Revision, 1953*.

74. Statement of Stanley Ruttenberg, U.S. House, *General Revenue Revision, 1953*, 69–70.

75. Minutes, LAC Meeting, May 15, 1953 (box 7, file 142, FM-SL); Caroline Davis to all UAW-CIO National Women's Advisory Council Members, memo, June 28, 1954 (box 1, file 5, LH-ALUA). For the support of the UE for such a tax provision, see Blackwelder, *Now Hiring*, 276, 61n. For IUE's support, see *IUE News*, Sept. 21, 1953, 9.

76. McCaffery, *Taxing Women*, 114–15; Michel, *Children's Interests, Mother's Rights*, 205; U.S. President's Commission on the Status of Women, *American Women* (Washington, DC: GPO, 1963), 21–22.

77. National Manpower Council, *Womanpower*, 326, 340–41.

78. Statement of Arthur Klein, congressman from New York, U.S. House, *General Revenue Revision, 1953*, 52–53.

79. Statement of Stanley Ruttenberg, U.S. House, *General Revenue Revision, 1953*, 69–70.

80. "Statement of AFL on Possible Amendments to Revenue Laws in Relation to Prepared Schedule of Topic," U.S. House, *General Revenue Revision, 1953*, 25, 71.

81. Betty Friedan's dramatic account of the hegemony of the domestic ideal in the 1950s has been effectively challenged by Joanne Meyerowitz in "Beyond the Feminine Mystique: A Reassessment of Postwar Mass Culture, 1946–1958," *JAH* 79 (March 1993): 1455–82. The quotes are from Elizabeth Rose, *A Mother's Job*, 194–96.

82. Henle and Pratt, "The Woman Who Works," 20–22.

83. Michel, *Children's Interests, Women's Rights*, 167–72; Pratt, "When Women Work," 7–9; National Manpower Council, *Womanpower*, 3.

84. National Manpower Council, *Work in the Lives of Married Women*, 15, 125–27, 133–35; 183–96, 211–15. See also National Manpower Council, *Womanpower*, 327–28.

85. Mirra Komarovsky, *Blue-Collar Marriage* (New York: Vintage Books, 1962), 78.

86. Rose, *A Mother's Job*, 5, 46; Michel, *Children's Interests, Mother's Rights*, 3.

87. Rose, *A Mother's Job*, 5–6, 181.

88. For an account of the centrality of work time issues to labor reform before World War II, see David Roediger and Philip Foner, *Our Own Time: A History of American Labor and the Working Day* (New York: Verso, 1989). Some writers puzzle over what they see as a fundamental discontinuity in labor history after World War II: the abrupt end of the century-old shorter hours movement and the dissolution of a fragile but enduring belief that shorter hours ultimately translated into higher pay. See Hunnicutt, *Kellogg's Six-Hour Day* for a discussion of the decline of the shorter hours movement.

89. For a discussion of the arguments made by Ira Steward, Samuel Gompers, and other labor leaders who linked shorter hours and higher wages, see Glickman, *A Living Wage* and Rosanne Currarino, "The Eight-Hour Day Movement and the Construction of Economic Rights" (Worktime Roundtable, Institute for Research on Women, Rutgers University, May, 2002).

90. The quote is from "Shorter Hours, 1929–31" (box 44, file 44, LD-GMMA). For secondary treatments, see Roediger and Foner, *Our Own Time*, and Glickman, *A Living Wage*.

91. "Shorter Hours, 1936–1950" (box 44, file 47, LD-GMMA).

92. For quotes, see George Brooks, "History of Union Efforts to Reduce Working Hours," 1271–73, and Seymour Brandwein, "Recent Progress toward Reducing Hours of Work," 1263–65. All of the papers presented at the AFL-CIO Conference on Shorter Hours, held Sept. 11, 1956 in Washington, DC, were published in *Monthly Labor Review* 79 (Nov. 1956). For earlier drafts of all the articles, see box 44, file 48, LD-GMMA.

93. CWA, *Proceedings*, 1955, 156–57; CWA, *Proceedings*, 1956, 35.

94. Interview with Sylvia Gottlieb by Anne Draper [c.1964] (box 9, file 1, AD-GMMA).

95. Jill Quadagno, "Women's Access to Pensions and the Structure of Eligibility Rules: Systems of Production and Reproduction," *The Sociological Quarterly* 29 (Winter 1988): 548–49. See also Beth Stevens, *Complementing the Welfare State: The Development of Private Pension, Health Insurance and Other Employee Benefits in the US*, Labor-Management Series no. 65 (Geneva: International Labour Office, 1986), 398, for the coverage gap.

96. Miller quote in "Transcript, April 1945 Conference," 165–66 (box 898, file "WM Conf, 1945," WB-RG86).

97. Mary Anderson, *Woman at Work*, 71.

98. USDL, Women's Bureau, *Child-Care Arrangements for Full-Time Working Mothers*, 31–32.

99. Unidentified newspaper clippings, Bertha Metro Collection, box 3, file 24, CHS.

100. Interestingly, some labor women, such as Mary Callahan of the IUE, argued that "voluntary overtime" was a workable concept if bargained in the context of a strong union presence. As president of her local, Callahan helped win "voluntary overtime" in 1946 as part of a overall contract that protected workers from employer recrimination against anyone exercising their right of refusal. It proved to be a popular and long-standing achievement. Callahan interview, TUWOHP, 23.

101. In explaining the divisions among working women over hour legislation, the insights of industrial relations scholar Alice Cook still appear persuasive. Women will resist such legislation, she argued, in industries where men and women work many of the same jobs, and in certain individual cases where women are primary wage earners and are available to work overtime. But where the majority of workers are "secondary," where they have young and school-age children, and where their "jobs are insulated to some considerable degree from competition with men," they will probably not assess the legislation as burdensome. Cook, "Women and American Trade Unions," *Annals of the American Academy of Political and Social Science* 375 (Jan. 1968): 127.

102. Interview with Dorothy Haener, TUWOHP; Nancy Gabin, "Time out of Mind: The UAW's Response to Female Labor Laws and Mandatory Overtime in the 1960s,"in *Work Engendered*, 355–65.

103. Mary Anderson, "Should There Be Labor Laws for Women?" 158.

CHAPTER 6
LABOR FEMINISM AT HIGH TIDE

1. Esther Peterson to Arthur Goldberg, Feb. 13, 1963 (box 53, file 1044, EP-SL).

2. *Congressional Record, House*, vol. 110, pt. 2, Feb. 9, 1964, 2581.

3. Cynthia Harrison, for example, writes that the federal initiatives "broke a critical stalemate among women's organizations, set much of the early agenda, legitimated the idea of women fighting for their rights, provided legislative tools, and helped establish a network of women nationwide who could be easily mobilized for the cause of women." *On Account of Sex*, 306.

4. Susan Levine makes a similar point in *Degrees of Equality*, 138.

5. Katherine Pollak Ellickson, *The President's Commission on the Status of Women: Its Formation, Functioning, and Contribution*, 6 (unpublished ms., Jan. 1976, box 90, file 1A, KPE-ALUA pt. 1).

6. For an overview, see William Chafe, *The Unfinished Journey: America since World War II* (New York: Oxford University Press, 1991), 146–246.

7. Arthur J. Goldberg, *AFL-CIO: Labor United* (New York: McGraw-Hill Book Company, Inc., 1956), and Dorothy K. Goldberg, *A Private View of a Public Life* (New York: Charterhouse Press, 1975), 222–23.

8. Bureau of the Census, *Historical Statistics of the United States, Colonial Times to 1970*; Bureau of Labor Statistics, *Employment and Earnings*, January, various years, 1983–2001.

9. See, for example, Dubofsky, *The State and Labor in Modern America*, 217–23.

10. Bureau of the Census, *Historical Statistics of the United States, Colonial Times to 1970*; Bureau of Labor Statistics, *Handbook of Labor Statistics*, Bulletin 2070, Dec. 1980, 62; Marten Estey, *The Unions: Structure, Development, and Management*, 2nd ed. (New York, Harcourt Brace Jovanovich, Inc., 1976), 2–13.

11. On Meany, see David Brody, "George Meany," *Encyclopedia of American Biography*, ed. John A. Garraty, 2nd ed. (New York: HarperCollins, 1996), 764–65; John Corry, "The Many-Sided Mr. Meany," *Harper's*, Mar. 1970, 52–58; and Archie Robinson, *George Meany and His Times* (New York: Simon and Schuster, 1981).

12. Edward D. Berkowitz, *Disabled Policy: America's Programs for the Handicapped* (Cambridge: Cambridge University Press, 1987); introduction by George Meany in "Plans for Pamphlet on Labor's Social Goals," Nov. 5, 1958 (box 49, file 10, KPE-ALUA pt. 1); Alice and Howard Hoffman, eds., *Chruikshank Chronicles* (Hamden, CT: Archon Books, 1989), 147–54.

13. For the increasing assertiveness of African-Americans within the labor movement and the growing tension between African-Americans and their white liberal allies, see Ray Marshall, "Unions and the Negro Community," *Industrial and Labor Relations Review* 22 (Jan. 1964): 187–93; Boyle, *The UAW and the Heyday of American Liberalism*, chs. 5–6.

14. "Chronology of AFL-CIO Activities on Federal Equal Pay Legislation for Women" (box 8, file 35, AD-GMMA); George Riley to Andrew Biemiller, memo, Feb. 27, 1959 (box 17, file 6, LD-GMMA).

15. Ruttenberg and Henle to VPs Mattthew Woll and David McDonald, memo, Feb. 6, 1956 (box 17, file 1, LD-GMMA). Ellickson had been one of the six staff members appointed to the 1956 AFL-CIO committee charged with recommending a policy on equal pay (box 8, file 35, AD-GMMA).

16. "Notes on Informal Discussion on Women's Labor Laws, July 16, 1958," prepared by Anne Draper (box 9, file 1, AD-GMMA); Anne Draper to Peter Henle, memo "Re Meeting on Women's Problems," July 18, 1958 (box 9, file 1, AD-GMMA).

17. *IUE News*, June 24, 1957, and Sept. 1975, 5.

18. GEB Report, ACWA, *Proceedings*, 1954, 349–50; 1956, 249–50; 1958, 219–20; 1960, 258–59.

19. "History Scrapbook" (box 20, AFWAL); *Labor's Daily*, Dec. 10, 1957 (box 3, file 2, LS-ALUA); AFL-CIO Auxiliaries, *Proceedings of the First Convention*, Dec. 9–12, 1957, 7–8 (box 3, file 4, LS-ALUA). I have not come across any estimates of CIO auxiliary membership apart from the national federation. Most likely, the numbers were far less than those for the AFL due to the AFL's long tradition of auxiliaries and the more decentralized voluntary structure of the federation.

20. Susan Ellis, "The Gentle Warriors of the Auxiliaries," *AF* 76 (July 1969): 21–22.

21. Anne Draper to Marcella Beatty, memos, Feb. 21, 1963 and Nov. 6, 1963 (box 9, file 9, AD-GMMA).

22. Patricia Sexton refuted this contention later, pointing out that among union members a smaller percent of union women than union men voted for Eisenhower. Patricia Cayo Sexton, "Wife of the 'Happy Worker,' " in *Blue-Collar World*, ed. Art Shostak and William Gornberg (Englewood Cliffs, NJ: Prentice-Hall, 1964), 84.

23. Joseph Gaer, *The First Round: The Story of the CIO Political Action Committee* (New York: Duell, Sloan & Pearce, 1944), 64; Margaret Thornburgh, "The Power of Women at the Polls," *AF* 61 (June 1954): 12–13.

24. Thornburgh, "The Power of Women at the Polls," 12–13, and Thornburgh, "Women and Elections," *AF* 62 (March 1955): 16–18.

25. Interview with Helen Berthelot, UIOHP; *Michigan CIO News*, Jan. 12, 1956, and *United Auto Worker*, Jan. 1956 (box 1, file 12, LS-ALUA); Callahan interview, TU-WOHP; Jeffrey interview, TUWOHP, 80–81; *United Auto Worker*, Sept. 1956 (box 1, file 4, LS-ALUA); *CIO News*, Nov. 9, 1953, p. 10.

26. Callahan interview, TUWOHP, 27–28.

27. *IUE News*, Aug. 4, 1958, 8; "Letter from Sec-Treasurer," n.d. (box 9, file 1, AD-GMMA).

28. AFL-CIO, *Proceedings*, 1961, 267–68; 381–83; Stebenne, *Arthur J. Goldberg*, 225–32.

29. AFL-CIO, *Proceedings*, 1957, 115, 332–33; 1959, 584–85; Davis interview, TUWOHP.

30. Sean Devereux, "The Rebel in Me," 272, 281–82; Selina Burch, "An Interview with Selina Burch," *Southern Exposure* (Spring 1976): 12; pamphlet for AFL-CIO Democratic Party Rally, New Orleans, Oct. 21, 1960 (file 429, EP-SL).

31. Box 22, file 392, EP-SL.

32. Peterson to "Dear Sister," Oct. 25, 1960, and "Labor Sets Up Committee of Labor Women for Kennedy and Johnson," press release, Oct. 24, 1960 (both in box 92, file 13, KPE-ALUA pt. 1). See also file 427, EP-SL.

33. File 425, EP-SL; Kornbluh and O'Farrell, "You Can't Giddyup by Saying Whoa," 56–57.

34. Peterson, *Restless*, 64; Kornbluh and O'Farrell, "You Can't Giddyup by Saying Whoa," 56.

35. Kornbluh and O'Farrell, "You Can't Giddyup by Saying Whoa," 56–57; Laughlin, *Women's Work and Public Policy*, 73; Peterson, *Restless*, 96. As her friend Julia Maietta from the ACWA wrote, "I hope you are letting them put your name in for the Women's Division—this should be one way of letting the Union-Men-folk know that women are considered by other groups if not by the union officials." Julia Maietta to Esther Peterson, Dec. 15, 1960 (file 427, EP-SL).

36. Dorothy Goldberg, *A Private View of a Public Life*, 47.

37. As quoted in Laughlin, *Women's Work and Public Policy*, 74.

38. Kornbluh and O'Farrell, "You Can't Giddyup by Saying Whoa," 57; Stebenne, *Arthur J. Goldberg*, 251.

39. Peterson, *Restless*, 98–99.

40. Box 3, file 34, EP-SL; Kornbluh and O'Farrell, "You Can't Giddyup by Saying Whoa," 57–58; Laughlin, *Women's Work and Public Policy*, ch. 3.

41. For Peterson's specific priorities, see Kornbluh and O'Farrell, "You Can't Giddyup by Saying Whoa," 57–58.

42. Transcript, "February 28, 1961, Discussion with Trade Union Women" (box 90, file 31, KPE-ALUA, pt. 1).

43. Peterson, *Restless*, 184.

44. Laughlin, "Backstage Activism," 174; Peterson, *Restless*, 100.

45. Peterson, *Restless*, 94. See also Interview with Esther Peterson by Martha Ross, August 13, 1978, TUWOHP, pp. 20–21.

46. Marshall, "Unions and the Negro Community," 187–93; Anderson, *A Philip Randolph*, 298–310.

47. For the rivalry between Reuther and Meany, see Boyle, *The UAW and the Heyday of American Liberalism*, ch. 4.

48. Walter Reuther and Jim Carey to "Sir and Brother," Apr. 25, 1961 and May 25, 1961 (box 6, file 12, WD-ALUA).

49. "IUD Holds Women's Conference," *IUD Bulletin*, July 1961 (box 92, file 12, KPE-ALUA pt. 1); "Problems of Working Women: Summary Report of a Conference Sponsored by the Industrial Union Department, AFL-CIO, June 12–14, 1961, Mayflower Hotel, Washington, D.C.," 55–57 (Publication no. 43, Industrial Union Department, AFL-CIO, Washington, DC, n.d., box 9, file 11, AD-GMMA); see also file 2409, EP-SL.

50. "IUD Holds Conference," 1.

51. "Problems of Working Women," 55–57.

52. Ibid., 58–60.

53. Ibid., 61–66.

54. "IUD Holds Women's Conference," 1.

55. Agnes E. Meyer, *Out of These Roots: The Autobiography of An American Woman* (Boston: Little, Brown & Company, 1953). I am grateful to Jim Livingston for pointing out Meyer's connection to the pragmatist tradition.

56. "Problems of Working Women," 17–19; italics added.

57. Ibid., 16–23, 49–51.

58. Isabelle Shelton, " 'Take to the Hills,' Chairman Advises," *Washington Evening Star*, June 15, 1961 (box 9, file 1, AD-GMMA).

59. Laughlin, *Women's Work and Public Policy*, 79–80.

60. "Discussion of the Possibility of Setting up a Commission to Study Discriminations Against Women," memo, Feb. 28, 1961 (box 90, file 31, KPE-ALUA pt. 1). See also box 91, file 7, KPE-ALUA, pt. 1.

61. Peterson to Goldberg, "Re Suggested Commission on Women," memo, June 2, 1961 (box 91, file 9, KPE-ALUA, pt. 1).

62. Ellickson took a partial leave from the AFL-CIO to work on plans for the PCSW. She later requested a full leave but was denied. She decided to resign. Interview with Katherine Pollak Ellickson by Philip Mason, 27 (ALUA).

63. Unprocessed file 699, EP-SL; "Attendance List, Women's Bureau Meeting," May 5, 1961 (box 91, file 9, KPE-ALUA, pt. 1).

64. "Confidential Background Paper on the PCSW," PCSW Document no. 4, Dec. 1961, (box 90, file 10, KPE-ALUA, pt. 1).

65. Ellickson, *The President's Commission*, 6–7; Esther Peterson, "The Kennedy Commission," in *Women in Washington*, ed. Irene Tinker (Beverly Hills, CA: Sage Publications, 1983), 25–28.

66. Peterson, *Restless*, 79–80.

67. Arthur Goldberg to President Kennedy, Dec. 13, 1961 (box 91, file12, KPE-ALUA, pt. 1).

68. Kennedy's motives remain somewhat obscure and were probably mixed. Cynthia Harrison suggests (in *On Account of Sex*) that Kennedy agreed to such a commission in an effort to deflect criticism of his administration's poor record on female appointments and to divert attention from the ERA. Patricia Zelman sees "the major shift in women's policy during the Kennedy years" as largely attributable to the efforts of Peterson, "whose authority stemmed more from Kennedy's confidence in her than any following of her own" (*Women, Work and National Policy*, 23–38, 58). Judith Sealander notes that "Kennedy received pressure from female trade unionists, the USDL, and prominent women leaders to formally consider women's status in America" (*As Minority Becomes Majority*, 133–39, 142). It is also possible that Kennedy gave very little thought to the PCSW and simply relied on the judgment of his staff. Dorothy Goldberg suggests as much in her book about her husband's life (*A Private View of a Public Life*, 259).

69. Seven technical committees and four consultations aided commission deliberations. Harrison, *On Account of Sex*, 109–15, 229–36; Ellickson, *The President's Commission*, 11–19; Wyatt interview, UPWA-OHP, tape 55, side 1; PCSW, *Report of the Committee on Protective Labor Legislation*, app. A; and Sealander, *As Minority Becomes Majority*, 142–48.

70. PCSW, *Report of the Committee on Protective Labor Legislation*, app. A; PCSW, *American Women: Report of the President's Commission* (Washington, DC: GPO, 1963).

71. *Congressional Record*, vol. 105, pt. 5, Apr. 13–-29, 1959, 6750–51, and vol. 105, pt. 3, Feb. 25–Mar. 16, 1959, 2929–4342. To build support for the bill, its advocates sponsored a White House Conference on Child Care, which brought together over 400 representatives from interested organizations. Michel, *Children's Interests, Mother's Rights*, 219–23; Quadagno, *The Color of Welfare*, 135–42.

72. Quoted in Michel, *Children's Interests, Mother's Rights*, 223. Quadagno, *The Color of Welfare*, 138.

73. Quadagno, *The Color of Welfare*, 138–42. Margaret Mead and Frances B. Kaplan, eds., *American Women: The Report of the US President's Commission on the Status of Women and Other Publications of the Commission* (New York: Charles Scribner's Sons, 1965), 113; Task Force on Working Women, *Exploitation From 9 to 5: Report of the Twentieth Century Fund Task Force on Women and Employment* (New York: Twentieth Century Fund, 1975), 169–71.

74. Kessler-Harris, *A Woman's Wage*, ch. 1.

75. Statement of Willard Wirtz, Secretary of Labor, U.S. House, *Hearings before the General Subcommittee on Labor of the Committee on Education and Labor, 89th Congress, on H.R. 8259, A Bill to Amend the FLSA, pt. 1, May–June 1965* (Washington, DC: GPO, 1965), 32–33; Dorothy Goldberg, *A Private View of a Public Life*, 69; Laughlin, *Women's Work and Public Policy*, 69–82. Estimates vary as to the number of workers covered by the FLSA. The 17 million estimate is based on Biemiller's testimony, U.S.

House, *Hearings to Amend the FLSA, pt. 1, 1965*, p. 426. For a higher estimate, see President's Commission, *Report on Protective Labor Legislation*, 3–4.

76. AFL-CIO, *Proceedings*, 1959, 243.

77. Correspondence file, 1959–61, NCEP-GMMA; "Chronology of AFL-CIO Activities on Federal Equal Pay Legislation for Women," n.d. (box 8, file 35, AD-GMMA); "Meeting in Esther Peterson's Office on Equal Pay Bill, March 2, 1961" (box 9, file 7, AD-GMMA).

78. George Riley to Arthur Goldberg, July 18, 1961 (box 17, file 8, LD-GMMA).

79. For union women's lobbying efforts in 1962, see Susan Hartmann, *The Other Feminists*, 25.

80. Statement by Caroline Davis, U.S. House, *Equal Pay for Equal Work Hearings, 1962*, 337–40. See also Davis's statement (read by Dorothy Haener) in U.S. House, *Equal Pay Act Hearings before the Special Subcommittee on Labor of the Committee on Education and Labor, 88th Congress, March 15, 25–27, 1963* (Washington, DC: GPO, 1963), 123–25.

81. Quotes from W. F. Strong, president, Maryland and DC AFL-CIO, to Biemiller, Jan. 3, 1962 (box 8, file 33, AD-GMMA), and statement of Jim Carey, president of the IUE and sec.-treas., IUD in U.S. House, *Equal Pay Act Hearings, 1963*, 108–10. See also press release, Mar. 26, 1962, and "To Senators/Congressmen from NCEP," letter, June 7, 1962 (correspondence files, 1960–62, NCEP-GMMA); statement of Esther Peterson, Asst. Sec. of Labor, U.S. House, *Equal Pay for Equal Work Hearings, 1962*, 215–21; statements of David Dubinsky, president, ILGWU, and Willard Wirtz, Sec. of Labor, U.S.House, *Equal Pay Act Hearings, 1963*, 6–10.

82. U.S. House, *Equal Pay for Equal Work Hearings, 1962*, 1.

83. Statements of Arthur J. Goldberg and Esther Peterson in U.S. House, *Equal Pay for Equal Work Hearings, 1962*, 9–11 and 215–21 respectively. See also Willard Wirtz, Sec. of Labor, and Jim Carey, in U.S. House, *Equal Pay Act Hearings, 1963*, 6–10 and 117 respectively.

84. NAM statement, *Equal Pay for Equal Work Hearings, 1962*, 166. Statement of W. Boyd Owens, Owens-Illinois Glass Co., 95–108; NAM statement, 290–95; statement of John Wayman (attorney retained by Corning Glass Works), 137–54; and American Retail Federation, 134–36; all in U.S. House, *Equal Pay Act Hearings, 1963*.

85. William Miller, on behalf of the U.S. Chamber of Commerce, in U.S. House, *Equal Pay Act Hearings, 1963*, 155–75.

86. Statement of Miss Sarah Jane Cunningham, National Legislative Chairman, National Federation of Business and Professional Women's Clubs, Inc., U.S. House, *Equal Pay Act Hearings, 1963*, 86.

87. U.S. Congress, *Congressional Record*, July 25–Aug. 3, 1962, 14767–68.

88. Ibid., 14768–69.

89. Ibid., 14769–70.

90. Statements of NJ congresswoman Florence Dwyer and Missouri congresswoman Leonore K. Sullivan, both in U.S. House, *Equal Pay Act Hearings, 1963*, 286–87 and 91 respectively; *Congressional Record*, House, Feb. 21, 1963, 2576–77.

91. Statement of Richard Lester, U.S. House, *Equal Pay Act Hearings, 1963*, 75–79.

92. Peterson, "The Kennedy Commission," 23.

93. U.S. House, *Equal Pay Act Hearings, 1963*, 58; Edith Green to Kitty Ellickson, Aug. 2 [c.1976] (box 90, file 31, KPE-ALUA pt. 1).

94. NCEP minutes, Aug. 6, 1962 (file "Minutes of the NCEP," NCEP-GMMA).

95. Statement of Esther Peterson, U.S. House, *Equal Pay Act Hearings, 1963*, 12. See also statements by William Schnitzler and Jim Carey, both in U.S. House, *Equal Pay Act Hearings, 1963*, 216–30 and 115 respectively.

96. See, for example, statements of Sonia Pressman, ACLU, and J. A. Bierne, both in *Equal Pay Act Hearings, 1963*, 211–16 and 180–81, respectively.

97. Anne Draper to William Schnitzler, Apr. 11, 1963 (box 17, file 9, LD-GMMA).

98. Kenneth Meiklejohn to A. Biemiller, internal memo, May 28, 1963 (box 17, file 9, LD-GMMA).

99. Harrison, *On Account of Sex*, 103–4.

100. John A. Grimes, "Kennedy Signs 'Equal Pay for Work' Bill, But Economic Emancipation Is Not Assured," *Wall Street Journal*, June 11, 1963.

101. Draper to NCEP Members, minutes and memo, June 20, 1963; minutes, Dec. 15, 1964 (both in file "1963–1964"); Membership Lists file; Clarence Lundquist, Administrator, Wage and Hour Division, to Anne Draper, Chair, NCEP, Apr. 9, 1965, and Anne Draper to Dr. Sara Feder, Feb. 14, 1968; Anne Draper to Gloria Johnson, July 9, 1974 (unprocessed NCEP files), all in NCEP-GMMA. See also file 1053, box 54, EP-SL.

102. Peterson, *Restless*, 110.

103. For discussions of the impact of the EPA, see Moran, "A Rate for the Job Regardless of Sex"; *Women Today*, July 23, 1973, vol. 3, no. 15; *IUE News*, Sept. 1972, 12; Jo Freeman, *Politics of Women's Liberation* (New York: David McKay Company, Inc., 1975), 174–75; Rosalind Rosenberg, *Divided Lives: American Women in the Twentieth Century* (New York: Hill and Wang, 1992), 184–85; Goldin, *Understanding the Gender Gap*, 201.

104. Kornbluh and O'Farrell, "You Can't Giddyup by Saying Whoa," 58; O'Farrell and Kornbluh, *Rocking the Boat*, 82; Laughlin, *Women's Work and Public Policy*, 86, quoting an oral history interview with Peterson by Ann Campbell, JFK Library, pt. 2, Feb. 11, 1970, 53. See also Peterson, "The Kennedy Commission," 23.

105. Beatrice McConnell, Deputy Director, Women's Bureau, to Clarence Lundquist, Administrator, Wage and Hour; Alice Morrison to Keyserling and McConnell, memo, Apr. 22, 1964; Keyserling to Mr. King Carr, Nov. 4, 1964; all in box 53, file 1052, EP-SL.

106. See PCSW, *American Women*, i–ii; "Meetings of Commission & Subcommittees" (box 93, file 2, KPE-ALUA pt. 1).

107. Esther Peterson, "The Work of the President's Commission on the Status of Women: An Evaluation," *Women's Education* 3 (Sept. 1964): 1 (box 116, file 2328, EP-SL).

108. Peterson, "The Kennedy Commission," 29.

109. Sealander, *As Minority Becomes Majority*, 147.

110. Mead and Kaplan, eds., *American Women*, 149.

111. PCSW, *American Women*, 27–34.

112. Ibid., 2.

113. Ibid., 44–46.

114. Ellickson, *The President's Commission on the Status of Women*, 13.

115. For the range of scholarly opinion on the PCSW, see, among others, Deslippe, *Rights, Not Roses*, 65; Blackwelder, *Now Hiring*, 181–82; Winifred Wandersee, *On the Move: American Women in the 1970s* (Boston: Twayne Publishers, 1988), 16–17; Susan Hartmann, *From Margin to Mainstream*, 49–52; Goldin, *Understanding the Gender Gap*,

200–205; Laughlin, *Women's Work and Public Policy*, 190–99; and Sealander, *As Minority Becomes Majority*, 147–48.

116. Mead also faulted the commission for its narrow conception of the proper family. "Epilogue" by Margaret Mead in Mead and Kaplan, *American Women*, 181–204.

117. PCSW, *American Women*, 18–26, 40–43; PCSW, *Report of the Committee on Protective Labor Legislation*, 15, 24; PCSW, *Report of the Committee on Social Insurance and Taxes* (Washington, DC: GPO, 1963); box 6, file 36, KPE-ALUA pt. 2; Sealander, *As Minority Becomes Majority*, 142–48.

118. Peterson, "The Kennedy Commission," 29.

119. PCSW, *American Women*, 49; box 6, file 36, KPE-ALUA pt. 2; Peterson, "The Kennedy Commission," 29–30.

120. For areas of disagreement, see Mead and Kaplan, *American Women*, 118–19, 159.

121. Ibid., 118–19; interview with Caroline Davis, TUWOHP.

122. Quotes from PCSW, *American Women*, 30–31. See also Zelman, *Women, Work, and National Policy*, 36–37; Gabin, *Feminism in the Labor Movement*, 157.

123. Callahan interview, TUWOHP, 31–32; quote from *IUE News*, Dec. 28, 1961, 1, 6.

124. Haener interview, TUWOHP. PCSW, *Report of the Committee on Protective Labor Legislation*, 22–26; Peterson, "The Kennedy Commission," 29–30.

125. PCSW, *Report of the Committee on Protective Labor Legislation*, 9–12; Mead and Kaplan, *American Women*, 128–35.

126. PCSW, *Report of the Committee on Protective Labor Legislation*, 11–12; PCSW, *American Women*, 35–39; Callahan interview, TUWOHP, 32–35; Mead and Kaplan, *American Women*, 128–35. Neither the committee nor the commission agreed with the AFL-CIO position that "double time after 35 hours" was necessary before any real change in employer work time practices would occur. Transcript of Labor News Conference, Program no. 40 on Shorter Work Week, Jan. 28, 1962 (box 44, file 49, LD-GMMA); "Reduction of Work Hours Resolution," AFL-CIO Convention Proceedings (box 44, file 49, LD-GMMA).

127. For further discussion and for Esther Peterson's views, see box 55, file 1082, EP-SL.

128. The Committee on Protective Labor Legislation also believed that men's hours should be regulated because it would help promote equality for women in the market place and because shorter hours helped distribute employment more equitably. For many in the labor movement, a shorter standard workweek was a remedy for "high and persistent unemployment" and "an alternative to cutting men." See Transcript of Labor News Conference, Program no. 40, Jan. 28, 1962.

129. For the quote, see Arthur J. Goldberg, *AFL-CIO: Labor United*, 195–202. Assessing organized labor's record on civil rights at mid-century is complicated, in part because of the great variety of racial attitudes and practices existing within the labor movement. Certain sectors of the labor movement, including the railway brotherhoods and many of the building trades, still excluded minority workers in their constitutions. Other unions had no such formal racial barriers, but they tolerated and at times reinforced racial segregation and second-class status for workers of color. In contrast, a number of unions had racially progressive politics and had taken up the cause of civil rights early on. See William H. Harris, *The Harder We Run: Black Workers since the Civil War* (New York: Oxford University Press, 1982) and more recent literature cited in ch. 3, note 40.

130. George Meany gained infamy for his opposition to the 1963 March on Washington, but he objected to its tactics, not its goals. His support for the proposed civil rights act held firm even when it was amended to include unions along with employers as potential defendants in cases alleging race-based employment discrimination. Draper, *Conflict of Interests*, 3–16.

131. Laughlin, *Women's Work and Public Policy*, 76.

132. White, *Too Heavy a Load*, 148–50 and ch. 6.

133. Ellickson, *The President's Commission on the Status of Women*, 13.

134. Press release, July 10, 1963 (box 95, file 2, KPE-ALUA pt. 1); files 1136–1160, EP-SL; Catherine Gelles, "Report on Visit to the White House, July 9, 1963" (box 3, file 15, WAC-ALUA); Women's Activities Division, COPE, *Keeping In Touch*, July 15, 1963 (box 60, file 1160, EP-SL). According to Jo Freeman, Nina Horton Avery of the NWP attended the first meeting to lobby JFK about the ERA but then declined further involvement. Freeman, "How 'Sex' Got into Title VII," 173.

135. "Summary: Second Consultation on Private Household Employment, Feb. 8, 1965," memo, and press release, USDL, Feb. 11, 1965 (file 975, unprocessed, EP-SL); press release, USDL, Mar. 13, 1968 (box 9, file 44, KPE-ALUA pt. 1).

136. Peterson, *Restless*, 79–80.

137. Laughlin, *Women's Work and Public Policy*, ch. 4.

138. MDK-SL, particularly the guide. Storrs, *Civilizing Capitalism*, 190–94.

139. The fullest account of the addition of the sex amendment to Title VII is Carl Brauer, "Women Activists, Southern Conservatives, and the Prohibition of Sex Discrimination in Title VII of the 1964 Civil Rights Act," *Journal of Southern History* 49 (Feb. 1983): 37–56. See also Donald Allen Robinson, "Two Movements in Pursuit of EEO," *Signs* 4 (Spring 1979): 413–20; Cynthia Deitch, "Gender, Race, and Class Politics and the Inclusion of Women in Title VII of the 1964 Civil Rights Act," *Gender and Society* 7 (June 1993): 183–203; and Freeman, "How 'Sex' Got into Title VII"; Susan Hartmann, *From Margin to Mainstream*, 54–56; Zelman, *Women, Work, and National Policy*, 55–71; Rosenberg, *Divided Lives*, 186–89; and Caruthers Gholson Berger, "Equal Pay, EEO, and Equal Enforcement of the Law for Women," *Valparaiso University Law Review* 5:2 (Spring 1971): 326–37.

140. *Congressional Record, House*, vol. 110, pt. 2, Feb. 8, 1964, 2577.

141. Quote from Brauer, "Women Activists," 41–42. For the attitudes of the NWP toward the Civil Rights Bill, see also Freeman, "How 'Sex' Got into Title VII."

142. As quoted in Brauer, "Women Activists," 43.

143. *Congressional Record, House*, vol. 110, pt. 2, Feb. 8, 1964, 2578–80.

144. Ibid., Feb. 8, 1964, 2582. Similarly, when the NWP adopted a resolution on Dec. 16, 1963, calling for the inclusion of sex in the Civil Rights Bill, it argued that "the CR bill would not even give protection against discrimination to a White Woman, a Woman of the Christian religion, or a Woman of US Origin." Quoted in Brauer, "Women Activists," 43.

145. *Congressional Record, House*, vol. 110, pt. 2, Feb. 8, 1964, 2583–84.

146. Edna Kelly, Democrat from Brooklyn, also supported the sex amendment. Brauer, "Women Activists," 46–50; Robinson, "Two Movements in Pursuit of EEO," 419; Brauer, "Women Activists," 46–47.

147. *Congressional Record, House*, vol. 110, pt. 2, Feb. 8, 1964, 2581–82.

148. For the vote count, see Freeman, "How 'Sex' Got into Title VII." Also see citations note 139, particularly Rosenberg, *Divided Lives*, 181–89.

149. Peterson, "The Kennedy Commission," 31.

150. Ibid., 31.

151. Brauer, "Women Activists," 51–53.

152. Ibid., 55. For a letter to Esther Peterson complaining about the Bennett amendment and the lack of attention to it from labor women, see Mrs. Macleod Simchak (Mac) to Esther Peterson, Nov. 8, 1965 (box 56, file 1088, EP-SL).

153. The term "divided citizenship" is from Mettler, *Divided Citizens*.

154. Draper to NCEP members, minutes and memo, June 20, 1963 (NCEP-GMMA).

155. Statements of Andrew Biemiller, Director, Department of Legislation, AFL-CIO, U.S. Senate, *FLSA Hearings, July 7, 1965* (Washington, DC: GPO, 1965), 89–129 (quotes from 95–96), and U.S. House, *Hearings to Amend the FLSA, 1965, pt. 1*, 419–86.

156. Biemiller, in U.S. Senate, *FLSA Hearings, 1965*, 89; statement of Willard Wirtz, Secretary of Labor, U.S. Senate, *FLSA Hearings, 1965*, 41.

157. Wirtz, in U.S. Senate, *FLSA Hearings, 1965*, 32–36.

158. U.S. Department of Labor, Citizens Advisory Council, Task Force on Labor Standards, *Report of the Task Force on Labor Standards to the Citizens' Advisory Council on the Status of Women* (Washington, DC: GPO, Apr. 1968), 22–23.

159. Phyllis Palmer also argues that an alliance of labor unions and civil rights groups were responsible. Palmer, "Outside the Law: Agricultural and Domestic Workers under the Fair Labor Standards Act," 418–26.

160. For further discussion of the impact of the commission, see Freeman, *Politics of Women's Liberation*, 52; Nancy Woloch, *Women and the American Experience* (New York: McGraw-Hill, Inc., 1994), 504–5; Zelman, *Women, Work, and National Policy*, 23.

CHAPTER 7
THE TORCH PASSES

1. Friedan and Clarenbach to Secretary of Labor Willard Wirtz, Apr. 9, 1967 (box 55, file 1075, EP-SL).

2. Myra Wolfgang testimony, U.S. House, *ERA Hearings, March–April 1971* (Washington, DC: GPO, 1971), 215.

3. Davis, *Moving the Mountain*, 106–8.

4. "Leaflet," Mike Friedman, AFSCME 1695, for Union WAGE, Apr. 8, 1971 (box 1, file 7, AD-CHS); Anne Draper testimony at IWC hearing, March 30, 1971 (box 2, file 10, AD-SUL). See also "Statement of Joyce Maupin at IWC Hearing," Mar. 7, 1972 (box 3, file 33, AD-CHS).

5. Joyce Maupin interview by Patricia Yeghissian, 1978, LARC, 97–98.

6. The phrase is from Ruth Rosen, *The World Split Open: How the Modern Women's Movement Changed America* (New York: Viking, 2000).

7. Materials in box 4, files 8 and 9, WD-ALUA; obituary in *Goshen News*, Dec. 30, 1988.

8. Box 1, file 1, AD-CHS; "Myra Wolfgang, Feminist Leader, 61," *NYT*, Apr. 13, 1976; "Gladys Dickason, Ex-Union Official," *NYT*, Sept. 1, 1971.

9. Mary Keyserling to Edith Cook, Associate Solicitor for Legislation, Oct. 8, 1964 (box 53, file 1052, EP-SL); Laughlin, "Backstage Activism," 208–24.

10. Stebenne, *Arthur J. Goldberg*, 514, 112n.

11. "Roosevelt Finds Sex Discrimination in Jobs is Big Problem," *NYT*, July 21, 1965; "De-sexing the Job Market," *NYT*, Aug. 21, 1965; Thomas Bray, "The Gripes of Rath: Laid-off Men Holler as Women Get Jobs," *Wall Street Journal*, Sept. 22, 1966. For a full

account of the early EEOC and its evolving policy, see Kessler-Harris, *In Pursuit of Equity*, 246–80.

12. "Third of Job Complaints Based on Sex Discrimination," *Washington Post*, Sept. 29, 1966; "It's Not a Man's World," Oct. 2, 1965, *Washington Post*, B6; Thomas Bray, "The Gripes of Rath"; Donald Allen Robinson, "Two Movements in Pursuit of EEO," *Signs* 4 (Spring 1979): 424; Deslippe, *Rights, Not Roses*, chs. 6, 7; Gabin, *Feminism in the Labor Movement*, 220–25; Ruth Needleman, "Women of Steel in the Calumet Region: Coalitions Create Power" (paper delivered at the North American Labor History Conference, Detroit, MI, Oct. 2000).

13. Esther Peterson, "The Kennedy Commission," in *Women in Washington*, ed. Irene Tinker (Beverly Hills, CA: Sage Publication, 1983), 32–33; Harrison, *On Account of Sex*, 164–65.

14. Laughlin, *Women's Work and Public Policy*, 99–108; Lerner, "Midwestern Leaders of the Modern Women's Movement," 11–15; transcript, "A Conference on California Women: Social Attitudes and Pressures in 1966," San Francisco State College, Nov. 19, 1966 (California State Department Industrial Relations Collection 1986/OB1, LARC).

15. Dorothy Pendergast, Boston regional director of the U.S. Women's Bureau, speaking to an IUE Conference in Apr. 1968, *IUE News*, Apr. 10, 1968, 10.

16. The discrimination against women in Johnson's anti-poverty programs and the anti-female bias of the Moynihan Report also helped spark a "new feminist consciousness among members of the Status of Women organizations," according to Zelman; see *Women, Work and National Policy*, 89.

17. Mary Keyserling, "Looking Ahead: Title VII and EEO," Apr. 5, 1965 address to Regional Conference on Civil Rights Sponsored by National Council of Women in U.S. (file 1077, EP-SL).

18. See, for example, Labor Advisory Committee minutes, June 4, 1946 (box 6, file 140), and "Rough Draft, Minutes," Feb. 14, 1949 (box 7, file 146, FM-SL).

19. After 1961, six states extended the minimum wage laws to men, and eleven amended their maximum hour laws to allow for more flexibility. See Harrison, *On Account of Sex*, 184.

20. Citizens Advisory Council, Task Force on Labor Standards, *Report of the Task Force on Labor Standards to the Citizens' Advisory Council on the Status of Women*, Apr. 1968 (Washington, DC: GPO, 1968), 23.

21. Munts and Rice, "Women Workers," 6–7; Gabin, *Feminism in the Labor Movement*, ch. 5.

22. FDR, Jr. to Frieda Miller, Dec. 21, 1965 (box 13, file 267, FM-SL).

23. Dorothy Height, NCNW President, to Luther Holcomb, Chair, EEOC, July 28, 1966 (box 55, file 22, LD-GMMA).

24. Ellickson interview with Dennis East, 1976, 26.

25. Haener interview, TUWOHP, 61–63; Biemiller to Margolin, Aug. 9, 1966 (box 55, file 22, LD-GMMA). The UAW Women's Department's position opposing woman-only hour laws, weight lifting, night work, and occupational limits was articulated as early as 1965. At this point, they did not see "seating laws, employment before and after childbirth, home work, minimum wage and equal pay laws" as "discriminatory." See Caroline Davis to FDR, Jr., Nov. 5, 1965 (box 56, file 1088, EP-SL).

26. For a condemnation of the behavior of the UAW women, see, for example, Margolin to Biemiller, Aug. 5, 1966 (box 55, file 22, LD-GMMA).

27. For the significance of the EEOC decision on want ads, see Kessler-Harris, *In Pursuit of Equity*, 257–59. On the origins of NOW, consult Haener interview,

TUWOHP, 59–60; Conroy interview, TUWOHP; Betty Friedan, epilogue to 1974 edition of *The Feminine Mystique* (New York: Dell Publishing Co., Inc., 1963), 367–71; Betty Friedan, *Life So Far: A Memoir* (New York: Simon and Schuster, 2000), 164–79; Freeman, *Politics of Women's Liberation*, 53–55, 71–102; Zelman, *Women, Work, and National Policy*, 36–37.

28. Freeman, *Politics of Women's Liberation*, 71–102; Susan Hartmann, *From Margin to Mainstream*, 58–69; Linden-Ward and Green, *Changing the Future*, 408–10; Woloch, *Women and the American Experience*, 516.

29. *1968 UAW Women's Department Report* (box 10, file 4, LH-ALUA); Carideo, "Stepping Forward with Catherine Conroy, 6–15.

30. "Woman in Society Resolution Adopted at the UAW Convention, April 20–25, 1970" (box 9, file 10, AD-GM); *1968 UAW Women's Department Report*; Betty Friedan and Kathryn Clarenbach for NOW to Willard Wirtz, Apr. 9, 1967 (box 55, file 1075, EP-SL); Kessler-Harris, *In Pursuit of Equity*, 275–76.

31. Kessler-Harris, *In Pursuit of Equity*, 258–59; Susan Hartmann, *From Margin to Mainstream*, 58–62.

32. The literature on the new feminism is vast. For a start, consult Alice Echols, *Daring to Be Bad: Radical Feminism in America, 1967–1975* (Minneapolis: University of Minnesota Press, 1989); Freeman, *Politics of Women's Liberation*; Davis, *Moving the Mountain*; Rosen, *The World Split Open*; and Myra Marx Ferree and Beth B. Hess, *Controversy and Coalition: The New Feminist Movement* (Boston: G.K. Hall & Company, 1985).

33. Peterson to Clifford Alexander, Jr., Chair EEOC, Sept. 7, 1957 (file 1100, EP-SL).

34. Citizens' Advisory Council, *Report of the Task Force on Labor Standards*. I have not come across any labor feminists who wanted to keep sex-based weight restrictions intact. Most favored replacing the fixed weight limits with "reasonable statutory requirements establishing flexible standards or limits related to the capacity of the individual." See legislative representative Kenneth Meiklejohn to Esther Peterson, Jan. 2, 1968 (box 55, file 22, LD-GMMA).

35. Ellickson interview with Dennis East, 1976, 26; *Daily Labor Report*, May 2, 1967 (no. 85), A9 (box 7, file 8, KPE-ALUA pt. 1).

36. *Daily Labor Report*, May 2, 1967, A9; "Statement of UAW to EEOC, May 2, 1967 (box 17, file 15, DH-ALUA).

37. The racial-ethnic breakdown of the industries affected belief as well. The civil rights ideology was less pervasive among women in retail and service work because of stricter racial segregation and the smaller numbers of minority women in these jobs.

38. Interview with Haener, TUWOHP. See also Caroline Davis to Esther Peterson, Mar. 22, 1967 (box 56, file 1099, EP-SL).

39. Anne Draper to Marvin Karpatkin, ACLU, Mar. 13, 1968 (box 9, file 5, AD-GMMA).

40. Wyatt interview, UPWA-OHP; Simmons interview, UPWA-OHP; Cobble, *Dishing It Out*, chs. 7–8; Sugiman, *Labour's Dilemma*, 5–6.

41. UPWA, *Proceedings*, 1968, 50–51.

42. Kitty Ellickson to Olga Madar, Apr. 22, 1967 (box 3, file 17, WD-ALUA).

43. In California, for example, the UAW, the Machinists, and the Steel Workers wanted changes in the hour laws that would allow women to work overtime. Unions opposing the amendments included those representing "women's industries" such as HERE, ILGWU, ACWA, CWA, and the IUE. See box 9, file 5, AD-GMMA.

44. Munts and Rice, "Women Workers," 9; "Letter to Honorable Paul Adams from Wolfgang, Chair, Planning Committee, C. Davis Dinner," June 19, 1963 (box 4, file 1, WD-ALUA); Wolfgang, "Statement of Policy of the Ad Hoc Committee Against the Repeal of Protective Labor Legislation for Women Workers in Michigan," Oct. 1967 (box 10, file 11, KPE-ALUA pt. 1); Robert A. Popa, "Two Union Women Wrangle over Female Work Limit," *Detroit News*, Jan. 17, 1969 (box 18, file 9, DH-ALUA); Wolfgang, "Statement of Policy Regarding Hours Legislation for Women Workers," n.d. (box 1, file 8, MW-ALUA); Wolfgang to "Dear Fellow Unionist," Mar. 11, 1969, and Wolfgang to Rep. James Del Rio, May 31, 1968 (both in box 1, file 3, MW-ALUA).

45. Gabin, "Time Out of Mind," 364–65.

46. Ibid., 367–68; Wolfgang Statement, *Congressional Record, Senate*, March 21, 1972, 4419.

47. Gabin, "Time Out of Mind," 367–68.

48. Citizens' Advisory Council, *Report of the Task Force on Labor Standards*, 1968, 29–31.

49. Munts and Rice, "Women Workers," 8; Citizens' Advisory Council, *Report of the Task Force on Labor Standards*, 29–31, 41. Draper's position reflected that of the AFL-CIO; see AFL-CIO *Proceedings*, 1967, 485–86. Keyserling also favored retaining hour limits for women but with increased flexibility in the laws so that those women who wanted overtime would "have the opportunity to earn extra money"; Keyserling, "Recent Developments with Respect to State Hours Laws and their Relation to Title VII," 5–7.

50. For example, AFL-CIO, *Proceedings*, 1967, 485–86.

51. *Daily Labor Report*, May 2, 1967 (no. 85), A9 (box 7, file 8, KPE-ALUA pt. 1); statement of Wolfgang, U.S. Senate, *The "Equal Rights" Amendment: Hearings before the Subcommittee on Constitutional Amendments of the Committee on the Judiciary, 91st Congress, May 5, 6, and 7, 1970* (Washington, DC: GPO, 1970), 21.

52. Wolfgang, "Address before the AAUW," Oakland University, May 1, 1971 (box 1, file 8); Wolfgang to Del Rio, May 31, 1968 (box 1, file 3); Wolfgang, "Statement of Policy of the Ad Hoc Committee against the Repeal of Protective Labor Legislation for Women Workers in Michigan" (box 1, file 8), all in WM-ALUA.

53. Munts and Rice, "Women Workers," 6–7; Gabin, *Feminism in the Labor Movement*, ch. 5.

54. Many "protective" laws were eventually extended to men. The Occupational Health and Safety Act (OSHA) passed in 1970, for example, extending certain health and safety protections to men. Yet as will be discussed in chapter 8, OSHA is another example of a gender-neutral law premised on male standards. Because of this bias, it failed to address adequately the reproductive differences between men and women and hence left sexual inequality intact.

55. A dozen states still had hour laws for women, for example, and a handful of other woman-only laws also existed that covered minimum wages, employment before and after childbirth, rest breaks, and other working conditions. Munts and Rice, "Women Workers," 4–7.

56. Brauer, "Women Activists," 36–40; Rupp and Taylor, *Survival in the Doldrums*, ch. 6. There had, of course, been some prominent women associated with labor and social feminism who "defected" before the 1960s. See Eleanor Roosevelt, "My Day," *Louisville Courier-Journal*, June 8, 1951, in which she argued that more could now be gained by removing the state laws that discriminate than fighting to keep those that protect. See also Alice Hamilton to Miss Magee, May 15, 1953 (box 92, file 5, KPE-ALUA pt. 1).

57. UAW women had pushed for the change and the leadership complied, in part because the UAW's withdrawal from the AFL-CIO in 1968 made a break with the official AFL-CIO line less controversial.

58. Madar testimony, U.S. Senate, *ERA Hearings*, May 1970, 592–93, 614.

59. U.S. Senate, *ERA Hearings*, May 1970; U.S. Senate, *Equal Rights 1970: Hearings before the Committee on the Judiciary, 91st Congress, September 9, 10, 11, and 15* (Washington, DC: GPO, 1970). For UAW testimony, see *ERA Hearings*, Sept. 1970, 402–6; U.S. House, *ERA Hearings*, Mar.–Apr. 1971.

60. On the Women's Bureau, see Sealander, *As Minority Becomes Majority*, 147; Laughlin, *Women's Work and Public Policy*, 122–23. For background on Koontz, see Percy E. Murray, "Elizabeth Koontz," in *Black Women in America*, 683–84.

61. Esther Peterson to Martha Griffiths, Oct. 12, 1971 (box 54, file 1061, EP-SL).

62. Jane Mansbridge argues convincingly that ERA activists on both sides of the debate in the 1970s exaggerated the likely effects of the ERA. It was a fight based as much on what the ERA symbolized as what it would accomplish. Mansbridge, *Why We Lost the ERA*, 1–7.

63. U.S. Senate, *ERA Hearings*, May 1970, 616–18; ACWA, *Proceedings*, 1968, 185. See also ACWA, *Proceedings*, 1970, 231–35.

64. U.S. Senate, *ERA Hearings*, May 1970, 103–22, and Sept. 1970, 29–64, 149–61, 229–33 (230 for Miller quote), 402–6; U.S. House, *ERA Hearings*, Mar.–Apr. 1971.

65. Doris Hardesty, "The Continuing Fight for Women's Rights," *AF* 78 (Jan. 1971): 12–16.

66. Eileen Shanahan, "Women Unionists Score Equality Plan," *NYT*, Sept. 10, 1970.

67. Wolfgang testimony, U.S. Senate, *ERA Hearings*, May 6, 1970, 52–55; U.S. Senate, *ERA Hearings*, Sept. 1970, 44. *Congressional Record, Senate*, Mar. 21, 1972, 4416–21. See also "Statement of Mrs. Esther Peterson before the Republican Platform Committee, July 21, 1960" (box 9, file 1, AD-GMMA). The same language appears in a draft of an earlier proposed letter from the AFL-CIO to each member of the Senate. "Draft of letter to be sent to each member of Senate opposing ERA, May 1956" (box 17, file 1, LD-GMMA).

68. Friedan testimony, U.S. Senate, *ERA Hearings*, May 1970, 491–93.

69. Local 705, HERE, press release, Oct. 22, 1970 (box 1, file 6, MW-ALUA).

70. Myra Wolfgang, "Address before the AAUW," Oakland University, May 1, 1971 (box 1, file 8, MW-ALUA). See also "Some of the Problems of Eve," address to the "Women and Work" Conference, Mar. 13, 1971, Los Angeles County Federation of Labor (box 9, file 10, AD-GM).

71. "Memorial Statement, Anne Lipow, President, Union WAGE" (box 1, file 1, AD-CHS); Anne Lipow to "Union and Women's Organizations," Sept. 30, 1972 (box 1, file 3, AD-CHS).

72. NCNW, the National Council of Jewish Women, and others joined the National Committee Against Repeal of Protective Laws. See Laughlin, *Women's Work and Public Policy*, 122–23.

73. Maupin interview by Yeghissian, 95, LARC.

74. Diane Balser, *Sisterhood and Solidarity: Feminism and Labor in Modern Times* (Boston: South End Press, 1987), 87–149; Anne Draper to "Dear Friend," Mar. 11, 1971 (box 1, file 3, AD-CHS); press release, Sept. 22, 1970 (box 1, file 14, AD-CHS).

75. Guide to Anne Draper Collection, AD-SUL; materials, box 1, files 1–3, AD-CHS; interview with Joe White, professor of history, University of Pittsburgh, by the author, Mar. 23, 2001.

76. Maupin interview by Yeghissian, LARC.

77. Balser, *Sisterhood and Solidarity*, 87–149; Maupin interview by Yeghissian, 51–96, LARC; box 2, file 10, AD-SUL; "Memorial Statement, Anne Lipow, President, Union WAGE"; Anne Draper to "Dear Friend," Mar. 11, 1971 (box 1, file 3, AD-CHS).

78. Maupin interview by Yeghissian, 99–100, LARC.

79. *Spokeswoman* 2 (Oct. 1, 1971), 6; Maupin interview by Yeghissian, 117–20, LARC; Anne Draper, "Equal Rights for All," leaflet, n.d. [c.1971–72] (box 1, file 7, AD-CHS).

80. "Memorial Statement, Anne Lipow, President, Union WAGE," and "Memorial Statement, John Henning, Sec-Treas, California State Federation of Labor" (box 1, file 1, AD-CHS); "Union Women vs. N.O.W.," *Union WAGE Newsletter* 1:4 (Aug. 1971) (box 1, file 7, AD-CHS); see also other materials in box 1, files 3, 14, and 17–19, AD-CHS.

81. Aileen C. Hernandez, "An Open Letter to the California Federation of Labor," May 20, 1972 (box 1, file 2, AD-CHS); Maupin interview by Yeghissian, 95, LARC; Balser, *Sisterhood and Solidarity*, 103–8.

82. *IUE News*, July 1972, 10; Dec 1972, 3; CWA, *Proceedings*, 1972, 203–9. For the AAUW debate, see Levine, *Degrees of Equality*, 164.

83. Linda Kerber and Jane DeHart Matthews, *Women's America: Refocusing the Past* (New York: Oxford University Press, 1982), 446–47; AFL-CIO, *Proceedings*, 1973, 388–89; ACWA, *Proceedings*, 1974, 202–8.

84. Andrew Biemiller to Mrs. Gereau, ERA Ratification Council, Dec. 6, 1973 (box 17, file 10, LD-GMMA). By 1972, the AFL-CIO was in coalition with the DAR, the Virginia Federation of Women's Clubs, and other conservative groups in their Stop ERA Campaign in Virginia. See box 55, file 22, LD-GMMA.

85. Peter Levy, *The New Left and Labor in the 1960s* (Urbana: University of Illinois, 1994), 175–76.

86. Leslie Bennetts, "6,000 Rally at the Virginia Capitol in Drive for Equal Rights Measure," *NYT*, Jan. 14, 1980, A12.

87. *IUE News*, Sept. 1978, 4.

88. For example, Addie Wyatt, UPWU-OHP, tape 55, side 1.

89. For the term "bread and butter equality" and her criticisms of the ERA approach, see Peterson's letter to the *Trentonian*, Oct. 6, 1968 (box 54, file 1056); also, Peterson to Willard Wirtz, memo, n.d. [1965] (box 55, file 1084), both in EP-SL.

90. Peterson, "The World Beyond the Valley," 21; for her continuing activities as asst. secretary of labor, see, for instance, materials in box 54, file 1066, and box 56, file 1099, EP-SL.

91. Peterson to Jacob Potofsky, June 13, 1967 (box 56, file 1100, EP-SL). See also her critical notes jotted on Jacob Potofsky's statement to the EEOC, May 24, 1967 (box 56, file 1100, EP-SL).

92. Katherine Ellickson, "Eleanor Roosevelt's Contribution to the PCSW," n.d. (box 6, file 40, KPE-ALUA pt. 2).

93. Although little political support existed for the goal of revaluing household labor, neither Ellickson nor Peterson lost interest in the issue. Peterson, *Restless*, 79–81, 100–102, 183–84; box 94, file 3, KPE-ALUA pt. 1; draft statement, "Recognition of the Economic Contribution of the Homemaker" (box 8, file 33, KPE-ALUA pt. 2); Ellickson interview by Philip Mason, 1974, ALUA.

94. U.S. Senate, *Hearing before the Subcommittee on Labor on S. 2068, 91st Congress, 1st Session, May 8, 1969* (Washington, DC: GPO, 1969), 6; "Statement of Howard Sam-

uel" and "Statement of Jacob Sheinkman," in U.S. House, *Hearing before the Special Subcommittee on Labor, 91st Congress, 1st Session on HR 4314 and HR 13520* (Washington, DC: GPO, 1969). Union support is discussed in *Alliance of Union Women Bulletin* 1:4 (Dec. 1970) (box 9, file 10, AD-GMMA); Biemiller to Mrs. A. J. Evans, Aug. 18, 1972 (box 18, file 28, LD-GMMA); *IUE News*, Oct. 3, 1968, 14, and Dec. 1971, 6; AFL-CIO, *Proceedings*, 1969, 375–78; AFL-CIO, *Executive Council Statements and Reports, 1956– 75*, vol. 3, ed. Gary Fink, 1878–79, 2115, 2237. For ACWA's early commitment to child care centers, see pamphlet, "A Report of a Conference on Day Care and the Working Mother," June 17, 1967, and *Issues in Industrial Society* 2:1 (1971): 13–15 (both in box 8, file 39, AD-GMMA); *Advance* 59 (May 15, 1968): 4. ACWA also won an amendment to Taft-Hartley allowing joint financing by unions and employers of day care centers. See Biemiller to Ralph Yarborough, Mar. 4, 1968 (box 13, file 36, LD-GMMA).

95. President's Task Force on Women's Rights and Responsibilities, *A Matter of Simple Justice: A Report* (Washington, DC: GPO, Apr. 1970).

96. Richard Nixon, "Veto of Economic Opportunity Amendments of 1971," *Weekly Compilation of Presidential Documents*, Dec. 13, 1971, vol. 7, no. 50, 1634–36. U.S. House, *Hearings, 92nd Congress, May–June 1971*; *Congressional Record*, May 1972, vol. 51, no. 5, 138–99; Task Force on Working Women, *Exploitation From 9 to 5: Report of the Twentieth Century Fund Task Force on Women and Employment* (New York: Twentieth Century Fund, 1975), 169–71; Quadagno, *The Color of Welfare*, 114–54. For assessments of the role of second wave feminists, see Davis, *Moving the Mountain*, 280–86; Weiner, *From Working Girl to Working Mother*, 137–40; Laughlin, *Women's Work and Public Policy*, 114–16; Michel, *Children's Interests, Mothers' Rights*, 247–48.

97. *Congressional Record, 88th Congress, vol. 109, pt. 18*, Dec. 4–12, 1963, 23253; "Legislative Series: New Law Liberalizes Child Care Deductions," USDL Employment Standards Administration, Women's Bureau (typed sheets, box 8, file 39, AD-GMMA); McCaffery, *Taxing Women*, 114–15. McCaffery notes that in 1976 Congress replaced the deduction with a credit. A credit offers everyone the same benefit; the amount of a deduction, however, depends on the taxpayer's marginal rate: the higher one's rate bracket, the greater the deduction.

98. Peterson, *Restless*, 79–80. For the earlier efforts of the Women's Bureau, see Frieda Miller, "On Domestic Service," *Vassar Alumnae Magazine*, Jan.–Mar. 1947 (box 15, file 283, FM-SL); "Statement of Frieda Miller," *Hearings on HR 2893, Social Security Act Amendments of 1949 before HR, 81st Congress* (Washington, DC: GPO: 1949), 1587– 93; Kessler-Harris, *In Pursuit of Equity*, 152–55.

99. Michel, "Motherhood and Social Citizenship in the U.S. Public/Private Welfare State," 16–17.

100. For a fuller account of the origins and history of this movement, see Dorothy Sue Cobble, " 'A Spontaneous Loss of Enthusiasm': Workplace Feminism and the Transformation of Women's Service Jobs in the 1970s," *International Labor and Working-Class History* 56 (Fall 1999), 33–39.

101. "Dorothy Bolden Portrait," in *Nobody Speaks for Me! Self-Portraits of American Working Class Women*, ed. Nancy Seifer (New York: Simon & Schuster, 1976), 136–77; "Dorothy Bolden Interview with Gerda Lerner," in *Black Women in White America*, 234–38; quote from *Nashville Tennessean*, Mar. 13, 1972 (clipping in box 1633, file 181, NDWU-SLA). The Detroit movement is also well documented. See Mary Upshaw McClendon Collection, Archives of Labor and Urban Affairs, Wayne State University, Detroit, Michigan.

102. For coverage of the conference, "Our Day Has Come," *NYT*, July 18, 1971, 1, 43; Jeannette Smyth, "Household Workers Organize," *Detroit News*, July 22, 1971; "Farewell to Dinah," *Newsweek*, Aug. 2, 1971, 67.

103. Miller, "On Domestic Service;" "Statement of Frieda Miller," in U.S. House, *Hearings on Social Security Act Amendments of 1949*, 1587–93. Peterson, *Restless*, 79–80, 100–101; U.S. Dept. of Labor, press release, Feb. 11, 1965 (file 1110, EP-SL); "Draft Foundation Proposal," Sept. 26, 1967 (box 12, file 253, and box 13, file 254, FM-SL); U.S. Dept. of Labor, press release, Mar. 13, 1968 (file 1115, EP-SL); NCHE, "Employer Training Manual," n.d., and other documents in box 1629, file 116, NDWU-SLA; Women's Bureau of the USDL, *Report of a Consultation On the Status of Household Employment* (Chicago, May 1967) (box 31, California Department of Industrial Relations Collection, LARC), in particular Peterson's remarks, 27–30. As chair of the NCL "Committee on Labor Standards," Ellickson developed model regulations for "alien live-in household employees" that included limits on hours, a statement of immigrant rights, and the use of written, not oral contracts. She argued that immigration policies should include domestics. See box 9, files 40–45, KPE-ALUA pt. 2.

104. Miller quote from letter, Miller to Christensen, Oct. 11, 1966 (box 12, file 253, FM-SL); Sloan quote from Darry A. Sragow, "Taking the Mammy Out of Housework," *Civil Rights Digest* (Winter 1971): 34–38. At the 1971 conference, the NCHE sponsored a new membership-based dues-paying organization, the Household Technicians of America (HTA), to effect many of its goals. The plan was for the NCHE eventually to turn over its staff to the HTA, which would "become in effect a sort of union." See Elaine Morrissey, "Household Workers, Today's 'Necessity,'" *Dayton Daily News*, Aug. 5, 1971; *NCHE News* 1:1 (Nov. 1970–Sept. 1972) (box 2, file 11, MM-ALUA); Ron Chernow, "All in a Day's Work," *Mother Jones* 1 (Aug. 1976): 11–16.

105. Sragow, "Taking the Mammy Out of Housework." 34–38; "Farewell to Dinah," 67.

106. Quote from Sragow, "Taking the Mammy Out of Housework," 38; "Farewell to Dinah," 67; Geraldine Roberts interview, TUWOHP; "National Domestic Workers," pamphlet, n.d. [c.1975], 9 (box 1628, file 102, NDWU-SLA); Jeannette Smyth, "Union Maid: A Two-Way Street," *Washington Post*, July 17, 1971.

107. Guide to the MM-ALUA, and box 1, files 4, 14–22, MM-SLA; Geraldine Roberts interview, TUWOHP, 65–70, 73–75,100–104.

108. Peterson, *Restless*, 101; Verta Mae, *Thursdays and Every Other Sunday Off: A Domestic Rap by Verta Mae* (Garden City, NJ: Doubleday & Company, 1972), 151–52; Elizabeth Koontz, "The Women's Bureau Looks Back to the Future," *Monthly Labor Review* 93 (June 1970), 3–9; Elizabeth Koontz, "The Progress of the Woman Worker: An Unfinished Story," *Issues in Industrial Society* 2:1 (1971): 30–31. See also box 18, file 28, LD-GMMA; Palmer, "Outside the Law: Agricultural and Domestic Workers Under the Fair Labor Standards Act," 426; Sylvia Porter, "1.4 Million Domestic Workers Have Big Stake in Pay Bill," *Miami Herald*, Aug. 24, 1973; Levy, *The New Left and Labor in the 1960s*, 174–76; NOW Legal Defense and Education Fund, *Out of the Shadows: Strategies for Expanding State Labor and Civil Rights Protections for Domestic Workers* (New York: NOW LDEF, 1997), 1–20; "Interview with Edith Sloan" (box 1, file 8, MM-SLA).

109. Box 1629, file 116, NDWU-SLA; Austin Scott, "Household Workers Ask for Economic Justice," *Washington Post*, June 29, 1977, C6; Joyce Kennedy, "Household Help Upgraded," *Washington Star*, January 30, 1976, B5; Geraldine Roberts interview, TUWOHP, 71–72, 94; Mary Romero, *Maid in the USA* (New York: Routledge, 1992) ch.

6, and Romero, "Household Workers," in *The Reader's Companion to U.S. Women's History*, 260–63; Garfinkle, "Occupations of White and Black Women Workers, 1962–74," 27, 31; "Farewell to Dinah," 1971; John Sweeney, *America Needs a Raise* (Boston, Houghton Mifflin Company, 1996), 22–27; Sara Mosle, "How the Maids Fought Back," *New Yorker*, Feb. 26 and Mar. 4, 1996; Dorothy Sue Cobble and Michael Merrill, "Collective Bargaining in the Hospitality Industry in the 1980s," in *Contemporary Collective Bargaining in the Private Sector*, ed. Paula Voos (Madison, WI: Industrial Relations Research Association, 1994), 447–90.

110. Callahan interview, TUWOHP, 38–39.

111. "Myra K. Wolfgang, Feminist Leader, 61," *NYT*, April 13, 1976.

112. Balser, *Sisterhood and Solidarity*, 151–210; "Planning Committee for Founding Conference" (box 1, file 13, BW–TL); newspaper clippings, box 1, file 1, CK–TL; Philip Foner, *Women and the American Labor Movement*, 505–6, 516; Jeffrey interview, TUWOHP, 128–30; "Black Women in the Labor Movement: Interviews with Clara Day and Johnnie Jackson," *Labor Research Review* 11 (Spring 1988): 79–86; Needleman, "Women of Steel in the Calumet Region: Coalitions Create Power," 1–9.

113. Ferree and Hess, for example, describe the early 1970s as a period in which "working-class women moved from a position of distanced neutrality into organizing on their own behalf." See Ferree and Hess, *Controversy and Coalition*, 85.

114. Address by Olga Madar, UAW, *Proceedings*, 1974, 203–9.

115. Ellickson to Howard Samuels and Myra Wolfgang, August 1, 1970 (box 8, file 7, KPE-ALUA pt. 1). See "Notes on Informal Meetings of Trade Union Women Who Have Been Active with Various State Commissions on Status of Women" (file 996, EP-SL); O'Farrell and Kornbluh, *Rocking the Boat*, 132.

116. Wolfgang, temporary chair, Ad Hoc Committee, Federation for Advancement of Women, to KPE, memo, July 30, 1970 (box 7, file 18, KPE-ALUA pt. 2); *Alliance of Union Women Bulletin* 1:1 (Sept. 1970) (box 9 file 10, AD-GMMA); "Statement of Myra Wolfgang," U.S. House, *ERA Hearings*, Mar.–Apr. 1971, 228–29, 724.

117. On black unionists in the 1960s, see Harris, *The Harder We Run*, 147–77, and for the Coalition of Black Trade Unionists, see Patrick Renshaw, *American Labor and Consensus Capitalism, 1935–1990* (Jackson: University Press of Mississippi, 1991), 160–66. On the beginnings of CLUW, see Balser, *Sisterhood and Solidarity*, 151–57, (Addie Wyatt quotes on 154–55) *Women Today*, July 23, 1973, vol. 3, no. 15; press release, Cleveland Council of Union Women, Jan. 29, 1974 (box 8, file 13, CLUW-ALUA); Callahan interview, TUWOHP, 38–39.

118. Balser, *Sisterhood and Solidarity*, 167; interview with Susan J. Schurman, president, George Meany Center for Labor Studies—The National Labor College, June 27, 2000, by the author. Some accounts of the convention also praise the "organizational talent" of the chairs for keeping grandstanding and disruption to a minimum. For example, Sexton, "Workers (Female) Arise," 384.

119. For the different styles of women's organizations, see Ferree and Hess, *Controversy and Coalition*, 48–62.

120. Balser, *Sisterhood and Solidarity*, 133–34, 186–89.

121. When faced with defining its boundaries, the Women's Trade Union League, also concerned with keeping labor women's issues primary, limited the number of "allies" who could hold office and insisted on loyalty to the principles of the organization, but allowed nonunion women to join. On the WTUL, see Payne, *Reform, Labor, and Feminism*.

122. Balser, *Sisterhood and Solidarity*, 133–34, 165–89.

123. Tory Rhodin, "Union Official Credits Women's Movement," *Morning Call* (Allentown, PA), Nov. 17, 1976 (box 8, file 18, CLUW-ALUA).

124. O'Farrell and Kornbluh, *Rocking the Boat*, 132.

125. CLUW-ALUA; Wyatt interview, UPWA-OHP, tape 56, side 1; Patricia Cayo Sexton, "Workers (Female) Arise," *Dissent* 21 (1974): 383; newspaper clippings, box 1, file 20, CK-TL; Deslippe, "Rights, not Roses," 316–23; Eileen Shanahan, "Union Women Hold Mainstream Course," *NYT*, Dec. 8, 1975; Balser, *Sisterhood and Solidarity*, 189–205.

126. Irving Howe, introduction, in *The World of the Blue-Collar Worker*, ed. Irving Howe (New York: Quadrangle Books, 1972), 4–5.

127. Anne Draper to Esther Peterson, Nov. 24, 1970 (file 1659 "20th Century Fund Task Force on Working Women," EP-SL).

128. AFL-CIO, *Proceedings*, 1975, 339–43; Leon Lunden, "AFL-CIO Focus: Economy, Farmworkers, and Women's Rights," *Monthly Labor* Review 98 (Dec. 1975): 42–46; AFL-*CIO News*, April 24, 1976.

129. Balser, *Sisterhood and Solidarity*, 49; Susan Reverby, "An Epilogue . . . or Prologue to CLUW?" *Radical America* 9 (Nov.–Dec. 1975): 111–14; Nancy Seifer and Barbara Wertheimer, "New Approaches to Collective Power: Four Working Women's Organization," in *Women Organizing*, ed. Bernice Cummings and Victoria Schuck (Metuchen, NJ: Scarecrow Press, Inc., 1979), 159–60.

130. For a discussion of some of these changes, see Dorothy Sue Cobble and Monica Bielski Michal, " 'On the Edge of Equality?' Working Women and the U.S. Labour Movement," in *Gender, Diversity, and Trade Unions: International Perspectives*, ed. Fiona Colgan and Sue Ledwith (London: Routledge, 2002), 232–56.

131. Erma J. Wiszmann, president, CWA Local 7117, Davenport, Iowa, to Linda Tarr-Whelan, Apr. 13, 1974 (box 8, file 15, CLUW-ALUA).

132. CWA, *Proceedings*, June 12–16, 1978, 29.

CHAPTER 8
AN UNFINISHED AGENDA

1. "The Woman in Society Resolution," adopted Apr. 20–25, 1970 (box 9, file 10, AD-GMMA); Wolfgang, "Address before the American Association of University Women, Oakland University, May 1, 1971" (box 1, file 8, MW-ALUA).

2. The response of unions to women who challenged the sexual division of labor in the late 1960s and 1970s varied considerably. In the construction trades the hostility was often intense and unrelenting. Yet in other situations, unions reacted more ambivalently, and at times were even supportive. The IUE, for example, set up a Social Action Department in 1965 with the aim of seeing to it that Title VII would be implemented fully throughout the international, and in 1970 they assigned Gloria Johnson to handle women's activities on a full-time basis. On construction, see, among others, *Hard-Hatted Women: Stories of Struggle and Success in the Trades*, ed. Molly Martin (Seattle: The Seal Press, 1988). On the IUE, Hartmann, *The Other Feminists*, ch. 2, and Deslippe, *Rights, Not Roses*, ch. 7; *IUE News*, Aug. 22, 1968, 10; Apr. 10, 1969, 10; Mar. 1972, 7.

3. "Sex Objects in the Sky Unite" is a quote from Elizabeth Rich in *Newsletter* 2:9 (Sept.–Oct. 1974) (box 2, file 52, SFWR-TL). She was expanding upon Paula Kane's title. See Kane, *Sex Objects in the Sky: A Personal Account of the Stewardess Rebellion* (Chicago: Follett Publishing Co., 1974).

4. "Our History . . . First in a Series," 20–21; *Intercom* (magazine of ALSSA, Local 550-TWU), Dec. 1966–Oct. 1967 (TL); Davis, *Moving the Mountain*, 16–25. For the charges

before the New York State Commission, see TWU news release, May 6, 1966 (box 32, file "1966," TWU-TL); Leonard Shecter, "Flying High," *New York Post*, Dec. 8, 1965; "Unfair to Fair Sex?" *World Telegram*, Dec. 8, 1965. Kathleen Heenan, "Fighting the Fly-Me Airlines," *Civil Liberties Review*, Dec. 1976–Jan. 1977, 49–50; J. Edward Conway, Investigating Commissioner, "In the Matter of Airlines Maximum Age Requirements," Exhibit 8, Mar. 23, 1966, in U.S. House, *Age Discrimination in Employment: Hearings before the General Subcommittee on Labor of the Committee on Education and Labor, 90th Congress, August 1–3, 15–17, 1967* (Washington, D.C.: GPO, 1967), 128–30. Frank Prial, "The Great Girl Shortage in the Sky, Pt. 2," *New York World Telegram*, Aug. 26, 1965, 2:17.

5. Fredric C. Appel, "Unions want airlines to break age barrier for stewardesses," *NYT*, Dec. 8, 1965.

6. ALPA press release, Sept. 22, 1965 (box 3, file 22); statement by Margie Cooper, particularly exhibits 17 and 23 (box 3, file 24) both in AFA-ALUA; Davis, *Moving the Mountain*, 20–22. Colleen Boland testimony, U.S. House, "Subcommittee on Labor Hearing," HR 10634, Sept., 1965 (box 32, file "1965," TWU-TL). See also statements of Francis O'Connell, Margie Cooper, and Colleen Boland, U.S. House, *Age Discrimination Hearings, 1967*, 104–129, 425–28. Cooper quotes on pp. 105–6, 109.

7. Gelder, "Coffee, Tea, or Fly Me," 89; Heenan, "Flighting the Fly-Me Airlines," 49–50; Nielsen, *From Sky Girl to Flight Attendant*, 100–101; Davis, *Moving the Mountain*, 22–25.

8. ALPA press release, Sept. 22, 1965 (box 3, file 22); statement by Margie Cooper, particularly exhibits 17 and 23 (box 3, file 24); *Betty Green Bateman and ALPA v Braniff*, Case no. 394 (box 3, file 23 and other materials, box 3, files 20–24, all in AFA-ALUA). Hugh Aynesworth, "Grounded by Marriage Rule, Hostess Fights to Fly Again," *Dallas Morning News*, Sept. 25, 1965; box 32, file "1965," TWU-TL.

9. "Picketing for Money and Marriage," *New York Tribune*, May 25, 1965; Gelder, "Coffee, Tea, or Fly Me," 89; Rozen, "Turbulence in the Air," 141–43; 170–98; Davis, *Moving the Mountain*, 16–25; Heenan, "Fighting the Fly-Me Airlines," 50–51; Patricia Moore, "Airlines Taking Lumps in Sex-Bias Cases," *Chicago Daily News*, July 31, 1973, 16; "News Clippings," box 2, file 64, SFWR-TL; Nielsen, *From Sky Girl to Flight Attendant*, 84–99; "Legal Task Force," box 1, file 15, SFWR-TL.

10. "Personhood" is from Cynthia Glacken letter, Oct. 1, 1975 (box 2, file 50, SFWR-TL).

11. An important segment of the women's liberation movement developed a pointed and angry analysis of the ways in which the so-called sexual liberation movement freed men but denigrated women. The women's liberation movement also stressed the importance of women's knowledge and control of their own bodies as evidenced in the Boston Women's Health Book Collective's best-seller, *Women and Our Bodies* (Boston: New England Free Press, 1970) or the oft-reprinted article by Anne Koedt, "The Myth of the Vaginal Orgasm: A Thesis for Further Study," in *Notes from the First Year* (New York: New York Radical Women, June 1968).

12. Frank J. Prial, "The Great Girl Shortage in the Sky," *New York World Telegram*, Aug. 25, 1965 (part 1), and materials, box 2, files 62–64, SFWR-TL.

13. Kane, *Sex Objects in the Sky*, 11–63; 102–3. For "geisha girl" label, see p. 19.

14. See "Clippings," box 2, file 64, SFWR-TL; quotes from Heenan, "Fighting the Fly-Me Airlines," 48–53; Anne Sweeney, "The Turn of the Screwed," *SFWR Newsletter* 2:5 (May 1974): 6–7 (box 2, file 52, SFWR-TL); Frank J. Prial, "The Great Girl Shortage in the Sky," Aug. 25–26, 1965.

15. Betty Liddick, "Tail Slogan Hits Bottom, Say Stews," *LA Times*, Jan. 25, 1974 (box 2, file 64, SFWR-TL); Kane, *Sex Objects in the Sky*, 11–15; 52–63; 155; Steven Pratt, "They're in a Stew about Discrimination," *Chicago Tribune*, Sept. 17, 1973, 2:6; Ed Cray, "The Barbie Dolls Revolt," *Air Fair*, Apr. 1975, 16–19.

16. Address by Sandra Jarrell, in *SFWR Newsletter* 1:2 (May 1973): 2 (box 2, file 51; see box 1, file 3 and box 2, file 51 for Jarrell's background, SFWR-TL). SFWR documents reveal a range of attitudes toward unions among members; it also appears that the tensions between SFWR and labor were greatest in its first few years. See, for example, "New Directions for SFWR," May 9, 1974 (box 1, file 5) and "Board Member Correspondence" (box 1, file 12, SFWR-TL).

17. Heenan, "Fighting the Fly-Me Airline," 58–59; *SFWR Newsletter* 1:7 (Dec. 1973): 3 (box 2, file 51, SFWR-TL). Gloria Steinem and other middle-class feminists profiled the organization and the problems of flight attendants in *Ms* magazine and at numerous New York City feminist conferences. Feminist leaders and organizations also spoke at conferences, provided legal counsel, and helped with fund-raising, office space, and getting media attention for SFWR.

18. "Stewardesses for Women's Rights Planning, Coordinating Meeting," handwritten notes, n.d. (box 1, file 1); "Section 2, Purposes," SFWR By-Laws, n.d. (box 1, file 2); *SFWR Newsletter* 1:1 (1973) (box 2, file 51, all in SFWR-TL); Kane, *Sex Objects in the Sky*, 84–95.

19. SFWR-TL, in particular Carol Ivy, "Stews Organized against Sexism"; Henrietta Leith, " 'Sexpot' Stereotype Angers Stews," and other unidentified clippings in box 2, file 64; also *SFWR Newsletter*, 2:9 (Sept.–Oct. 1974): 1–2 (box 2, file 52).

20. Cynthia Glacken to *Time*, Feb. 14, 1974 (box 1, file 22, SFWR-TL).

21. "Press Release, July 19, 1973, S&S Division, ALPA" (box 1, file 16, SFWR-TL); "Press Release, Association of Flight Attendants, June 25, 1974" (box 1, file 22, SFWR-TL); Prial, "The Great Girl Shortage," and Ed Cray, "The Barbie Dolls Revolt" (box 2, file 61, SFWR-TL); Nielsen, *From Sky Girl to Flight Attendant*, 97–99.

22. Carolyn Childers, "Stews Challenge Airlines," *Christian Science Monitor*, n.d. [c.1974–75] (box 2, file 64, SFWR-TL); Nielsen, *From Sky Girl to Flight Attendant*, 106–16.

23. On public-sector organizing, see Deborah Bell, "Unionized Women in State and Local Government," in *Women, Work, and Protest*, 280–99; Thomas R. Brooks, *Toil and Trouble: A History of American Labor* (New York: Dell, 1971), ch. 23; Richard R. Freeman, "Unionism Comes to the Public Sector," *Journal of Economic Literature* 24 (Mar. 1986): 41–86.

24. For the leading occupations among women, consult Rosalyn Baxandall, Linda Gordon, and Susan Reverby, eds., *America's Working Women: A Documentary History* (New York: Vintage, 1976), 406–7; Women's Bureau of the U.S. Department of Labor, *1975 Handbook on Women Workers*, Bulletin 297 (Washington, DC, 1975), 96.

25. On the historical transformation of clerical work, see Harry Braverman, *Labor and Monopoly Capital: The Degradation of Work in the Twentieth Century* (New York: Monthly Review Press, 1974); Margery Davies, *Woman's Place Is at the Typewriter: Office Work and Office Workers, 1870–1930* (Philadelphia: Temple University Press, 1982); Angel Kwolek-Folland, *Engendering Business: Men and Women in the Corporate Office, 1870–1930* (Baltimore: John Hopkins University Press, 1994); Jean Tepperman, *Not Servants, Not Machines* (Boston: Beacon Press, 1976); Mary Benet, *The Secretarial Ghetto* (New York: McGraw-Hill, 1973).

26. Margie Albert, "Something New in the Women's Movement," *NYT*, Dec. 12, 1973, op-ed page; *Congressional Record*, Dec. 12, 1973, 41255.

27. Albert, "Something New"; Philip Foner, *Women and the American Labor Movement*, 557.

28. Dorothy Sue Cobble and Alice Kessler-Harris, "Interview with Karen Nussbaum," in *Talking Leadership: Conversations with Powerful Women*, ed. Mary S. Hartman (New Brunswick, NJ: Rutgers University Press, 1999), 135–55; John Hoerr, *We Can't Eat Prestige: The Women Who Organized Harvard* (Philadelphia: Temple University Press, 1997), 47.

29. For more on the various organizations and their issues, see Seifer and Wertheimer, "New Approaches to Collective Power," 152–83, and Judith Sealander and Dorothy Smith, "The Rise and Fall of Feminist Organizations in the 1970s: Dayton as a Case Study," *Feminist Studies* 12 (Summer 1986): 321–41.

30. See note 29 above and Tepperman, *Not Servants*, 40, 63–78; Benet, *The Secretarial Ghetto*, 1–2; Hoerr, *We Can't Eat Prestige*, 47–51; Cobble and Kessler-Harris, "Interview with Karen Nussbaum," 138, 140; Joyce Moscato, "Hard Day at the Office: The Pitfalls and Promise of Clerical Organizing," *Union*, Dec. 1988–Jan. 1989, 22–26; "Rebellion behind the Typewriter," *Business Week*, Apr. 28, 1980, 86, 89–90; Roberta Wyper, "Secretaries Dictate New Images," *Worklife*, Sept. 1976, 29–31.

31. "Rebellion behind the Typewriter," 86, 89–90; Cobble and Kessler-Harris, "Interview with Karen Nussbaum," 139–41; David Plotke, "Women Clerical Workers and Trade Unionism: Interview with Karen Nussbaum," *Socialist Review* 49 (Jan.–Feb. 1980): 151–59; Tepperman, *Not Servants*, 81.

32. 9to5 and the National Association of Working Women, *Anniversary Celebration Commemorative Journal* (New York, 1988); Judy Kelmesrud, "Jane Fonda to Office Workers: 'Organize'," *NYT*, Sept. 26, 1979; "Rebellion behind the Typewriter," 86, 89–90; Moscato, "Hard Day at the Office," 25.

33. Stuart Garfinkle, "Occupations of Women and Black Workers, 1962–1974," *Monthly Labor Review* 98 (Nov. 1975): 31; Susan Sliver, "Women in the Workplace: A Variety of Viewpoints," *Monthly Labor Review* 97 (May 1974): 85–89; M. C. King, "Black Women's Breakthrough into Clerical Work: An Occupational Tipping Model," *Journal of Economic Issues* 27 (Dec. 1993): 1097–1125.

34. Tepperman, *Not Servants*, 96–97; Hoerr, *We Can't Eat Prestige*, 57–59; Margie Albert, "What Can be Done to Change Things," *Ms*, May 1973, 82.

35. Quote from Cobble and Kessler-Harris, "Interview with Karen Nussbaum," 142–43.

36. Gail Toes, "Flight Attendant Fights Back," *SFWR Newsletter* 4:2 (Mar.–Apr. 1976) (box 2, file 54, SFWR-TL).

37. Heenan, "Fighting the Fly-Me Airlines"; Nielsen, *From Sky Girl to Flight Attendant*, 112–16, 132–33; Lukas, "The Evolution of the Flight Attendant in the United States," 33–42; Jerry Flint, "Flight Attendants Break Away from Union," *NYT*, Feb. 28, 1978; Cindy Hounsell, "Stews Moving towards Independent Unions" and other documents in box 2, file 62, SFWR-TL.

38. Anne Sweeney, "Broadside," *SFWR Newsletter* 2:4 (Apr. 1974): 7–8 (box 2, file 52, SFWR-TL).

39. Plotke, "Women Clerical Workers," 153–55; Philip Foner, *Women and the American Labor Movement*, 562; Richard Hurd, "The Unionization of Clerical Workers in Colleges and Universities," in *Power Relationships on the Unionized Campus*, ed. Joel M. Douglas (New York: National Center for the Study of Collective Bargaining in Higher Education and the Professions, Baruch College, CUNY, 1989), 40–49; Dorothy Sue Cobble, "Willmar, Minnesota, Bank Strike of 1977–79," in *Labor Conflict in the United*

States: An Encyclopedia, ed. Ronald Filippelli (New York: Garland Press, 1990), 571–74; *AFL-CIO News*, Mar. 7, 1981.

40. Bell, "Unionized Women in State and Local Government," 280–99.

41. For the helpful distinction between civil and social rights, see Boris and Michel, "Social Citizenship and Women's Right to Work in Postwar America," 207.

42. "Third of Job Complaints Based on Sex Discrimination," *Washington Post*, Sept. 19, 1966.

43. "Clippings," box 1, file 15, SFWR-TL; Van Gelder, "Coffee, Tea, or Me," 86–91; Heenan, "Fighting the Fly-Me Airlines," 50–52; Margaret Ann Sipser, "Maternity Leave: Judicial and Arbitral Interpretation, 1970–1972," *Labor Law Journal* 24 (Mar. 1973): 182–83; Anderson, *Changing Woman*, 194; *IUE News*, Nov. 1973, 12.

44. "The Woman in Society," UAW Resolution Adopted 22nd Annual Convention, Apr. 20–25, 1970 (box 9, file 10, AD-GMMA); Anne Draper to Peterson, Nov. 24, 1970 (temporary file, "Twentieth Century Task Force Controversy," EP-SL); Boris and Michel, "Social Citizenship and Women's Right to Work in Postwar America," 211–12.

45. Marisa Chappell, "Rethinking Women's Politics in the 1970s: The League of Women Voters and the National Organization of Women Confront Poverty," *Journal of Women's History* 13 (Winter 2002): 170; Theda Skocpol, *The Missing Middle: Working Families and the Future of American Social Policy* (New York, W.W. Norton, 2000), 43–44.

46. For a discussion of the division within the women's reform community over the Family Assistance Program proposed by Nixon in 1969 and the eventual triumph of NOW's more individualistic perspective, see Chappell, "Rethinking Women's Politics," 157–69.

47. AFL-CIO, *Proceedings*, 1975, 219–20.

48. Robinson, "Two Movements in Pursuit of EEO," 413–33; "Memo for NY CLUW Model Contract Committee," 1975 (box 1, file 4, BW-TL).

49. Carole Seidman, "San Francisco Waitresses Union Sues to Gain Maternity Benefits," *Militant*, Oct. 20, 1972, 16.

50. Quote from *IUE News*, Dec. 1976, 2. See also Apr. 1972, 7; Jan. 1973, 2; Aug. 1973, 11–12; Winn Newman and Carole Wilson, "The Union Role in Affirmative Action," *Labor Law Journal* 32 (June 1981): 328–29.

51. CWA, *Proceedings*, 1973, 74; CWA, *Proceedings*, 1976, 49–50; CWA, *Proceedings*, 1977, 61–62.

52. Patricia Moore, "Airlines Taking Lumps in Sex-Bias Cases," 16; *SFWR Newsletter* 1:2 (May 1973): 3 (box 2, file 51) and 2:2 (Mar. 1974): 2–3 (box 2, file 52), in SFWR-TL; Nielsen, *From Sky Girl to Flight Attendant*, 94–97, 101; box 33, file "1971–1972," TWU-TL.

53. *GE v Gilbert* (429 US 125); *IUE News*, May 1974, 1, and Dec. 1976, 2.

54. CWA, *Proceedings*, 1977, 61; Newman and Wilson, "The Union Role in Affirmative Action," 328–29; Davis, *Moving the Mountain*, 298–301; prepared statement, David J. Fitzmaurice, President IUE, U.S. House, *Hearings to Prohibit Sex Discrimination on the Basis of Pregnancy, June 29, 1971*, 96–130; *IUE News*, Apr. 1977, 3; May 1977, 12; Aug. 1978, 9; ACWA, *Proceedings*, 1978; statement of Ruth Weyand, Associate Counsel, IUE, in U.S. House, *Legislation to Prohibit Sex Discrimination on the Basis of Pregnancy, Hearing before the Subcommittee on Employment Opportunities of the Committee on Education and Labor, 95th Congress, Apr. 6, 1977* (Washington, DC: GPO, 1977), 199–228.

55. CWA, *Proceedings*, 1978, 53–54; Joanna S. Lublin, "More Women Enroll in Unions, Win Office, and Push for Change," *Wall Street Journal*, Jan. 15, 1979; Conroy interview, TUWOHP, 98; Nielsen, *From Sky Girl to Flight Attendant*, ch. 4.

56. Vogel, *Mothers on the Job*, 69–84.

57. Ibid., 2–4.

58. Tamar Lewin, "Debate over Pregnancy Leave," *NYT*, Feb. 3, 1986, D1; Stuart Taylor, Jr. "Job Rights Backed in Pregnancy Case," *NYT*, Jan. 14, 1987, A1; Vogel, *Mothers on the Job*, 80–90.

59. For an excellent deconstruction of the limitations of both the "equity" and the "protectionist" paradigm in the Johnson Controls case, see Daniels, "Competing Gender Paradigms," 221–36.

60. For the AFL-CIO's continuing support of child care and the quote concerning the Chicago conference, see *AFL-CIO News*, Oct. 21, 1972; also, Andrew Biemiller telegrams and letters in box 13, file 36, and box 18, file 28, LD-GMMA; AFL-CIO Executive Council statements, Feb. 14–21, 1972, 2237–38, and Feb. 17–24, 1975, 2693. The second quote is from AFL-CIO, *Proceedings*, 1975, 521–22; 219–20. On the commitment of labor women to child care, see box 8, file 39, AD-GMMA; *Clue-In, Newsletter of NYC CLUW*, 1974–78; "Union Women Press Congress for Quality Child Care Centers," *AFL-CIO News*, Aug. 27, 1977, 6; Boris and Michel, "Social Citizenship and Women's Right to Work in Postwar America," 207–11; Susan Cowell, "Family Policy: A Union Approach," in *Women and Unions*,115–28. On the women's movement as a whole, see Susan Hartmann, *From Margin to Mainstream*, 74–77.

61. Weiner, *From Working Girl to Working Mother*, 139; Linda Greenhouse, "Of Rocking the Cradle and the Legislative Boat," *NYT*, July 3, 1986; Cobble and Michal, " 'On the Edge of Equality?' " 239–40.

62. "Union Women Press Congress for Quality Child Care Centers," 6.

63. Susan Hartmann, *The Other Feminists*, 25; "The Woman in Society Resolution," adopted Apr. 20–25, 1970, UAW Convention, and other clippings, box 9, file 10, AD-GMMA; *IUE News*, Apr. 1973, 8; Dec. 1975, 5; Linda M. Blum, *Between Feminism and Labor: The Significance of the Comparable Worth Movement* (Berkeley: University of California, 1991), 46–53.

64. *AFL-CIO News*, Feb. 19, 1972 (box 9, file 7, AD-GMMA); Mary Dresser, "Rosie's Daughters: Still Underpaid," *IUE News*, Mar. 1980; Johnson, "Comments," 93–99.

65. Materials, box 8, file 23, KPE-ALUA pt. 1.

66. CWA *Proceedings*, 1980, 281–84; *IUE News*, Dec. 1978, 10; Mar. 1979, 8; Linda Tarr-Whelan, "Women Workers and Organized Labor," *Social Policy* 1 (May 1978): 15; Balser, *Sisterhood and Solidarity*, 202–5; materials, box 1, file 25, CK-TL.

67. Heidi Hartmann and S. Aaronson, "Pay Equity and Women's Wage Increases," 71–73. In 1980, AFSCME also published the labor bible of comparable worth, *Pay Equity: A Union Issue for the 1980s* (Washington, DC: AFSCME, 1980).

68. Margaret Hallock, "Unions and the Gender Wage Gap," in *Women and Unions*, 27–42; Blum, *Between Feminism and Labor*, 46–53.

69. Jean Ross, "Comments," in *Women and Unions*, 49–53; Robert L. Nelson and William P. Bridges, *Legalizing Gender Inequality: Courts, Markets, and Unequal Pay for Women in America* (Cambridge: Cambridge University Press, 1999), chs.1, 6, 9; Hallock, "Unions and the Gender Wage Gap," 27–43.

70. See table 1 (pp. 56–61) in Richard B. Freeman, "Spurts in Union Growth: Defining Moments and Social Processes," Working Paper 6012 (Cambridge, MA: National Bureau of Economic Research, Apr. 1997).

71. Cobble and Kessler-Harris, "Interview with Karen Nussbaum," 145; see also Richard Perras, "Effective Responses to Union Organizing Attempts in the Banking Industry," *Labor Law Journal* 35 (1984): 92–102.

72. Cobble, "Willmar, Minnesota, Bank Strike," 571–74.

73. Moscato, "Hard Day at the Office," 25.

74. Hurd, "The Unionization of Clerical Workers in Colleges and Universities," 40–49; Hurd, "Organizing and Representing Clerical Workers: The Harvard Model," in *Women and Unions*, 316–36; Hoerr, *We Can't Eat Prestige*.

75. Hallock, "Unions and the Gender Wage Gap," 27–42.

EPILOGUE
THE NEXT WAVE

1. U.S. Department of Labor, Bureau of Labor Statistics. *Employment and Earnings*, January 2002.

2. For a fuller discussion of the biases of the New Deal legal and institutional framework, Cobble, "Making Post-Industrial Unionism Possible," 285–302.

3. New independent worker-run organizations now exist in many cities across the country: worker-run hiring halls among casual day laborers in Los Angeles, associations of day care workers and providers, living wage alliances, immigrant rights groups, and fair trade producer cooperatives (meeting minutes and participant list, Rockefeller-Ford Conference on Low-Wage Work, July 21–24, 2002, Aspen, Colorado, in possession of the author); remarks by Ruth Milkman, Dana Frank, Kirsten Spalding, "Roundtable on the Future of the Labor Movement," at "Justice at Work: A Conference Honoring David Brody" (University of California, Santa Barbara, Aug. 8–10, 2002).

4. P. T. Kilborn, "Union Gets the Lowly to Sign Up: Home Care Aides Are Frequent Target," *NYT*, Nov. 21, 1995; Cobble and Michal, " 'On the Edge of Equality?' " 243–44.

5. Quotes from Jim Green, "Union Victory: An Interview with Kristine Rondeau," *Democratic Left*, Sept.–Oct. 1998, 5; Kris Rondeau, "Organizing Harvard Workers," lecture given at the University and College Labor Education Association Annual Conference, Miami, Apr. 23, 1991. On HUCTW, see also Richard Hurd, "Organizing and Representing Clerical Workers: The Harvard Model," in *Women and Unions*, 316–36; Hoerr, *We Can't Eat Prestige*; Dorothy Sue Cobble, "The Prospects for Unionism in a Service Society," in *Working in the Service Society*, ed. Cameron Macdonald and Carmen Sirianni (Philadelphia: Temple University Press, 1996), 333–58; Susan Eaton, " 'The Customer Is Always Interesting': Unionized Harvard Clericals Renegotiate Work Relationships," in *Working in the Service Society*, 291–332.

6. Eaton, " 'The Customer Is Always Interesting,'" 304–6.

7. Hochschild, *The Managed Heart* (Berkeley: University of California Press, 1983), 3–8, 185–198. For other examples, see Cobble and Michal, " 'On the Edge of Equality?' " 242–45.

8. For a feminist perspective on welfare reform, see Randy Albelda and Chris Tilly, *Glass Ceilings and Bottomless Pits: Women's Work, Women's Poverty* (Boston: South End Press, 1997).The literature on the problems of balancing work and family is extensive. Recent overviews that pay attention to class differences include Jody Heymann, *The Widening Gap: Why America's Working Families Are in Jeopardy and What Can Be Done About It* (New York: Basic, 2000); Eileen Appelbaum, ed., *Balancing Acts: Easing the Burdens and Improving the Options for Working Families* (Washington, DC: Economic Policy Institute, 2000); and Joan Williams, *Unbending Gender: Why Family and Work Conflict and What to Do About It* (New York: Oxford University Press, 2000), ch. 5.

ACKNOWLEDGMENTS

LET ME ACKNOWLEDGE here the many debts I have accumulated in the writing of this book. Ruth Milkman, David Brody, Alice Kessler-Harris, Ava Baron, and Eileen Boris provided crucial encouragement in the early unsteady stages of this project. My long—but never quite long enough—research stints at various archives were eased by the assistance of able and hospitable staff. Lynn Bonfield and Susan Sherwood at the Labor Archives and Research Center, San Francisco State University; Mike Smith and Tom Featherstone at the Archives of Labor and Urban Affairs in Detroit; Jane LaTour at the Tamiment Institute, New York; Pete Hoeffer at the George Meany Memorial Archives; and Kathy Kraft at the Schlesinger Library, Radcliffe Institute, Harvard University, deserve special mention. Teresa Poor and Haejin Kim, two graduate students in Labor and Employment Relations at Rutgers University, rescued me from some of the most painstaking of the early research endeavors. Haejin unfurled raft after raft of copies of the Packinghouse Workers' newspaper for me to read at my leisure. Teresa culled through the *CIO News* and other labor papers with an eye ever alert to articles on women or women's issues. Her master's thesis on the Women's Auxiliary of the Typographical Workers' Union also proved to be another delightful collaboration and an excuse for us to catch happy hour at the Frog and Peach.

Way before I was ready, I visited versions of my arguments on audiences at the Rutgers University Center for the Critical Analysis of Contemporary Culture, where I was a fellow, and in seminars held by the History Department and the Labor Studies and Employment Relations Department at Rutgers. I also benefited from delivering portions of my research to groups at York University, McMaster University, Smith College, University of Illinois in Champaign, University of Nevada in Las Vegas, University of Pittsburgh, University of California at Berkeley, and University of California at Los Angeles. Ruth Gilmore, Dan Horowitz, Kim Voss, Craig Heron, Bettina Bradbury, Julie Guard, Linda Briskin, and Maurine Greenwald deserve to be singled out for their hospitality and their critical engagement with the project as it visited their campuses.

Arlie Hochschild in *Second Shift* (1989) describes working mothers as dreaming of sleep the way a hungry person dreams of food. As a *writing* working mother, my dreams have centered on time, time alone, time uninterrupted, time to write. I was thus ecstatic to receive a Woodrow Wilson Fellowship in 1999 that allowed me a year of writing time and brought me into contact with an amiable and stimulating group of scholars. Thanks go to Dan Rodgers, Paula Baker, Paul Gootenberg, Michael J. Lacey, and many other fellows and "sisters" for their friendly and helpful advice.

The School of Management and Labor Relations, Rutgers University, has been generous in supporting my sabbatical requests and in providing me with research funding. In this regard, thanks are due to Deans John Burton and Barbara Lee as well as to Paula Voos, Chair of the Labor Studies and Employment Relations Department. Not only did their financial support of the project allow me time to write, but it also made it possible for me to hire Jennifer Pettit, a Ph.D. student in the History Department, as a research assistant during the later stages of this project. She proved to be a truly gifted researcher with an indefatigable memory, a keen intelligence, and an uncanny ability to decode and synthesize primary texts, including congressional debates over the tax code. I especially appreciate her willingness to see this project across the finish line, even in the midst of graduate school exams, dissertation proposals, conference papers, and the birth of a new baby.

Those friends and scholars who interacted with the project in its final stages, that is, with the bulky penultimate manuscript, deserve special praise. My heartfelt thanks to Kathryn Kish Sklar, Alice Kessler-Harris, Linda Gordon, Gary Gerstle, Jim Livingston, Dee Garrison, Nancy Hewitt, and Deborah Gray White for reading and commenting on the full manuscript. I am grateful for the time and effort they put into the project, and I regret the occasions where I have not been able to meet their high standards.

Brigitta van Rheinberg and the staff of the Princeton University Press have been models of responsibility and good sense. Brigitta offered astute advice on how to shave extraneous material from the manuscript and how to create a visible and cleared path for the reader. Jodi Beder touched her editorial wand to virtually every page, saving me from innumerable missteps. Mary Beth Corrigan, a curatorial consultant now with the AFL-CIO, worked hard to ensure that the book had the best visuals possible. Ellen Foos and Jim Curtis eased the stresses of final book production and indexing.

On the home front, I have been blessed (and at times cursed) with the loud noises and incessant desires that are inseparable from life with three teenagers, two "real" and one "aspiring." My daughter Ava is a never-ending source of joy, pride, and amazement. Thank you Ava for all your gifts of love, for your tolerance of your cranky writer mom, and for never letting me stray too far from reality or from laughter. My step-children are also each remarkable in their own way. Thank you, Evan, for being the last to anger and the first to smile, and Jayna, I hope you never lose that remarkable capacity for flexibility and empathy.

My greatest debt is to my husband, Michael Merrill. I have never known anyone with more kindness, generosity, and intelligence. He has been my teacher, my co-parent, my muse, and my dearest friend. Thank you, Michael. Your love showed me the way.

PERMISSIONS

PORTIONS OF THIS research appeared, in somewhat different form, in two essays previously published by the author. " 'A Spontaneous Loss of Enthusiasm': Workplace Feminism and the Transformation of Women's Service Jobs in the 1970s," *International Labor and Working-Class History* 56 (Fall 1999): 23–44 and "Lost Visions of Equality: The Labor Origins of the Next Women's Movement," *Labor's Heritage* 12:1 (Winter/Spring 2003): 6–23. I want to thank Cambridge University press and the George Meany Center for Labor Studies-National Labor College for permission to reprint this materail.

Landon R. Y. Storrs and Bruce Fehn graciously allowed me to cite and quote from their unpublished manuscripts. Addie Wyatt and Marian Simmons granted permission to cite and quote from interviews with them conducted by Rick Halpern and Roger Horowitz as part of the UPWA-OHP at the State Historical Society of Wisconsin.

Joyce Kornbluh and Lawrence S. Root of the Institute of Labor and Industrial Relations, University of Michigan, offered permission to cite and quote from the TUWOHP interviews conducted under the auspices of the Institute.